SATHER CLASSICAL LECTURES

Volume Thirty-seven

THE ANCIENT ROMANCES

THE
ANCIENT ROMANCES

A Literary-Historical Account of Their Origins

by BEN EDWIN PERRY

UNIVERSITY OF CALIFORNIA PRESS

BERKELEY AND LOS ANGELES 1967

University of California Press
Berkeley and Los Angeles, California
Cambridge University Press
London, England
Copyright © 1967 by The Regents of the University of California
Library of Congress Catalog Card Number: 67-63003
Printed in the United States of America

Preface

IN THIS VOLUME the lectures which I had the honor
of giving as Sather Professor of Classical Literature at the
University of California in the spring of 1951 have been greatly
enlarged, and in most cases freely rewritten, although no essential change has been made in the substance of what I tried to
convey in much briefer compass to my audiences on that occasion. I regret the long delay in the making over of those lectures
into the present book; but the form in which they now appear,
as the result of a slow-going process of revision and extension,
represents, in my judgment, an improvement worth the cost.
What is added to the original lectures, even in the matter of
bibliographical notes, is meant to be either strictly relevant to
the argument in the text, or of practical use to the studious
reader. Much that might have been cited for the sake of completeness in illustration or reference has been deliberately
omitted. It has not been my intention to provide anything
like a handbook of ancient romance, nor to deal with any topic
more fully than is warranted by its place in the central scheme
of things as indicated in my subtitle. Questions of broad import, relating mainly to origins, have been raised and an effort
made to answer them in a lucid and positive manner. This
involves, along the way, the putting into perspective of a good
many facts of literary history which are often necessarily
repeated, consideration of the principles and methods by which
such inquiries should be guided, and the interpretation of particular texts against the background of their literary, cultural,

and personal environment; but all this is focused on the main problems.

The nature of these problems is such that they cannot be solved by purely objective, mechanical, or analytical methods, such as that of Aristotle in his *Poetics*. For that reason they are often avoided by classical scholars, who tend to regard them as hopeless or insoluble. The inquiry seems likely to lead one into long and dangerous paths of historical and philosophical speculation, while most of us prefer to play safe by concerning ourselves with matters that are more objective by nature and not so elusive. Yet the challenge is there and ought to be met. I offer my solutions for what they are worth, in the hope that they will prove to be enlightening. Those who are well versed in ancient literature may judge their value as historical explanations. There is no book in English dealing specifically with the origin of the Greek sentimental romance, and I know of no article or essay on the subject in our language which I can recommend as worthy of serious consideration.

The book falls naturally into two parts. Part I, consisting of chapters I–IV, deals with a single historical problem, the origin of the ideal romance of love and adventure, considered as a type of literature produced in quantity in response to a continuous popular demand. Part II, consisting of chapters V–VII, relates to what I call comic romances, in a broad, literary-historical sense of the word "comic," with reference to the spirit or tone in which a story is told, or to its purpose, including anything narrated in a spirit of jesting, mockery, farce, or burlesque, or anything satirical, scornful, mimic, or "picaresque" in its underlying tendency. Comic romances, unlike the serious or ideal species, to which they are traditionally unrelated, are not produced in quantity in response to the steady demand of a naïve reading public, but are put forth on isolated occasions by highly sophisticated authors addressing themselves ostensibly to the learned world of fashion for purposes of their own; which purposes may vary substantially between one individual writer and another, as is the case with

Petronius, Lucian, and Apuleius, whose comic romances are described in the second part of this book. Here we have three different kinds of books, no one of which can be understood in terms of another of the three, or in terms of traditional literary practice. Instead, the origin and *raison d'être* of each must be explained differently with reference to the special motive by which its author as an individual was inspired and the circumstances under which he wrote.

The distinction between comic and ideal orientation is the most fundamental distinction that can be made in the history of narrative forms, because each kind has its own proprieties and laws for what may or may not be admitted. These, although rarely stated explicitly, are always strictly observed, or at any rate meticulously reckoned with, in ancient literary practice. After the ideal novel had been invented by and circulated among the poor-in-spirit—long afterward in the ancient world, as seen in the romance of Achilles Tatius, but almost immediately afterward in modern times, as manifested in Fielding's *Joseph Andrews* and *Tom Jones*—the proprieties and liberties thitherto restricted to comic varieties of fiction, including the picaresque novel, were fused with those of ideal fiction, and vice versa; and it was this fusion of the two conventional traditions, ideal and comic, with their respective proprieties and liberties, that gave to the novel its potentiality of extension in all directions, and its universality, which we see outstanding in its latest representatives.

In this connection some apology is due, I suspect, for the fact that throughout this book the conventional requirements of different kinds of ancient writing are often restated and to some extent, unavoidably, in the same words. For these repetitions I beseech the reader's indulgence. They are not otiose. They have seemed to be necessary to make it clear to the reader in each new context, by way of reminder, how the controlling forces of ancient literary convention, forces which prevailed in literature before the birth of the novel and are today too often forgotten, bear importantly upon the matter under discussion. Failure on the part of modern scholars to reckon with those forces and all that they imply has often led to false explanations being given for this or that phenomenon in the history of ancient fiction. I have pointed out specific instances of this here and there in the notes.

The subject of ancient romance, in various of its aspects, is one upon which I have meditated a great deal from time to time in the past; but, owing to deterrents of one kind or another, the summing up of my views in what is meant to be their final form in this book—something that I had always intended to do—would probably never have been realized had it not been for the invitation kindly extended to me by the University of California to give these lectures and to prepare them for publication. That furnished the necessary incentive; and it is with much pleasure and gratitude that I recall the stimulation of that occasion, the very friendly hospitality shown me by colleagues at Berkeley, both within and without the Department of Classics, and the quickening of intellectual interests which I enjoyed through association with the fine scholars and personalities there.

To the Harvard University Press I am gratefully indebted for permission to quote, in chapter V, a number of passages from M. Heseltine's translation of Petronius in the Loeb Library edition. Other translations of ancient or modern texts are my own, except in cases where a different translator is mentioned.

Urbana, Illinois   Ben Edwin Perry
July, 1965

Contents

Abbreviations

(See also the classified Bibliography on pp. 379–385 below)

AJPh	*American Journal of Philology*
BZ or *Byz. Ztschr.*	*Byzantinische Zeitschrift*
Christ-Schmid or Christ-Schmid-Stählin *Gr. Litt.*⁶.	Wilhelm von Christ, *Geschichte der Griechischen Litteratur*, sixth edition, Part II revised and extended by Wilhelm Schmid and Otto Stählin, München (C. H. Beck Verlag), 1920 (II 1) and 1924 (II 2). Part I, by W. Schmid, 1912.
CPh	*Classical Philology*
Diss.	B. E. Perry, *The Metamorphoses Ascribed to Lucius of Patrae; Its Content, Nature, and Authorship*, Lancaster, Pa., 1920. Copies obtainable from W. H. Allen, Bookseller, Philadelphia, Pa. 19103.
Krumbacher, *Byz. Litt.*²	Karl Krumbacher, *Geschichte der Byzantinischen Litteratur*, second edition, München (C. H. Beck Verlag), 1897.
Oxy. Pap. or *Oxy. P.*	*Oxyrhynchus Papyri*, ed. B. P. Grenfell and A. S. Hunt, London, 1898–.

Migne, *Patrol. Gr.*   J. P. Migne, editor, *Patrologiae Cursus Completus. Series Graeca*, Paris, 1857–1866.

Migne, *Patrol. Lat.*   J. P. Migne, editor, *Patrologiae Cursus Completus. Series Latina*, second edition, Paris, 1878 ff.

PSI   *Papiri greci e latini* (*Pubblicazioni della Società italiana per la Ricerca dei Papiri greci e latini in Egitto*), Firenze, 1912– .

RE   Pauly-Wissowa-Kroll, *Real-Encyclopädie der classischen Altertumswissenschaft.*

RhM.   *Rheinisches Museum für Philologie*

Rohde, *Gr. Rom.*[3]   Erwin Rohde, *Der gerichische Roman und seine Vorläufer*, third edition with an *Anhang* by W. Schmid, Leipzig, 1914.

Schanz, Röm. Litt.[3]   Martin Schanz, *Geschichte der römischen Litteratur*, third edition in collaboration with Carl Hosius and G. Krüger, München (C. H. Beck Verlag).

TAPhA   *Transactions of the American Philological Association.*

PART ONE

The Ideal Greek Romance of Love and Adventure

I

Greek Romance and the Problem of Forms and Origins

For English and American readers the general type of ancient book with which we are here concerned, whether it be the serious or the comic variety that is in question, would be somewhat better indicated by the term *novel*, with its implications of modernity, than by the broader term *romance*, which we are likely to associate with something old-fashioned. Nevertheless the latter term, as used on the continent of Europe (*roman, romanzo*), includes everything that we mean by novel, along with other and kindred varieties of narrative which we shall have to consider; and the word romance, in this wider, continental sense, is so convenient in various contexts and has become so familiar and well-established in the critical writing about our subject, even in English, that I have been inclined to use it most of the time. Nothing, of course, is made to depend upon a precise definition of either term, but both are used in a broad sense as equivalents for convenience in the absence of a more exact terminology.

1

Today the novel is well recognized as a literary form and so familiar as such, in spite of its many varieties and the many uses to which it is put, that no one is likely to confuse it with other genres. It has become the principal medium of literary expression, enlisting in its service as practitioners authors who represent every degree of intelligence and artistic capacity from the lowest to the highest. It has come to include every kind of entertainment or interpretation of society and human experience, ranging from what is profoundly philosophic or sublimely poetic to what is inane, vulgar, or merely sensational, thereby embracing what, in earlier and more disciplined ages, would normally have been cast into such various literary forms as tragedy, comedy and mime, history, biography, epic, essay, satire, dialogue, elegy, etc., or circulated orally for amusement with no pretense to being art and therefore never written down. But this epic-like universality of the novel is something relatively new in the Western world—in a strict sense, no older than Balzac. In Graeco-Roman antiquity, on the other hand, as also in the time of Shakespeare, what we call novels or romances were far more restricted in the range of their substance, quality, and pretension than they are today. Among the ancients, furthermore, books of this kind were so persistently ignored by literary critics, and so far from being recognized as constituting a distinct or legitimate form of literature fit for discussion, that no proper name for them as a species, such as the modern words novel and romance, ever came into use. On the rare occasions when romances are mentioned by Greek and Latin authors—and this is only at a late date—they are either spoken of in terms that belong to other and better-known types of literature, chiefly history and drama, or their nature is indicated by various phrases made up to describe their contents.

This vagueness and reticence on the part of the ancients in speaking about novels, the disdain with which such works were regarded by educated men (when regarded at all), the humble nature of the entertainment which they provided, and the fact that the form itself, in spite of its great potentialities as a medium for the expression of all kinds of intellectual and artistic values, was nevertheless confined, in Graeco-Roman antiquity, to a narrow range of uses, tending either to become stereotyped as melodrama for the edification of children and the poor-in-spirit, or employed by intellectuals on isolated occasions for the ostensible purpose of satire or parody—all these aspects of the ancient novel may be regarded as more or less typical of the initially restricted scope of the genre in any literature at an early stage in its history. The novel appears first on a low and disrespectable level of literature, adapted to the taste and understanding of uncultivated or frivolous-minded people. As such, it is ignored or despised as trivial by the prevailing literary fashion of the time, because that fashion honors only traditional or academic forms, usually more concentrated forms, and insists upon a higher standard of artistic or intellectual value than what is to be found in a string of fictitious adventures, or a love affair that ends in complete felicity.[1]

Nevertheless, the newborn novel is something genuinely popular and true to the real, if often subconscious, spirit and taste of the new individualistic age which creates it; and, because of this inherent strength, it is destined, sooner or later, to become recognized and extended upward and outward in its uses indefinitely, so long as the society in which it is born and nourished continues to be an open one, more and more agitated by spiritual and intellectual forces of a centrifugal and disintegrating nature, as in Roman imperial times and at present. Had the outward-looking, pagan society which engendered the Greek romance continued to move forward on its open path of cultural dissolution for a few more centuries, or at a faster tempo than it actually did, before being closed up and brought to an end by the triumph of Christianity as a unifying spiritual force productive of cultural solidarity, it would probably have produced a novel as broad in its scope and as dominant among other literary forms as the novel of today. This was the direction in which the ancient novel had begun to move when it came to an end, after a career of some four hundred years (*ca.* 100 B.C.–A.D. 300), along with the open society which had produced it. The extent of its progress, however, whether upward in the scale of artistic or intellectual quality, or outward in the range of its subject-matter and ideas, was very small in comparison with what has been achieved by the modern novel in the last two hundred years, a period of cultural history which is, in a Spenglerian sense, with reference to the nature of its expanding social and intellectual outlook, "contemporary" in the main with the era of Greek romance.

Why was it that the ancient novel evolved so much more slowly than the modern and failed to reach similar levels of quality? No doubt the principal reason lies in the fact that the spirit of men in western Europe since 1800 has been generally forward-looking, hopeful, and energetic, despite the centrifugal nature of thought in this period with its hostility to traditional forms of culture and fixed beliefs. By contrast, the spirit of Roman imperial times, the age of Greek romance, was essentially backward-looking, negative, and moribund in worldly affairs and prospects. In that age the hopes of common men and their visions of a happier future (when they had any) were directed not, as in modern times, to such things as Science, Progress, and a new life for the emancipated Everyman— destined to become forever better by a supposed law of evolution—but, instead, to some form of divine revelation or authority, which, by solving the problems of men and once more congregationalizing their souls, would bring them home, as it were from their spiritual wanderings and isolation and re-establish in effect, as the Christian church finally did, howbeit on an international basis, the cultural poise, solidarity, and unity of the old city-state. For men living in the Hellenistic world the old regime of political independence in small states, where the way of life was communal and fixed by custom, was something dear which they had lost through no will of their own, but by a fatality. The new order of things, which had deprived them of the normal functions and aspirations of citizenship by making them subjects of a big empire on a par with vast numbers of foreigners and expatriates, provided no incentive for ambition in civic affairs and no hope for improvement of conditions in the future. The age of Greek romance was similar to that of the modern novel in the centering of thought and feeling about the private concerns of the individual man apart from society, and the tendency to look outward in a spirit of wonder upon the endless varieties of nature and human experience, rather than inward to the nature of man in his more universal or more heroic aspects. Both ages worship the Many rather than the One; and what is particular, personal, abnormal, strange, or sensational is more than ever played up in preference to what is normal in kind, or generically significant. In the absence of an inner spiritual satisfaction, and of a sense of meaning in life, such as the city-state had once given them, men had perforce to amuse themselves as well as they could with the external novelties of a big, strange world full of accident, and above all, when it came to matters of real feeling, with their own purely personal hopes and concerns. On the other hand, the romantic movement of the nineteenth century, having originated in reaction against the too-great formalism of the *ancien régime*, which it had recently overthrown, was animated by a dynamic enthusiasm for new and untried things and for exploration in all directions, which has not yet spent itself; and this positive spiritual energy has carried literature, along with the science which expands its boundaries and its outlook, both higher and further afield than was possible in the moribund period of classical civilization. In *Daphnis and Chloe* the ancient novel approached the top level of literary quality for its time, probably the late second century after Christ. If nothing better was produced in that century or the following, it is probably because no form of literature can rise above the ceiling of the culture that projects it; and if more novels of a similar quality were not written, this must be ascribed to the fact, already noted, that the writing of such books never became fashionable in the ancient world of letters, as it has been in the modern, and could seldom, therefore, attract authors of first-rate talent or artistic ambition. Longus, the supposed author of *Daphnis and Chloe*, is exceptional in this connection, but he is a man about whom we have no ancient or medieval testimony. There is nothing to indicate that he had, in his time, any reputation as a literary man, at least not under the name Longus. Normally, men of cultivated understanding, if they cared for their reputations among the intelligentsia, would express themselves in a literary medium other than that of prose fiction, but now and then able wits may show themselves outside the Academy in disregard of its frowns. In Graeco-Roman antiquity the restraining force of a dominant academic fashion, which refused to recognize anything that was not classical in kind, or learned, or intellectual, or informative, was much stronger than any similar force of opinion has been since the birth of the modern novel in the eighteenth century; and this is the main reason why the Greek romance was so much slower to develop than the modern, and was rarely if ever exploited by the best minds of the age in which it flourished. As serious literature it did not rate the respectful attention, much less the authorship, of such intellectual spirits as Lucian and the outstanding prose writers of his day, although it had flourished on the obscure lower levels of ancient literature for two hundred years previously. Contrast with this the rapid rise of the serious or ideal modern novel, which even at an early stage in its career could claim the artistic efforts of no less a man than Goethe.

2

The student of classical literature who reads a Greek romance for the first time is bound to be surprised by the novelty of the thing and by its apparent modernity; for there is nothing else in ancient literature so much like our present-day movies with their glamorous heroines and heroes, the rapid succession of breathtaking adventures, nearly always ending happily, often with a wedding, and their highly conventionalized morals, gestures, and techniques, as these Greek romances. Some students, on making this discovery, are much pleased with the thought that ancient writing can be at times as exciting and trivial as much of what is written today, as if that were all to the credit of the ancients. My own reaction on first reading these romances, apart from the usual surprise, was one of strong curiosity about their place in the history of literature. Here was a difficult but fascinating problem to be solved. How did such things as modern novels come to emerge upon the surface of ancient literature, which is elsewhere so very different? What were the precedents for this type of writing, and what was the relation between it and other literary forms and traditions? How did it get started, and under what theory, or rationale, as literature?

For a long time I pondered these questions imaginatively, but in vain. I was unable to formulate for myself any theory concerning the origins of Greek romance that seemed adequate, or even plausible, and what others had conjectured on the subject likewise failed to convince me. At last, however, I came to realize that this perplexity of mine was due in very large measure to the fact that I could not free myself from the pervasive tyranny of those fashions of thinking about literary history which prevailed in the nineteenth century, and which I now believe to be as false in principle as they are misleading and frustrating to those who follow them. Like many others, I was asking the wrong questions, looking for the wrong kind of data, making false assumptions, and failing to understand what the real forces are that create new literary forms. Such forms, I am convinced, never come into being as the result of an evolutionary process taking place on the purely literary plane, but only as the willful creations of men made in accordance with a conscious purpose. That purpose, in the case of the more important and well established genres, is to satisfy the new spiritual or intellectual needs and tastes that have arisen in a large part of society in a given period of cultural history. Without such needs no new literary form of any importance will arise; and when those needs are present and have come to be felt, a new and suitable vehicle for their expression will be easily devised, *ad hoc*, and inevitably. This new thing will not be the end-product of a series of accidents, or of successive imitations, or of rhetorical experiments, or even of a gradual shifting of emphasis on the part of those who write in a traditional and already established form. One form does not give birth to another, but is separated from it by a logically unbridgeable gap. In terms of literary form as generally understood, historiography, for example, cannot become romance without passing through zero, that is, through the negation of its own *raison d'être*, the thing which defines it as historiography. That which generates the new form, and at the same time identifies it, is a new purpose or a new ideal, which acts from without in a horizontal direction upon what is traditional. Literature itself can influence literature only through the medium of human thought. Once it has entered into that medium, which is the mind of the prospective writer, its values are mingled with those of many other intellectual and spiritual forces, and it is these in their aggregate that determine the nature of what will be written— not the mere substance of what has been written before. The latter is of minor consequence in the question of origins. What the old form supplies is not motivation or causation, or inspiration, but only a loose structural pattern and building materials of one kind or another which may be used at will to a greater or less extent in the construction of the new thing. A Christian church may be made of stones taken from a pagan temple, but the temple does not explain the church, nor do the separate stones. The first Greek tragedy was, I should say, invented for the purpose of giving expression to some aspect of the new and "tragic" outlook on life (however one may define it) that had been created and fostered by the historical experience of the Greek world in the sixth century B.C. It had nothing to do with Dionysus by its intention; but the old Dionysiac chorus, itself already transformed to some extent by the impingement of Dorian and Apolline lyric, was used as the clay, so to speak, out of which the new vessel was molded, and from which it received its necessary but purely conventional sanction as an institution. The molding process in itself was nothing wonderful or difficult to manage, so long as there was a dynamic purpose and ideal back of it; although the *means* by which this new idea was implemented might be improved and developed in the course of practice, provided the artistic aim itself remained unchanged, or seemingly so.

Such, in general, is the way in which, according to my own hard-earned view, the rise of any literary form should be explained; and many today will probably agree with me in principle.[2] But this is not at all the method followed by the great majority of those who have written on the origins of tragedy, or of the romance. They concentrate on the process of creation and the materials used, while ignoring or taking for granted (as though it were something unimportant that could be assumed for any time or place) the idea that motivates it. All they ask is *how* the thing was made, not why, nor what for, nor whether it was wanted or not at the time, or how much it was wanted. Human will by their way of thinking is not worth reckoning with, because it is *immaterial*, a word to which our age has given the meaning of inconsequential. Nothing spiritual or teleological matters; only the techniques and the materials by which things are made are felt to be worthy of the scientist's attention. In this atmosphere of thought one is led to infer that men living in the time of Deucalion would gladly have written tragedies and novels if they had only known *how*, and that, owing to their presumable want of inventive ability and their ignorance of technique, only an accident comparable to that by which roast pig was discovered (according to Lamb) could have taught them how, and so started them on the road to production. These critics—not to dismiss them just yet—think of a literary species as having come into being in much the same way as a biological species, namely, through a long series of evolutionary accidents. Mistakenly, they look for "connecting links," "forerunners," and "intermediate stages of development." They try to see how the parts or "elements" of which a literary form is composed were put together one at a time naturally (which is to say aimlessly) in such a way as to produce in the end the form as they know it or choose to conceive it. When all the parts of the literary organism have been accumulated fortuitously in the tide of history—for like attracts like—the idea which it embodies becomes apparent for the first time, being the result of the process instead of its cause.

It is unlikely, of course, that anyone would defend this method of inquiry consciously and on principle in the radical form in which I have here stated it; but I find much of it to be implicit, nevertheless, in what has been written about the growth of literary forms, and I myself in the past have often been misled by it. In the absence of a positive and well-recognized theory as to how literature evolves, the familiar concepts of biological evolution, with all their prestige as science, have moved into the vacuum as it were by default, unnoticed and unchallenged, so that what is conceded to be valid in the method of the one discipline is often thoughtlessly assumed to be so in the other.

The analogy of biological evolution is false and misleading in the realm of literary history, because it ignores the human will and capacity to create new forms at frequent intervals in response to its own spiritual or intellectual needs.[3] These needs, which vary greatly with time, place, readers addressed, and the author's personality, broadly considered, may be either those of society as a whole or a large part of it, corresponding to important phases of its outlook and interests, or they may be only those of an individual writer. It is only in response to a continuing popular demand, or to one that is fostered by a numerous group or class of persons with common interests, that the more important and enduring literary forms, such as romance and tragedy, have been created. Those which were current in the classical period of Greek literature, when society was relatively homogeneous, belong almost entirely in this category and are few in number; but in the Hellenistic period, when much of literature was artificial and out of touch with the public at large, the number and variety of literary forms produced by individual authors and the practitioners of art for art's sake was very much greater. Here the willful nature of literary creation, and its ready adaptation to all kinds of contemporary fashions of thought and taste are especially evident, as they are in the modern world of letters. In writing on the history of the English novel no one would attempt to trace a line of development by successive stages of imitation or precedent running through all the separate novels from Richardson to Joyce, because—and perhaps only because—too many of the varieties would be seen at once to be simultaneous in appearance, or eccentric, or reverse in their tendency, with the result that the supposed line of descent, instead of being straight or perpendicular, as in normal biological evolution (and in what is often assumed for the less-known Greek romance), would run back and forth and laterally in many directions, to say nothing of its being broken at many points by the absence of any plausible connection in causality. Nor would the result of our quest for a generative principle be any better if the novel were divided into a number of separate species and an effort made to trace each of them back through intermediate stages of growth to an ancestral form. What about *that* form? Was it purposely created, as we are maintaining that all forms are, or was it inherited by evolution from the first literary form on earth? The last mentioned could not be the result of evolution, since no literary compositions preceded it, and literature itself, being a man-made thing, cannot, like flesh or inanimate matter, be traced to an origin earlier than man. It did not spring from the oak or the rock. The first literary composition, or its oral equivalent, which constituted at the same time what we call a literary form, was made by a human artist acting deliberately under the guidance of a preconceived purpose. That is something that cannot be denied, and would not be denied by any student of literature; not even by one of those whose habits of thinking in this field have otherwise been damaged by the analogy of biological evolution, and by the equally misleading notion of progress and gradual development toward perfection (perfection of what?). But if the willful creation of a literary form can and must be acknowledged to be humanly possible, and to have actually occurred in the beginning of literature, why should anyone be reluctant to suppose that the same process of spontaneous generation, miraculous though it may seem to be from the biological point of view, has in fact been often repeated, and never more frequently and easily than in the open societies of Hellenistic and of modern times, when the urge to create something new is a primary condition of men's minds and the materials at their disposal with which to create it, more abundant than ever before?

Few will deny the truth of this as a general proposition, and some may wonder why anything so obvious and axiomatic is here painstakingly set forth. The reason is that the principle, though generally admitted to be valid, is often ignored or denied in the practice of literary historians, who as a class are seldom willing or able to recognize the application of it in any particular case. They fail to realize the amount of transforming power inherent in a new idea, which is capable of making radical changes all at once in the content and orientation of an antecedent form, thereby creating a new one. They seem to feel that their pronouncements on a problem relating to the origin of a literary form will be plausible and scientific in proportion to the degree in which they succeed, first, in avoiding the supposition that anything more than a trifling change, unconsciously introduced, is due to any one writer, and secondly, in making it appear that the aesthetic ideal represented by the new form is the result of a series of blindly groping experiments on the part of "forerunners." In this way a process of gradual growth is exhibited analogous to that which takes place in plants and animals. For literature this analogy is false and fatally misleading; but its prestige in modern times has been great and seldom challenged, owing partly to the authoritative example of Aristotle in discussing the origin of tragedy, and partly to the influence of biological science in the nineteenth century. Thus Rohde devoted, irrelevantly, some 275 pages of his great book on the Greek romance to what he called *Vorläufer*, these being the authors of Alexandrian erotic poetry on the one hand and, on the other, those who from the earliest times had written about travel in strange lands; because the principal parts of romance (μέρη as Aristotle would say) were supposed to be love and travel. Formula: Divide the mature literary product into parts and say all you can about the previous history of each. Rohde is only one of many scholars who have proceeded in this manner, without realizing the futility of it.

In explaining the appearance of a type of book or composition for which no plausible forerunners can be cited in extant literature, it is customary to assume the loss of a number of ancient writings—or forms of a legend, in cases where literature is confused with folklore—each of which presumably showed an advance beyond its predecessor in the appropriate direction. This is that *development*, which students under the mere spell of the word so often feel obliged to discover wherever they can, as if it were a necessary clue to the understanding of all literary history, or the same thing as what may be loosely (if not without some danger), called the evolution, i.e., the changing, or the flux of literature. Owing chiefly to the influences mentioned above, namely Aristotle, biological thinking, and modern ideas of progress in general, this concept has become so familiar and so sacred an idol that even the best of scholars and critics are liable to bow before it without thinking, or do it lip service, to the extent of disregarding the ordinary dictates of logic, common sense, and literary realities of which they themselves are well aware when they meet them in any other context, or alone. Here let us dwell for a moment on a concrete example, one which happens to be of peculiar significance in connection with the origins of Greek romance which we shall discuss more fully in a later chapter.

In a papyrus fragment, Ninus and Semiramis, aged 17 and 13 respectively, are represented, for the edification of little girls and boys, as cousins who are violently in love with each other. Ninus, who seems to be on vacation for a few days from his duties as royal field marshal of the Assyrians, is pleading earnestly and piously with his Aunt Dercy (elsewhere the goddess Derceto of Ascalon) for permission to marry her daughter Semiramis, although he has already conquered a large part of Asia and has had the opportunity, as he himself points out, of behaving otherwise, had he so desired, than as the model young man that he is, so careful of his morals and above all of his chastity. As for our dear little heroine, Semiramis, her bashfulness is such that she is unable to tell her aunt, the mother of Ninus, that she is in love, but is overcome by embarrassment in her efforts to do so. Since we do not find here anything like the Ninus of saga, who takes Semiramis away from her husband by force, quite incidentally, nor the Semiramis of the popular stage, who, as a scheming royal concubine, coaxes Ninus into letting her rule Asia for one day and thereby supplants him, the question has arisen how this difference can be explained, and the typical answer is given by a recent writer on the subject who comments as follows: ". . . in the romance such a radical transformation of the characters has taken place that we must assume intermediate steps of development which have been lost to us." [4] Note the word "must." This is equivalent to saying that it is impossible for an author to make a radical change in the representation of legendary characters, even when he deals with a period in their lives about which legend has been silent. Or are we to suppose that Ninus and Semiramis, at the same time that the patriotic saga about them as mighty rulers of divine parentage was elsewhere in circulation, were being celebrated in folklore as a pair of adolescent lovers with strictly conventional, middle-class mores? But folklore is concerned with action, and with what is extraordinary or picturesque, not with character, nor with social and moral correctitudes or what is commonplace in contemporary society; and the text of this romance, however naïve its *thought* may be, is, by common consent, as obviously rhetorical and artificial as anything well could be. It represents the studied effort of a writer seeking to please a certain class of readers by his own invention. He wanted to tell them what he imagined to be an ideal love story. He was not recording any folklore about Ninus and Semiramis, other than what was already current in the vague saga about them as mature persons and conquerors, and that, in *his* scheme of things, could have been only background material. He was not writing as an historian, nor as a patriot extolling the ancient glories of Mesopotamia. He was no more concerned about the patriotic or national significance of his legendary lovers than was Euripides, let us say, about that of Hippolytus or Iphigenia, or Ovid about that of Pyramus and Thisbe. Intermediate steps of development? Obviously there can be no such thing between a folk-saga or a history which relates to one period of a man's life from an ethnical point of view, and a literary composition, belletristic by nature, which relates to a different and antecedent period of that man's life and concentrates upon his personal and domestic affairs. These two accounts of Ninus aim at two totally different objects or ends; and progress, or development, is something that takes place only in relation to a single end. The story of Ninus as national hero, like that of Alexander, might have been told any number of times in any kind of society without becoming anything like an erotic romance. Only an act of will on the part of an individual can account for that creation, not the aimless gossiping of people at large. This romance is not a development from the saga, any more than the representation of Jason as a poor husband and a hypocrite in Euripides is the outcome of a gradual process of literary or folkloristic development from the conception of Jason in Pindar as a splendid hero in the prime of his physical and ethical glory.

3

In every literary composition what we have in reality is the projection of a separate idea. This idea, the soul of the thing and at the same time its *raison d'être*, is a spiritual entity so personal, so inimitable, and so volatile by nature that the exact reproduction of it in literary expression would be very difficult of achievement even by one and the same author, and quite impossible for anyone else. "L'arte è intuizione," says Croce, "e l'intuizione è individualità e l'individualità non si repete." [5] From this it follows that every piece of literature, strictly considered, is *sui generis* and represents a distinct literary form of its own, even though the differences between some of these countless forms, or artifacts, each of which is in some degree a law unto itself, may be so slight in appearance, or so subtle, as to defy one's powers of definition, or even of aesthetic perception. In such cases, and in others, where the similarities are not so great, we are prone to ignore or deny the differences, and to transfer to the group, collectively and abstractly, for the sake of convenience, that concept of literary form which belongs in strict reality only to separate works. [6]

In this connection it must be observed—also with Croce— that there is no such thing as a literary form, or genre, in the *prescriptive* sense in which these terms have commonly been used by critics from Aristotle down to the present day. For what these critics have nearly always meant by *genre* or *form* is not just a group of literary phenomena which have many conspicuous features in common with each other, and thus may be given a generic title for convenience in describing their collective appearance, but, instead, something that lies deep-seated in the nature of things and is defined and controlled, like things in the physical and biological world, by unchanging laws of nature. By this view, the form (εἶδος in Aristotle and Plato) is the ultimate reality, a universal pattern in relation to which any particular work of art must be judged and thereby approved or rejected. The philosopher, by an analysis which proves to be objective and external in method, separating part from part like the elements in a chemical compound, may discover and proclaim what the fundamental laws and specifications are which nature has established for a particular form or genre (εἶδος, γένος); after which, all that the poet has to do is to follow the rules, and the critic to insist that others do likewise. This defining of the genres—and a definition in Aristotle is always a statement of what he believes to be a law of nature— is the main business of Aristotle in his *Poetics* and of Horace in the *Ars Poetica*; and the concept of literary form as it appears in those famous essays has shaped and dominated the thinking of literary historians and critics ever since. Thus error became standardized.

A principal tenet of this false doctrine, shared by ancients and moderns alike, is that the literary form, fixed by nature as something eternal and unchangeable, predetermines the content of a given work. And modern critics have doubled the error by putting the same proposition into reverse, concluding that the contents of a given work, or a plurality of its parts, externally considered—for they cannot be considered otherwise, being parts—are reliable criteria by which to identify the form to which it belongs, or that from which it has been derived. Such are the premises, for example, on which romance, according to a well-known theory about its origins, is derived from the exercises on sensational themes assigned by rhetoricians to their pupils in the schools, the so-called *controversiae*.[7] Herein, as in many similar speculations, content is derived from content, in naïve disregard of the mind which rises above it, controls it, and manipulates it for its own purpose. Everything is carefully scrutinized except the main idea, which is left severely alone. Another critic, who seems to think that certain types of subject-matter and technical procedure belong in fee simple each to one or two of the well recognized genres, has found in the romance what he calls the "debris" of all the other genres;[8] and still another *Quellenforscher* has taken the pains to catalogue these *disiecta membra*, along with the indication of their respective sources, in a book dealing with the manifold "elements" of which Greek romance is composed, as represented by Chariton. This listing of elements and the tracing of their sources is a popular philological game, but not much more profitable than the working out of a crossword puzzle. For the truth is that these elements, or parts, with which critics have been so curiously and so exclusively concerned, as if they were reliable clues to the origins of a literary genre, or to the identification of one, are almost as free of movement in the world of literature, and as adaptable to different purposes, as are the letters of the alphabet. By the same method and logic by which romance is derived from school exercises, one may derive the word *smile* from the word *mile;* the former contains all the elements of the latter, plus *s*, which may be explained as due to "development"; and as for the meaning of the combination as a whole in each case, think nothing about it! It is true that certain types of content are sure to be found in a given genre; but that is because we ourselves, not nature, have already defined that genre in a purely arbitrary manner as something that embraces that content. To infer genre from content (externally considered), or content from genre, is to argue in a circle, and to beg the primary question of what constitutes the genre, and whether there is any such thing or not. It is useful and legitimate to speak of literary forms or genres only so long as we understand those terms in a purely *descriptive* sense as referring to arbitrary categories of literary phenomena, categories which may be greatly varied, multiplied or restricted at will, according to the criteria on which one chooses to base them. But a genre in this sense of a category cannot have a genealogy; and genre in the prescriptive Aristotelian sense does not, I submit, exist. It is true that a genre in the descriptive, *ex postfacto* sense may represent (and usually does) a strong literary fashion, which in turn may influence a subsequent genre; but such influence is strictly secondary and superficial. It does not belong among the forces that create new forms and is therefore irrelevant to a large extent in questions relating to their origins.

The Aristotelian doctrine of literary forms is false because it goes contrary to the self-evident fact that individual fancy, no matter what shapes it or prompts it, is the mother of artistic invention; and that this creative force, which is purely psychological and subjective by nature, is far too complex, manifold, variable, and unpredictable in its manifestations to be seized upon by objective science and confined within the narrow limits of a few simple patterns or formulas made up on the analogy of what nature has ordained for the behavior or the constitution of physical and biological, not spiritual, phenomena. What Aristotle imagines to be nature's unchanging requirement for the genus tragedy is a combination of parts abstracted from those particular tragedies which best suited his fourth-century Aristotelian taste, his special fondness for plot and action, and his admiration for organic structure.[9] Such a definition necessarily depends upon a subjective process of reasoning, in spite of the fact that the method is made to appear objective. In comparison with the objectivity and certainty of a genuine scientific law, say in physics or biology, the law for tragedy, as he defines it, fades into a shadowy and unreal abstraction incapable of verification. Almost every critic feels obliged to define the "law" in a different way. It has no objective validity. But in the misguided effort to make it appear objective, and thereby "scientific," it positively misrepresents the nature of the subject, which is not objective but subjective. It fails to take the measure of any real tragedy, because it views tragedy externally as a mechanism, describing and cataloguing (with arbitrary restrictions) only its parts, which are the means and instruments by which the artist achieves his end —not the end itself, not the total effect, not the aesthetic quantum, and not, therefore, the tragedy itself, which is indivisible. In attempting to explain literature in terms of exact science, Aristotle was attempting the impossible; and his example has had a ruinous effect, direct or indirect, upon the thinking of innumerable students of literature in modern times. Those who externalize a literary form or composition, by dividing it into parts and concentrating their attention on those parts instead of upon the purpose which they serve, are all victims of that ancient error.

"Respect for distinguished teachers is often a hindrance in the path of those who would learn," says Cicero.[10] That Aristotle should underestimate the range and potentialities of literary art, which vary widely with human emotion according to time, place, and the individual, by confining it within a straitjacket of natural law, is understandable in the light of three special circumstances. (1) Much of his thinking had been in the field of biology, whence the concepts and methods appropriate to that discipline tended to carry over into his thinking on other subjects. (2) His was the first attempt that had ever been made to classify literature systematically, and the data on which his inferences were based (classical literature from Homer to Euripides) were few in number as compared with what the modern student has to contemplate, and more uniform and communal in kind, as being the products of a relatively closed society. (3) He was so strongly influenced by the doctrines of Plato, his teacher, that those doctrines conditioned his reasoning even when he opposed them. This last point is one of prime importance for the understanding of Aristotle's whole theory of literature. Why he conceived literature and art as imitation (*mimesis*), why he maintained that catharsis of the emotions of fear and pity was the virtue of tragedy, and why he spoke of a literary form as a universal pattern under the control of natural law, and thereby limited in its possibilities of variation—all this hinges on Plato's theory of ideas and the place to which poetry is relegated therein, as has been truly explained by R. K. Hack in his brilliant and masterly essay entitled "The Doctrine of Literary Forms." Hack rightly observes in summary that "the laws of the genres are nothing but the expression in the sphere of literature of the Platonic doctrine of ideal forms." [11]

This relationship between the theories of Plato and Aristotle relative to literature deserves a fuller exposition than can here be given to it, but the main points are as follows. Plato valued only the ultimate truth or reality which underlies all earthly appearances, and which, like the modern scientist's "laws of nature," is eternal and unalterable. The knowledge of this scientific truth could be attained, he believed, by means of dialectic, and this knowledge was, in his opinion, the only knowledge worth having or worth seeking. Everything that seems to be real in this world—and that excludes literature and art—is an imperfect *imitation*, according to Plato, of a corresponding ideal form (ἰδέα or εἶδος) in the world of permanent reality. Man's highest function is to discover by scientific methods, that is by dialectical reasoning, what the eternal and immutable forms are and, by fixing his gaze on these alone, to copy them as nearly as possible. The greatest hindrance to men in the pursuit of this real knowledge is emotion in all its forms— love, pity, fear, anger, laughter, hope, despair, pleasure, desire, grief, etc. These are impurities, the deplorable falsities with which poetry is concerned. They must be "purged" from the soul in order to sterilize it and render it fit for the apprehension of purely scientific truth. Man has no need for poetic feeling, sentiment, imagination, or creative activity. His only business is to learn and conform. He can have no real history, and his whole world is, or should be, and would be in the ideal state outlined in the *Republic*, a mere mechanism. Literature and art, like freedom, have no value for Plato, because their sanction is purely humanistic. Plato saw clearly that poetry, which, as he complains, "feeds and waters the passions instead of withering and starving them" (*Resp.* 606), was antagonistic to his whole system of philosophy and irreconcilable with it. If the poets were right in their claim of instructing men and making them better, then Plato's philosophy was fundamentally wrong. In defense of his own philosophical life, he felt obliged to put the poets out of business by denying the validity of their craft. He argued that poetry, like everything else in the world, was imitation; but it was inferior to all the respectable kinds of imitation, because what it imitated was not the ideal reality, but only what people on earth do and think, and that in turn was already an imperfect imitation of the truth. Thus poetry is twice removed from reality and the poet as teacher is an impostor. He is also immoral and injures the souls of men by his poetry, because he stirs up the emotions and fosters them, instead of withering and starving them, and, like Homer, he violates (Platonic) propriety by failing to represent gods and heroes as morally perfect; in other words, by failing to make them conform as nearly as possible to the everlasting and unchanging ideal forms (ἰδέαι), which alone are true, and thereby morally perfect. The theory of imitation is inseparable from the theory of ideal forms. Once it has been accepted as applicable to poetry, as well as to everything else, that which is imitated in poetry must be conceived either as a *particular* act or emotion, as Plato said it was, thereby spelling the ruin of poetry, or as a universal, virtually equivalent to Plato's ideal form. Aristotle, beginning as usual with the fact of poetry, and feeling that it must be a good thing and therefore defensible on philosophical grounds, undertook to defend it against the strictures of his teacher. The only way in which he could have done so successfully would have been to reject the theory of imitation altogether and to recognize the fact that poetry, and with it all belletristic literature, is the expression of a man's soul, something to which the writer individually gives birth, by bringing it out of himself creatively, not something which he makes in conformity with an established pattern, earthly or otherwise. If what he writes is a "form," in any other sense than of a mere structural pattern such as narrative or drama, it is one that he himself, not God or nature, has created. But, instead of this, Aristotle made the fatal mistake of accepting Plato's premise that poetry was imitation. Thereafter in his efforts to avoid Plato's conclusions, which were inescapable, he ran into the error, momentous in the history of literary criticism, of positing the literary form (εἶδος) as something shaped and controlled by nature, a universal, therefore, which the artist is bound to imitate. In this way he made poetry as imitation respectable, by bringing it into accord with ultimate reality. He was refuting Plato, as it were, by Plato. As for the charge that poetry was impure and immoral, because it fed and watered the passions, Aristotle, in his defense of tragedy, tried save the patient by the use of more Platonic medicine, though applied in a different way. When Plato "purged" the soul of emotions—as being impurities—it was a surgical operation by which poetry itself was cut out and perished; but Aristotle maintained that tragedy had the healing virtue of "purging," by homeopathic treatment, the impure emotions of fear and pity, and was therefore beneficial to moral health and had a right to exist. Tragedy was valuable as a moral cathartic, and that was its principal function. This was not a profound observation concerning the effect of tragedy upon the spectator or reader, arrived at on the basis of independent contemplation of the subject, but rather a sophistical makeshift (honest though it was) by which to defend tragedy on the false premises concerning poetry already laid down by Plato.

Change in literature is geared to change in the way men think and react to life, both as groups and as individuals. If we wish to understand what causes the appearance of a new type of writing, we must not look for it in literature itself, which has no procreative power and is seldom more than a tool in the hands of a literary workman, but in the ever-changing world of thought and feeling which underlies literature, causes and controls its movement, or evolution, and acts upon it constantly from without. This generative force is in the process of changing its direction all the time; partly because the outlook and interests of society as a whole change with the passage of time and historical experience, and partly because every writer has a mind of his own which differs more or less in its ideals and purposes from that of any of his contemporaries. No two works of literature can represent exactly the same idea or aesthetic value, but each modifies its predecessors of a similar type by the application of a new and unique psychological force, the direction of which is arbitrary (within certain broad limitations imposed by cultural environment) and seldom predictable. This modification, taking place in a single work, may be either radical and conspicuous, amounting to a sharp change of purpose and direction, whence the birth of what is recognized as a new literary form, that is, a distinctive though broad fashion of writing; or it may be so slight as to be scarcely noticeable, in which case we say, conveniently but inaccurately, that it belongs to the same form, although in reality it is a new one. The only *exact* sense in which we can use the word "form" in this connection is in referring to a single composition. When the term is used abstractly in referring to a group or class of writings, its precise connotation is arbitrary and uncertain, and it cannot be adequate for any one text.[12]

A group of texts, each of which is more or less unique in its own way, though very similar to the others in its principal features, determines what we call a literary form or genre; but this form or genre, being only an *ex postfacto* classification, does not determine anything about a particular text. How then shall we account for the great similarity that exists between the separate members of one of our groups? Not by the concept of form as a prescription and a regulation, in the Aristotelian sense of εἶδος, consciously premeditated by writers, but by the unformulated and unmeditated force of contemporary thought, taste, and literary fashion. This, in its fundamental aspects, is obeyed by writers instinctively, and has as many different facets, both within and without the same social or intellectual stratum, as there are at the time literary forms or classifications, each of which is a projection from one of them. Every writer's expression has two aspects: what is peculiar to himself as an individual, and what belongs in kind to a more or less popular pattern of thought and style. Much the greater part of his expression falls normally into the last-named category, hence the genres; but the potentialities of individual expression are wide and only loosely controlled by the social and intellectual milieu as a whole, and the degree in which it is exercised by different authors varies greatly, especially in such an age as the Hellenistic, or that of today. Many literary works defy classification according to genre, except in the widest and loosest interpretation of what constitutes a particular genre. Critics have been much perplexed, for example, in their efforts to decide whether Horace's *Ars Poetica* is an *ars* (εἰσαγωγή), by form, or an epistle; whether the *Wonders beyond Thule* by Antonius Diogenes was a romance or an aretalogy; whether the *Satyricon* of Petronius was a Menippean satire or a romance; to what genre, if any, the so-called epyllion belongs;[13] and why Satyrus wrote biography in dialogue form, or is it dialogue with biographical content?[14] What the individual writer does with his composition seems to show little respect for the critically established canons of literary form, but to override them at will, and Horace the poet disagrees in practice with Horace the critic.

4

The concept of development in literature, which assumes that one kind of writing necessarily precedes or follows another by an interval of time, allowing for change in the way people think, often tends, by misapplication, to prevent our realizing the virtual simultaneity in appearance of many diverse kinds of composition, both within and without a literary genre so called. At the very beginning of the modern English novel we have such spiritual opposites as *Pamela, or Virtue Rewarded* on the one hand and *Tom Jones* on the other; and, far off from these, though not in time, the mysterious *Castle of Otranto*. Richardson, Fielding, and Walpole are three different minds catering to three different facets of contemporary taste; yet all three are writing "novels." Consider too how very different in their outlook and character are the novels of Stevenson, Thackeray, Dickens, Scott, and Hardy in the nineteenth century; but they are all spokesmen of a culture that we think of

as the same, something distinct from what preceded and followed it. It was so likewise in the beginning of the Greek
romance, and later on in its career. The sentimental romance
of *Ninus and Semiramis*, written in a spirit somewhat similar
to that of Richardson, has been dated with some probability
around the year 100 B.C., although it may be a little later or
earlier; and it was just about that time that Aristides of Miletus wrote his scandalous erotic stories entitled *Milesiaca*. In
the second century after Christ, if our dating of the Greek
novelists is approximately correct, we have such different kinds
of romantic narratives as the idyllic *Daphnis and Chloe*, in
which there is a minimum of adventure and a maximum (for
romance) of psychological interest; the sophistic *Babyloniaca*
of Iamblichus, in which a long series of sensational and meaningless adventures, interspersed with digressions on pseudo-
scientific subjects, is everything, and sentiment or character
apparently very little; the *Clitophon* and *Leucippe* of Achilles
Tatius, bordering on parody; and the *Ephesiaca* of Xenophon
of Ephesus, which is crowded with fast-moving adventures but
written in a spirit of naïve sentimentality. This variety is not
due to the evolution of literary fashion but to the fact that the
authors have different aesthetic ideals and purposes before
them and are addressing themselves to different kinds of contemporary taste. What a romance would be in the second century, when many were produced, depended primarily, as it
does today, upon what kind of an author had undertaken to
write it and what interested him most. Men representing many
different attitudes and tastes might be writing romance at the
same time, with corresponding results.

The plots of Greek romance tended to become stereotyped
so as to represent a pair of lovers separated from each other and
traveling about the world in adversity until they were finally
and happily reunited; but this uniformity of plot is no necessity
of the genre, any more than a similar stereotyping of plots was
necessary or inevitable in New Comedy, where there is prob-

ably no more variety, proportionately, than there is in the extant romances. Would anyone maintain that a play could not be classed as New Comedy unless it centered around a young man in love with a slave girl who later proved to be well-born? Neither love nor travel is a necessary feature of romance, even in Rohde's canon; *Apollonius of Tyre* is not primarily a love story, and there is no travel in *Daphnis and Chloe*. Comic or picaresque novels were probably scarce in antiquity, as they are relatively so today; but serious romances of adventure without the conventional pair of lovers, like *Apollonius of Tyre* and the *Recognitiones* of Ps. Clement, may well have been numerous and varied in kind, and it seems likely that some of them are represented among our papyrus fragments.

Of all the recognized literary forms, the romance, or novel, is by nature the most unbounded and the least confined in the range of what it may include. It is the most genuine and most characteristic expression in literature of the open society, whether Hellenistic or modern.[15] As such it is always expanding to meet the new and widening interests and outlook of its time, tending to absorb and to supplant in popular favor all other forms, especially poetry and drama and whatever in artistic literature is intense or concentrated, and to become for the open society of the cosmopolitan world what the old epic was for the closed society of tribal and patriarchal days—everything. In this sense (and also because it is concerned primarily with action viewed as concrete experience, paratactically presented, rather than with symbolical action as in tragedy), romance has been very aptly and significantly called "latter-day epic." Although the ancient romance, for reasons mentioned above, could not have expanded as far as the modern in the direction of universality, yet it was natural, if not inevitable, that it should adapt itself to the principal interests of the unlearned reading public for whom it was intended, and those interests were not confined to ideal love stories of the conventional type represented by Chariton or Heliodorus. Love in

ancient romance, as I conceive it, was not an essential element
but only a favorite theme in one of many possible varieties of
plot and subject matter.

5

Side by side with the secular romances, dealing with worldly
love and adventure and written only for entertainment, we
have the Christian romances, so-called, contained in such apocryphal books as the *Acts of Paul and Thekla*, the *Acts of Thomas*,
the *Acts of Andreas* (in the land of cannibals), the *Acts of Xanthippe and Polyxena*, etc.[16] These narratives are crowded with
sensational and miraculous episodes, and there is a beautiful
but fanatical heroine, either married or about to be, who attaches herself to the apostle as a religiously consecrated follower. Her renunciation of carnal love, and her efforts to save
herself and others from the "filth" of marriage, make much
trouble and lead to many narrow and miraculous escapes from
death and persecution, although the ending purports to be a
happy one. The content of these narratives, externally considered as usual, has led to their being classified by many as
"romances." Certainly the subject matter is romantic in the
sense that it includes much that is wonderful, thrilling, glamorous or sensational; but this is only a means by which simple
souls might be overawed and led into the way of salvation.

The purpose of an author, not his means nor the specific
content or mechanical features of his book, is the only feasible
criterion by which to classify it among genres. Any other
method leads to endless confusion and nullifies the value and
usefulness of the classification itself. There are books, to be
sure, though they are relatively few in number, in which the
author's main purpose in writing seems doubtful to us, or cannot be defined with certainty. We may be unable to decide,
for example, whether the philosophical, religious, or scientific
implications of a story, or simply the entertainment which it
affords, is uppermost in the author's intention. Such books

belong on the periphery of our classifications, or outside of them all, as you please. The limits of what constitutes a genre are necessarily arbitrary; but the most satisfactory basis on which to draw them, if they are to be clear, sharp, and deep reaching, is the author's intention; even though, in the nature of things, this criterion may sometimes elude us. To classify on the basis of anything else than the author's primary intention is to lose one's way in the labyrinth of means and materials, which are endlessly variable and complex and of minor consequence. In the case of the apocryphal *Acts*, which are all alike in their tendency, it ought to be clear to anyone that the principal purpose of the writers was to propagate the ideal of Christian asceticism, and not, as in the secular romances properly so called, simply to entertain the reader by a series of adventures of whatever kind.

Now it is very easy to understand how this Christian type of writing, whatever one may choose to call it, originated. Nothing but the *idea* of the Christian faith can account for it. No one has tried to trace its development through forerunners reaching back to the *Odyssey*. What it owes to antecedent literature, romantic or otherwise, is no more important or significant in explaining its origin than is Greek aretalogy or historiography or biography for explaining the origin of the canonical Gospels and the message of Jesus. Those who write anything make use of traditional patterns and take suggestions for episodes and illustrations wherever they find them, guided always by their own ideas and purposes. Greek romance is written in the basic structural pattern of narration, which is also that of historiography, biography, and epic. Its conventional features and its formal theory (its *décor*, not its purpose) are mainly those of historiography, but many of its mannerisms and stylistic conceits may be referred to epic and dramatic, and, in one case, to bucolic poetry. As for the stuff of which its plots and episodes are molded, this could be found almost anywhere in the Hellenistic world, in real life and in folklore as well as in books and on the stage. Such matter was never the exclusive property of any literary genre; and even if we knew the sources which prompted or supplied every episode, we should not be any nearer to understanding why books of this kind came to be written. We must look for the idea or purpose that motivated the writing of them, locate this in its historical setting, and show that it was alive and actively asserting itself at the time, bearing in mind that an old idea, though it may be well known to students of antiquity, can have no creative power unless it has been reborn and reactivated through having become part of life in the new age. When that happens, or seems to happen, it is really a new idea that is born, however much it may look like the old one; and with it a new literary form may come into being as its expression. We must explain the rise of every literary form in essentially the same way that we explain the appearance of the apocryphal *Acts*; for all such forms spring from specific ideas, or ideals, which are dynamic entities and just as real, even though they seldom take the form of an organized religion and are not so easily recognized, as Christianity itself. The trouble with so many searchers after origins has been that they know not the way of the spirit until it is institutionalized, and when that is the case, they are so impressed by it that they tend to overwork it. On the basis of fanciful and farfetched analogies, Buddhism has been proclaimed as the source of Aesopic fables and of the (Pythagorean) silence of Secundus and Syntipas; the Greek romance, according to Kerényi (and now Merkelbach and Altheim), developed from the sacred story of Isis and Osiris;[17] and Lord Raglan can account for hero-legends only on the supposition that they originated as misinterpretations of religious rituals. It is unfortunate for the understanding of literary history that, with few exceptions, the ideas which generate new forms have not all been branded by large and unmistakable labels.

6

In spite of the persistence here and there of perverse and outmoded ways of thinking about the nature and origins of Greek romance, it is nevertheless true that a great deal of new light has been thrown upon this subject since the beginning of the present century. Many papyrus fragments of new romances have been published; other newly found fragments belonging to extant romances have shown us that these must be dated earlier than had previously been supposed; and there have appeared two stimulating and instructive interpretations of our accumulated data. Here I refer to Bruno Lavagnini's *Le Origini del Romanzo Greco* (1921) and to J. Ludvíkovsky's *Rečky Roman Dobrodružny* (Greek Romance of Adventures, 1925) respectively. Apart from these, many other valuable books and articles have appeared in recent years which deal with partial aspects of the subject or with particular texts; but the two monographs just mentioned are those which are most relevant to the central theme of my chapters on the ideal romance, and it is from them that I have learned most.

With Lavagnini I find myself in almost complete agreement insofar as concerns the main points in his thesis. He first laid the triple foundations upon which any sound theory of the origins of Greek romance must be based. First, he emphasized the originally humble and demotic character of this kind of writing, in significant contrast to that of the great body of formal literature which moves on a separate and higher intellectual level, and in terms of which the ideal romance in its origin cannot be explained at all. Secondly, he identified the spiritual values embodied in these romances as something peculiar to the cultural outlook of Hellenistic times, historically conceivable only in that age, and a characteristic expression of it which is manifested contemporaneously through many other media, apart from these lowly romances of love and adventure, and on all levels of literature and thought. Thirdly, he demonstrated in copious detail the now somewhat obvious, but nonetheless interesting and significant fact that the early erotic romances were in many cases built upon local historical legends or myths. These are the basic lines in my own sketch of how the Greek erotic romance came into being; but, beyond this, much remains to be done by way of filling in the picture so as to make it more complete, definite, and convincing. Granted that the erotic romances were built chiefly on local myths of a national and once sacred character—and this proposition needs some qualification—how shall we explain the process which has transformed the meager outlines of these obscure myths into a long story of adventure with many episodes and complications? On this point Lavagnini is vague and almost silent; and yet it is just here, as it seems to me, that we are most in need of an explanation. Is it a gradual growth of some kind that confronts us, or an outright act of literary creation, or both? Must we suppose that a good part of the story in outline was already shaped for the romancer by local historiography or oral tradition, as Lavagnini seems to imply, or may we assume that the romancer invented almost everything except the names of his principal characters? In the latter case, what literary sanction did the author have for treating his matter so freely? These and similar questions have to be considered against a wide background of literary convention in ancient times.

Ludvíkovsky, who otherwise has much in common with Lavagnini, makes no fundamental distinction between the erotic type of romance as represented by Chariton and the earlier so-called romance of Alexander by Pseudo-Callisthenes, which tells of a military hero of national significance who is not in love. Both books, according to Ludvíkovsky, are only varieties of what is defined in its essentials as romance of adventure, or latter-day epic; and the transition from one variety to the other, that is, from a story about a famous military hero to one about an unknown lover, is explained as due to a gradual evolution taking place within the genre after its origin. This view, in my opinion, is fundamentally wrong, and I note that Lavagnini in a recent essay also objects to it. The error lies in supposing that the telling of adventures on their own account is the ideal purpose by which in both cases the romancer is motivated in his effort, rather than a favorite *means* which he employs for pleasing his readers in the pursuit and development of a different ideal. That different ideal in the case of the Alexander romance was the glorification of Alexander the Great as a national hero, the son of King Nectanebus II of Egypt and the Macedonian Olympias, the Graeco-Egyptian founder of the city of Alexandria, where Greeks and Egyptians lived together in harmony as his political heirs on a relatively equal footing. The spirit in which this book is written is strongly patriotic; and although the facts of history are distorted and mingled with much fiction, yet the central purpose of the composition as a whole is eminently historical and propagandistic. It is historiography by intention, not romance. It expresses the sentimental, civic idealism of a particular society, at a particular moment in history, in line with a familiar type of short-lived, local patriotism looking to the past which asserted itself apologetically and simultaneously throughout the Graeco-oriental world as the aftermath of Alexander's conquests.[18] It is this background of nationalistic ideas and impulses, historically well known, that explains the appearance of such things as the Alexander biography by Ps.-Callisthenes. Herein the romantic adventures are something incidental to the main idea, not an end in themselves.

In strong contrast to the motive which inspired the patriotic efforts of Ps.-Callisthenes, vulgar as they are, stands the motive which prompts the writing of those later books which are more properly called romances. In this category of romance in the stricter sense of the word we include the extant novels of love and adventure by Chariton, Xenophon of Ephesus, Longus, Heliodorus, and Achilles Tatius, along with the non-erotic stories of *Apollonius of Tyre* and the *Recognitiones* of Ps.-Clement in its pre-Christian environment.[19] In this kind of book the author aims at nothing more than outright entertainment by means of imaginative fiction; his purpose, like that of the dramatists is purely literary and aesthetic, not informative. He has no concern with history or nationality for its own sake (not even in the Ninus romance), and his principal character, or characters, although they must have the conventional sanction of belonging to some myth or legend—the more obscure the better, so long as it is recognized as official, or said to be, by someone somewhere—are practically unknown to the world at large, even by name. They can therefore be written about with the utmost freedom, very nearly as much freedom indeed as would be the case if the characters had been invented outright as in the average modern novel. Thus the reader is entertained at length by an account of plainly fictitious experiences which are, in effect, those of a private individual devoid of historical significance. This is the most distinctive thing about the seven books mentioned above as belonging in the category of real romance; it is the one radical feature that they all have in common both with each other and with the modern novel, and it is the principal thing that marks them off in a class by themselves in sharp contradistinction to such national hero-legends as that about Alexander. The latter, in its original form, was the product of a time and place in which men were still thinking about their corporate interests, and had not yet become so accustomed to thinking in terms of purely private persons and private fortunes as to write about these in an ideal way, or to use them as symbols for the presentation of popular sentimental or ethical values, except in poetry. The romantic biography of Alexander on the one hand and the erotic romances on the other stand in a purely paratactic relation to each other. They are parallel and independent projections from relatively low strata of Hellenistic culture; and it is this fact alone that accounts for the aesthetic similarities between them. There is no direct genetic relationship between the two, and no discernible influence of one upon the other. Probably the nearest thing in kind to Ps.-Callisthenes, although this too is a parallel, independent, and unrelated literary phenomenon that deals with a famous cultural hero instead of with a military hero, is the vulgar *Life of Aesop*, written in Egypt in the first century after Christ.

In explaining the relation of romance to historiography Ludvíkovský applies the well-known principle of Brunetière, according to which a literary form in its origin is a *démembrement* of a preceding form. This is generally true as a statement of what takes place externally and mechanically at the birth of a new form, and it is true, I believe, of romance in relation to historiography; but it passes over the important matter of causation, and on this point Ludvíkovsky satisfies himself by invoking the vague and magical concept of development, which is supposed to take place under the influence of popular taste and literary tendencies, without the intervention of any new and conscious purpose on the part of vulgar historiographers; they thought that they were writing history, but instead they had stumbled into writing romance. "A son école" says Ludvíkovsky, referring to Brunetière in the French résumé of his book (p. 149), "nous nous representons le roman se développant, sans intervention d'une force extérieure, comme un démembrement de la forme précédente, c'est à dire de l'historiographie qui, en Grèce, fut toujours plus un art épique qu'une science." By denying the intervention of a new purpose on the part of the romancer, which would be a force acting from without, Ludvíkovsky is saying that romance is historiography extended along its own lines as an epic art. Half-educated authors, writing in accord with popular taste, exploited that side of historiography which was least concerned with matters of historical truth or consequence. In so doing, they made their histories worse and worse, by intermediate steps of development, or rather degeneration, until at last they became so bad, as histories, that we call them romances. Thus romance in origin was only a disease of historiography, which broke out in the intellectual slums of antiquity and became endemic.

Superficially considered, there is something plausible in the theory that Greek romance is a specialized offshoot of historiography (or historical biography), developed under the influence of popular taste and sentiment in Hellenistic times; especially so if, with Lavagnini in opposition to Ludvíkovsky, we think of this historiography as primarily that which was concerned with the legendary founding of cities and local cults in faraway times. The idea in general, without the emphasis on local myth, has been endorsed by others besides Ludvíkovsky, as he himself observes, and notably by Edward Schwartz, although only in an offhand way. What makes it deceptively plausible is the undoubted fact that it was from historiography that the romancer derived a large part of his manner and method in writing, as well as the purely conventional theory under which his new kind of composition was put forth before the world, and by which it received that minimum of sanction as literature which was necessary for its debut. Owing to the nature of literary conditions at the time, under which outright, 100-percent fiction made up in the service of ideal *Dichtung* was unheard of and almost inconceivable, a long and serious narration written in prose was bound to make the purely formal pretense (by which no one was deceived) of relating historical events, and of being a "history"; hence our word *story*. But this convention, though necessary, was only an externality, which could cover artistic and creative fiction as well as informative history. In the case of romance presented outwardly as history the author's intention was no more historiographical than was that of the Greek poets and tragedians, who had been bound by similar convention, and whose plasmatical manipulation of "history" for their own artistic purposes was exactly the same in kind, though not in degree, as that employed by the earliest romancers in prose. The romancer, unlike all the historiographers, no matter how mendacious, epic, rhetorical, or dramatic some of these might be in their procedure, was intent *only* upon producing an artistic composition; and in that respect his purpose is far more like that of the tragedian than like that of the historiographer, whose business, however he may manage it, is always to inform his readers about persons and events of public importance and significance. For the romancer, as for the poet, the data of history, legend, or myth serve only in the subordinate capacity of supplying characters, starting points, and background for the work of literary art, and are rarely dwelt upon in their entirety; but for the historiographer —and that means Ps.-Callisthenes and his kind as well as the more critical historians—these same materials in all their completeness and continuity are the principal thing; and whatever is untrue, or stylistically epic, romantic, dramatic, or rhetorical in the presentation of them is incidental to the main undertaking, the purpose of which always, whether or not it is seriously and honestly pursued, is to tell the truth about important events and persons of the past insofar as it can be known. Many historians tell lies, and make mistakes about what really happened in the past, some much more often than others; but romancers and poets never lie about such things, because their business is not with matters of factual occurrence, and no one is or need be deceived by their representations. The real romance, as we defined it above, is falsehood ($\psi\epsilon\hat{v}\delta os$) only when judged by the alien standards of historiography; when judged with reference to its own standards as a literary genre, it is a legitimate artistic creation ($\pi\lambda\acute{a}\sigma\mu a$). Although much of the manner and substance of historiography was used in the making of romance, it is an illusion to suppose that the former gave birth to the latter or was responsible for its appearance.

What I regard as Ludvíkovsky's failure, in his attempt to explain how the Greek romance originated, is due to the evolutionary nature of his and Brunetière's way of thinking, the fallacies of which in general have been described in the earlier part of this chapter.[20] The purpose which guides the romancer and defines the genre romance is entirely different from that which guides the historiographer and defines his genre, and there can be no development or gradual transition from one purpose to another, at least not on the plane of results, which in this case means the surface of literature. What are the intermediate steps of development between writing and not writing, or between writing in verse and writing in prose? There may be a gradual transition in the mind of the prospective writer, but it cannot be gauged in terms of what he actually does. Change in direction in literary practice can come only from without, by the intervention *d'une force extérieure* in the form of a new idea. Ludvíkovsky, like many others, regards it as a scientific virtue not to recognize the operation of consciously new ideas and purposes appearing suddenly in the formation of literature. Under the narcotic influence of concepts shaped on the analogy of biological change, which is accomplished in disregard of human or animal will in the course of millions of years, he prefers to explain a relatively momentary phenomenon in Hellenistic literature by positing the activity of a series of miraculously confused writers, whose accumulated mistakes revealed to the ancient world the concept of romance, rather than to admit that the first romance was produced by a man who had a conscious purpose and a plan of his own. It is true that a writer may not know what he is actually doing in effect; but unless he is crazy he knows what he is trying to do, and so do his readers. Pseudo-Callisthenes thought that he was doing the same kind of thing as the real Callisthenes and some thirty other historians of Alexander whose books are known to us by quotation; but what the author of the Ninus romance, properly so called, has done in his composition is recognized by all critics as being the same in kind as what the later romancers beginning with Chariton do in theirs. Between these two books, the one about Alexander, the other about Ninus, lies all the difference between historiography and romance, as much difference in the fundamental concepts of purpose and orientation as there is between Plutarch's *Life of Caesar* and a novel by Sir Walter Scott. The resemblances between the Greek books are purely incidental, being due not to the influence of one upon the other as an example or precedent, but mainly to the fact that both were written by naïve or ignorant authors to suit the taste of half-educated, or perhaps juvenile, readers. The absence of any known connecting links in the supposed evolution of historiography, as represented by Pseudo-Callisthenes, into romance as represented by the story of Ninus is not due to the loss of ancient texts, but to logical necessity; for such links are practically inconceivable. Like many others who speak about "development," with the easy feeling that the word of itself will carry conviction or pass unchallenged, Ludvíkovsky does not realize what it implies in terms of actual literary practice and human behavior. In the sense in which he uses it in ex-

plaining the origin of romance it will not bear examination.
"The essential element of romance," says Ludvíkovsky, "is
action and fantasy. One must find a common definition applicable to both the historical romance (Pseudo-Callisthenes)
and the erotic romance. These are merely two categories of the
romance of adventures, which may be defined [*qu'on peut carac-
tériser*] on the same principle of ἀρετή [valor or virtue] and of
Τύχη φιλόκαινος [novelty-loving Fortune]." The fallacy of this,
as an argument, lies in ignoring the positive intention or purpose of the authors (unless it was merely to entertain the reader
with adventures), and of representing as a causative force
operative in the formation of literature a mere description or
category of *external* features which the critic has succeeded in
"finding." If these romancers, including Pseudo-Callisthenes
along with Chariton, had been intent only on giving the reader
adventures, instead of being inspired by different and more
fundamental artistic purposes and ideals, it would not have
mattered to Pseudo-Callisthenes whether he wrote about Alexander the Great or an unknown girl named Callirhoe. This
choice of characters could *not* have mattered with the author
of the Ninus romance, Chariton, Heliodorus, or any of the
other *erotici*; but it would be absurd to suppose that it was a
matter of indifference to Pseudo-Callisthenes.[21] Moreover, if
romance originated in the desire to exploit action and fantasy
per se, instead of in the service of a *sentimental* ideal, why is it
that these features are so much more conspicuous in the latest
of the erotic romances than in Chariton's, which is the earliest
extant specimen that we have? Chariton's plot is much simpler
than that of any of the later romances, *Daphnis and Chloe*
excepted, and its sentimental inspiration is obviously much
stronger, more genuine, and more naïve than that of his followers. More of the interest is on the inside of things, on the
characters and their responses to circumstances, and less on
the external novelties of plot and incident. Action for its own
sake at the expense of character and inner meaning is something which, like rhetoric for its own sake, encroaches upon the

various forms of Hellenistic literature not as a purposive ideal capable of changing the theory of the genre, but as a weakness due to poverty of spirit in mediocre authors. It increases in prominence in proportion to the degree in which the original purposes and ideals of the genre, with its emphasis on inner meaning, cease to inspire the practitioners of it and are maintained only as empty formalities. This happened, with notable exceptions here and there, in the history of Greek drama from Euripides on through New Comedy and late tragedy down to pantomime, wherein acting was everything; and, as Ludvíkovsky observes, the same tendency was rife also among the inferior writers of history during the same period. But historiography and romance, as we explained above, move along parallel lines, which have not yet met.

Although I cannot accept Ludvíkovsky's theory of how the romance originated, I wish, nevertheless, to repeat that his essay contains much that is vital and stimulating; especially in what relates to the environment and aesthetics of Greek romance, conceived in the words of Karel Čapek, writing about its modern equivalent, as "la dernière épopée, ou le roman à l'usage des servants," and to the peculiar influence exerted by Xenophon's *Cyropedia* as a precedent, upon the earliest romancers.

Ludvíkovsky objects to Lavagnini's theory that romance originated in the popular elaboration of local myths, on the ground that these myths were dead at the time and no longer cultivated among the people themselves, but only in learned antiquarian literature. This objection is valid, in my opinion, if by "popular elaboration" Lavagnini referred to the growth of myth into romance by a folkloristic process. I am not sure that such was his meaning, or, if it was, how much of the development of local myths into romances he would attribute to the popular manipulation of them either in written texts or in folklore. However that may be, the point made by Ludvíkovsky, that the local myth was "dead" in Hellenistic times, deserves some emphasis in this connection, as well as a word of explanation, lest there be any doubt in the reader's mind concerning what the present writer believes to have been the part played by myth in the making of romance. I cannot believe that local patriotism had anything to do with the making of myths into romances; or that the local myths furnished any different kind of inspiration to the romancers, who may just as well have been foreigners, than they did to Ovid when he exploited their erotic themes in his poetry. Knowledge of these myths, many of which were very obscure, comes to us almost entirely from learned poets and antiquarians. Although they were locally advertised now and then in an official way, as a matter of civic pride or an attraction for tourists, it is very unlikely that they had any real popularity, or any potential of growth and expansion as folktales. In that sense they were dead, even though "humanized," and belonged only in the realm of erudite things. They were inert materials which could be used, and were used in the making of romances. Rohde, in referring to the use made of these local myths by Alexandrian and Roman poets, aptly calls them "pretexts, under which one might tell a graceful or a clever story on its own account as such." [22] Lavagnini says in ambiguous language that the romance could easily develop, or be developed from one of these short stories, provided there was already inherent in its texture, or was introduced, a structural principle allowing for the dramatic unfolding of events and of progress from an initial situation to a final one; to which he adds that historiography might furnish that "germ of action," when it was otherwise wanting. All this is true and noteworthy, but what needs to be emphasized more especially in this place is something that Lavagnini himself observes in another and somewhat broader connection, namely, that "il romanzo e il carattere romanzesco non sta nella materia in sè, ma nel modo in cui questa è sentita e trattata." [23] We must study the *creator* of romance; first the spiritual impulse that moved him to write, and after that the way in which he worked and the literary concepts and precedents that guided or conditioned his procedure. *Materiam superabat opus.*

II

The Form Romance
in Historical
Perspective

1

For the purpose of understanding the nature of Greek romance and how it came into being, it is essential to look at it from the outside as a totality, lest we wander about among the trees without seeing the forest itself and the landscape on which it stands, as so many investigators of this subject have done. We shall try to put into perspective a wide range of narrative literature, if not the whole of it; and, in so doing we shall have to consider other forms of literature in their bearing upon it. Nothing can be understood historically in isolation. We begin with a definition of romance as a whole.

What should be included and what not under the term romance as applied to a literary species, or under any subspecies thereof, is a matter of arbitrary choice, owing to the fact mentioned above (p. 18), that the only logical limit to divisibility in the classification of literary forms is the single composition. With this qualification in mind, we may define the form romance, all varieties included, as follows: *an extended narrative published apart by itself which relates—primarily or wholly for the sake of entertainment or spiritual edification, and for its own sake as a story, rather than for the purpose of instruction in history, science, or philosophical theory—the adventures or experiences of one or more individuals in their private capacities and from the viewpoint of their private interests and emotions.*

The foregoing definition applies to almost everything that the present writer would call romance or novel, ancient or modern. It describes the romance or novel in its *original* and proper character, when its outward form and substance is not made to serve an ulterior purpose. Although it has the advantage of delimiting the term in certain important respects, which will be discussed later on, yet it is necessarily very inadequate as a description of any one kind of romance, and it applies to "epic" as well as to "romance." The reason for this inadequacy in our definition, or in any conceivable substitute for it, lies in the fact that romance as a whole is made up of heterogeneous groups of literary phenomena, which have in common with each other and with epic (to distinguish them from other kinds of literature) only such radical features of structure, purpose, method, and potentiality as do not determine anything in particular about the aesthetic ideals, minor techniques, or subject-matter which may be characteristic of any one group or subdivision. That which determines the specific nature of any large and well-recognized variety of romance, or of epic, or of romance as a whole in contrast with what we call epic in a narrow sense, is the nature of the society for which it is produced and whose taste, temper, and experience it reflects.

2

Romance and epic are basically the same genre, as much so as ancient and modern drama. If we call this elemental narrative genre *epic*, then the best-known varieties of it in the Western world, each of which is the independent creation of a different culture in a different historical era, may be designated as follows: national warrior-epic I (*Iliad*), romantic epic I (*Odyssey*), latter-day epic I (Greek romance), national warrior-epic II (*Beowulf, Song of Roland*, etc.), romantic epic II (romance of chivalry, broadly so called),[1] latter-day epic II (modern novel). The forms here mentioned are only those which have been projected by familiar and well-known types of *Weltanschauung*, and which have repeated themselves conspicuously in the history of European literature, ancient and modern. Each arises from the historical conditions under which men have lived in different ages. But many other cultural entities—some of them simple, some more complex or artificial, some only temporary or local, some purely individual—have, within the same period of time, so acted upon the negative primeval form as to produce many special varieties of it.[2] The idea of indefinitely continued narrative relating to the actions of an individual is at least as old as literature itself. It is the common property of the human race, and nothing that needs to be explained historically. It may be used in different ages and clothed with new values so as to become what we call a new literary form, or it may remain unused and neglected, as in the classical period of Greek literature, according to whether or not it is found to be suitable for the expression of thought and feeling in any particular age.

In the long run of history certain fundamental types of society recur, and from each of them is projected a characteristic kind of narrative literature. What we have called national warrior-epic has twice appeared in the Western world as the principal literary expression of its time, and the same is true for what we have called latter-day epic, or the novel. It is well recognized that the simple, heroic, war-conditioned, tribal society that produced such epics as *Beowulf*, the *Song of Roland*, or the *Niebelungenlied* (in their earliest forms) is fundamentally the same kind of society as that which is reflected in the *Iliad*; and it is likewise clear that the cultural conditions of the Hellenistic age, in their broad essentials, were profoundly similar to those of the modern world since the French revolution. In both these "modern" ages the cultural solidarity of an earlier period, in which the life and thought of men had been shaped and controlled by relatively fixed customs and standards of value, has been gradually dissolved into a world-wide megalopolitan civilization which has no soul of its own, nor any direction other than that of sheer nihilism, and in which all the forces of thought and feeling are centrifugal. There are no common ideals, interests, or viewpoints among men, save those which have become provincial in the new world-society or confined to small groups where the cultural values sanctioned by tradition or communal life can be fostered for a while, though they continue to ebb into the spiritual void and the intellectual chaos by which they are surrounded. In such a world anything that has high quality—be it moral, aesthetic, or intellectual—is understood and cultivated by only a few people. Whatever in literary or dramatic art is meant to be accommodated to the understanding and taste of the cosmopolitan masses is thereby debased in proportion to the degree in which it is popularly exploited. Quality cannot be spread abroad in a *big* world without losing itself in mere quantity, variety, and extension. Literature made popular in an open society, such as that of the Hellenistic age or the present, is progressively externalized, mechanized, sensationalized, and impoverished, as regards its moral and aesthetic quality, while the range of its content is extended outward ever more to embrace the vagaries unlimited of the spiritual and intellectual nomads for whom it is intended. That which reaches out for everything loses its own shape; hence the novel, like the epic, is the least defined, the least concentrated, the least organic, and the most formless of all the so-called literary forms. It is the open form *par excellence* for the open society, as the early epic is the open form for the closed society. Like the epic in its day, it has everything for everybody, and the range of its thought-content is, or tends to be, coextensive with that of the world for which it is produced. But the world of the early epic, with its compact cultural uniformity of outlook and its refraction of experience into generic patterns of thought and action,[3] is a very much smaller and simpler world than that which projects the novel, and the quality of its thought and expression *on the popular level* is as much higher and more intense than that of the modern age as its range and dispersion into equalitarian multiplicity and confusion is less. It is only in a relatively small world that the individual man can be thought of as poetically great and heroic and his experience or fate felt to be symbolical of that of mankind in general at its best or most typical. The hero, epic or tragic, must signify, to the instinct of a popular audience, something that is fraught with more meaning than his own curious particularity. He must represent ideal values that no one questions and that everyone feels to be noble. This is possible and natural in a relatively closed society, where the principal concepts and values of life are typed by custom, tradition, faith, and uniform experience; but that condition of things passed away in the lifetime of Sophocles, and thereafter in the old Greek world neither an epic nor a tragic hero, in the original sense of these words, was possible. Nor is he possible today. In the vastly expanded world of Hellenistic and Roman times the individual lost nearly all his quondam importance and representative significance, having become too tiny to be tragic, or heroic, or poetic, or symbolical of anything more than himself or a particular segment of contemporary society. He could play the part of Dicaeopolis, Davus or Chremes, Chaereas the young lover, or the pathetic Willy Loman in Arthur Miller's *Death of a Salesman* (mistaken for tragedy), but he could not wear the tragic mask of Ajax, Agamemnon, or Oedipus, not though he were Caesar himself.[4] The bigger the world the smaller the man. Faced with the immensity of things and his own helplessness before them, the spirit of Hellenistic man became passive in a way that it had never been before, and he regarded himself instinctively as the plaything of Fortune. All this is conspicuous from first to last in the Greek romance.

Viewed as latter-day epic for Everyman, the romance or novel was, owing to its preoccupation with action, its particularity, its extension and looseness, its unconcentrated nature, and its adaptability to the expression of all kinds of values high and low, the one literary form which was best suited to the Hellenistic age. It would have prevailed over all others, tending to absorb them all as it does today, and as the old epic had done, had it not been suppressed by the force of a learned academic tradition more powerful, howbeit rarely proclaimed, than any that has since prevailed in Europe.

With greater intercourse among nations, and the widening of geographical and political horizons due to manifold contacts with an outside world larger and more varied than that which fostered the purely national saga, epic poetry in Europe passes into a romantic stage, where it dies as poetry. Afterwards it is succeeded as narrative by historiography, which is written at first in epic verse but later in prose, and as poetry by lyric and drama. In Northern Europe, among the Germanic and Celtic peoples, the first stage of epic poetry, comprising national war-rior-epic, was still young and immature when its natural devel-opment was thwarted by influences from without and it passed prematurely into the romantic stage of epic poetry, which is fundamentally analogous, expecially in its beginnings, to what we have in the *Odyssey*. In this second stage Northern epic, embracing many types of romance, mostly chivalrous, flour-ished abundantly for more than three hundred years, nourished and standardized in its substance and ideals by the culturally consolidated but international world of Christianity and feu-dalism, and frequently enriched by the importation of legend-ary materials from abroad. The culture which sustained and quickened this romance of chivalry, though self-contained, positive, and dynamic, was peculiar in that it had resulted from the fusion of two very different worlds of ideas: one the simple and relatively barbarous world of the earliest national epic, the other the highly civilized and sophisticated world of Rome and Christendom. Owing to historical conditions of a more normal and less complex nature, the corresponding phase of epic poetry in early Greece, which we may recognize in the

Odyssey and presumably also in a few lost poems, was of only brief duration, as compared with that of its counterpart in medieval romance; but the nature of the evolution through which it passed, and the causes of it, were very much the same.

The *Odyssey* has often been called a romance, and reasonably so. It has a definite plot with a background of private and domestic life, a long series of wonderful adventures undergone by the hero in struggling to achieve his goal, and a happy triumph and reunion at the end. Indeed, there may be no generic difference at all, as concerns content and structure, between the *Odyssey* or a romance of chivalry on the one hand and a late Greek or modern novel on the other. But one must not be deceived by this similarity into supposing that there is any causal or genetic relationship between these two types of narrative—or rather these two literary institutions—either in the ancient world of Greece or in the medieval and modern world of Western Europe. In neither case is one the "forerunner" of the other, except accidentally and in the purely chronological sense of that word. They are as isolated and disconnected from each other as the several cultures which projected them in widely separated periods of history. When the conditions under which men live and think in different ages and places become similar, through the tendency of history to repeat itself, the types of narrative which are engendered by those conditions, and which reflect them, will be correspondingly similar.

The conditions under which the story of the *Odyssey* was told were distinctly different from those which had inspired the story of Achilles in the *Iliad*. This difference in the outlook, experience, and taste of the respective audiences, and their times and places, is fundamentally similar in kind, though not in degree, to the difference in social, political, and cultural conditions which lies between those reflected in the later, more romantic and more biographical *chansons de geste* with their world-wide theater of action and those which are implicit in the *Chanson de Roland*, and similar early warrior-epics. The later type of epic narrative presupposes an audience and a minstrel whose political, social, and geographical horizons have been widened and whose outlook on the world is more international in character, more wonder-seeking, more interested in action or adventure as such, and less concerned with the ethical idealism and patriotic pride of the relatively small and isolated ethnic group to which the earlier and more tragically colored epic songs were addressed. With its happy ending and its background of domestic life, the *Odyssey* is much less tragic in tone than the *Iliad*. Its elevation of a multitude of adventures into the foreground of dramatic interest represents a movement away from early epic poetry, whose ideal values are intensely ethical and usually tragic, in the direction of prosaic narrative, wherein, as in the cyclic epics that followed, the episode *per se* —what a French critic aptly called the *machine*[5]—becomes the main thing, and the poetry of character is lost in a lengthy catalogue of events garnished with heroics that are only conventional. In the *Odyssey*, to be sure, much of the old poetry of character is still retained, and Odysseus even at the court of Alcinous is a greater attraction in his own person than the adventures which he relates; but, in spite of the poet's *relative* closeness to the ideals of the heroic age, the direction of advance in epic narrative from *Iliad* to *Odyssey* is unmistakeable. Whatever may be the date of origin of the *Iliad* in the form in which we have it, the story of Achilles pictures the ideals of a comparatively isolated, patriarchal society on the mainland of Greece, while the *Odyssey* reflects the outlook on the world of a later age, in which the interest in sea voyages has been stimulated by the beginnings of colonization and contact with Phoenician traders, and in which the social organization has advanced toward the dissolution of the old kingship and the predominance of the nobility, as it appears in Hesiod and Archilochus. That curiosity about the wonders of the world, which gives to the *Odyssey* so much of its romantic quality, was a transitory state of mind fostered by recent Greek experience in the colonizing, first of the Northeast and later of the West, in the eighth century. As such it was strong enough to make a conspicuous mark upon the contemporary shaping of epic legends. The newest song, as Homer himself in the *Odyssey* (I 352) tells us, in referring to stories about the return of the heroes from Troy (*nostoi*), is always most welcome to the audience of the minstrel. In the *nostoi* the old hero, originally the idol of a local and patriotic tradition, and chiefly a warrior, becomes, like Huon de Bordeaux or Ogier the Dane, an adventurer in strange and faraway lands, even fairyland. But this romantic outlook on the world, together with the maintenance of the old epic poetry which had been revitalized by it for a while even in the moribund stage of its own career, was bound to pass away and become impotent, literarily, as soon as the Greek world of city-states became what it was geographically, politically, socially, and commercially at the end of the seventh century. Even before that time, by half a century at least, it would have been difficult or impossible for an epic minstrel to picture Sicily and its environs as the outlying fairyland of the *Odyssey*, peopled with gods and giants. The kind of living experience and thoughts by which men's minds were dominated in the middle of the seventh century, and which determined the basic nature of the only genuine and spontaneous literature that they would produce, may be seen in the poetry of Hesiod, Archilochus, and Alcman. Lyric poetry, on the one hand monodic and personal, and on the other choral and communal, was a natural product of life in the new city-state, with its keen political and social rivalries, which brought to the fore such individuals as Archilochus, and its well-established communal institutions, mainly religious but also secular, whose needs were best served by choral singing of one kind or another according to the occasion. Under these conditions the epic recitation could not thrive as poetry, because it no longer had a monopoly of public interest as entertainment. It could be admired and enjoyed on occasion, as always afterwards, but the spirit necessary to create it and keep it renewed was no longer existent in the Hellenic world of that time. Owing to the uniformity of its subject-matter and meter, its length and its impersonal objectivity, epic narrative was inadequate either for the expression of individual thoughts and emotions, which called for a variety of other moods and meters, or for choral singing on state occasions.

Literature was by now distributed into specialized and, for the most part, concentrated and intensified forms cultivated separately, to meet the needs of a more varied and more self-conscious society whose ideas and interests were of a new kind. So poetry departed from epic narrative and found its truest expression in other forms; and those narratives about the heroes of old became data for writers who sought, by means of systematizing and rationalizing the ancient traditions and genealogies, to construct a history of the past. Although they wrote in the meter and dialect of the epic, yet the purpose by which they were guided was informative and didactic rather than inspirational or poetic, and their spirit, by comparison, prosaic. The historiographical approach to and treatment of legendary materials, as opposed to the epic and poetic, appears first in the catalogues of the *Iliad* (Bk. II) and the *Odyssey* (Bk. XI), which are Hesiodic in character and relatively late; and this exploitation of the ancient traditions *as history* was continued in the so-called epic cycle as described by Proclus, and later on in the prose chronicles of the rationalizing Ionian logographers. Hesiod, unlike Homer, with whom he contrasts himself by implication in the *Theogony* (1. 27), and whose art he misunderstands, writes to instruct men in the knowledge of *true* things. His attempt to explain how the world came into being and evolved on the principle of birth is animated by a scientific impulse of fundamentally the same nature as that by which the Ionian philosophers were inspired from Thales on to Democritus. In the Greek world after Homer the minds of men —and that is what one must reckon with first of all in literary history—were dominated by two moods: one, the poetic, found its genuine expression in lyrics of various kinds and later in drama, and the other, which may be described as the intellectual and pedestrian or informative mood, manifested itself in the pursuit of historical and scientific truth. Under these conditions, as under broadly similar conditions in the sixteenth and seventeenth centuries when lyric poetry, drama, and scientific and critical writings predominate, there was no real place for romantic epic in the manner of the *Odyssey*, or of *Lancelot du Lac*, or of Sidney's *Arcadia*; and whatever was written in this tradition was bound to be artificial and precious. Real romance was dead. Hence the *Odyssey* had no successors in kind, unless one takes into account the lost *Telegony*. It represents not the beginning of a new literary fashion, but the last phase of an old one; that is, the last phase of narrative literature with a poetic, rather than a historiographical orientation.

3

Early epic poetry embodies the almost complete ethical, aesthetic, religious, historical, and scientific ideas and ideals of the simple society to which it is addressed. It has no literary competitors in its time, because it contains within its own ambit all the spiritual, educational, and entertainment values that the age requires. But later on, when society has become more complex, self-conscious, sophisticated, and urban, the various elements of history, ethics, science, tragedy, comedy, lyric, etc., which had been only parts of the simple epic or implicit or incidental in it, are each cultivated on their own account and intensified as separate literary forms. In these conditions, which prevail throughout the long cultural interval that separates early epic from latter-day epic (novel), the importance or value of a story *per se* as an independent form of literary art is enormously reduced. All its principal values have been preempted by other more concentrated forms of literature, which alone are in honor; so that a mere story as such, however interesting or charming, as in Aeschylus, Pindar, Herodotus, Plato, or Xenophon, can only be incidental and subordinate to something else, not an end in itself. The principal forms of classical poetry, which is popular poetry, are lyric, tragedy,

and comedy, presented to the public orally under keenly competitive conditions and meant to be heard rather than to be
read; while the prose-writing which is contemporary with this
poetry is employed for the utilitarian purpose of instruction in
history, philosophy, and science of one kind or another, or the
keeping of records. The appeal of this early classical prose is to
the intellect almost exclusively, rather than to the emotional
or to the artistic sense, and it is not used, at least not con-
consciously, as a medium by which to convey poetic or inspirational or sentimental values. Nor is it as yet *Kunstprosa*; for
literary artistry as such still belongs, theoretically at least,
only to poetry. A narrative of personal adventure could have
no place of its own within the framework of these firmly established conventions, since it was in theory neither *Dichtung* nor
Wahrheit, neither art nor science, poetry nor instruction. It
was only when these sharply defined and mutually exclusive
forms of classical literature had been broken down and their
aesthetic and intellectual proprieties redistributed among a
multiplicity of forms in both prose and verse, and with little
distinction between these two, that the story of personal adventure with its poetic, sentimental, and dramatic virtues could
once more be exploited on its own account as an independent
form of literary art as it had been in the time of Homer. As
Dichtung in Alexandrian times, both historiography and romance took unto themselves artistic aims of a kind that had
once belonged only in drama or epic poetry. In historiography
these dramatic and poetic features, although extensively cultivated in accordance with the taste of the age, were incidental
and illegitimate and secondary in theory to the main purpose
of the genre, which never changed; but in romance these features were exploited on their own account and for no other purpose; and it was for their sake alone that romance, as a new
form, was invented. In respect to the kind of literary values
that it purveyed, this new form, romance, like its older contemporary, New Comedy, was a natural successor to Euripidean
drama. That drama, continued on the Hellenistic stage, was

made at first to suit the taste of a cultivated and intellectual public, but it was succeeded thereafter by mime and pantomime, in which sheer action was everything with a minimum of meaning or of attention to character; and the same evolution took place on a lower intellectual level in the romance, which became in course of time likewise externalized. In the big world of Alexandrian times there were sharply defined strata in society and intellectual aptitude which had not existed in the old city-state, and in these circumstances literature had to take on additional forms and be accommodated as never before to different classes of readers and spectators. In order to fill the gap left in the field of fictional and dramatic entertainment for everybody, caused by the passing of the city-state with its uniform, theater-going public, it was necessary in late Alexandrian times to provide two separate forms of literature, each addressed to a different class of people, conveyed by a different medium, and marked by a wide degree of difference in aesthetic quality and potentiality, in accordance with the understanding and taste of the public to which each was addressed. One of these forms, the earlier, more intellectual and more sophisticated of the two, though still popular, was New Comedy, which was the direct heir of Euripides on the Athenian stage, and later on the Roman. The other was the lowly romance of love and adventure, meant for a reading public composed of young or naïve people of little education, most of whom presumably lived in small towns or rural districts, rather than at Athens or in other cities, and would seldom be near a theater. These are the forgotten people of literary history; and, although the expression of their taste and ideals in written form was slow in making its appearance and was long ignored by men of intellectual or literary pretensions who always look back to what is classical, yet it is to them that we owe the creation of the novel both in ancient and modern times.

Like the modern novel, the ancient, which had the same potentiality of extension upward and outward, succeeded the drama as the dynamic form of fictional entertainment and edification. The literary and social conditions, which brought about this change in the principal medium by which literature as a genuine interpretation of life was henceforth expressed, were very much the same, fundamentally, in both cases. The drama had declined to a low level of effectiveness in two respects: the values that it had to convey, which were normally trivial and narrow as compared with those of Euripidean or Menandrian drama in the ancient period, or with those of Elizabethan in the modern;[6] and its capacity for communicating even those values to the literary public at large, whose center of gravity so to speak had shifted from the cities to the country as a whole, and from theater-goers to readers. By the beginning of the first century B.C., the approximate date to which the origin of Greek romance may be reasonably referred, comedy proper in the style of Plautus and Terence was giving place to mimes and farces as the principal forms of popular entertainment on the stage; and tragedy, being an intellectual exercise in emulation of the classics, could have little or no meaning for the mass of common people at this time.

4

Drama in general, and especially tragedy, is the peculiar product of the *polis*, or city-state, in which the life of man in all its mundane variety is conceived as a homogeneous, well-rounded, and fully comprehensible whole, the boundaries of which, like those of the state itself, are more sharply defined and are brought into much smaller compass than they can possibly be for us of the greatly expanded and complex modern world of knowledge and experience, or for the men of later antiquity who lived in a similar world. It is only in the microcosmic cultural environment of the city-state, or of its medieval and early modern approximations, that human life, not yet a "problem," can be conceived by a poet and his audience as a totality, which is then contemplated and meditated upon, poetically, musically, religiously and metaphysically, not with reference to its mundane morphology, which is assumed as self-evident and is not a matter of primary concern, but with reference to what lies beyond it, what controls it, and what its place is in the transcendental scheme of things. Tragedy in its original character, like the contemporary pre-Socratic philosophy, looks outward from life on earth, rather than into it, and seeks to find the meaning of earthly things within the framework of a cosmic or universal order. What Socrates did for philosophy, in bringing it down from the heavens to the market-place, was accomplished by Euripides for the tragic drama. In him it was no longer metaphysical but empirical. Its values had become primarily epic and Socratic, concerned on the one hand with action as sensation, and on the other with psychoanalysis and the newly discovered problems and sentimentalities of ethics and social justice—symptoms of cultural disintegration and of the expansion of social and intellectual horizons. The Greek mind was on its way to becoming "emancipated." The Euripidean protagonist is no longer a mask for humanity, but may be a pathological exhibit, a romantic heroine, a victim of man's inhumanity to man, a melodramatic villain, or a dialectician. Euripides, like Homer and the later novelists and comedians, studies life in its varied and concrete manifestations. He never gets on the outside of life so as to contemplate it in transcendental perspective. His art, like Homer's and the novelist's, is controlled by life, to which it is subservient and of which it is a description, complete as such, if ever, only when a large number of separate pieces, as in Balzac's Comédie Humaine (planned to contain 138 novels), have been added together and totalled.[7] But in the metaphysical tragedy characteristic of the early stage, the poet does not aim to describe life in all its thrilling, curious, pathetic, or problematical aspects, nor indeed in any one aspect, except incidentally and subordinately; and the point at which this metaphysical poet begins in his contemplation of human life is just that at which Balzac, or Balzac plus Zola and their kind, necessarily leave off. Early drama took an overall, collective view of human life without examining it critically or taking it apart, because it was made for an age in which not philosophy, but custom grounded on faith, instinct, and tradition, was the guide to life, and because it was the institution, characteristic and well-adapted, of the compact, closed society of the city-state, in which only what was representative of civic man and so of mankind in general seen in his image, was felt to be worthy of artistic presentation at a public festival. Brought on the stage before the entire public in daytime, wearing a mask and attended by a chorus—nothing private about *that*—the tragic hero became a symbol of humanity in a much higher and more abstract degree than is the case with the hero of either epic or romance, both of whom by comparison are only individuals. In the city-state, even under a *tyrannos*, no one man is regarded as indispensable, or towers greatly in the popular imagination above his fellow-citizens. He is an inseparable part of the body politic, neither above it nor outside of it. And this conception of man as inseparable from the group is reflected in the drama. But it is a different light in which the hero of an action is viewed in the Homeric world of narrative, as in the Hellenistic. The Homeric hero is pre-civic, the Hellenistic or romantic post-civic. Neither is attended by a chorus or anything resembling it in significance. The former overshadows the state (of which the poet is scarcely conscious), and is therefore of more importance and more interest for what he does and wills on his own account as a particular man; for the state, if the patriarchal community of which the epic hero is the head and leader can be so called, is only the hero's following and counts for little in the poet's imagination. That imagination is cast in the mold of the myth-maker, who, by a childlike process of simplification, sees history only as the exploits of individual men, with scarcely any awareness of such abstract things as states, empires, dynasties, or cultures. Cretan history is reduced to the exploits of King Minos, its art to the accomplishments of one Daedalus in person. The direction of the mythmaker's thought and instinct, inherited by the epic poet, is directly opposite to that of the tragic poet, in that the latter, instead of reducing generalities to particulars in the form of individuals and their actions, consciously uses his hero as a symbol either for humanity in the large or for man in one of his principal aspects. Hence it is that the epic hero, unlike the tragic hero, whose function and significance are shaped by the communal view of life, is primarily an individual. In the Hellenistic age, on the other hand, the individual man has been cut loose from the state of which he was once an integral part but which is no longer a controlling force in his life, so that what concerns him privately, apart from any group-relationship, is now of paramount interest. "The great Epic," says Spengler, ". . . belongs to *Pfalz* and *Burg*, but the Drama, in which *awakened* life tests itself, is city-poetry, and the great Novel, the survey of all things human by the *emancipated* intellect, presupposes the world-city." [8]

5

The forms of literature which are dominant and truest to the mood of their time throughout the cultural interval that separates romantic epic in verse from latter-day epic in prose (novel) are these: lyric poetry, choral and monodic; drama, religious and metaphysical at first, but later becoming secular and empirical; and historical and scientific writing, first in verse, then in prose. This is plainly evident in the history of Greek literature, and I think that it is true also, in a fundamental sense, of northern European literature from the beginning of the fifteenth century, or earlier, to the middle of the eighteenth, in spite of many confusing blots on the map of genuinely popular and dynamic literature in this period due to the cultivation in learned circles of classical and medieval forms, including narrative. The dominant forms of literature in any age are those which are best adapted to the intellectual and cultural conditions of the time. When those conditions have undergone a fundamental change, the new order of things, which comes about gradually, must sooner or later employ a new form of literature as its principal artistic expression. But even after the new order with its new form, or forms, has been established, the older forms (the structural patterns of composition used by previous generations as their principal and most effective media of expression) continue in most cases to be cultivated, though only in a narrower and more restricted capacity. They are no longer a natural or adequate means by which to convey the real thought, spirit, and temper of the times, and there is always something more or less artificial, academic, or precious in the continued exploitation of them by literary men. Such, generally speaking, was the status in the sixteenth and seventeenth centuries, when drama or spectacle in some form was the most natural medium of expression for an artistic world that centered about a court in a capital city like London or Paris, of the long story of ideal adventure, such as Sidney's *Arcadia* or the romances of Scudéry, which carried on the loose formal traditions of medieval romance, and were ill-adapted, in spite of their up-to-date *lyrical* virtuosities, to the intellectual and dramatic temper of the new urban society. Literature in the time of the Renaissance, from Boccaccio on, had followed the directions given it by scholarly circles in which learning was fashionable, and traditional forms, both classical and medieval, were cultivated more because they met with academic approval, as being either classical or sanctioned by tradition or by learned theory, than because they were actually in line with the spirit of the times—as might or might not be the case. Drama and lyric poetry were so in line, and for that reason they prospered and reached great heights, without owing anything more than the externalities of form and occasional subject matter to the ancient classical models on whose patterns, in the mid-sixteenth century and before, they had been studiously constructed by scholarly poets. With epic and romance the case was quite different. They too, like the drama, had been sponsored and cultivated, although in a lesser degree, by learned writers who emulated the ancients and the medieval romance; but both forms were artificial and without popular support in the temper of the age, and neither therefore could make its way against the tide of contemporary taste in competition with the forms that were naturally favored by it and thereby truly dynamic. The classical epic had long been dead, as regards its popular appeal, no less in the time of Petrarch with his *Africa* or Ronsard with his *Françiade* than in the time of Apollonius of Rhodes in the third century before Christ. And because the social, cultural, and literary conditions were not yet favorable to it, and did not demand it, latter-day epic, which we have called novel or romance almost indifferently, according to whether it was ancient or modern, was destined by historical necessity not yet to be born, in the one case until the advent of the "complete English tradesman," [9] Samuel Richardson, as author and friend of the servant girl and of all proper young ladies, in the mid-eighteenth century, and, in the other, until the almost unnoticed entrance upon the stage of ancient letters of such humble and naïve sentimentalists as the unknown (and probably pseudonymous) author of the Ninus romance at the end of the Alexandrian period.

6

The novel or romance, as we know it today, or as it was in the days of the Roman Empire, can arise and flourish only when a much larger public is concerned with literature than was the case either in the Elizabethan age or in the early Alexandrian. In the last-mentioned periods of history, fictional entertainment in narrative form (unlike early epic and medieval romance, both of which were recited by minstrels and meant to be heard as well as read) was communicated exclusively by the written page; and the number of people who could or would read for entertainment in those days was very much smaller than it was 150 or 200 years later in either case, when the genuine ancient and modern novels, respectively, began to appear. This means that literature in the time of Shakespeare, as in that of Callimachus in the early third century B.C., was produced by and for relatively few people; that these few were either themselves highly educated, or sophisticated, or they emulated the intellectual standards, moods, and fashions of those who were of that quality, like the gravedigger in *Hamlet*; and that common people had no representation in literature for their own unformulated notions of value, except insofar as these coincided, as they might to a large degree in some cases, with the broadly human interests of their intellectual superiors. These bonds, by which written composition was confined and regulated in the learned ages, were broken down in later times with the increase of literacy among common people, the greater production, distribution, and commercializing of books (in antiquity as well as in the eighteenth century), and the rise to prominence of a morally and realistically minded, middle-class citizenry, which was so numerous and so conscious of its own concerns, tastes, and problems of living that it was bound to find fuller expression for them than was possible within the limits of a literature controlled by intellectual fashion and tradition. The result was the novel as we know it in modern times, or the Greek romance, as it is usually called in its ancient manifestations. Both are, in the social sense of the word, *democratic* institutions. Owing to the more restricted and more severely classical nature of its immediate literary environment, which was not influenced by an immediately preceding age of romance, and to the absence of printing, the ancient novel was much slower than the modern to win recognition at the court of letters and to advance in the range of its quality and uses; but it was the same institution fundamentally, and its potentialities, though never so fully exploited, were precisely the same.[10] The most distinctive thing about this new form, the novel, in comparison with the narrative forms that precede it in either case, is the nature and orientation of its aesthetic values: here for the first time in a bookish world the private adventures of an individual, whatever their moral or philosophical implications may be—and these will vary greatly with the author—are elaborated and dwelt upon sympathetically and in detail for their own dramatic interest, as an end in themselves. The long story of ideal personal experience in prose is thus accepted as a new and independent medium for the serious criticism or interpretation of life (however sentimental, intellectual, trivial, or profound that may be), having been elevated by new concepts of artistic value arising from a democratic public to the rank of a major form of literary art. Previously it had not had that status nor that function. In the modern age the long story, controlled by essentially academic traditions, had been an artificial epic, a mock-epic, a satire, a picaresque narrative, or a romance addressed to a small circle of cultivated readers whose taste was precious or determined by courtly fashions and the medieval inheritance. But in antiquity, previous to the appearance of the Greek romances, the long story of personal experiences had taken the form either of an epic poem or, with less similarity of content and structure, that of an historical biography or an account of travels, either of which was put forth under the aegis of history, science, or philosophical theory, not of simple entertainment or of *belles lettres* like the epic, drama, or modern novel.

The short story, on the other hand, which represents a different concept of literary value and of which we shall say more later on, has always been fashionable in classical and intellectually controlled literature, although in medieval and early modern times it enjoyed a greater degree of independence and prestige on its own account, and was likely to be somewhat longer than in antiquity. Literary fashion in the time of the Renaissance, in spite of its learned environment and classical restraint, was necessarily conditioned to a considerable extent by the traditions of the immediately preceding age of romance, in which stories of all kinds, both long and short, had been propagated as independent forms of literary art. For that reason a Boccaccio or a Chaucer could offer to the educated public of his time a story, or more often a collection of stories, which, unlike the ancient narrative of personal experience (apart from the Greek romance), was its own sanction and required no context or frame of reference other than its own value as entertainment for ladies and gentlemen. But the story in Boccaccio and his followers in Italy and abroad, however great the skill and charm of the narrator might be, was essentially light reading, intended rather as relaxation and amusement for an idle hour—what Lucian called in effect a literary vacation—than as a serious or idealistic interpretation of life, like *Pamela* or the Ninus romance, or Chariton's novel. The great majority of those short stories were witty and unmoral and more concerned with clever and amusing actions as such than with any moral or philosophical implications that might be drawn from them. Their conventional counterpart in ancient literature is well represented by the collection of Milesian tales made by Aristides in the second century B.C. In the Greek romance, as in the modern novel, the story of personal adventure in prose aspires to a much higher plane of literary dignity than had previously been accorded to it. Before the appearance of the novel proper, serious literature in which the author aims to edify his readers in one way or another or to instruct them is either confined to such classical forms as drama, lyric, essay, dialogue, historiography, or outright allegory, or, if put into a narrative, is something incidental to the context, like the digressions in *Robinson Crusoe*. These classical restrictions could not be abandoned all at once. The patterns of thought and feeling that prevail in the public at large, and depend mainly upon sociological forces, are bound to change and make their mark in many ways upon the established institutions sooner than the forms and conventions of literature, which tend to remain static, can be reshaped to accommodate them and to give them their fullest expression. Hence what are sometimes called the elements of the novel are found abundantly in literature before the appearance of the novel itself, being admitted in varying degrees and aspects into the framework of forms that maintain the orientation and theory of older and more academic fashions.

7

What signals the birth of the genuine novel more than anything else is, as we have already suggested, a transvaluation of narrative values. A much greater premium than before is put upon the close-up description of persons and events as such, so that these representations, being prolonged, magnified, and multiplied out of proportion to their total significance, become an artistic end in themselves—the main part of the entertainment, which may be continued indefinitely—rather than, as in a short story by a classical author, the means economically managed by which to convey a main idea or a total dramatic effect. Ancient classical authors, and all who emulate their standards in prose narrative, are concerned primarily with the sum of an action or of a series of related actions, and this they give us only in broad outlines and in general terms, with mention of only such details as are essential for the understanding of the whole. This is because their method of approach, whatever they may think or feel about the matter temporarily in hand, is the traditional one of the historian bent on recording in summary fashion things that have happened, or are supposed to have happened in the past, and *not* that of the dramatist nor of our modern story teller, whose principal purpose in writing in either case is to entertain his readers, or his listeners, with an artistic creation. In Herodotus, for example, this kind of artistry is something incidental and secondary, however conspicuous and important it may seem to us who live in the age of the novel and have lost the ancient perspectives. Among ancient critics Herodotus got more blame than praise for what we admire in him. He is not a story teller in the sense in which this word is understood in relation to such writers as Boccaccio or Edgar Allen Poe, nor is he a dramatist in the way that Sophocles would be even if his plays were written in prose and without a chorus. The purposes and hence the direction of effort are very different. This is not to deny that Herodotus is eminently tragic and dramatic in his presentation of historical events and persons, and that he has the epic genius of Homer in narration; but he is all this only in the way in which Plato is a poet—not because of what he aims to do but in spite of it. Born into a Greek world whose thought for centuries had been molded in the forms of high poetry, nursed at home in the epic tradition of Ionia, and living in the prime season of the tragic culture, it was inevitable that Herodotus should leave the impress of these epic and tragic patterns of thought, and of his own highly artistic instincts in very large measure upon whatever he undertook to write. But the central purpose of Herodotus, clearly stated in his first sentence, is the same as that of all historians, including such wide varieties as are represented by the dullest of the logographers who preceded him, by Thucydides, Ctesias, Polybius, Ps.-Callisthenes, Dares and Dictys, and the medieval chroniclers. All these are doing essentially the same thing: giving their readers an informative account, which they want them to believe, of important things that took place or existed in the past. The differences that we note between these writers severally are only the accidents of time and place and, above all, of individual mentality. In the Hellenistic age, as in the time of Herodotus, such dramatic, poetic, or rhetorically artistic values as were currently fashionable or fostered by the spirit of the age, or by that of the particular author, were imposed in various degrees and proportions upon the writing of history without ever changing its direction, its primary purpose, or its *summary* manner of dealing with the actions or adventures of an individual person.

This *historical* attitude, with its summary fashion of dealing with everything that we should call a "story," however plainly fictitious the substance may be even in the mind of the author himself, pervades all ancient prose writing outside the romance proper and the traditionally comic genres of mime (hence dialogue) and fable. It is the governing framework within which, throughout the long period that separates Homeric epic from latter-day epic, all prose fiction in the form of narration is contained and controlled in respect to its length, the extent and nature of its invention, and its general orientation. It is this that prevents a story of personal action in classical authors, and in all who emulate their style, from becoming an independent form of literary art parallel in its aims and orientation (like the modern novel or *novella*) to the early epic, to the drama, or to poetry of any well-recognized kind, narrative or not. In this classical environment a story in prose is *formally* treated not as an artistic creation (which for us is implied by the very words "story" and "fiction") but as factual information about what has happened or what someone somewhere has actually done. Incidentally, this is the reason why, in any kind of ancient prose writing outside the romance, an incredible narrative is nearly always told either on the authority of someone other than the author himself, or as the author's own personal experience, which no one else can verify or refute because he wasn't there.[11] There must be a sponsor for the *truth* of the narrative (which is not important in poetry), because the primary business of the historian, unlike that of the dramatist, the poet, or the romancer, is to tell the truth; and any self-respecting author who writes in this broad prosaic tradition, be he orator, sophist, scientist, pseudo-scientist, or philosopher, must be careful about what he vouches for in his own person. So sensitive was the feeling of the ancient academicians in this matter that the rhetorician Theon, while appealing to Aristotle as authority for the principle, recommends that even an Aesopic fable, in spite of its obviously utilitarian function and the comic license which always belonged to it, should be told, for the sake of decorum, "in the accusative case," that is, that it should be represented as the substance of what somebody other than the speaker or the writer himself has affirmed.[12] Beware of declaring outright on your own authority (in the nominative case) that the frogs asked Zeus for a king, lest you seem to be making untrue statements. But this important convention, which belongs to historiography and its numerous intellectual heirs and kindred, and which assumes that the actual occur-

rence or nonoccurrence of something is a more important consideration than enjoyable contemplation of it, does not concern
the genuine romancer or novelist, just as it does not concern the
poet. The novelist's is a fundamentally different business, and
essentially a poetic one. Unlike other prose writers he employs
very freely, and without apology, in the cause of art and regardless of historical plausibility, the inventive license proper to the
tragedian or the epic poet. His characters, like theirs, must
indeed be presumably historical (unlike those of comedy, which
may be invented), but beyond that he is free to ascribe to those
characters anything that he pleases in the way of actions as
well as of words, just so long as what he predicates of them does
not run into open conflict with what is familiar to his public
from tradition. In order to avoid this, the romancer picks out
quasi-historical characters—obscure figures of myth or local
legend, like Ninus in his teens or Callirhoe the daughter of
Hermocrates, about whose lives as youngsters his readers could
have heard practically nothing from any other source. Contrast
the procedure of learned prose writers, whose way of looking at
persons and events of the past is never that of the creative
artist but always that of the historian talking about *famous*
things, regardless of whether the persons and events to whom
they allude are real according to our reckoning or purely and
patently mythical. When they deal with the obscure figures of
local myth, it is in the spirit of the antiquarian exhibiting his
erudition and explaining the origins of cities and institutions;
when they address themselves to the public on general topics,
they are careful in most cases not to allude to anything by way
of illustration or comment except what has long been celebrated in ancient history and mythology. "Perhaps," says Dio
Chrysostom in one of his orations, "you hold me in contempt
and think that I am talking foolishly because I do not speak
about Cyrus and Alcibiades, the way learned men do even today, but instead I make mention of Nero and more recent affairs, which are not considered respectable." [13] How can a story
in our literary sense of the word, something which exploits as

of primary consequence the dramatic and sentimental values and the pathos of private experience, fail to be stifled in such an atmosphere?

Here we must repeat that throughout the formal prose literature of antiquity, exclusive of the romance and of the traditionally comic or mimic genres, what we call fiction or story is conceived either as history or as the recording of presumably actual occurrences. In this fashionable environment, moreover, from the standpoint of dramatic development, a story is always depressed by being subordinated to something else, either to the larger framework of a history, within which it is only one incident, or to a philosophical idea which it serves to illustrate. Ordinarily in such a context the story is told only in bare outlines, even when its substance is romantic; and although it may be spun out and dramatized in varying degrees, according to the mood or motive of the author in his progress towards a larger end, nevertheless it remains under the control of the historiographical viewpoint and thus can never become a prose drama in the sense in which a Greek romance or a modern short story is such. A writer in the later academic tradition, such as Dio Chrysostom, or for that matter Xenophon the Athenian in the early fourth century B.C., knows very well *how* to dramatize a story, even in the modern fashion; but he chooses, as a matter of principle, not to regard that process, or its aesthetic result, as an end in itself. Dio's *Hunters of Euboea*, about nineteen pages long, reads so much like a high class modern novel, in respect to its dramatic manner of presentation, its attention to character, and the social and ethical implications of its incidents, that one might as easily suppose it to have been written in the twentieth century as in the first. There is nothing stiff or old-fashioned about it. Dio had the know-how of the professional novelist, but, like many a sophist who preceded or followed him in the academic tradition, he chose not to use it in the service of the novel as an independent literary form. The *Hunters of Euboea* may be called a romance or a novellette in respect to its manner and substance, but it is not such in terms of literary form. It is only the first half of an oration on the character and resources of poor men, serving to illustrate that theme concretely and followed by some eighteen pages of philosophical exegesis, mingled with references to other examples drawn from ancient literature and mythology. At the beginning the speaker, Dio, takes pains to assure his audience that what he is about to relate is not something that he learned from others, but something that he himself actually saw and lived with, "some men I met practically in the heart of Greece, and the kind of life they lived." This amounts to an explicit statement on the author's part that he is *not* doing what the serious romancer always does, and on principle, with the implication that he has no right to do so. Whatever may have been the actual extent of his invention in this case, Dio does obeisance to the historiographical law of prohibition, which denies to any prose writer of his intellectual standing the privilege, exercised freely and with no apology by poets and novelists, of inventing what he pleases.[14] He holds himself morally responsible for the literal truth, in substantial outline, of the things he relates. Fiction with him, and with all the prose writers of antiquity who aspire to a similar dignity as educated men, is a strictly bootleg article. With "truth" uppermost in their consciences, they find Homer, with Strabo an accurate geographer, with Lucian a liar. Some of them smuggle in more fiction than others, according to occasions and individual temperaments, or the opportunities for a cover-up; but all alike respect the unwritten law against the use of arbitrary invention, upon the nominal observance of which their reputations depend.

This prohibitive attitude towards ideal fiction in prose has been almost as persistent in modern times, both prior to and for some time after the upstart appearance of the real novel, as it was throughout the Hellenistic age. Comic or picaresque fiction, on the other hand, has been easily tolerated in the sophisticated world of letters, whether ancient or modern, because it is looked upon as so much jesting or relaxation. It has the saving grace of being clever, amusing, or nonsensical, or at the most ancillary to a sermon or a satire, but that is the extent of its dignity. It is not something to be taken seriously on its own account as dramatic narrative, and not the kind of composition to which, as to poetry, one looks for spiritual edification. The sense of it in some cases may inform our understanding, but it does not stir or warm the heart, nor is it intended to do so. It is only in fairly recent times, when the ideal novel in its ascendency overshadows all literature and blinds us to the older distinctions of form and fashion, that narrative fiction in prose has ceased to be regarded as falsified history, when not seen as comedy, and has come to be accepted without question as a form of literary art having the same sanction and legitimacy as fiction in poetry and drama. Failure on the part of literary historians to realize the full force and meaning of those older distinctions is responsible for many a futile attempt to derive romance from historiography, or to trace its development from some kind of sophistic literature, practice, or technique.

8

The ideal novel as a literary form does not come into being until, through the agency of a new class of writers morally and sentimentally inspired by a new middle-class idealism, a complete and sudden break has been made with traditional literary practice. The nature of the innovation thus made, on its formal side, consists in nothing more or less than the transference to prose narrative, the natural medium for a reading public, of the principal artistic aims and sanctions of serious drama. Chief among these sanctions is the plasmatic license, which allows an author to invent for art's sake speeches, actions, and characters on the basis of mythical or historical events. In theory this belongs more properly to tragedy, where it is moderately exercised, than to comedy, where, from the start, everything might be invented; but the unlimited *extent* to which it is carried in the idealistic Greek romance had a conspicuous precedent in Hellenistic comedy, which was essentially serious in its overall meaning and in which the exploitation of action *per se* regardless of other values, in the direction begun by Euripides, was much greater than it had been with the earlier tragedians. For New Comedy, which might more truly be called, with reference to its traditions, New Tragedy, owes far more to the Euripidean stage for its orientation towards the serious criticism of life than to the Aristophanic; and there can be little doubt that many of its plots, like those of tragedy, elegy and romance, were originally made up on the basis of local myths or historical legends. The tendency of serious drama to veer away from the famous characters of mythology (as well as from tragedy in the stricter sense of the word) and to deal instead with the obscure figures of *local* myth, if not with outright inventions on the analogy of such local myths as in much of the New Comedy, is already seen in the case of Agathon's play called *Antheus*, the plot of which, according to Aristotle (whose statement I cannot believe in its exact literal sense), was entirely invented. An obscure myth or historical legend was better suited to the needs of most Hellenistic *Dichtung*, especially drama and narrative whether in prose or in verse, than was a famous story; for, in dealing with characters about whom little or nothing was known, an author could represent them as typical citizens of his own middle-class society without making them appear incongruous to one familiar with their representation in classical literature. The scope offered by such myths for the free invention and exploitation of novelties in the way of action and plot—the main direction of drama after Euripides—was much greater. Under those conditions it was natural, if not inevitable, that the plasmatic license, which the early tragic poets had need to employ only in moderation, should later be carried to great lengths in order to meet the requirements of drama and romance in the Hellenistic Age. It is probable that the evolution of plasmatic invention in the history of Hellenistic comedy took the same course that we know it to have taken in the Greek romance. In the latter the earliest plots, those of the Ninus romance and of Chariton, are very clearly legendary at the base, while some of the later ones are so freely invented that we cannot identify them with any known tradition, however meager. When this stage of the plasmatic practice is reached, the results are indistinguishable from those of outright invention, except perhaps that the name Daphnis may tell us that the romance was built on the analogy of a bucolic myth, and that the exposure of an infant in the comedy was patterned after a similar motif in some local legend. Owing to the need for ever more action and adventure, there was a development from quasi-historical plots to completely invented plots; but the *theory* of these plots— that they dealt with historical persons in their private lives— remained always the same, regardless of the practice. Real tragedy, like comedy in its original character, was dead by the end of the fifth century, but its formal conventions were retained in part and variously modified in the only dynamic species of drama that succeeded it. This drama was called "comedy" mainly because it did not seem to be "tragic"; but in reality it is a new kind of basically serious, middle-class drama which has never been properly named. Insofar as it was something serious, rather than a farce, it would tend to build its plots on something at least quasi-historical, in the tradition of Euripidean drama.

When ancient writers speak of tragedy, comedy, or drama, they are as likely to be thinking of the nature and quality of a composition as of its structural pattern, which may be that of prose narrative or bucolic poetry or some other form of writing, as well as what we call in a narrower and more formal sense tragedy, comedy, or drama. And because they thought more about the inner nature of literature than about its outward form, those ancient critics who deigned to take notice of prose fiction were well aware that it was essentially "drama," that is, action, most of which was made up by the writer. The ancient ideal romances are generically called dramas or dramatic nar-

ratives by Photius in the ninth century; and the authors themselves, especially Heliodorus and Achilles Tatius, often refer
to parts of their own works as dramas.[15] Hermogenes in the
second century tells us that the plasmatic narrative, by which
he means a narrative invented in large part, but on a quasi-
historical or mythical base, "is the same as what they call dramatic narrative (δραματικόν), like the plots of the tragedians."
Similar statements, in which the plasmatic narrative is equated
with the dramatic, are made by the rhetoricians Aphthonius
and Nikolaos. Nikolaos in the fifth century recognizes three
kinds of narratives, other than that which is employed in law-
suits: namely, the mythical (μυθικά), the historical (ἱστορικά),
and the plasmatic (πλασματικά). He adds that the first and last
of these are alike in that they are both invented (πεπλασμένα),
but that the plasmatic, unlike the mythical, is of such a nature
that it could have happened, even if in fact it did not. This
hocus-pocus is found already in Cicero's De Invent. I 27 (see
below p. 144) and in Quintilian (II 4, 2), who says that fabula
(= μῦθος) "used in tragedies and poems, is remote not only from
truth but from the semblance of truth," and that the argumentum (= ὑπόθεσις) "which comedy invents resembles something
true even though it is false." How about the Amphitryo of
Plautus and the Old and Middle Comedy in general? In none
of these definitions is there anything technical or fundamental
in the way of literary classifications or terminology, only an attempt to define different kinds of narrative descriptively on the
basis of their comparative truth or plausibility, and to illustrate them with reference to comedy or tragedy; all of which
is necessarily vague, subjective and indeterminate, when not
in part false or contradictory. Hermogenes illustrates plasmatic
narrative by reference to tragedy, Nikolaos by reference to
comedy "and other dramas," and Quintilian's statement, in
effect, that there is no semblance of truth in myths, tragedies,
and poems, is much exaggerated and only partially true to the
facts as we know them.

The trouble with these commentators, from our point of

view, is that they are not thinking about the theory of composition that lies back of the various literary forms, but about the concrete results to which that theory has led in the practice of the particular authors or compositions which they happen to have in mind. The theory, or rather the principle of composition, to which I refer, is implicit in much of what the ancient grammarians have to say about plasmatics, and no student of classical literature can fail to recognize the reality of it, once it is stated. Here it is again: all ideal or poetic narratives must deal, and do deal with *presumably* historical characters and events, however mythical, unreal, or impossible these may seem to be from a factual point of view. "I sing of nothing that is not attested" (by someone somewhere), says Callimachus;[16] and all the ancient writers who concerned themselves with ideal *Dichtung* in narrative or dramatic form were with him in principle as in practice. But that which is completely unattested, in other words *freie Erfindung* from the bottom up, which Rohde, along with Nikolaos and many moderns, confuses with invention on a mythical (i.e. theoretically historical) base—this, in the words of Edward Schwartz, had "no right to exist in the kingdom of the Muses," except, as we noted above, in the kingdom of Thalia, who presides over comedy. When Trygaeus in the *Peace* of Aristophanes goes to heaven on the back of a beetle, that, in spite of Aesop's authority, is obviously pure invention, and thereby comedy. On the other hand, the exposure of Oedipus as a babe, his encounter with the Sphinx, his slaying of his father, and his marrying of his mother, are regarded as history; but what Oedipus says to Tiresias and other characters in the play of Sophocles, the introduction of Manto, daughter of Tiresias, in Seneca, the pair of lovers associated with the family of Oedipus in the plays of Corneille and Dryden, or the marriage of Electra to a peasant in Euripides—all this is understood to be *plasma*, that is, invention on the basis of traditional data. That kind of invention, as opposed to outright comic invention, was always legitimate in drama and poetry, and the first Greek romances were constructed on that principle and under the cover of that time-honored sanction. The convention of tragedy and other poetry, unquestioned in its own field, was simply transferred to prose narrative, where it had never before been openly exercised. The practice of the romancer in the matter of invention differs from that of the tragedian, not in kind nor in theory, but only in the extent to which it is carried. Since the artistic aims of the tragedian are very different from those of the romancer, being more concerned with a central idea or the musical reflections of the chorus than with action as such, there is a correspondingly wide difference in the degree in which the two artists exercise their plasmatic license. For the tragedian, action in the form of episode was originally something added to the drama from without, as the name itself indicates; but for the romancer it was almost everything that he had to offer, and for that reason he was bound to carry the process of plasmatic invention to great lengths.

At the end of this progression outward from legendary materials one cannot discover what, if anything, is really traditional in the whole story, although the mythical pattern of its core remains to tell us that the romance was conceived on the analogy, at least, of a myth or legend dealing with presumably historical persons and events in a far-off age. Modern critics, with their incurably scientific bias, are too apt to forget that the ancients thought lightly and seldom about history in our sense of the word, and especially about remote history. For them the world was primarily a world of ideas, which could be put to practical use in the instruction and edification of living men, rather than a world of facts valued only as such, and thereby useless. What moral or spiritual good is there in a mere fact? On some occasions the ancients became antiquarians and were at pains to distinguish what was probably true in the distant past from what was mythical and false; but this was not their habitual way of looking at traditional data, and least of all when they were concerned with *belles lettres*. With all his critical zeal, not even Thucydides challenges the historical reality of Deucalion and the patently eponymous Hellen; and from the Greek poetical point of view (which was that of drama and romance) Inachus, Candaules, Xerxes, Alcibiades, Ninus, Nireus, and Daphnis are alike historical and belong in the same category. All Greek romances, except the fundamentally comic variety, are what would be called today historical novels.

In the preceding paragraphs the point has been made that Greek romance is essentially Hellenistic drama in narrative form, and that it was recognized as such in late antiquity. The fact was also recognized that the *outward* form of romance is that of historiography, as we observed above on another occasion. The emperor Julian, in a letter recommending suitable reading matter for priests of the ancient religion, comments as follows: "It would be fitting for us to make acquaintance with those histories which are written about deeds actually done in the past; but we must deprecate those fictions put forth by previous writers in the form of history (ἐν ἱστορίας εἴδει), that is, love stories (ἐρωτικὰς ὑποθέσεις) and, in a word, all such stuff." (*Epist.* 89, 301b, ed. Bidez et Cumont p. 141). This is one of very few passages in the extant ancient literature where we have an undoubted reference to the Greek erotic romance, and the phrase by which Julian refers to it, quoted above, is the same as that used by Photius in speaking of romances which have come down to us. Of course it is obvious from many things in the romances themselves, including such titles as *Ephesiaca, Aethiopica*, etc., that their outward form and *décor* was intentionally that of historiography; but it is interesting to note, in addition to the testimony of Julian, that Suidas calls the romancers ἱστορικοί, and that he says of a book by Ptolemy the son of Hephaestion, which was entitled *Sphinx* and was very probably a romance, as Rohde infers, that "it is an *historical drama*" (δρᾶμα ἱστορικόν). That designation is very fitting for the ideal Greek romance as a whole, when we consider both its nature and its place within the history of literary convention as explained above. Both drama and history are important aspects of epic, whether it be early Homeric or latter-day epic.

9

We have stated that the genre romance, as we choose to define it and as it is popularly conceived, includes only *extended* narratives, what one would call long stories rather than short ones. Why, one may ask, is this qualification necessary? What difference does it make in the nature of a story and its literary classification whether it is three pages long or a hundred? As concerns the nature of the story, its method, style, and subject-matter, there may indeed be little or no qualitative difference between a long one and a short one; but when it comes to the classification of stories within the framework of literary history, theory, and practice, and the question of origins, this matter of comparative length, within broad limits of course, is one of cardinal importance. The two types of story, long and short, represent two separate literary institutions which have nothing to do with each other. Each is cultivated in line with definite artistic ideals and purposes, which are always consciously present and are very different from those by which the other is motivated; and it is for this reason only, not because of anything inherent in either the quality or the organic structure of the short story, or in its subject-matter, that the latter can never develop in the course of literary practice into the long kind of story which we recognize as a romance.

The misapprehension that such a development can take place in literature is due partly to the false analogy of agglutinative tendencies in folklore, and in literature where the genre-concept remains unchanged, and partly to the mistaken notion, carried over from biological thinking, that literary forms grow slowly out of literary "seeds," like vegetables. On the contrary, everything depends upon the writer's ideal intention. The materials with which he works have no potentiality for growth within themselves. It is not a matter of mechanics that confronts us here, nor one of gradual, unconscious progression, but a matter of human will and conscious artistic purposes. If a writer *wants* to make a long story out of a short one he can easily do so; and it matters little for the success of his project, since he can make changes and additions to suit his own needs, what kind of a short story it is upon which he chooses to build. If he is writing an ideal or sentimental romance he will naturally build upon a short story or upon a myth in bare outline that is already cast in that mold or can be easily adapted to it; but the spirit of a story, whether ideal, realistic, or burlesque, depends much more upon the author who shapes it than upon the outlines of legendary action with which he begins. Such outlines may be quite neutral as concerns the direction that their development can willfully be made to take. In some short stories consisting of a single episode the structure seems to be organically closed, in the sense that there is logically no room for the addition of further episodes; but a little ingenuity on the part of a writer can open up even such a story, so as to make it elastic and capable of indefinite expansion. In many *novellae* consisting of one or more episodes this elastic framework is already present. The clever thief, for example, who steals from the treasure-house of King Rhampsinitus in Herodotus (II 121), is waging a war of wits with the king until such time as the latter becomes reconciled with him; here any number of episodes might easily be added to the three that are given, without any organic readjustment. But those additions will never be made in any considerable quantity, so as to produce a picaresque novel, until the Herodotean conception of where such a story belongs, and what it is worth in the scale of literary value and of history, has been completely and deliberately abandoned. Again, if by the terms of a simple folktale a man is temporarily changed into an ass or some other animal, how many adventures will he undergo in that condition before being restored to his original form? The number will depend upon the will or fancy of the story teller or the literary artist, as the case may be, in relation to the circumstances under which the story is told or exploited as literature. Normally such a story is short and contains only a few episodes; but when a writer expands it to the length of Lucian's *Onos* (ca. 40 pages), composes it artistically, and publishes it as a separate book, he is doing so in accordance with a conscious artistic purpose which is foreign to all the *short* stories in prose that have come down to us from Greek and Roman literature. There is no gradual transition in literary practice from one purpose to another; and the thing that we have to explain, in accounting for the origin of that lengthy kind of narrative which we call romance, is the artistic intention that lies back of it, not the how nor the what of its make-up, which are secondary matters.

Rohde maintained that a *novella*, by which he meant a short realistic story, could never become a romance, either ideal or realistic.[17] This proposition, which, as stated by Rohde, is very ambiguous in what it implies, has been opposed by a number of critics; but these critics (including the present writer) seem not to have realized why or in what sense Rohde was wrong, and Rohde himself apparently did not know why he was right. He was wrong insofar as he implied or meant to imply that, owing to structural or qualitative differences between the long and short types, romances cannot be made, or have not been made, on the basis of short stories. On the other hand, he was right in the more important sense that authors who compose short stories do not, in the course of literary practice, drift aimlessly into the habit of making their stories longer and longer and more and more romantic until they become "romances," because those authors are always sophisticated men who know very well what they are doing artistically, for whom they are writing, and to what canons of taste and fashion they are addressing themselves. It is their positive intention *not* to be lengthy in dealing with such matter, and to keep it always in a subordinate place relative to some other leading idea or purpose. It must be short and it must be in a context of some kind, if only in a collection of stories; it could not stand alone because it was never recognized as a literary genre in its own right.[18] That is the classical conception of where prose fiction belongs in the realm of art and of how much it is worth; and this concept was dominant throughout the formal or intellectual literature of Graeco-Roman antiquity, as opposed to the genre romance, from the time of Herodotus onward to the Byzantine age.

In the plots of New Comedy, for example, we find imbedded and depressed within the prologues and narrative statements about what has happened off stage, many stories of adventure and intrigue which involve much travel about the world and are thronged with most disastrous chances—such stuff as no story teller would fail to describe in detailed episodes strung along one after the other, although they are necessarily left undescribed in the play. It is obvious that these stories were originally not made for the theater, because they transcend its scenic possibilities. They are much too long in substance. And the fact that some of them, as we happen to know definitely, have continued to live widely diffused as folktales in oral and written circulation up to the present, indicates that the majority or all of them likewise were current as folktales told at full length in the fourth century B.C. or earlier. These had to be shortened and reduced to summary outlines; they could not be long stories on the stage or in the written text of a stageplay.[19]

What we need to ask ourselves, in this whole inquiry into origins, is not such questions as where a certain kind of subject-matter comes from, what its precedents are, or how it can grow or be manipulated, all of which is irrelevant and inconsequential, but rather the all-important question of when, why, by whom, and for whom the fictitious story of personal adventure in prose was first elevated to the dignity of an independent form of literary art—one to which an author would devote a sustained artistic effort, dwelling with care upon the dramatic possibilities of all its parts, thereby carrying the story to such length and such importance on its own account that it was suitable, or so considered, for publication as a separate book.

It is the *independence* of the story as a form of art that leads to its being long, instead of short.

There never was a time in the history of Greek literature when a good story of personal adventure of any kind, erotic or non-erotic, tragic, comic or scandalous, wonder-seeking or realistic, was not welcome to readers or listeners, so long as it was presented within the context of an approved literary form, or on a suitable oral occasion. The Greeks from the earliest times were familiar with all kinds of stories and enjoyed them.[20] But what the Greeks of the classical period were familiar with as narrative substance, and what they chose to exploit in literature, are two very different things. Unlike the multifarious literature of today, which easily adapts itself in specialized form to anything or everything that may be interesting, the literature of the Greek city-state, being presented for the most part orally and publicly on state occasions and under competitive conditions, or else as a contribution to knowledge intended for permanent record, was of necessity very much restricted in the range of what it could admit. Only what was high in the scale either of poetic and musical art or in that of historical, political, philosophic, or scientific meaning was felt to be worth communicating to the public at large either orally on a state occasion, or in books, which were for most people in the fifth century neither accessible nor desirable as a source of entertainment. A farce, a fairy tale, a love story, an Aesopic fable, or a story of remarkable personal experience of any kind might be included as something subordinate or incidental or illustrative within the framework of a comedy, a tragedy, an artistically wrought poem of some kind, a history, an oration, a philosophical essay or dialogue, or even a collection of similar items; but it could not appear in *classical* literature outside such a context. So long as it remained inside, as it did for many centuries among fashionable authors owing to the force of classical tradition and the intellectual temperament of the authors themselves and their well-educated readers, it was bound to be short. Only the mounting pressure of a hitherto inarticulate popular taste, representing a different standard of aesthetic value and supported by a large body of intellectually undisciplined readers, can, under these conditions, lead to the popular exploitation of a serious story of personal adventure in prose as an independent, and thereby considerably lengthened form of literary entertainment. When that happens for the first time in the world of letters, it is a revolutionary act on the part of a single author heralding the birth of romance as latterday epic. This has twice happened in the history of Western literature, once with the advent of the ideal Greek romance (probably erotic at first) in the late Alexandrian age, and once with the publication of Samuel Richardson's *Pamela, or Virtue Rewarded* in 1740.

Outwardly considered with reference to length and subject-matter *Pamela* was not so new a thing for its time as was the first Greek romance, but its significance as a new kind of literature created in line with the moral and sentimental idealism of a middle-class reading public was equally great. It marked a change in the orientation of fictional literature on the dynamic level from drama to novel, from poetry to prose, from a theater-going public to a reading public, and from a small public ruled by a smart set to a greatly enlarged one which included all kinds of people and was predominantly middle-class. It is with reference to these aspects of Richardson's work that the modern English novel is commonly reckoned by critics as beginning with *Pamela*; and it is with the same considerations in view that the appearance of *Pamela*, rather than that of any so-called novel or romance that preceded it, must be reckoned as the true parallel in modern literary history to the appearance of the first Greek romance in the late Alexandrian age.[21]

10

In our definition of romance (novel) as a literary form, stated at the beginning of this chapter, it was stipulated that in order to qualify for this category the narrative of personal adventure

must be written for its own sake as a story, rather than for
the purpose of instruction in history, science, or philosophical
theory; and under these terms, used in their broadest sense,
we mean to exclude also religious, social, or political propaganda. Now "romance" in the sense of a quality of subject-
matter, like the qualities "tragedy" and "comedy," is found
in all kinds of books and transcends many distinct and well-
recognized literary genres; hence it cannot serve as a criterion
by which to define a particular literary genre, or form, if that
form as a category is to have any meaning: and the all-too-
common practice of labeling books as romances on the basis of
this criterion, namely that they contain romantic stuff, much
or little, leads to endless confusion and to the misunderstanding
of much literary history. Only the principal artistic or intellectual purpose of an author, viewed in relation to literary conventions, can guide us in this matter—not the materials that
he may use in implementing that purpose. Defined on these
principles, and with these qualifications above mentioned, romance or novel, as a literary form, includes along with thousands of modern specimens only a handful of ancient books
among those known to us that can be put in the same category.
Among the many other books and types of books or compositions that have been loosely called romances, the following are
excluded by the terms of our definition and do not belong to
romance or novel as a literary form: the biography of Alexander
by Pseudo-Callisthenes, the *Sack of Troy* ascribed to Dares the
Phrygian, the *Journal of the Trojan War* ascribed to Dictys of
Crete, the *Letters* of Chion of Heraclea (called a novel by their
latest editor), and, generally speaking, in the words of Juvenal,

> . . . Quidquid Graecia mendax
> Audet in historia.

Others are the *Life of Aesop* and the biography of the philosopher Apollonius of Tyana by Philostratus; the apocryphal
Acts of Christian martyrs, such as those of Paul and Thekla or
of Xanthippe and Polyxena with their theatrical exploitation

of miracles and sensational events as propaganda for a fanatical, antihumanistic creed; and the numerous accounts that were written from time to time about travels into strange and far-away lands and the wonders that they contained. These travelogues and utopias, most of which are known to us only indirectly through the testimony of ancient writers, were written in some cases, apparently, only for the sake of their interest as popular "science," as with Ctesias and Antonius Diogenes, who lie for entertainment; but in other cases, as in that of Plato's story of Atlantis or the *Sacred Register* of Euhemerus, the author makes use of the popular interest in paradoxology as a means by which to propagate a religious, political, or social theory. All these books must have been very romantic, in the sense that they were full of strange and wonderful things; but, whatever reasons their authors may have had for writing them, they were always put forth under the pretext, however thin or transparent, of informing the reader of things that presumably existed in the world of reality, either on the basis of a personal experience that no one could verify or refute or upon the report of others, real or fictitious. In the matter of literary form they came under the banner of scientific or philosophical writing, and not, like our romance, under that of artistic creation. Their orientation was toward the outer world of phenomena, whether geographical, political, social, physical, or biological, rather than inward toward the characters themselves and their emotional or dramatic experiences.[22] After the birth of romance proper as a literary form, and toward the end of its career, material of this kind was superimposed upon stories of love and adventure in the form of digressions by sophisticated novelists.

What is a novel in all other respects may be used at times to convey a message which is more important and more central to the author's purpose than the dramatic entertainment of the story as such, and there will be cases where we cannot decide whether the story is written principally for its own sake

as entertainment, or for the sake of a philosophical message, or
for both alike. Such cases defy classification and bring us back
to the ultimate reality that every composition is *sui generis;*
but, if we are to speak of genres or classifications at all, we
must restrict any term for such to a group of literary phenomena governed by what we can conceive as a common purpose,
and that, in the case of romance or novel, has been set forth
in our definition. Inasmuch as a genre in this sense is defined
by the author's primary purpose, it can *originate* only in that
purpose, and not as a means for the implementation of some
other purpose. The structural pattern and substance of a novel
can be used in an ancillary capacity not only after, but also
before the time when the novel as a genre or an independent
literary institution has come into being. It is only a particular
use of an age-old pattern of composition, though one long
familiar to us moderns, whose origin and *raison d'être* we seek
to explain in this book.

11

Broadly speaking, a romance or novel in the fundamental sense
of our definition may be either serious or comic, including under
the latter designation anything that one would call burlesque,
picaresque, satirical, realistic, disillusioning, unmoral, or unideal. These two types of ancient romance, the serious or ideal
on the one hand, and the comic or unideal on the other, have
radically different origins and different proprieties. The cultural and intellectual soils on which the two species grow are different and entirely apart from each other. The occasions for
their production vary widely: the serious is produced in quantity in response to a steady popular demand, which tends to
stereotype the product, while the comic appears only at long
intervals and on special occasions, or from personal motives,
as the unconventional but formally legitimate *jeu d'esprit* of an
individual. And, finally, there is no genetic relationship between

the two types historically considered. Any educated man in antiquity would know how to write a novel, either comic or ideal, but what we have to account for is the will to do so.

The spirit that pervades a comic or satirical novel, such as the *Satyricon* of Petronius, the *True History* of Lucian, or the *Metamorphoses* of Apuleius, presupposes an author with a sophisticated and critical outlook on the world; and the authors of this kind of book who are known to us are all highly educated men with reputations for achievement in other fields than prose fiction. The intellectual world to which they belong, and whose formal and aesthetic standards they acknowledge, is that of literature and learning on the high level of classical and academic tradition, which dominated the literary scene both after and before the birth of the ideal sentimental novel, and was unaffected by the latter. Since the creation of it presupposes only a sophisticated and formally educated author, or one who acts on the principles of such authors, a novel written in the spirit of comedy could make its appearance in any age of Greek literature when an occasion suitable for it happened to arise. Such an occasion, which was unique in early literature and almost the only one conceivable for the preclassical or classical period, arose when the old epic saga in scientific Ionia, like the romance of chivalry in the time of Cervantes, had become overripe and was inviting parody. The structural pattern of the epic (which is also that of the novel), was naturally retained in the parody of epic called *Margites*, while the burlesque substance of the narrative was the invention of a playful author responding, like Cervantes, to a genuine crisis in the literary taste of his age. The fool Margites, as antihero—as Odysseus in reverse—"knew many arts, but knew them all badly." So far as our information goes, there was only one *Margites* in its season, and one was enough; although similar parodies were written *invita Minerva* by pedants in later antiquity.[23] Has there been more than one *Don Quixote*, or more than one *Hudibras* or one *Gargantua*? Possibly so, but it lies in the nature of things that they are not produced in quantity, like stories of love or of strange or thrilling adventure. Like the *Margites*, these comic romances of the early modern period appeared sporadically upon the broad surface of classical or academically controlled literature without violating any of its principles or ideals of propriety, and in times when there was nowhere as yet any incentive for the writing or reading of an ideal novel in the spirit of Chariton or Richardson. The very nature of comedy is such that it tends to put beyond criticism or objection on formal grounds any piece of writing that comes under its banner. A man may be looked upon as a trifler for concerning himself too much with things fit only for amusement, but so long as he is jesting, or seems to be, he is not bound by any strict rules of procedure in so doing, and no one is likely to censure him on the grounds of his form. Trifling can be fashionable when serious sentimentality is not. It is only when an author undertakes to write something in a serious, ideal, positive, or poetic vein that he comes under the dominion of literary laws, and there he is bound by heavy pressure to conform, if only nominally, on pain of losing his reputation as a respectable writer. If Cicero, Seneca, or Apuleius (or anyone in their time with a similar reputation for intelligence and good taste) had written an ideal novel on the formal pattern of *Chaereas and Callirhoe*, the event would have caused a scandal in the ancient world of letters, or at any rate amazement, no matter how superior the novel may have been artistically in comparison with those that have survived. The writing of that ideal kind of romance in prose, at least in the early stages of its practice, was left to authors who were nobodies (as Philostratus says of Chariton), and of these and their readers in the Greek-speaking world there were many. Since Roman literary men were very conscious of being such, and were careful as a rule to emulate only what was correct and respected in the Greek academy of letters, they could not afford to vie with the nobodies of the Hellenistic world in composing ideal romances. They wanted to win reputation as high class writers, not to disbar themselves from it. It is mainly for this reason that Latin literature, with one late exception, *Apollonius of Tyre* in the third century, admits only comic romances, which were fashionable in Greek. There may have been many Latin-speaking people who would have enjoyed an ideal novel, but the literary language of the poor-in-spirit was not Latin but Greek.

All the comic romances of antiquity with which we have any direct acquaintance were written with an ulterior purpose transcending that of pure entertainment. This purpose may be either real, personal, and unheralded, as in the case of Petronius, which we shall explain in a later chapter, or it may be only a nominal purpose which is secondary in reality to that of amusing the reader, as is the case with Lucian's *True History*, or his story of *Lucius the Ass* in its original form (chap. VI below), both of which were put forth in the guise of satires or parodies. An excuse of this nature is usually necessary to justify the publication in fashionable society of an *extended* narrative of personal adventure. But the laws of propriety that govern the *short* story in prose, which is a fundamentally different genre, are not quite so severe. Here the story, besides being only a part in a larger whole, justifies itself in large measure by its very brevity, which is essential to its wit and tends to produce an effect similar to that of an epigram. It is in this connection that we must consider the literary-historical problem which confronts us in the interpretation of the ancient testimony relating to the *Milesiaca* of Aristides.

It was the common practice among Alexandrian scholars and their successors to make more or less extensive collections of homogeneous items:—epigrams, *bon-mots* (χρεῖαι), quotations from the poets, proverbs, myths, fables, etc. In theory these collections were utilitarian or informative in purpose. Some of them were meant to be of practical use as repertories for poets, rhetoricians, orators, historians, antiquarians, or philologists; but others served only as repositories of scientific, pseudo-scientific, or merely curious facts or supposed facts, like the compilations of Athenaeus, Aelian, and the paradoxographers. The subject matter of such books could be very trivial, so long as the separate items were short; but not even Aelian, with all his bad taste in matters of detail, would have thought of publishing a separate book containing in expanded form any one of his own stories, unless it were introduced or concluded with some claim or insinuation that the story was more significant in terms of philosophic or scientific meaning than the contents alone would otherwise indicate. Dramatic narratives in any composite compilation of this kind are viewed as parts of a larger whole, as they are in Herodotus or Livy, and the orientation of this whole is toward science or history in the broadest conception of those disciplines. A collection of relatively short items was regarded as a legitimate form of book, no matter what the items themselves, taken separately, might be. One by one they might have no other value than that of idle amusement, as the items in the compilation of jests known as *Philogelos*. The framework into which the contents of a collection were put might be one of several different schemes. The simplest consisted in a straight-forward presentation of separate units in paratactical order, with or without divisions according to some kind of classification, as in the Aesopic fables, the love stories of Parthenius, the classified jests of the *Philogelos*, or the paradoxical stories of Damascius in four divisions, as described by Photius.[24] Other favorite frames were the symposium, in which each of the banqueters would contribute a discourse or story of his own to the sum total of discussion on one or more topics of a general nature, as in Plato and in Athenaeus; and the philosophical dialogue, which was often arranged on the same pattern, as in Lucian's *Ship*, his *Philopseudes*, or his *Toxaris*. In the last of these, ten short but dramatically narrated stories illustrating friendship, five Greek and five Scythian, are contributed jointly by the two interlocutors. This is *Rahmenerzählung* in the true Greek style, wherein, as in Boccaccio and Chaucer, the framework is very simple and the separate stories are presented as coordinate units, which they really are, instead of being tied together or subordinated one to the other by some kind of artificial and unreal logic, as in the

Metamorphoses of Ovid or of Apuleius. Unlike Ovid, a Greek author never tries to bind together, in logical connection one to another, a mass of items which are separate and independent by nature; and unlike Apuleius, he never so far abuses the privilege of digressing from his main story as to make of digression a system by which a multitude of nominally subordinate but really independent stories are allowed to overwhelm and obscure the primary story into which they are inserted. This process, which is carried much further in the Indian storybooks than in Apuleius, is due to a lack of feeling for organic structure or an inability to manage it. The author views his materials paratactically in spite of himself; and his attempt to subordinate one story to another as an illustration is as unnecessary as it is unsuccessful. That a hybrid, pseudo-organic form of this kind should be employed by a Greek writer in the second century B.C. is most improbable, unless, like the Cynic Menippus with his mixture of prose and verse, his purpose was to mock at the conventions instead of observing them.

At the beginning of the dialogue called *Erotes*, which has come down to us under the name of Lucian although it is probably not his work, one of the interlocutors speaks as follows: "Early this morning, before sunrise, I was so delighted by the sweet and seductive appeal of your naughty stories that I almost thought that I was Aristides listening spellbound to the Milesian tales." Plutarch in the *Life of Crassus* (c. 32) tells us that the Parthian general Surena, after defeating the Romans in battle, called a meeting of the senate of the Seleucians and showed them "the licentious books of the *Milesiaca* of Aristides," which had been found in the baggage train of Roscius the Roman general. This, says Plutarch, gave Surena an opportunity to heap many insults upon the Romans and to ridicule them, charging that they couldn't keep their minds off such things and such reading, even when they were at war. Plutarch goes on to say, in effect, that people who live in glass houses ought not to throw stones: Surena himself was as great a whore-monger as anyone could be, and the Seleucians knew

it and were not fooled. They bethought themselves of Aesop's
fable about the two wallets, and how different the one in front
looked from the one behind. Surena would go forth to battle
with a brave and fearful array of spearsmen, archers, and cav-
alry in front; but in his rear were many wagonloads of *filles de
joie*, with whom he spent the nights in carousal. Roscius indeed
was blameworthy, but it was mere impudence on the part of
the Parthians, says Plutarch, to scold about things Milesian
when many of their own kings, the Arsacidae, had been born
of Milesian and Ionian pleasure girls. A Latin translation of
the *Milesiaca* was made by the Roman historian Cornelius
Sisenna, who died in 57 B.C. From this translation a total of
sixty-seven words in ten different fragments, all purporting
to be from the thirteenth book, are quoted by the grammarian
Charisius; but the only word preserved from the Greek original,
a gloss in Harpocration, is referred to the sixth book. It is possible that Sisenna, who inserted *turpes iocos* into his histories
(Ovid, *Trist.* II 445), added a great deal of his own that was
not in the Greek original, as did Apuleius in his *Metamorphoses*;
but the book of Aristides in any case was a lengthy one. Its
publication created something of a scandal in the world of letters, not so much because the stories were immoral—the contemporary Greek mime was often equally so—as because
Aristides had elevated into prose writing, as if it were suitable
for literary exploitation in that form, a type of narrative which
the ancients regarded as trivial and fit only for street-corner
gossip or barber-shop entertainment.

Nothing is known concerning Aristides personally, except
that he wrote this book. It is probable that he lived in the latter part of the second century B.C. The title of his book seems
to have been *Milesiaca*, on the analogy of such titles as were
very commonly given to serious historical works, but we do not
know just what the author meant to imply by it in this case.
It is clear that the work was contained in at least six books, if
not thirteen or more, and that the contents were mainly if not
entirely erotic, and of a very licentious nature. Beyond this, we

may conclude with some assurance (in view of the generic sense in which Roman writers use the term *Milesia fabula* and on grounds of artistic probability), that many of the stories or episodes were of a clever and witty nature, featuring such things as adulterous intrigues in which a husband is outwitted or a lover caught in the act with comic consequences, or the surprisingly easy virtue of women with a reputation for chastity. The famous story of the Widow of Ephesus in Petronius is one of numerous ancient tales that might be cited as typically "Milesian," and we know that plots of this kind were common in the Roman and Greek mimes.

In what form, or in what kind of literary framework, was the matter of the *Milesiaca* presented? Here scholarly opinions are bound to differ on many points, owing to the scantiness and the ambiguity of the ancient testimonies. The only question that need concern us here, in our survey of ancient romance as a whole, is whether the work was a lengthy and continuous novel, or a large collection of short stories. Either conclusion is possible when the issue is made to depend upon nothing more than the phraseology used by ancient writers in referring to the book; but when we consider the nature and limitations of comic romances, as outlined above, and the conventions which governed the exploitation of short stories in a sophisticated environment, the balance of probability inclines very heavily toward the conclusion that the *Milesiaca* was not a continuous story, but a series of short stories. There is no hint in our ancient testimony that Aristides had, or pretended to have, any other purpose before him than that of amusing his readers with a popular kind of material. Without such a pretense of satire or parody, a long story of erotic adventure in a comic or burlesque vein is hard to imagine, even for modern literature. Brevity is essential for the artistic effect of a story in the Milesian style. Such a story could not be extended to the length of an ordinary novel without losing its effect and becoming a bore. And, if we assume that the stories were short, consisting only of separate episodes in the career of one or two characters (as in Petronius), we assume a structural form for which the author had no apparent need, and which is without parallel elsewhere except in writers who have a special purpose of their own other than that of presenting a miscellany. Since the practice of bringing short stories of one kind or another into a collection was common in ancient literature, and since this form was very well suited to the only purpose that Aristides is believed by anyone to have had or to have professed, there can be little doubt that the majority of modern critics have been right in assuming that the *Milesiaca* consisted of a long series of short stories.

What was the framework on which they were hung? We cannot know with certainty, but it is reasonable to infer from the passage in Pseudo-Lucian quoted above that the author Aristides represented himself in his book as listening to stories told by others, and if so, the form may well have been that of a symposium on the subject of erotic experience, or of women in general. This would be like Lucian's *Toxaris*, which has the form of a dialogue on friendship. The title *Milesiaca* further suggests that the scene was laid in Miletus and that the storytelling banqueters were either Milesians themselves (which alone would explain the title *Milesiaca*) or that they were telling things which were presumably representative of Milesian culture or of local Milesian tradition. The author might well have published his book under the formal pretext that it was scientific sociology, a documentary report, as it were, on the sexual behavior of the Milesians, or on what they knew about the subject—in six volumes or more.

III

Chariton and the Nature of Greek Romance

1

THANKS TO the recovery of fragments written on papyrus in the second century after Christ, it is now generally believed that Chariton's story of *Chaereas and Callirhoe* is the earliest of all our extant Greek romances. The nature of the book itself, considered from a literary-historical viewpoint in comparison with the other extant romances, is such as to confirm this belief in a positive way; so much so that the relatively early dating of Chariton which we now accept on the basis of documentary evidence was maintained on grounds of style and content alone by one scholar, Professor Wilhelm Schmid, before the papyri were discovered, and at a time when historians of literature had long been unanimous in supposing that Chariton was the latest of the ancient romancers and that he lived in the fifth or sixth century.[1] This misconception about the date of Chariton, which prevailed throughout the nineteenth century, was largely responsible for what we now know

to have been an upside-down orientation of the whole problem
of Greek romance. For Rohde, influenced by the prevailing
conceptions of his day, placed Iamblichus, Heliodorus, and the
other "sophistic" romances at the base of his system, assuming
that they were typical of the romance in its pristine character,
and that the distinctive features of Chariton's work were
merely so many aberrations from an originally sophistic norm,
due mainly to decadence. On this assumption we were told, for
instance, that the simplicity of Chariton's plot was a deficiency
due to want of imagination or ingenuity in the invention and
multiplication of episodes, that he imitated the substance of all
the other romancers, and that the historical background of his
narrative, instead of being due to an early literary convention,
was only a bit of arbitrary decoration—or flavoring, as a recent
writer calls it in effect—superimposed on a story that was pure
invention from the bottom up. In Rohde's theory of development the romance passes from Antonius Diogenes at one pole
to Chariton at the opposite, from the complex, unreal, sophistic,
and externalized at the beginning of its career to the simple,
naïvely sentimental, and quasi-historical at the end. This
theory does not need to be refuted today, since no one accepts
it in principle; but its baleful influence still lives, particularly
in the tendency to regard ancient romance as a by-product of
professional rhetoric, and in certain other misconceptions which
have not yet disappeared from what is casually or perfunctorily
written about the Greek romances.

What was the rational basis, in the nineteenth century, for
this completely erroneous dating of Chariton? Was it inferred
from any internal evidence of a positive nature, or from any
external testimony? The answer is no. It was only a hazy guess,
fostered by historical accidents in the textual transmission of
the several romances, and by the vogue which the sophistic
romancers, Heliodorus, Longus, and Achilles Tatius, had enjoyed among the *precieux* of the sixteenth and seventeenth
centuries, and, before that, among the Byzantines. What might
be called the canon of Greek romance, comprising the authors

just mentioned, had been established some two hundred years before the text of either Chariton or Xenophon of Ephesus was discovered and published (Chariton in 1750 and Xenophon in 1726). The fact that Chariton was the latest of the romancers to be made known to the modern public, and that Heliodorus, Longus, and Achilles had for many years been accepted as standard, created the false impression, strong though not consciously reasoned, that his romance was also the latest of its kind to be written; and the complete absence of any sure reference to this author in either ancient or Byzantine writers encouraged the belief that he was unimportant and so, presumably, late. We owe the preservation of his book, along with that of Xenophon of Ephesus, to a single manuscript of the thirteenth century, which remained the property of a small Florentine monastery until late in the eighteenth century, when it was transferred to the great Medicean library.[2]

2

It is probable that Chariton's romance was well known in the second century after Christ and that it was read by many people, particularly, we may suspect, by young people of both sexes. There is such a thing as juvenile literature even in our own highly sophisticated age; and in ancient times the ideal novel must have catered to that obscure but far-flung literary market long before it became adapted in some measure to the taste and outlook of mature or educated minds. This is evident from the nature of the idealism in the romances themselves. Age levels, as well as cultural levels, mark off different strata in literature as determined by its psychological outlook. Our belief that Chariton's romance was a popular one is confirmed by the fact that since 1900 four fragments of it have been found on papyri in different towns of Egypt.[3] It seems probable, moreover, that the author of *Chaereas and Callirhoe*, rather than some unknown person, is the Chariton addressed by the sophist Philostratus in a short epigrammatic letter (no. 66 in the collection) which reads as follows: "To Chariton. You think that the Greeks are going to remember your stories (λόγων) when you are dead; those who are nobodies when they are living, what will they be when they are not living?" This letter stands in the neighborhood of at least two others, namely no. 67 to Philemon and no. 72 to Caracalla, which were addressed by Philostratus to well-known persons who were not living when he wrote. It is apparently an open letter to a dead author. It implies that Chariton's writing was well-known and widely acclaimed, and that the sophist looked upon this popular writer in the same spirit of jealous contempt that he shows for a certain Epictetus in the preceding letter and in letters 42 and 69. To this Epictetus, conceivably the slave-born philosopher but more probably a rival sophist, Philostratus says: "Fear a people with whom you have so much power" (*Ep.* 65); and "the Athenians by their applause drive you so frantic that you forget who you are and of whom you were born" (*Ep.* 69).

The principal virtue of Chariton's novel, apart from the element of manifold adventure which it has in common with the others, though in a smaller degree, lay in its sentimental idealism, its *inner* force, which was meant for the edification of naïve readers in a middle-class, pagan society. Since this society had passed away or disintegrated with the coming of Christianity, what the Byzantine ages would see or relish in any pagan romance would be only its externals; and these, the novelties of plot and episode, the affectations of learning and of rhetorical style, and the ascetic or mechanically exaggerated virtue of the heroine, were much less evident in Chariton, who was the spokesman of an earlier culture on a non-academic plane, than in the later romances of Heliodorus and Achilles Tatius. The two last mentioned, which represented Greek romance in its latest and most artificial phase, came to be looked upon in Byzantine times as the standard and almost the only known specimens of the ancient genre, to the exclusion of its more genuine but more humble representatives, which for their part had never been recognized as literature by the intelligentsia,

and on that account were more easily and more quickly forgotten. The greater the degree in which a romance was popular
and reflected the psychological outlook and taste of the un-
academic readers for whom it was written, the less chance it
would have of surviving in a literary world whose fashions were
dominated by the academic standards of scholars, pedants, and
professional rhetoricians. It was not until late in the second
century after Christ that romances of love and adventure began
to emerge upon the surface of sophistic literature; and it was
only then, when the genre had been elevated in a few cases to
that higher and more arid plane of literature, whereon it was
transformed and sophisticated by such authors as Iamblichus,
Longus, Achilles Tatius, and Heliodorus, that it became conspicuous enough to attract attention in the world of formal
learning. What appeared in that environment, or even on the
edge of it, had a much better chance of being preserved than
what lay beyond its pale, no matter how popular the latter may
once have been. This explains why such authors as Heliodorus
and Achilles Tatius, instead of such as Chariton and Xenophon
of Ephesus, came to be the principal representatives of ancient
romance in the Greek middle ages: they owed their survival to
the attention given them by scholastics. But why Heliodorus
and Achilles were elected, instead of Longus and Iamblichus or
others of their kind no longer known to us, is not so clear. It
must have been due, however, more to random historical
accidents than to the nature of the romances themselves. There
seems to be no good reason, for instance, why the book of
Achilles Tatius, whose realistic eroticism was scandalous in the
eyes of the patriarch Photius, should have been more favored
by early Christians on account of its actual content and style
than *Daphnis and Chloe* or the *Babyloniaca* of Iamblichus. It
appears that the nature of a romance could not assure its
survival, and that other factors, depending on whim or circumstance, could be more decisive. It so happened, although we
know not just why, that as early as the fifth century, if not
sooner, both Heliodorus and Achilles Tatius were believed in

some quarters to have been Christians; and this conception of
them as Christian writers may account in large measure for
their celebrity in Byzantine times, and for the fact that their
romances were transmitted through more manuscript copies,
from antiquity on, than any of the others. Concerning Heliodorus in this connection more will be said later on. The evidence
that Achilles Tatius was believed to have been a Christian
is derived partly from Suidas, who states explicitly that he
"finally became a Christian and a bishop," and partly from the
fact that persons bearing the same names as those of the
principal characters in his novel, the lovers Cleitophon and
Leucippe, were represented as the parents of St. Galaktion in
an early legend dealing with the two saints Galaktion and
Episteme.[4] Pointing in the same direction, moreover, is the fact
that Ps.-Eustathius in the late fourth or early fifth century,
in his hexaemeral commentary on *Genesis*, uses Achilles as
one of his sources for the description of peculiar animals,
along with such other authorities as Origen, Eusebius, Clement
of Alexandria, Josephus, Philo, and the *Physiologus*—as if he
saw Achilles Tatius, though dimly, in the same religious light
as the others, presumably as a Christian writer.

3

The bridge over which the Greek romance passed on its way
from the ancient world to the Byzantine was purely scholastic
and had almost no support in popular favor. The ideal love
story, or the story of worldly adventure, was no longer cultivated as a literary form. It had passed out with the pagan
culture that had fostered it. What replaced it on the dynamic
level of literature was the biography of a saint. Hundreds of
these are known to us, and the highest development of the type
is seen in the immensely popular "romance" of *Barlaam and
Joasaph*,[5] which was made for the eighth century, the age of the
iconoclastic struggle, when metaphysical contemplation and
renunciation of worldly affairs could inspire men to write books,

but not the assertion of such things. Primary concern with the hopes, fears, passions and manifold experiences of life in its purely mundane aspects, and with the exploitation of these on their own account in an intellectually wide-open society, was the force that sustained and made possible the proliferation of the ancient novel, as of the modern. When that outlook on life and its values passed away before the onset of otherworldliness, the ancient romance passed away with it. The things that the latter held in honor and exploited were the things that the early Christians renounced on principle. This is not to deny that many people in the early Middle Ages might enjoy reading a Greek romance, just as many of us today may enjoy reading a tragedy of Sophocles or the *Barlaam and Joasaph* ascribed to St. John of Damascus. But reading an ancient book, even with pleasure and profit, is a very different thing from having the inspiration and incentive necessary to create others like it and propagate them in one's own environment, and unless that is done to a notable extent, the literary genre is dead in our sense of the word.

The age of asceticism in the East, which is sometimes called the Dark Age, from a humanistic standpoint, extended from the fourth century, approximately, to the middle of the ninth. In terms of the basic literary pattern which we have called epic, meaning thereby any extended narrative of personal adventure exploited on its own account, the truest expression of this age was the saint's life. Latter-day epic, as we called the Greek romance, had been succeeded by martyr-epic, or saintly epic, which was generated by a new culture with a new *Weltanschauung*. This age of asceticism, in which theological thinking was dominant and tended to exclude concern with anything of a purely secular nature, was followed by an era extending from the ninth century down to the fall of Constantinople in which the interest of men in worldly things became ever more pronounced and more varied. In literature, as well as in scholarly activity, this oncoming humanism, which ran deep in the tides of instinct and action, manifested itself in many ways and on both cultural levels, the level of genuinely popular and spontaneous expression on the one hand, and that of learning, and learned affectation or pedantry on the other. What concerns us here is primarily the popular expression in epic medium—narratives in a new, unclassical verse, which were in the unscholarly vernacular, sung and recited in part by minstrels, as well as written down. In this kind of narrative we can see, more clearly than elsewhere, the cultural ideas and forces which created new forms and modified the old ones. Even the learned world of Byzantium, hitherto always formal and backward-looking in secular matters, was affected by it. Tzetzes in the twelfth century poured out the copious erudition of his *Chiliads* in 15-syllable "political" verse, to the tune of "A captain bold of Halifax who lived in country quarters"; which was the meter of popular epic and romance. The humanistic outlook of the later Byzantine ages, insofar as it was romantic, found its fullest and truest expression on the popular plane of song and story, much of which still lives in the Greece of today; but it is only a pale reflex of this romantic stir that we observe in the slavish imitations of Achilles Tatius and Heliodorus which were written in the twelfth century by such miserable pedants as Eustathius Macrembolites, Theodorus Prodromus, and Nicetas Eugenianus, trying to write romance in what they thought was the ancient manner.[6] Of these no account need be taken.

The real Byzantine epic and romance begins with the *chanson de geste* dealing with Digenes Akritas, the hero of border warfare in the tenth century against Moslems and robber knights on the eastern outskirts of the Empire.[7] This warrior-epic is closely analogous in many fundamental respects, including its ballad-like meter, to the old Spanish *Cid*, the story of "el mas famoso Castellano"; and it stands at the head of a line of epic-romantic development in the East, which is profoundly similar to that represented in the West by the *chansons de geste* from beginning to end, and the romance of chivalry as a whole. In the East, as in the West, warrior-epic,

as we called it, was succeeded, under the influence of feudalism
and the presence of Frankish knights and kingdoms throughout
Greece in the thirteenth century, by romantic epic. Like their
ancient counterparts, the *Iliad* and the *Odyssey* respectively,
but unlike the latter-day epic known as novel which arises only
in a literate environment and is a written composition from the
start, both types of medieval epic, in the forms preserved to us,
rest upon a broad and fertile substratum of oral minstrelsy.
They were sung or recited in substance and variously adapted
to listening audiences by wandering rhapsodists before they
were written down, whether in the form of relatively short
poems, or combined into larger unities by a conscious literary
effort. In the process of being cast into literary form, and later
reworked, these epics and romances acquired some formal
features of language, style, and structure, and perhaps also
of substance, which were not native to them but superimposed
by learned convention and the literary education of their
editors. Thus even *Digenes Akritas* shows verbal imitation of
two descriptive passages in Achilles Tatius, although the
inspiration that underlies the poem is everywhere fresh and
original, and its thought and substance independent of book
learning.[8] The influence of formal education upon these popular
stories was only superficial; and between the two cultural
spheres, popular and academic, osmosis, so to speak, took place
in both directions. Greek romance in the medieval period,
generated by the ideal impulse which first appears in the epic
of *Digenes Akritas* and was later modified by the mingling of
peoples and cultures after the fourth Crusade, comes out in a
variety of forms. Some of these are lengthy, some relatively
short. In date of composition they range from the thirteenth
century to the mid-sixteenth. The themes may be either ancient
in origin or medieval; in nationality, Greek, French, Italian,
Oriental or mixed. Some are only adaptations of romances of
chivalry current in the West. The hero may be historical,
quasi-historical, fictitious, or folkloristic; and his wanderings
may be in a known region of the world or mainly in fairyland,

where things happen by magic. To illustrate these points would take us too far from our course.[9]

In the West during the period of the Renaissance, and onward to the eighteenth century, there was no genuine ideal romance. As a dynamic literary form it had been replaced chiefly by the drama, which belongs to the microcosm of the city (where the currents of thought and fashion are centripetal) rather than to the castle in the distance, the wars of the barons, the knight on his journey of adventure, and the wandering minstrel who sang of his exploits. Concentration in the forms of artistic expression, rather than extension, were in honor, and literature in fashion was under the control either of intellectuals and classicists, or of a smart set, all of whom in the aggregate exercised the function of an academy. In this environment ideal romance, being at the base mainly an inheritance from the past, could be cultivated only as a tender plant in a literary hothouse. More favored by the intellectual temper of the times was a short story, usually witty or picaresque, told in a light vein for the amusement of smart society; if such a story was long, it would be a satire weighted with philosophical meaning or criticism of some kind. As we have noted before, the real novel, comparable to the Greek romance in its time, did not appear until the middle of the eighteenth century. Latter-day epic, martyr-epic, warrior-epic, romantic epic and, once more, latter-day epic—such, in broad outline, are the forms successively assumed under the impact of different cultures by the primeval pattern of epic narrative from the time of Heliodorus to the present day.

4

A fitting epitaph for the Greek erotic romance was penned by Nietzsche: "Christianity," he says, "gave Eros poison to drink; he did not die of it, certainly, but degenerated to Vice." [10] How true this is will be realized by anyone who reads the apocryphal *Acts* of Christian martyrs or the lives of the saints. Eros, healthy, pagan, and not yet poisoned, had been the principal prop of Greek romance in its beginnings and in its prime; and when that prop weakened and decayed, by degenerating into vice or into trifling, the form supported by it collapsed therewith, inevitably, and died. The sickening of Eros is already evident in Heliodorus and Achilles Tatius.

Achilles treats love objectively in a spirit of critical realism, and more as a sporting proposition, or *ludus*, as the Romans would say, than as a sentimental ideal which he honestly shared with his lovers as a motive for their actions, as does Chariton. For him love is one of many sophistical topics upon which he likes to dwell learnedly and rhetorically, and, it must be confessed, with a good deal of understanding. His Melitte, for example, a minor character, is pictured with more insight into human nature and is thereby more real and interesting than his own Leucippe or almost any other heroine of Greek romance. Achilles has his virtues, but they are those of a highly sophisticated writer which appear as something incidental or tangential to the conventional type of plot with which he deals *invita Minerva*, and with which he seems to have little sympathy. He was better qualified by nature for the writing of a picaresque novel than an ideal one. From the ideal standpoint of other Greek romances many of his episodes are close to burlesque, and some critics have maintained that he was deliberately mocking at the extravagances of the conventional romance.[11] His realistic eroticism was bound to appear as sinful in the eyes of Christians, as it did to Photius (cod. 87), and as trifling, or disillusioning or cynical in the eyes of those simpleminded pagans whose idealistic sentimentality had been the chief support of romance as a literary institution at the beginning, insofar as it was a love story. The novel of today may deal with love in any manner whatever, without weakening the impulse to write novels; because in our own degenerate society the very negation of moral and spiritual values has become a fashion and a cultural power. But this was far from being the case in the time of Achilles Tatius. He lived in the late second century, a climactic age, when negation of any kind was sheer weakness and the only thing that could survive was something very serious, positive, and idealistic.[12]

In Heliodorus love as an ideal or as something to be attained and enjoyed is decidedly secondary in interest to religious mysticism, sacerdotal solemnities and strategies, and the implication that a grandiose epic scheme of things, too complicated to be more than dimly understood, is being worked out by the design of an inscrutable Providence. The idealized persons in Heliodorus are likely to be either priests or ascetics: Calasiris, who comes close to being the real hero of the story, Sisimithres, Charicles, and the latter's daughter the heroine Chariclea, who was a priestess of the virgin Artemis in the beginning and never quite got over it. She remains a celibate at heart, and is more interested throughout in managing things by means of deceptions and roundabout methods, in which she is expert, than in love or loving, although she is willing to marry under priestly guidance after all the proprieties of courtship have been rigidly and ostentatiously observed. From the way in which she and Theagenes behave, especially near the end of the story, one gets the impression that neither of the two is really in love or anxious to possess the other. Here Eros is failing. Heliodorus is what Nietzsche might have called "preëxistently Christian," with reference to his religiosity and his priestly character as seen in the *Aethiopica*, as well as to the cultural outlook of the transitional age, mid-third century, in which he lived.[13] He was devout by nature, howbeit in the cause of a pagan cult, and there is something sanctimonious and pontifical about his manner of writing. Those qualities of mind caused him to be looked upon as a kindred spirit by pious Christians; and that view of him, together with the fact that his name happened to be the same as that of a reputed bishop of Trikka in Thessaly, gave rise to a popular rumor that he was the same man and that he had written the *Aethiopica* in his youth before he became a convert to Christianity and thereafter a bishop. This popular rumor is reported by the ecclesiastical historian Socrates in the

early fifth century, writing as follows in his *Hist. Eccl.* V 22
(Migne, *Patr. Gr.* 67, col. 63): "The first to institute this
custom in Thessaly [the custom of requiring celibacy of the
clergy] was Heliodorus who became bishop there, and who is
said to have been the author of a love story in several books
which he composed when he was young and to which he gave
the title *Aethiopica.*" The unqualified statement here made by
Socrates about what a bishop named Heliodorus had done in
Thessaly is such that we have little reason to doubt the truth
of it; but, whether or not it was true as church history, it was
at all events something that the historian believed to be true,
and it was obviously on the basis of that belief, taken as fact
by himself and by his informants, that the identity of the
bishop with the romancer had been inferred. That inference,
however, unlike the matter-of-fact reference to Bishop Heliodorus of Trikka, is subject to grave suspicion, because its
pattern is that of a familiar type of myth of which we have
many examples.[14] In the case of Achilles Tatius it is difficult to
see how popular tradition could have fancied him to have been
or to have become a Christian bishop; but in the case of
Heliodorus it was almost inevitable that he should be mistaken
for such. He was a kindred spirit. In him, more easily than in
any other ancient romancer, they could find spiritual values of
the kind that they wanted to find, while enjoying at the same
time that element of sensational adventure which is always
popular with readers who have time for it, and which was
abundantly featured—though not on its account—in their own
biographies of the saints and martyrs.

5

In the evolution of the Greek novel there are two large phases
which must be clearly distinguished one from the other in our
contemplation of the genre as a whole. Failure to make this
distinction in the past has resulted in many misconceptions
concerning both the nature and the origins of the Greek

romance. The two phases to which I refer have already been mentioned (sec. 2). They may be called the presophistic and the sophistic, respectively, in order to indicate their historical sequence;[15] but since the difference between the two kinds is due less to the age in which they appear than to the mentality and educational background of the authors themselves, and the class of readers for whom they wrote, it follows that romances of the presophistic type (or the non-sophistic), may be produced in the same age as that in which the sophistic type is coming to the fore, as they were in the second century after Christ. Both types, broadly conceived as such, are historically significant and deserve our attention: the sophistic because it signalizes an upward and outward movement in the range of the novel, comparable to that which has taken place in modern times, and the presophistic or relatively simple type because it alone can reveal to us what the fundamental nature of the genre was in its beginnings. Since our study relates primarily to origins, the later part of this chapter will deal with the earlier phase of Greek romance as exemplified by Chariton. Meanwhile some attention must be given to the nature, implications, and potentialities of the sophistic romance.

What may be called the formal trade-mark of the sophist, the writer whose concepts of literary propriety are shaped by classical and academic standards, in contrast with the defiance of those standards by the earlier romancers, is clearly seen in the methods by which, respectively, Longus and Achilles Tatius introduce their stories. Both stories, unlike those of Chariton and Xenophon, are told on the authority of someone other than the author himself, in what the rhetorician Theon calls the accusative case. "Most of the ancients," says Theon, "introduced their fables in this way, and very rightly so, as Aristotle remarks: for they do not tell them in their own person, but refer them to ancient authority, in order to mitigate the appearance of relating impossible things." [16] This reveals the conscience of the historian who feels responsible for the truth of what he states in his own person, in contrast with that of the earliest romancers who thought of themselves as creative artists, like the dramatists, and had emancipated themselves accordingly, as prose writers, from the bonds of historiographical convention.

Technically considered, the *Daphnis and Chloe* of Longus is an *ecphrasis*, a form of writing which was much in favor with professional rhetoricians and about which they have much to say. An ecphrasis, properly so called, might be a description of almost anything visible—a landscape, a battle, or a person, but it often took the form of an exegetical interpretation of a picture or a statue, as in Philostratus and other sophists, and that is what we have in Longus. The author tells us that he saw a beautiful painting in a grove of the Nymphs on the island of Lesbos, that he was delighted with the varied scenes of rustic life and love therein depicted, that he inquired for an interpreter of the picture. After finding one, he wrote up the story which it represented in four books, "as an offering to Eros, the Nymphs, and Pan, and as a delightful possession for all mankind. It will remedy disease, bring fond recollections to him that has loved, and instruct him that has not loved. [Cf. *cras amet qui nunquam amavit, quique amavit cras amet.*] None, indeed, has escaped love or ever shall, as long as beauty survives and eyes to see it. May the god vouchsafe me to retain prudence as I write of the vicissitudes of others." Longus presents his love story for its own sake and makes no pretense of its being anything else than an artistic creation of his own. For that reason he is as truly a novelist as any of those who preceded him; but unlike the latter he has the sensibility of an educated man trained in the academic tradition, for whom a narrative in prose, unlike a drama, is necessarily a history in theory. It must be formally vouched for as true in substance, either by the author himself in his own person, like Dio in his idyllic account of the country folk of Euboea, or by some other authority, man or document, in this case a picture, to which the author refers. There is as large a proportion of pure fiction in Longus as in Chariton, and probably larger. Both writers feel

free to invent as much as they please, but they differ profoundly
in respect to the sanctions on which their narratives rest.
Chariton tells the story of Callirhoe in his own person, with
the self-assurance of a creative artist, poet or dramatist, elabo-
rating a kernel of historical legend. Longus will not take that
liberty, through fear of violating the conventions of formal
prose literature. Instead he professes to describe events which
an unknown artist outlined in a picture. By this technicality
he aligns himself with the contemporary sophists, but his
exploitation of poetic values on their own account in prose
narrative marks him as a romancer.[17]

Achilles Tatius, like Longus, and for the same reasons, is
careful not to tell his story of *Clitophon and Leucippe* on his
own authority, as a poet or dramatist would do, and as the
earlier romancers had done. Instead, he introduces Clitophon
himself, whom he says he met at Tyre, relating his adventures
in the first person. The author, Achilles, poses as only a listener
to the story, although he often forgets that Clitophon is
speaking and makes him say things that presuppose an overall
knowledge such as only the author himself could assume.

Since the protagonist Clitophon is a young man whom the
author meets and talks with personally, we see that the action
described in the romance takes place supposedly within the
lifetime of the author himself. That is something new. In all the
other ideal romances of antiquity of which we have any
knowledge, the actors live in a distant past; they belong, in
theory at least, to saga, and not to the contemporary world of
the writer, however thoroughly they may be conceived and
represented in the likeness of contemporary men and women.[18]
Achilles has broken away from a tradition of long standing,
which was dominant not only in the earlier romances but also
in tragedy and other forms of objective poetry, namely, that
ideal narrative must relate to saga, myth, or history. His
writing about a serious love affair, freely invented, as about
something that happened in his own time (but not to himself
personally) is without parallel, insofar as I can recall, in ancient

literature. It is important for us to realize the significance of this innovation. By it all the essential difference in form and potentiality between the ancient and the modern novel is bridged. In the modern novel the practice of writing ideally about the emotions and experiences of an imaginary third person who lives in the same age as the author has been cultivated ever since Fielding. This approximate contemporaneity of the fictional characters is so common in our own literature that the historical novel (which is the only kind known to us in ancient books apart from Achilles Tatius and the comic romances) is looked upon as something exceptional and in a class by itself. The ratio between the two kinds of novel in ancient practice might easily have become what it has been in modern times, had the need for contemporaneity been similar. But it was not. The needs of the novel in the matter of form are determined to some extent by the nature of the ideas of which it is made to be the expression. The ideas and aesthetic values which the ideal ancient novel had to convey, among them love and adventure, for example, were always of such a general, broadly human, and timeless nature (even when scientific or critical as often in digressions) that a theoretically ancient setting for the characters, in line with the long-established tradition of objective poetry, would serve as well as a modern one.[19] This is true also of many modern novels, which could easily have been shaped as historical novels, and of the *Clitophon and Leucippe* of Achilles Tatius. Contemporaneity in the latter is not called for by the nature of its subject-matter, but is an accident due to the method employed by the author in launching a nominally true story. If Achilles, or Richardson, had combined this contemporaneity with the method followed by other ancient romancers—all of whom tell the story on their own authority about other characters in the manner of historians—there would have been no formal difference at all between their methods of story telling and that of the average modern novelist. As it was, contemporaneity in both the ancient and the modern novel was introduced, not to meet any requirement of the novel itself, but by the author's desire to observe the proprieties of classical literature, still dominant in his time. To tell a story, however fictitious, about one's own personal experience or emotions, as do Clitophon and Pamela, had been proper in formal literature from Homer onwards, and it did not matter whether or not the narrator was identical or contemporary with the author himself. The incredible adventures of Odysseus are told by himself to Alcinous and are not vouched for by Homer; Sappho and many of the lyric poets, including Petrarch and Shakespeare in early modern times, write freely about their own emotions or experiences, at least ostensibly; and when an elegiac poet at Rome writes about his own love affair, as Propertius says,

Maxima de nihilo nascitur historia.

The license that went with subjective writing of any kind was far greater than that which was allowed to the historian, or even to the poet in writing objectively about a third person. Narrative in the first person always bordered very closely on undisguised fiction, and was generally seen either as such or as comedy or trifling (*ludus*).[20] A writer in the classical tradition might say whatever he pleased about himself, or represent another person so doing; but what he could not do, without violating all literary propriety or lapsing into farce, was to write out on his own authority an extended account in prose of the fictitious experiences of another person, especially if that person did not belong to myth or saga, but was presumably a contemporary. That is what the modern novelist has usually done, beginning with Fielding; but neither Achilles Tatius nor Richardson ventured to break with literary convention to that extent. Achilles, instead of writing the history of Clitophon on his own authority, only reports the autobiography of that character, and Richardson puts his romance into the well-recognized form of personal letters wherein Pamela tells of her own experiences.

The modern fashion of bringing ideal fiction into a framework of contemporary life, regardless of whether or not such a setting is actually needed, is probably due in large measure to the precedents set by Richardson and his followers in eighteenth-century England. The temper of those authors was as peculiarly realistic, and English, as it was moral. They were prone to preach, not in the relatively abstract manner of philosophers, poets, and essayists who address themselves to an intellectual few, but in terms of the concrete aspects and particularities of social life in their own time. Their message, which was more moral and positive than that of the earliest Greek romancers, and less concerned with the novelties of external adventure, needed to be dramatized in a familiar, realistic setting in order to be brought home to the masses of middle-class people for whom they wrote. In the communication of ideas or the description of events Greek writers, on the other hand, are likely to be more abstract than Romans or Englishmen, except in comedy, and are less inclined to illustrate their thought or meaning with an abundance of concrete details. The precedent of contemporaneity in the early modern novel opened up the form for the exploitation through its medium, in more recent times, of a wide field of ideas involving the studious criticism or description of contemporary social phenomena on their own account. The ancient novel as it appears in Achilles Tatius had the same potentiality, so far as form is concerned; but the writers of that time had no need for the extension of the novel in that direction.

In ancient literature the convention that restricted ideal fiction, whether in prose or in verse, to a setting distant in time or place was stronger than it has been in modern times; and, conversely, what was close-up and contemporary was associated more inevitably with what was broadly comic by nature and literary tradition, or else trivial and playful. Normally the ideal romance, like Sophoclean tragedy, was a bit of ancient history in theory, solemnly related in the third person; the comic was a story of contemporary experience told subjectively by the protagonist speaking about himself in the first person. Moreover, the protagonist in the ideal romance, as in tragedy, was usually a person of high estate, or one known to myth or legend; whereas the protagonist in a comic story would often be a nonentity. Neither of the two categories of epic narrative, thus described with reference to their traditional conventions, is broad enough to contain either the *Clitophon and Leucippe* of Achilles Tatius, or the novels of Henry Fielding. For that purpose, the two categories will have to be fused into one which admits the proprieties of both. It is obvious that Achilles is writing in the ideal tradition of Greek romance, but the contemporaneity of his story, the use of a Tom-Dick-or-Harry (specifically an unknown Clitophon) speaking in the first person as the protagonist, and the nature of the episodes, many of which border on burlesque and are thought by some to have been intended as parody—all this signifies that in his book the comic or picaresque tradition of epic narrative has been grafted onto the ideal, thereby greatly widening the scope of the genre romance and its capacity as an artistic medium for the criticism or interpretation of life in all its aspects. It was natural that this should happen when a relatively sophisticated author and one of realistic and skeptical temperament, such as Achilles, undertook to write in the ideal tradition of Greek romance. Such a man would react to the naïve conventionalities and sentiments of his predecessors in much the same way that Fielding reacted to Richardson's *Pamela*. Achilles stands in about the same relation to Chariton, Xenophon of Ephesus, and the author of the Ninus romance as Fielding does to Richardson, except that the Greek writer's reaction was not so strong, positive, and explicit as the Englishman's. Thus the ancient novel on the eve of its eclipse attained to just that point in its *formal* development which the English novel reached, only two years after its birth, in Fielding's *Joseph Andrews*.

The full title of the book just mentioned is significant: *The History of the Adventures of Joseph Andrews, and of his Friend Mr. Abraham Adams. Written in Imitation of the Manner of Cervantes, Author of Don Quixote* (1742). The central purpose

with which Fielding began in the writing of this book was to
ridicule Richardson's *Pamela* by transferring that heroine's
embarrassments, caused by the love-making of her master, to
a hero who purported to be her brother, Joseph Andrews,
bravely resisting attempts made upon his virtue by the amorous
Lady Booby. But this initial purpose, stated explicitly in the
first chapter, quickly fell into the background and became
unimportant when the author, with his genius for the sketching
of character-types, his moral seriousness, and his interest in the
contemplation of human nature *per se* as a great subject,
warmed to his theme. The secondary characters, such as Parson
Adams and Mrs. Slipslop, became more interesting than the
principals. Although the story begins and ends outwardly as
parody, the greater part of it, in spite of many ludicrous scenes,
is concerned with a serious and sympathetic study of human
nature as it appears against the background of contemporary
society. It differs from a purely picaresque, satirical, or burlesque novel—what we have called in ancient literature a comic
romance—in much the same way that the comedy of Menander
and Terence differed from that of Aristophanes. It is more
serious and sympathetic in its underlying tone and tendency;
it is written for the sake of ethical instruction, instead of for
satire or amusement only; the characters are made fallible in
order to be real and human; and the burlesque element is a
means rather than an end. It was not until he had come to the
close of his first volume that Fielding realized that he (like
Apuleius) had created a new kind of fiction; and in the preface
to the second volume he explained very truly what the new
form was in terms of the older classical conventions. He defines
his work as "a comic epic poem in prose." It is epic, because it
is an extended narrative of personal adventure or experience;
it is comic in the sense that it is realistic and admits ludicrous
actions and commonplace characters, unlike the serious romance; and it is a poem (so he implies) in the loose sense that,
unlike a burlesque or picaresque novel, it contains ideal values
comparable to those of the *Odyssey* and other epic poems. The

more precise implications of this definition need not detain us. The important thing to note is that Fielding combined the two main traditions of prose fiction which went into the making of the modern novel: the sophistical literary tradition, which allowed only novels of a burlesque, satirical, picaresque, or trifling kind, with which he began in *Joseph Andrews*, and the serious, ideal tradition which he shared with Richardson in spite of his disagreement with that author in matters of taste and ethical perception.[21] The same combination, as we have observed, is found also in Achilles Tatius; but there the ancient sophistical or intellectual tradition in prose fiction, which, like the modern, was fundamentally comic, is the superimposed element, instead of being, as in Fielding, the formal conception with which the author begins.

The serious Greek romance had originated with naïve authors who were of small understanding, and whose moral sentiments, like those of Richardson, were narrowly conventional and jejune. They were not addressing themselves to educated readers whose sense for ethical values would be cultivated and discriminating; and, apart from that, they had no such positive and absorbing interest in morality and problems relating to the conduct of life as did most English writers in the eighteenth century. Virtue, or heroism, for those obscure Greek romancers was usually a negative quality, meaning little more than sexual respectability, conformity to middle-class *mores* generally, and the heroic(?) readiness on the part of lovers to give up and commit suicide whenever external circumstances seemed to triumph over their struggles. This passive and negative outlook on the world was characteristic of the Hellenistic age, but not of the age of Richardson. In that respect the culture that projected the ancient novel was different in kind from that in which the modern novel grew up. What interested the early Greek romancer positively, the inspiration that moved him to write, was not a moral problem, as it was primarily with Richardson, nor the artistic exhibition of ethical qualities, as in much of the higher literature of antiquity, but a sentimental ideal centering about young love and the sensational buffetings of Fortune that interfered with its realization and prolonged the dramatic suspense. Preoccupation with such childishly fanciful and spectacular themes tended to preclude any concern with the portrayal of character or the study of human nature on its own account. These restrictions in the range and quality of Greek romance originated with the earliest exponents of the genre and became stereotyped features of it before the time when authors trained in the higher fashions of literature and thought, expressed in other forms, entered upon the writing of romance.

In our so-called sophistic romances the banalities of the earlier and more naïve type of romance are retained in varying degrees as a matter of traditional form; but much is added thereunto which stems from the educational background of the sophistic writer and his sense of literary or philosophical value. What is added in substance, or changed in respect to orientation and emphasis, whether inwardly or outwardly, depends upon the taste and talent of the individual writer and may be shaped in accordance with any concept of artistic value known to the higher literature of antiquity. Here the potentialities of the situation are more significant than the actualities as known to us, for the latter depend upon the identity of only a few romances that have survived by chance out of the many that were once written, while the former are implied by the nature of the innovations which we know to have been made.

These innovations in the techniques employed by Longus and Achilles in launching their stories, and in the admission of comic proprieties into ideal romance by Achilles, have already been noted and their literary-historical significance considered. Certain others, consisting mainly of digressions superimposed on the story, seem not to have any value for the development of the novel as such but to be carried over into it from the curricula of academic prose writing, the orientation of which in that age was scientific by pretension, or rhetorically epideictic. Iamblichus, Achilles Tatius, and Heliodorus seek to entertain their readers with disquisitions on a variety of topics which they regard as edifying or instructive, but which contribute nothing to the artistry of the main story, either outwardly as drama or inwardly as psychological experience. For them the story of love ending in success is a perfunctory theme of which they are almost ashamed. They tolerate it because they know that it is popular and will bring them readers, but they try to improve upon it as much as they can by the injection of a more respectable kind of subject-matter and artistic display. They do not tell the love story for its own sake, as a poet would do, and as the earlier romancers had done, but rather use it as a framework within which to display their sophistical wares. These may consist either of digressions upon topics of an informative kind, the tendency of which is scientific, pseudo-scientific, philosophic, or paradoxographical, or of rhetorical displays of one kind or another where the subject matter, as in nearly all the great sophists of the day, is of less consequence than the word-working and is looked upon almost with indifference by the authors, provided only that it is academic in kind or pretension. After reading the *Babyloniaca* of Iamblichus, Photius praises the author's prose style and thinks it a pity that one who was so capable a rhetorician should have stooped to childish fiction as a medium for the display of his rhetorical talents, instead of writing about matters of serious concern.[22] The digressions in these sophistic romances, which often take the form of philosophical or scientific discussions, are fundamentally analogous, in their literary-historical meaning, to the critical and philosophical essays which appear at the beginning of almost every book or chapter in Fielding's *Joseph Andrews* and *Tom Jones*. What these non-organic features signify in both cases is that the novel, when it first comes into the hands of authors trained in the intellectual or classical traditions, does not yet stand entirely on its own feet as a work of art, and has not yet cut its connections with those other forms which dominated the literary scene before its birth. In antiquity the novel stood on its own feet as an artistic creation mainly, though not entirely, in the presophistic or non-sophistic stage of its cultivation, when it was ignored or despised by the intelligentsia.

What were the possibilities of the ancient novel as a medium of artistic expression in the age of the Antonines? Judging only by what we have in the extant romances, including those which are reckoned among the non-sophistic, the variety of plots, aesthetic viewpoints, and orientation in this ancient species of novel was considerably greater than what is commonly supposed to be typical of the Greek romance, heretofore too narrowly defined. The plot is not necessarily concerned with a pair of lovers, as it is not in *Apollonius of Tyre* or in the *Recognitiones* of Pseudo-Clement, both of which are genuine romances in a sense which is not true of the apocryphal *acts* of the martyrs; travel and hazardous adventures by land and sea are not a necessary ingredient, as they are not in Longus; the main interest may be centered in the characters and their psychological experience, rather than in external events, as is the case in the *Daphnis and Chloe* of Longus, and in many parts of Chariton. Beyond this, we have to consider what must have been the aesthetic viewpoint and orientation in those erotic romances which are mentioned by ancient authors but which have not come down to us. Did the love story always end happily in those books, or might the ending have been tragic, as is the case in almost every story that is told by the elegaic or dramatic poets about mythical lovers (and even in Richardson's *Clarissa*)? Might it not be that in some of those lost romances the comic or realistic proprieties were as much blended with the fundamentally ideal and serious tendency as they are in Achilles Tatius or in Fielding?

Suidas mentions a Xenophon of Cyprus who wrote a book entitled *Cypriaca*, concerning which he ways: "It too [like the *Ephesiaca* of Xenophon of Ephesus just mentioned] is a story (ἰστορία) dealing with an erotic theme, concerning Cinyras, Myrrha, and Adonis." It is hard to imagine how this myth, which told about the incestuous relations of Myrrha with her father Cinyras, could have been shaped into a romance in which the ending was a happy one, rather than tragic, as elsewhere. This story of incest was too well-known to be completely ignored or avoided by any author writing about Cinyras and Myrrha. One may suppose that the main part of the romance dealt, as in Ovid, but more extensively, with the inner conflicts, passions, contrivances, and adventures of Myrrha herself, being, so to speak, a psychological novel. However, even if both parties were represented as innocently unaware of each other's identity, in any case the ending must have involved the recognition of incest and would thereby be tragic. The love of Myrrha for her father Cinyras had been elaborated in Alexandrian fashion by the Roman poet C. Helvius Cinna in his famous *Smyrna* (= Myrrha), to the writing of which he had devoted nine years; and the incestuous love of Byblis for her brother Caunus was told by Parthenius in hexameter verse.[23] The treatment of love in the Alexandrian and Roman poets, when it related to mythical or historical persons, was psychoanalytical in character and the story ended almost always in calamity or tragedy. No sophisticated writer in antiquity was likely to deal seriously and objectively with love as his principal theme in any other fashion; and this was the fashion in which a formal prose writer of the second century, one trained in the learned or academic tradition, would naturally handle a love story *if it were the principal topic to which his artistic effort was directed.* Such, as we noted above, was not the case with Iamblichus, Achilles Tatius and Heliodorus. For them the conventional story of love and adventure with its happy ending, taken over from the presophistic romance, was a perfunctory theme of secondary interest used as an attractive framework for the exhibition of other more sophistical wares; but the nature of the myth chosen by Xenophon of Cyprus is a clear indication that love in his prose romance must have been treated in essentially the same fashion as it was in the Alexandrian poets and in Ovid. These poets were not "forerunners" of the Greek romance in the sense intended by Rohde. They had no influence on its origins, and their conventions in writing about love were not brought into it from above until long after the species romance, as a new literary form with a happy ending, had been born and propagated in a lower intellectual environment. In order to invent the kind of drama that *they* wanted, namely an externalized story of love and adventure with a happy ending, the earlier presophistic romancers, who were men of naïve sentiments uncontrolled by intellectual standards, would choose for their theme either an obscure myth about whose principals next to nothing was known, or, like the author of the Ninus romance, they would deal with that part of a mythical hero's or heroine's life concerning which tradition had been silent. That was not the method of poets and sophistic writers generally. What the latter chose to deal with, if it was to be their principal subject, was nearly always either a famous myth or the essential part of an aetiological myth, however obscure it might be; and it is clear that Xenophon of Cyprus must have followed their example in writing a romance in prose about the love of Cinyras and Myrrha. Once the methods, values, and viewpoints of the ancient poets in dealing with a story of personal experiences had been carried over into prose narrative, as was probably the case in Xenophon of Cyprus, the potentialities of the form romance, as literature with a tragic, or ethical, or psychoanalytical orientation, were greatly extended. The rigid convention of the happy ending, along with other restrictions due to the environment in which this literary species had originated, was broken down and the form was open henceforth, by precedent, for the exploitation of all such narrative values as are represented by the ancient poets early and late on the one hand, and by such modern novelists as Thomas Hardy and James Joyce on the other.

Strict loyalty of the lovers to each other outwardly unto death was not so inevitable a feature of Greek romance as modern students, with Heliodorus in mind, have been inclined to assume. That convention is observed, as a matter of fact, in only two of the six erotic romances whose contents are known to us entire or in outline, namely, in Heliodorus and in Xenophon of Ephesus. Chariton's Callirhoe is induced by hard circumstances, though not compelled, to marry a second husband, whom she cherishes with affection and respect until her first husband, Chaereas, whom she prefers and has never ceased to love, is finally restored to her. Sinonis, the heroine in Iamblichus, marries another man for no other purpose, apparently, than to spite her first husband, Rhodanes, and to take revenge upon an imaginary rival; but in the end Rhodanes gets her back by defeating her husband, the king of Syria, in war. The innocent Daphnis, in the pastoral romance of Longus, is given a practical lesson in love-making by a neighbor's wife, a young woman married to an old man, who takes him into the woods apart from Chloe; and Clitophon in Achilles Tatius, though in love with Leucippe, satisfies the passion of the widow Melitte on the floor of his prison.

The behavior of lovers in Achilles Tatius (including their attempted premarital union) is described realistically and sympathetically, and there is nothing in his representation of their passions which would seem immoral or cynical to a cultivated man of antiquity or to the average modern novelist, however shameless it might seem to Photius the patriarch in an age of Christian asceticism, or to a small-minded person like the author of the Ninus romance for whom morality in all its aspects consisted, apparently, in nothing more than the mechanical observance of social respectabilities and taboos.

The manner of dealing with love in a Greek romance in the last half of the second century must have depended, as it does in the modern novel and in most of ancient literature, much less on conventions observed by the pioneers of the genre than on the taste and fancy of the individual author and the kind of readers for whom he wrote. The orientation of an erotic romance might be either inward or outward, tragic or sentimentally ideal, contemplative or sensational, realistic or extravagant, puritanical, prurient, or pornographic. Suidas mentions the *Rhodiaka* in nineteen books of one Philip of

Amphipolis, which, he says, was "very indecent"—ἔστι δὲ τῶν πάνυ αἰσχρῶν. The same author also wrote *Koaka* and *Thasiaka*, each in two books, according to Suidas; and the physician Theodorus Priscianus at the beginning of the fifth century recommends the erotic writings of this Philip of Amphipolis, along with those of Iamblichus and a certain Herodian, as prurient reading good for stimulating the sexual energy of partially impotent males.

The potentialities of the ancient prose romance as a literary form, once the writing of it had been taken over by sophisticated authors, were as great, therefore, as those of the modern novel; seeing that the varieties which it naturally admitted in the exploitation of a story of personal experience were as manifold as those of ancient literature itself. The only limitations in this direction were those imposed by the nature of thought and feeling in late antiquity. As it happened, this completely open stage in the development of the ancient romance was not attained until that worldly pagan culture upon which the species itself depended for its life was very close to its end. The ancient romance died almost as soon as it reached its maturity.

The nature of Greek romance in its earlier presophistic stage may be seen in Chariton's *Chaereas and Callirhoe*, an outline of which here follows.

6

"I, Chariton of Aphrodisias, secretary to Athenagoras the advocate, will describe a love affair that came about in Syracuse.

"Hermocrates the Syracusan general, he who conquered the Athenians, had a daughter named Callirhoe, who was a wonderful prodigy of a maid, and the idol of all Sicily. Indeed her beauty was more than human; it was divine; and not the beauty of a mere Nereid or mountain nymph, but of Aphrodite herself, the maiden's goddess. Reports about her astonishing beauty spread abroad everywhere and suitors came pouring into Syracuse, men of power and the sons of kings, and not from Sicily alone but from Italy and Epirus and the mainland of Greece. But Eros wanted to make a match to his own liking. There was a certain young man named Chaereas who surpassed all the youth of his generation in beauty, being such a one as sculptors and painters represent Achilles to have been, and Nireus and Hippolytus and Alcibiades. He was the son of Ariston, the second greatest man in Syracuse after Hermocrates. And there was a certain political jealousy existing between these two men, so much so that they would have promised their children in marriage to anyone rather than to each other's offspring. But Eros is fond of strife and rejoices in victories of a paradoxical nature."

At a festival of Aphrodite almost all the women in Syracuse went out to the temple, and among them Callirhoe accompanied by her mother. On that occasion Chaereas, returning home from the gymnasium, shining like a star with the ruddy glow of youth, met Callirhoe on a narrow path, the god Eros having strategically arranged this meeting. Chaereas went home deeply wounded, "like a champion in battle who has been dealt a fatal blow, ashamed to fall down but unable to stand up." Callirhoe, likewise affected, fell at the feet of Aphrodite praying for possession of the lover thus revealed to her. Both thereafter spent a terrible night of anxiety. The girl suffered more because of her enforced silence; but Chaereas, already wasting away bodily from love-sickness, ventured to tell his parents that he loved Callirhoe, and that he could not live without her. His father urged him not to woo Callirhoe because Hermocrates would never consent to the marriage, and his refusal would be humiliating to the whole family. Chaereas was too ill to go to the gymnasium any more, and when his friends there found out the cause they all pitied him. He was in danger of death. Something had to be done about this alarming situation. A public assembly was held of the citizens of Syracuse, and as soon as the crowd was seated they all called out to Hermocrates, urging him to save Chaereas by allowing his daughter to marry him. Hermocrates felt obliged to consent, and the wedding was arranged amid great public rejoicing. When the bride and groom appeared in public, many people bowed down before them, as though they were deities. Even such was the wedding of Thetis on Mt. Pelion as the poets tell it. But an evil demon, jealous of felicity, attended upon this occasion, as they say that the goddess Discord was present at the other.

For the numerous unsuccessful suitors, being angry and considering themselves insulted because a private citizen had been preferred to them, made common cause and held an indignation meeting. The first man who rose to speak was a young Italian, son of the tyrant of Rhegium, who, after denouncing Chaereas, proposed that plans be made to kill him. This was approved by everyone present except the tyrant of Agrigentum, who said in effect that he too would be

"much for open war, as not behind in hate,"

were it not for the fact that Hermocrates was a dangerous man to oppose. Guile must be used. "For it is by guile and intrigue, rather than by outright force, that we rulers manage our kingdoms. Elect me as your general in the war against Chaereas and I promise to break up this marriage. I will arm Jealousy against him, and she, with Passion as her ally, will do great havoc." The first scheme tried by the suitors fails, but on the second attempt they succeed by bribing Callirhoe's maid. Chaereas is told confidentially by one who pretends to be his friend that his wife is unfaithful to him and that she entertains a lover in secret. In order that he may see this for himself, he is brought upon a scene carefully arranged by the suitors to frame Callirhoe as an adulteress. Chaereas is completely deceived and, in his fury at what he supposes to be Callirhoe's treachery, he kicks her so violently that she swoons and appears to be dead. Thereafter he spends the whole night cross-examining the servants and, after discovering the truth, is so filled with remorse that he wishes to commit suicide. He is restrained from so doing by his friend Polycharmus, who performs the same office on several later occasions, his only function in the story being to console Chaereas whenever the latter despairs, and to marry his sister at the end. On being tried for murder the next day, Chaereas makes no effort to defend or excuse himself, but instead pleads vigorously for his own condemnation. Hermocrates, however, has learned the truth and through his influence our hero, Chaereas, is acquitted in spite of himself. Thereupon follows the funeral of Callirhoe, carried out with great pomp and splendor. Still alive, although presumed to be dead, she is entombed in a large vault near the seashore, and with her is deposited a great deal of wealth in the form of gold, jewelry and fine raiment. At this point the villain of the story is introduced. His name is Theron, a wicked and lawless fellow who, under the pretense of running a ferry business, heads a band of robbers who make their headquarters around the docks of Syracuse. Theron is very anxious about the treasure that he had seen buried with Callirhoe. Lying in bed that night, he was unable to sleep, but said to himself, "Here I am risking my neck in fighting on the sea and killing live men for the sake of paltry gains, when I might just as well get rich quick from a single corpse. Let the die be cast! I'll not let go this chance of profit. Well then, what men shall I pick for the job? Stop and think now, Theron, who is the most suitable of those you know?" This soliloquy continues in lively fashion, and in the end Theron plans to break into the tomb with his men on the following night and carry away the booty upon the sea. "Waiting until the very hour of midnight," says Chariton, "Theron silently and with muffled oars drew near the tomb." Meanwhile Callirhoe has recovered consciousness, and her emotions on realizing the situation are effectively put forth in a soliloquy. When Theron finds Callirhoe alive in the sepulchre, he decides, after some hesitation and a lively debate among his men, to carry her off with the rest of the booty and sell her for a high price.[24] On arriving overseas in the neighborhood of Miletus, he brings his ship to shore some ten miles outside the city, for it was dangerous to be selling a freeborn woman, and he has to go about the business secretly. With two companions he enters the city and begins looking about for a wealthy buyer. At first he has no luck and is much worried, lying awake nights and talking to himself. But one day he happens to be sitting in a shop in Miletus when a wealthy man dressed in mourning passes along attended by a crowd of servants. Theron inquires of one of the servants "Who is that man?" "You must be a stranger around here," replies the servant, "if you fail to recognize Dionysius, who is the foremost of all the Ionians in wealth, family, and education, and a friend of the great king himself." "But why is he dressed in mourning?" "Because his wife died recently, and he was very fond of her." Theron, having come across a man who was both wealthy and uxorious, follows up this conversation and becomes well acquainted with the servant, whose name is Leonas. He is the chief steward of Dionysius and the business manager of his estate. He becomes much interested in the possibility of purchasing Callirhoe for his master Dionysius, and with that in mind he takes Theron to his own house where the two men talk things over. It appears that Theron's ship has been moored off Dionysius' own land, so that the whole transaction can be carried on privately. Theron explains to the steward Leonas that Callirhoe is a servant girl whom he bought from a Sybarite woman who was jealous of her beauty and wanted to be rid of her. This was necessary in order to satisfy the conscience of Dionysius, who, as a man of honor and moral principle, would not buy Callirhoe if he knew the truth about her. Theron goes to the ship to fetch Callirhoe, but does not let her know what is going on. When he returns with her to the house of Leonas, all present are astounded by her beauty. Some thought that they were really looking at a goddess, because a rumor was abroad in the country that Aphrodite at that time was making her epiphany. More anxious than ever to clinch the deal, Leonas insists on making a down payment of a silver talent to Theron until such time as a formal contract of sale can be drawn up in the city. But Theron, after receiving the talent, makes off in his ship immediately, resolved to take no chances of becoming involved with the magistrates of Miletus. Callirhoe, left alone to rest in a comfortable apartment in Leonas' house, bewails her misfortune. Gazing at the image of Chaereas on her ring, she kisses it and exclaims, "Now indeed am I dead to you, Chaereas, separated by such an expanse of sea. You mourn for me and repent, sitting by an empty grave and bearing witness to my loyalty after death. And I, the daughter of Hermocrates, your wife, have been sold this day to a master." So lamenting, sleep came upon her at last.

Book II tells how Dionysius, at first uninterested, meets Callirhoe and falls deeply in love with her, although it occasions some struggles with his conscience; and how Callirhoe, finding herself two months pregnant by Chaereas, feels obliged to consent to marriage with Dionysius in spite of her very great love for her husband. For her child's sake, lest he be born in slavery, as well as for her own interest, it was about the only thing that she could do. Here no *deus ex machina* intervenes, as is so often the case in other romances. The hard circumstances which induce, though they do not compel Callirhoe to marry Dionysius, remain unalterable, and our heroine has to solve her own problem on the basis of things as they are. These developments are described by the author in a very effective way and with much dramatic irony. Here the interest of the story is focused throughout upon the characters themselves and the emotional struggles which they undergo. Dionysius is a kind man with good instincts who wants to do the right thing both legally and ethically. His dealings with Callirhoe are marked by much delicacy and consideration for her feelings. Although he is madly in love with her, he will not take advantage of the fact that she is actually in his power, but rests his whole hope on the chance of winning her love, or at least her willing consent to marry him. Failing that, he is ready to commit suicide. During this time Callirhoe has been under the care of a middle-aged servant woman named Plango who takes a friendly interest in her and advises her confidentially. She arranges a

meeting between Dionysius and Callirhoe, in which the latter
tells Dionysius the principal facts about herself and her recent
experiences, without, strange to say, making any mention of
her marriage to Chaereas. It is only later, when Dionysius is
married to Callirhoe, that he learns about Chaereas accidentally, when Callirhoe talks about him in her sleep as though
he were no longer living. It seems hardly plausible under the
circumstances that Dionysius should continue throughout to
believe, as he does, that Callirhoe's child is of his own beget-
ting, especially after he learns that Callirhoe was married to
Chaereas shortly before she came to him. This is one of several
loose ends in Chariton's story which seem to indicate that he is
following, in part at least, a popular legend in which some of
his data were already fixed for him. Callirhoe's child, the successor to Hermocrates, as he is repeatedly called in this romance, had to be fathered ostensibly by Dionysius of Miletus,
apparently, as Naber suggests, in order to become the famous
Dionysius I, tyrant of Syracuse. But of this more later.

"Now," says Chariton (III 2 end), "I want to tell you what
happened meanwhile in Syracuse." When the Syracusans discovered that the tomb had been robbed, they sent out searching parties in many directions with the hope of capturing the
pirates. But human effort was altogether weak, and it was only
good fortune that finally solved the problem, as may be inferred
from what happened. The robbers, after disposing of Callirhoe
in Miletus, set sail for Crete, where they hoped to sell the rest
of their cargo very easily. But a heavy wind came upon them
and drove them out into the midst of the Ionian Sea, where
they drifted about aimlessly thereafter. "Then thunder and
lightning and a long night overtook the unholy rascals, Providence revealing thereby that their previous fair sailing had
been due to the presence of Callirhoe. Though they were often
on the verge of death, yet God would not free them from the
fear of it, but prolonged their distress. Earth would give no
welcome to these unholy men; but being tossed about upon
the sea for a long time, they found themselves in sore need of

provisions and especially of drink. Their unjust wealth availed them naught; they were dying of thirst in the midst of gold. Slowly they repented of what they had done, and made accusations one against the other; but it was too late. Now all the rest were perishing of thirst, but Theron even in this crisis proved himself a scoundrel, for he kept filching the drink apportioned to his companions, robbing even his fellow robbers. In this he fancied he was doing a neat little bit of professional work; but in reality it seems that this was the will of Providence in order that the man might be spared for crucifixion." (III 3) Meanwhile the Syracusan trireme with Chaereas on board was approaching. Their main purpose was to recover the body or person of Callirhoe. On boarding the pirate ship, Chaereas found Theron half dead and began to question him. Theron said that it was only by accident that he had boarded the ship; he had not known that it was a pirate ship; and he alone of all those on board had been spared, owing to his piety. Afterwards Theron is taken before the assembly of the Syracusans where he is again questioned and where he repeats the same story; but in spite of his protestations, that he had "never done anything wrong in his life," he is found out and crucified, much to the gentle reader's edification. "For," says Chariton, "if he had succeeded in persuading the Syracusans that he was innocent, as he came very near doing, it would have been the most outrageous thing that ever happened."

From Theron the inquisitors learned that Callirhoe was sold to someone in Miletus, but to whom is not known. Hermocrates in a public assembly proposes that an embassy be sent to Miletus, at that time under Persian rule, for the purpose of recovering Callirhoe. Hereupon the crowd shouts, "We'll all sail to Miletus." Hermocrates decides that five envoys will be enough, these to include Chaereas. When the Syracusan trireme comes to shore, by chance just where Theron had landed, on the estate of Dionysius, his steward Phocas, the husband of Plango, after learning from a sailor what the Syracusans have come for, takes it upon himself to have the ship destroyed by a Persian garrison in the neighborhood, on the ground that it has come with hostile intent. Some of the crew are killed, but among the rest, who are taken captive, Chaereas and his friend Polycharmus are sold as slaves to Mithridates, the satrap of Caria. From the account of this affair given by Phocas, who implies that all the Syracusans were killed, Callirhoe concludes that Chaereas is dead and Dionysius holds a public funeral in his honor, erecting a cenotaph. Mithridates, Chaereas' master, attends this funeral ostensibly to honor Dionysius but really for the purpose of seeing Callirhoe, the fame of whose beauty has spread over all Western Asia. On this occasion the effect of her beauty upon those who beheld it was literally stunning. Those who tried to look upon it with the naked eye were compelled to turn aside their gaze, as though they were looking at the sun; even children suffered somewhat, and Mithridates the governor of Caria fell down in a faint. Mithridates makes a friend of Chaereas, after discovering who he is, and presently joins with him in sending letters and presents to Callirhoe. By helping Chaereas and pitting him against Dionysius, he hopes somehow to step in between the two and carry off the prize. As soon as Chaereas learns from Mithridates that Callirhoe is married to Dionysius, he is eager to go to Miletus right away and demand back his wife; but Mithridates restrains him, saying, "How can you, a lone stranger, go into a great city like Miletus and deprive the foremost citizen there of his legal wife? In what power are you trusting? Your only possible allies, Hermocrates and Mithridates, will be a long way off and better able to mourn for you than to bring you aid." On the advice of Mithridates Chaereas writes a letter to Callirhoe telling her that he is living, thanks to the kindness of Mithridates, his benefactor. He tells her what has happened to him and begs her to return his love. This letter, along with one from Mithridates, in which the latter offers to help Callirhoe regain Chaereas, even at the cost of making war on the Milesians, is intercepted and given to Dionysius, who infers that Mithridates is the author of both letters, and that he has forged the name of Chaereas. Soon the quarrel between him and Mithridates is reported to King Artaxerxes, who summons both men to Babylon for trial and orders Dionysius to bring Callirhoe with him. Her triumphal procession through Asia to the king's court and her sojourn there are full of incidents that bring anxiety and torment to both her husband and herself. Dionysius was pained by being congratulated so much, and the greatness of his good fortune (in having Callirhoe) only made him the more miserable. For, "being an educated man, he reflected that love is fond of change." He feared every man as a possible rival, and even the king proved to be such.

Mithridates, whom Dionysius has accused of plotting adultery, takes Chaereas and Polycharmus with him to Babylon as star witnesses; but this is unknown to Dionysius, who thinks that Chaereas is dead. The trial scene, which is the culminating point of a suspense which has been long and steadily gathering momentum, is much superior in dramatic effect to anything that one meets with elsewhere in the Greek romance. All the factors in the situation are clearly before the reader, as in a Greek tragedy, and the surprises are all for the characters. Dionysius in his opening speech, accusing Mithridates, is very eloquent and very confident that he can prove his case, because he thinks that Chaereas is dead; but the reader knows that Chaereas is present in that very courtroom, though concealed. Dionysius ends his speech with these words: "I have stated the case under trial. The demonstration is sure. One of two things must be; either Chaereas is living, or Mithridates is proved guilty. He cannot say that he is unaware of Chaereas' death, for he was in Miletus when we built his tomb and he joined in mourning with us. But when Mithridates wishes to commit adultery, he brings the dead to life. I will conclude by reading the letter which he sent by his own slaves from Caria to Miletus. Take it and read: 'I, Chaereas, am living.' Let Mithridates prove *that*, and he may be let off. But consider, O king, how shameless this adulterer is who gives the lie even to a dead man." On hearing this, everyone in the crowded courtroom inclines strongly to the side of Dionysius, and the king looks hard at Mithridates. But what the latter has to say in his own defense is no less eloquent and persuasive. "Even if I were guilty," he says, "I could avoid conviction; for Dionysius is not complaining on behalf of a legal wife, but one that he bought for a silver talent. The law of adultery does not pertain to slaves. If Dionysius maintains that Callirhoe was free when he married her, that only means that he enslaved her, since he acted against the will of her husband and without the consent of her father. I have not injured Dionysius either as husband or as master. He accuses me of intended adultery, and not being able to prove the act, reads you meaningless letters; but the law is aimed at the deed, not at the intention." Then turning to Dionysius, he continues: "I might say that I did not write that letter, that it is not in my hand, that it is Chaereas who is making the advances to Callirhoe, and that he is the one that you should be charging with adultery. But you claim that Chaereas is dead and that I am only using his name. You are challenging me, Dionysius, in a way that is not to your interest. You'd better withdraw your charge. If you don't, you'll be sorry for it. I'm warning you, you'll lose Callirhoe; and it won't be me whom the king finds to be an adulterer, but you." When Dionysius persists as before, Mithridates lifts his voice in prayer to the gods, asking them to reveal Chaereas, if only for this one occasion; and while he is still speaking Chaereas walks in. "Who could begin to describe the scene in that courtroom?" exclaims our author. "What poet ever brought so wonderful a story upon the stage? You would think you were in a theater filled with a thousand passions. Callirhoe herself was astounded and stood speechless, gazing with wide-open eyes at Chaereas. It would seem to me that even the king at that moment wished he were Chaereas." As the result of this trial Mithridates is dismissed with honor and the date is set for a new trial between the rival husbands Chaereas and Dionysius. But King Artaxerxes, having fallen in love with Callirhoe and wishing to protract her stay in Babylon, keeps postponing the trial until, as it happens, he is suddenly obliged to march out with his army against the Egyptians, who have revolted and already overrun most of Syria. With him on the march he takes Dionysius and all the women of the court, including Callirhoe and Statira, the queen. Chaereas, having heard a false rumor that the king has awarded Callirhoe to Dionysius, joins the Egyptian army, takes Tyre by strategem from the Persians, captures the island of Arados, where Artaxerxes had left the women for safe keeping, and so gains possession of Callirhoe. Chaereas, the commanding general, at first does not know that his wife is among the captives, nor does she know who the conqueror is; and this situation gives rise to some scenes remarkable for their dramatic irony. Here, at the beginning of Book VIII, the author once more takes us into his confidence: "I think," he says, "that this last chapter will be most pleasing to our readers, for it is a purging of the gloomy events that have gone before. No longer piracy, slavery, litigation, war, hardship and captivity, but legitimate love and lawful nuptials. And now I shall tell you how the goddess revealed the truth, and made the lovers known one to the other. It was evening," etc. The reunion of the lovers is described by the author with immense enthusiasm and no little felicity of style. Afterwards, Callirhoe, unknown to Chaereas—for she realized how prone to jealousy he was—wrote an affectionate letter to Dionysius, as follows: "Callirhoe to Dionysius, her benefactor, greetings. You are the one who saved me from pirates and slavery. Please don't be angry with me. I am with you in spirit on account of our child, whom now I leave with you to bring up and to educate worthily of us. Have him married, when he gets to be a man, and send him to Syracuse to see his grandfather. Give my best to Plango. Farewell, good Dionysius, and remember your Callirhoe." Chaereas had thought of taking Queen Statira, wife of King Artaxerxes Mnemon, back to Syracuse with him as a handmaid for Callirhoe, but the latter would hear of no such thing. No, indeed. She and Statira had become quite chummy during their association in Babylon, and Callirhoe had arranged for a ship to take her good friend immediately back to the king. And now was the moment of parting. Callirhoe, taking her friend by the hand, escorted her on board the ship and said, "Goodbye, my dear Statira. Remember me, and write to me often at Syracuse . . . I shall tell my parents how grateful I am to you, and shall make the fact known to the gods of Hellas. I send my little child in your care. . . . Consider him a pledge in place of myself." As she said this the tears began to flow, and the women about her were moved to lamentation. Then, as she was leaving the ship, Callirhoe bent over toward Statira and blushing put a letter in her hand, saying, "Give this to Dionysius, poor man. Try to console him." Chaereas and Callirhoe arrive safely in the harbor of Syracuse, accompanied by three hundred Greek mercenaries, who had helped Chaereas in his campaigns, and twenty triremes laden with the rich spoils of war. The Syracusans are suspicious of these ships, although they are said to be Egyptian merchantmen; and Hermocrates allows only one of them, that on which Chaereas is aboard, to land. On this ship an elaborate stage scene has been arranged under a covering of Babylonian tapestry. It is claimed that under the covering are the wares of the Egyptian merchants. A great crowd of curious people are gathered on the shore wondering about what is going on. When Hermocrates comes on board, the tapestry is suddenly removed and there, behold, the incomparable Callirhoe reclining upon a gold-studded couch, clad in scarlet robes of Tyrian dye, and beside her Chaereas, our hero, in the uniform of a general. "No peal of thunder ever broke upon the ears of men so loud, no lightning such did ever blind the eyes of those who see, nor, treasure found of gold, did ever man cry out so lustily as that great crowd, when they beheld a sight so strange, so far beyond belief." Hermocrates leaped onto the stage and throwing his arms about his daughter exclaimed, "Child, are you living, do my wits deceive me?" "I am alive, father; now in very truth, since I behold you living." All wept tears of joy. After this, the Syracusans, one and all, hurry into the theater for a public meeting, in order to hear all about Chaereas and Callirhoe, to see them in person, to praise them, and to pass such official decrees as are recommended by Chaereas in the interest of his soldiers.

In order to add to the felicity of the occasion, Chaereas proposes to the assembly that his sister be married to Polycharmus, and that a part of the spoils of war be given to her as a dowry. This is joyfully approved; although this sister of Chaereas has not hitherto been mentioned, and Polycharmus has not been consulted about the marriage. Meanwhile Callirhoe goes to the temple of Aphrodite to offer thanks to the goddess for the happy outcome of her trials, praying that she may never again be separated from Chaereas, or outlive him.

"So much," says Chariton in the last sentence, "have I composed (συνέγραψα) on the subject of Callirhoe." What Thucydides did for the Peloponnesian War, that Chariton has done for the daughter of Hermocrates!

The ideal sentimental values which Chariton puts forth in this story, and the psychological attitudes which it reveals, obviously belong to those spiritual and cultural forces which brought about the birth of romance as a new literary form.

7

The substance of Chariton's book, our earliest extant specimen of Greek romance, is much more closely connected with historical persons and events than is the case in any of the later romances. This is true with reference to the pattern of many episodes and to the actors and names of actors who play a part in the story;[25] and—what is more significant—with reference to the identity of the principal character Callirhoe, who is the daughter of the famous Syracusan general Hermocrates. The name Callirhoe, which had various mythical and poetical associations, may have been invented by Chariton; but some of the principal experiences which this heroine undergoes in the romance are closely parallel to things which are told by Diodorus and Plutarch concerning an unnamed daughter of

Hermocrates: namely, that she married the famous Dionysius I of Syracuse (instead of an unknown Dionysius of Miletus); that she was assaulted by rebel soldiers (instead of by a jealous husband Chaereas, doing what Nero did to Poppaea), and that she died, or was believed to have died, as a result of those injuries (compare the apparent death of Callirhoe). It is aptly surmised by Professor Wilhelm Schmid that the nucleus of a legend about Hermocrates and his daughter, which may have concerned his connection with Dionysius I and the latter's lineage, was to be found in the historians of Sicily, in Timaeus perhaps, or in Philistus, a contemporary of Dionysius, who wrote about him at great length in his history and flattered him. However this may be, there are some loose ends in Chariton's story which are hard to account for otherwise than on the assumption of a pre-existing popular or historiographical tradition which is not elsewhere attested. We are assured, for example, that the infant son of Callirhoe, really by Chaereas, but ostensibly by Dionysius of Miletus in the romance, shall one day sail to Syracuse, when he grows up, and see Hermocrates (II, 9 and 11; III 8; VIII 4, 5, 8); he is to be the successor of Hermocrates, as was the famous Dionysius I, and great hopes are held out for his future. But it is strange that this child should have been sent to Miletus to be brought up by Dionysius (VIII 4), when his parents, after the capture of Arados, could just as well have taken him with them to Syracuse. This episode is so purposeless insofar as the story is concerned, and so peculiar or unnatural in the conduct of the lovers—especially of Chaereas, who is not even consulted about the sending away of his child—that it seems unlikely to have been invented by Chariton. The same is true of such other episodes as the marriage of Callirhoe to Dionysius, and the brutal and almost fatal assault made by the otherwise ideal lover Chaereas upon his bride. Such episodes seem to owe their presence in the romance, not to the purely arbitrary invention of the author bent on telling an ideal story, but to the historical or legendary materials with which he worked, and whose patterns he followed, however much he may have altered those traditional data in terms of time, place, and the identity of the actors. It has been very plausibly suggested, by S. A. Naber,[26] that Chariton was thinking of Callirhoe's child as the future Dionysius I of Syracuse, who is said to have been the son of an earlier Hermocrates (otherwise unknown) and who won his way into power, as we know from the historians, by championing the faction of the famous Hermocrates. The tyrant's well-known literary aspirations may have suggested the intellectual qualities of his presumable Milesian foster-father in the romance, and the tradition that he was of low birth and obscure origin may have led to the creation by his followers of some such myth as Chariton seems to have in mind.

In choosing an historical character, the daughter of Hermocrates, as his heroine, Chariton was proceeding on artistic principles which were inevitable for the earliest romancers. They were bound, by the long-established conventions of serious or ideal narrative, whether in poetry or in prose, to write about *presumably* historical persons; and this artistic requirement was equally well satisfied whether the subject of a poem or a romance was a person well known to history, or purely and patently mythical; whether he was Xerxes or Inachus, Gyges or Oedipus, the daughter of Hermocrates or Daphnis the herdsman, Alcibiades or Nireus, Semiramis the queen of Assyria (ca. 809–782 B.C.) or Parthenope the siren who died and was enshrined at Naples. All these are equally historical from the artistic standpoint of ancient writers. The two characters last mentioned are the heroines of erotic romances of which we have fragments on papyrus dating from the second century. It is probable, as Lavagnini has demonstrated, that many of these heroines of romance, like those in Ovid and the Alexandrian poets, were taken from local myths, the bare outlines of which had already been rationalized and the characters humanized to some extent by historians and antiquarians who had recorded them briefly in connection with the founding of cities and the origins of cults and local institutions. Some of the myths used by romancers were better known, or closer to real history than others; but even a well-known legend, like that of Ninus and Semiramis, could be made to contain a completely new and lengthy story of love and adventure without contradicting what was known to tradition about its principal characters. The more obscure and recondite a myth was, the more easily it would serve as a base on which to construct a series of invented episodes and characters of whatever kind. Once the formal pattern of romance writing had become established and conventional, it was no longer necessary to select a real myth as the starting point for one's fictional narrative, and only the semblance of such would serve the purpose. All the extant romances, except that of Achilles Tatius, which relates—in the comic tradition—the experiences of a contemporary individual, are based either on real myths or local legends, or else they have the appearance of being so founded, as in Xenophon and Heliodorus.

8

Greek romance, as a new literary species with a purpose and direction all its own, was, as we noted above (p. 178), fundamentally drama in substance and historiography in its outward form. This is true also of the early modern novel, and the fact is historically significant. The novel is the necessary successor to stage-drama on the popular level for a reading public; and since its subject matter is theoretically historical, and its form that of prose narrative, it naturally follows the conventions of historiography, some of which in turn were fundamentally dramatic. Except for its form as narration, the novel is drama in a new quantitative dimension, not different in the nature of its substance and purpose from stage-drama, whose limits it transcends, but multiplied in respect to the number or length of its acts and capable of indefinite extension. Its tendency, like that of many folktales and of the early romantic epic, is away from organic structure in the direction of agglutinative parataxis. It is possible of course for even a lengthy novel to be constructed on organic principles with a strong inner synthesis; but such novels are exceptional, since multiplicity of action, which is the primary demand of the reading public, does not lend itself easily to that kind or degree of organic unity which, for example, Aristotle admired in the *Oedipus*. Only a loose framework with arbitrary limits of extension, allowing for the insertion of an indefinite number of successive episodes, as in the *Iliad* or *Odyssey*, will serve the main purpose well enough. All the plots of Greek romance known to us have an elastic framework of this kind, consisting usually in an initial separation of the principals followed by their reunion at the end. The episodes which are brought into an open plot of this nature may vary greatly both in number and in the motivation by which they are introduced and connected one with another. Some authors show more regard for organic structure than others, and are thereby more truly dramatic. In comparison with the later romances of Xenophon, Iamblichus, Achilles Tatius, and Heliodorus, that of Chariton, the earliest, is relatively very simple and compact. Its episodes are few in number, comparatively, and well motivated. Things seldom happen by accident, but are brought about usually by the willful and plausible actions of the main characters. The device known as *deus ex machina*, by which a lucky and purely fortuitous event resolves one situation and leads to another, is rare in *Chaereas and Callirhoe*, but very common in all of the later romances. Chariton's plot, unlike that of any of the authors above mentioned, has the structural economy, the inner motivation, and the overall unity of a drama in five acts, as follows:

I. Marriage of Chaereas and Callirhoe at Syracuse. The fortunes of Callirhoe: her apparent death; her abduction by the pirate Theron, who sells her to Dionysius in Syracuse; the courting of Callirhoe by Dionysius and their marriage.

II. Adventures of Chaereas: He pursues the pirates in the effort to recover Callirhoe. Learns from the pirate Theron that Callirhoe was sold in Miletus. Lands at Miletus, but his com-

pany is destroyed by a Persian garrison, and he himself is sold
as a slave to Mithridates, governor of Caria. Mithridates becomes a friend to Chaereas, when he learns who he is, and the
two write letters to Callirhoe. Dionysius, having intercepted
these letters, concludes that Mithridates is plotting to get
possession of Callirhoe, and that the letter from Chaereas,
whom he supposes to be dead, was forged by Mithridates. The
complaint of Dionysius against Mithridates becomes known
and both are summoned to Babylon for trial before the king.
Mithridates takes Chaereas with him as a witness.

III. The action that has gone before is recapitulated for the
first time (V 1), by way of introducing the climax of the drama.
The trial of the case of Dionysius *vs*. Mithridates, on a large
stage-setting at the king's court, results in the elimination of
Mithridates and the introduction of Chaereas as the real opponent of Dionysius. The case of these two rivals is then sched-
uled for trial at a future date; but the king, having himself
fallen in love with Callirhoe, postpones this trial indefinitely
in his own interest, until, owing to a revolt of the Eygptians,
he is compelled to take the field along with all the people of
his court (Bks. V and VI).

IV. The military triumphs of Chaereas fighting as a general
on the Egyptian side against the king. In the end he gains
possession of Arados, along with all the king's women, including Callirhoe; but he does not know that Callirhoe is among
his captives, nor does she know that the victorious general is
her dear husband Chaereas (Bk. VII).

V. Before the curtain rises, at the beginning of Bk. VIII,
the author bows before his readers and says: "I think that this
last chapter (act) will be most pleasing to our readers (audience); for it is a purging of the gloomy events that have gone
before," etc. Then follows the joyful and highly dramatic recognition scene between Chaereas and Callirhoe, and their triumphant return to Syracuse.

The close inner connection between the episodes in this romance, their natural character, and the gradual leading up

through a series of plausible complications to the main climax toward the end, will be evident to anyone who has read the outlines given above. In most other romances the effect of the main climax, when there is one, is greatly weakened by the large number of crises that have arisen and been disposed of by a *deus ex machina* in the preceding narrative; but in Chariton the trial scene, which is the culminating point of a suspense that has been gathering momentum for the space of an entire book (IV 3 to V 6), and in which the fortunes of all the principal characters are directly involved, overshadows in interest and importance everything that has preceded, and what follows consists in the unravelling of the situation thereby developed. Moreover, for recognizing Chariton's dramatic method it is significant that, unlike Heliodorus and Achilles Tatius, he makes no attempt to surprise the reader, or to keep him in ignorance of the true state of affairs. The variety of incident in his story serves to keep up interest in the plot, but always, as in the trial scene, it is one or more of the *characters* who are ignorant of the real situation, and not the reader. Chariton puts his readers in the same exalted position as the spectators of an ancient tragedy; they see all the factors involved in the action and are thereby able to appreciate its ironies. While Heliodorus and Achilles seek to entertain us with sensational surprises, as in a mystery story, Chariton, in the manner of the Greek tragedians, appeals primarily to our contemplative sense.

The analysis of *Chaereas and Callirhoe* as structurally equivalent to a drama in five acts, which we outlined above, was first made by R. Reitzenstein in his *Hellenistische Wundererzählung* (Leipzig, 1906), pp. 95 f. In this part of his book Reitzenstein describes first the rhetorical theory of artistic narration, as set forth explicitly by Cicero and other ancient writers, and, secondly, the concrete manifestations of this theory as seen in the practice of Sallust in his historical monographs, the *Jugurtha* and the *Catiline* (both of which are also divided by Reitzenstein into five acts, pp. 87 f.), as well as of Chariton in his romance.

The theory as outlined by Cicero in the *De Inventione* (I 27 = *Auct. ad Herennium* I 12–13) relates to *narratio* apart from that used in pleading cases in court (*tertium genus, a causa civili remotum*), irrespective of the literary forms in which it might be employed, and of prose or verse. The specifications for all this non-forensic *narratio* are here formulated on the patterns of stage-drama in respect both to the action, or plot, and to the characters and their emotions. They were also applicable in Cicero's view to narration in history writing, as we see from his letter to Lucceius quoted below; but the illustrations here mentioned and quoted are drawn only from Terence. The substance of the action, we are told, may be one of three kinds: *fabula*, as used in tragedy, which has neither truth nor the likeness of truth (contrary to Aristotle, who reckons the myths of tragedy with historical things); *historia*, something which actually occurred (*res gesta*), but distant in time from the present; and *argumentum*, which is fictitious, but of such a nature that it might have occurred, as the plots of comedy. Here Cicero and the *Auctor ad Herennium* are recommending, by implication, rhetorical exercises in imitation of well-known literary forms, which Cicero illustrates by reference to tragedy and comedy. The same applies to the second aspect of non-forensic *narratio*, which relates to the characters in action in any kind of plot. On this side there should be, in the words of Cicero: *multa festivitas confecta ex rerum varietate, animorum dissimilitudine, gravitate, levitate, spe, metu, suspicione, desiderio, dissimulatione, errore, misericordia, fortunae commutatione, insperato incommodo, subita laetitia, iucundo exitu rerum.* In other words *narratio*, wherever employed, should have all the emotional appeal along with the characteristic devices of stage-drama as an artistic entertainment.[27] In the field of historiography this prescription was followed out most commonly in the historical monograph, where unity could be attained by concentrating upon a single group of closely related events. Before Cicero's time Polybius had had much to say in protest about the disposition of those who wrote particular

histories (i.e., monographs) to cast their matter into the form
of sensational tragedies, thereby obscuring or misrepresenting
the truth of historical events and their real meaning. The purpose of history, he reminds us, is to tell the truth, unlike that of
tragedy, which is to entertain. Cicero honestly agreed with this
in principle; but, like many other prose writers of his time and
earlier, he was so fascinated with the artistic effects of dramatic
narrative that he would recommend it to the writers of history
in spite of its tendency to distort the truth of events. He wanted
a history to be true, but *also* full of dramatic entertainment.
In a well-known letter he urges his friend Lucceius to write a
special monograph on the subject of his (Cicero's) consulship,
instead of waiting to deal with it later on in a general history
of the Civil Wars which he was then writing. In this way, he
says, Lucceius would be concentrating on a single well-defined
theme centering around one man (*uno in argumento unaque in
persona*), and that would enable him to embellish the subject.
Cicero's fortunes would furnish Lucceius with a great variety
of matter fraught with a kind of pleasure that would take a
strong hold on the minds of readers (*plenam cuiusdam volup-
tatis, quae vehementer animos hominum . . . tenere possit*).
"Nothing," he continues "is more apt to delight the reader
than the variety of events and the vicissitudes of fortune . . .
When we look upon the misfortunes of others, without suffering ourselves, our very feeling of pity is something pleasurable.
The continuous series of events in an annalistic history holds
our interest only in a mild degree, like the listing of acts in an
official register; but often the hazardous and varied fortunes
of a distinguished man arouse feelings of wonder, suspense,
joy, uneasiness, hope and fear. Then, if the conclusion is a
memorable one, the reader's mind is filled with a most agreeable
pleasure." I hope therefore—says Cicero in effect—that you
will devote a special monograph to what I may call the drama
of my career (*quasi fabulam rerum eventorumque nostrorum*);
for it falls naturally into different acts, and contains many
actions arising from the counsels of men and the nature of the

times (*habet enim varios actus multasque actiones et consiliorum et temporum*).[28]

Cicero's fondness for dramatic narrative reflects the universal taste of his age, when writers were prone to exploit the dramatic possibilities of any narrative that they might have occasion to use, regardless of the literary form in which they were writing. The great tide of drama, that is to say fondness for the spectacle of men and women in action with all its excitements, peripeties, personal emotions, and character displays, had long since overflowed the dike of the stage, which had once contained it, and was now pouring into all the literary forms where narrative could be anywise employed. The new form romance was made—and just about this time—for the sole purpose of exploiting this drama on its own account; and it was, for that reason, the only form fully capable of containing it. In all the other prose forms, the central purpose and direction of which was informative or hortatory in theory, rather than artistic, drama or romance had to be something subordinate or incidental, and might be, as often in the historical monograph, positively injurious to the confessed aim of the book. As for the poetic forms, the long epic was much too artificial and learned in kind to satisfy the popular demand, and elegy and epigram were too small, as well as too smart and specialized in their conventions. It is noteworthy, however, that in the poetry dealing with Greek myths, the dramatic treatment of the narrative, which had been almost absent in Callimachus, where the story was only a curious and erudite antiquity told objectively in bare outlines, became the principal thing in Ovid, where it is exploited on its own account. This importation of drama into what had once been antiquarian mythology, or some form of *poésie verbale*, is parallel to the influence of drama on historiography in the same period. It was a powerful force entering from without into forms whose orientation had been different.

Chariton's romance has the outward form of an historical monograph, a biography, in part, of Callirhoe, the daughter of

Hermocrates. Still more significant for the purely formal relation of romance to historiography is the fact that Chariton
makes much more use of historical persons and events in the
invention of episodes than does any of the later romancers
whom we know. His romance is also closer to stage-drama than
any of the others, with the partial exception of *Daphnis and
Chloe*, in its organic structure, its economy of episodes, its
dramatic ironies, and its lively mimetic representation of character. All this is what we should expect in the early stages of
the writing of romance. The earliest authors, like Fielding in
modern times, were necessarily influenced to a greater degree
by the fashions and precedents of formal historiography and
drama (in honor before the invention of the romance genre)
than were their successors, who wrote at a time when the romance as an independent form catering to the popular taste
for a multitude of adventures had been further extended along
its own lines by many practitioners. It is probable that the
early romances as a whole were shorter and more organic in
their structure than those of later times; and the transition
from historical, or supposedly historical, characters at the
beginning to unheard-of characters near the end is evident in
our extant specimens.

The historical monograph, dealing with the career of a famous man, as in Xenophon's *Cyropedia*, the historians of
Alexander, Sallust's *Catiline* and *Jugurtha*, and Plutarch's
Lives, was the conventional pattern of composition into which
the Greek romancers chose to put their new product with
its entirely new orientation. This was a natural choice, because historiography, whatever its stylistic modifications may
be here and there, is basically narrative relating to men in
action and capable of indefinite extension. It was not quite a
necessary choice, because this dramatic narrative, of which
the novel as we know it is only one specialized form, could
have been put into other forms of composition, mechanically
so defined, which were no less conventional and respectable in
antecedent literary practice. The first ideal English novel,

Richardson's *Pamela*, was presented in the form of personal letters written by the heroine; and, in antiquity, the same form was used in what purports to be the autobiography of Chion of Heraclea, which is called a "novel" by its latest editor.[29] Longus, being a sophistic writer who was very conscious of the formal literary proprieties, put his love story of *Daphnis and Chloe* in the well-sanctioned technical form of an *ecphrasis* —the exegetical description of a picture or a series of pictures. He would not use the outright historiographical form employed by Chariton, lest he seem to the fashionable world of letters, whose standards he acknowledged, to be writing bad history.

In speaking about the nature of Greek romance in its beginning, we have confined our attention to only two aspects of it, its substance as drama and its outward form as historiography, because these features are most significant for our understanding of where the romance belongs in literary history and why it came into being. Other aspects of the early Greek romance, such as the happy ending, and the affinity of the romance in various of its qualities with the folktale, as opposed to formal literature, are omitted, lest the necessarily lengthy explanation of them should distract the reader's attention from the main subject of this book, which is the origin of the Greek romance.

IV

The Birth of the Ideal
Greek Romance

1

AFTER MLLE. DE SCUDÉRY's death, Boileau held up
to ridicule her distortion of history as exemplified in her lengthy
romance entitled *Artamène ou le Grand Cyrus*. In his satirical
Dialogue des héros de roman (1664), the famous French critic
introduces Diogenes the Cynic conversing with Pluto in Hades
as follows about Cyrus the Great of Persia:

DIOGENES (to Pluto): Don't be calling him Cyrus.

PLUTO: Why not?

DIOG.: Because that's not his name. Nowadays he is called Artamène.

PLUTO: Artamène? Where did he get that name? I don't remember
ever to have heard it.

DIOG.: I see well that you don't know your history.

PLUTO: Who? Me? I know my Herodotus as well as anybody.

DIOG.: No doubt; but for all that, could you tell me why Cyrus conquered so many provinces, overran Asia, Media, Hyrcania and
Persia, in fine, more than half the world?

PLUTO: That's a fair question. It was because this prince was ambitious and wanted to rule the world.

DIOG.: Nothing of the kind! It was because he wanted to deliver his
princess who had been carried away.

PLUTO: What princess?

DIOG.: Mandane.
PLUTO: Mandane?
DIOG.: Yes. And do you know how many times she was carried off?
Eight times.

And presently Cyrus himself is brought on the scene sighing and apostrophizing the beautiful and cruel Mandane.

What Scudéry did with the historical Cyrus in composing her romance of chivalry is the same kind of thing precisely that the authors of romances in medieval times do with other men whom they choose as protagonists for their love stories and who are famed in ancient history, legend or literature, as warriors, or as conquerors and builders of empire. It is the same kind of arbitrary invention, unrelated to either ancient or medieval tradition about the man himself, that we find in the Byzantine *Achilleis*, and in the French *Roman d'Hector*, not to mention many other similar inventions in the same age; and— what most concerns us here—the same kind of arbitrary invention, relative to all previous tradition, that we have in the Ninus romance. This analogy is very significant, I think, for the history of ancient fiction as well as for the medieval.

In the *Achilleis*, as in the *Roman d'Hector* and in *Ninus*, it is the early *youth* of the famous hero that is dramatically described; while the deeds for which he was famed in ancient legend, insofar as these are mentioned at all, are far away in the background, and only briefly and abstractly alluded to. The second stage in the παιδεία of this Frankish Achilles, begun at the age of 8, consists of training in the knightly arts of chivalrous combat, and he becomes, phenomenally, an invincible champion while still in his early teens. One day, on learning that a foreign prince is threatening the land, Achilles leads twelve chosen knights into the battle against him, sees Polyxena the beautiful daughter of the enemy king, and courts her with numerous *billets doux* (πιττάκια). Reconciliation with her father follows thereafter and Achilles and Polyxena are joyfully married. At the festivities in celebration of the wedding a Frankish knight overcomes all the knights of Achilles, including Patroclus, but is at last unhorsed by Achilles himself. Six years after her marriage Polyxena dies, and one year later Achilles leads his Myrmidons into the war against Troy. Paris the Trojan prince, promises to give him his sister in marriage on terms of reconciliation, and Achilles trusts him; but in the church at Troy, where the wedding was to take place, he is attacked by Paris and Deiphobus and treacherously murdered. Such was the great Achilles, who, as Dante puts it, "with love fought to the end"—*che con amore al fine combattéo* (Inf. V,66). The author mentions Homer, Aristotle, and Plato as his sources and ends with some moral reflections on worldly fortune; but the real sources of his inventions, of the plan of his romance as a whole, and of the patterns on which the episodes are shaped, with all their local coloring, are to be found, not in ancient authors, but in the Frankish romances of chivalry that proliferated on Greek soil among the feudal Latin rulers after the Fourth Crusade, and earlier in the Byzantine epic cycle of *Digenes Akritas*, with which this particular romance shows some striking similarities. What belongs to the ancient epic tradition in this medieval *Romance of Achilles* consists of little more than the names of the protagonists, as Krumbacher aptly observes.[1] Herein again we have an illustration of the fact that all a romancer needs for the creation of a new and dramatic story of love and manifold adventure is a name, or a group of names which are known to history, legend, or obscure myth, even when the actions ascribed to such characters by tradition, often vague and meager, are contradictory to what the romancer chooses to tell about them. This is the method by which romances were invented in Greek antiquity no less than in the Middle Ages.

In either age the names of the protagonists in a romance are little more than pretexts needed by the author for launching his story of love and adventure. If the actions for which the protagonist and his associates were originally famed are extensive, as in the case of Achilles, Cyrus, or Ninus, these actions are pushed into the background or in large part ignored, and what remains is the author's arbitrary invention, what the ancients called *plasma*. Plasmatic invention on the basis of a received myth or historical legend was recognized as legitimate by ancient critics and was widely practised by the Greek tragedians, especially by Euripides, although the tragedians in shaping their plots for the stage did not need many new episodes or characters and hence exercised their privilege of invention only to a small extent. By contrast, the romancer, in exercising the same privilege, carries it a great deal farther, because his principal stock-in-trade, so to speak, is the multiplication of adventures and for that purpose many new episodes must be added to what he finds in the original myth or legend, or to such parts of it as he can use in his own ideal scheme of things. It is not the *nature* of the thing that the author of the first Greek romance did by way of arbitrary invention that puzzles the student of origins, and so causes him mistakenly to assume antecedent stages of development, but simply the *extent* to which a well-sanctioned literary practice has here been carried. That excess was something unprecedented; and it was through the free and unbounded exercise of the plasmatic license that the Greek romance came into being.

In the medieval French *Roman d'Hector*, as in the Byzantine *Achilleis* and in the ancient *Ninus*—to take one more illustration—it is the *youth* of the hero that is described, and what is related about him shows very little resemblance to the Homeric account. Gaston Paris in his *La Littérature Français au Moyen Âge* (p. 77 f.) says of this romance that it is "une oeuvre de pure invention, qui raconte la jeunesse du héros, et appartient à la littérature franco-italienne."

The romance of Ninus, classified with reference to the orientation of its biographical narrative, has been aptly termed a *Ninopedia*. What this classification may mean historically, concerning the use made by the earliest romancers of Xenophon's *Cyropedia* as a classical model, will be discussed later on in section 3. Meanwhile we must explain what the text is of which we shall be speaking: the papyrus fragments containing it, the publications of them, their contents severally and the order in which they should be read, and the approximate date to which the composition of the romance itself may be referred.

2

What has survived of the Ninus romance consists of three fragments on papyrus leaves found in Egypt, herein designated A, B, and C respectively. Fragments A and B, first published by Ulrich Wilcken in 1893 (*Hermes* 28, pp. 161–193), are on papyrus no. 6926 in the Berlin Museum and come from the same manuscript (where found in Egypt not known), but fr. C, discovered in 1932, comes from a different manuscript found at Oxyrhynchus and was published definitively, although not for the first time, by Medea Norsa in *PSI* 13 (1949) as no. 1305 on pp. 82–86. Fragment A has the remains of five columns of 38 lines each, and fr. B the remains of only three such columns. A's columns are much better preserved than B's. On the verso of fr. A (or B?) is written a business document dated in the year A.D. 101, which shows that the recto of the papyrus, containing the romance, must have been inscribed much earlier. All three fragments, according to M. Norsa (p. 83) are copied in a style of handwriting (calligraphic uncials) which she and other expert palaeographers tell us cannot be later than the middle of the first century after Christ, and some would allow that this writing might be as much as a hundred years or more older. A dating close to the year 100 B.C. for the original composition of the romance, leaving aside the evidence of the handwriting, may be inferred from the type of romance which it represents, one which is much closer to Xenophon's *Cyropedia* as regards the orientation of its matter toward military education and warlike exploits than is any of the extant romances, including Chariton's, which may well have been written, as I think, in the late first century after Christ, if not earlier. For this reason most students of the problem, among them Rattenbury, date the composition of *Ninus* around the year 100 B.C.;

which is plausible in view of the literary conditions of that time, following the decline of drama on the stage after Terence and the spilling over of it into historiography and romance (above, p. 146).

Much has been written by various scholars on the interpretation of fragments A and B, which cannot be reviewed here. The text has been published with restorations, commentary, and translations (so far as possible) by H. Weil in 1902 (see below), by S. Gaselee in 1916 (Edmond's *Daphnis and Chloe* in the Loeb library, pp. 382–389), by Bruno Lavagnini in 1922 (*Eroticorum Graecorum Fragmenta*, Leipzig, Teubner), by R. M. Rattenbury in 1933 (*New Chapters in the History of Greek Literature*, third series, edited by J. U. Powell, Oxford, pp. 211–223), and by Franz Zimmermann (without translation) at Heidelburg in 1936 (*Griech. Roman-Papyri und verwandte Texte*, pp. 11–35). The order in which the fragments A and B should be read is not indicated by any external evidence, because the condition in which the leaves were found *in situ* is not known. Wilcken, the first editor, printed A before B but was not sure that this was the right order.[2] The question before us, whether the author's sequence was AB or BA, can be decided, if at all, only on the basis of internal evidence supplied by the narrative substance of the two fragments and what that seems to indicate concerning the inner relationship of the one to the other. Scholarly opinion on this question is divided. Gaselee (*op. cit.* p. 385) and Garin (*Stud. Ital. di Fil. Class.* NS. I, 1920, pp. 165–167) have preferred the order BA, and their judgment of the matter was formed before the discovery of fragment C. The last mentioned fragment has some bearing on the question of the order of fragments A and B, because it pictures a scene of shipwreck in the course of naval operations (ναυτιλίαι), which are mentioned in A as future hazards. It is certain, therefore, that fr. C belongs to a later part of the romance than A. That it is also from a later part than that to which B belongs is evident from the fact that B describes military campaigns on the mainland of Asia, which must have preceded the operations by sea, according to the nature of Assyrian conquests and to what is said in A about the futurity of naval operations as opposed to the warfare on land which has already been carried on extensively. In the light of these facts, I suppose, the latest commentator on the problem, R. Jeništova, advocates BAC as the order in which the three fragments of the Ninus romance should be read; and I agree with him.[3]

In the first column of B about one-half of the letters in each line are missing and there are only seven or eight lines which can be entirely restored with some approach to certainty. The two lovers are present, apparently at home at the royal court with the girl's mother, and the girl (Semiramis), though not named,[4] is lying or sitting on a couch. When Ninus approaches her in a state of agitation, something that he has done or, more likely, something that she has heard about him, causes her to jump up in alarm, as if he had intruded upon her privacy, and to reproach him; but Ninus restrains her with his hands and succeeds in quieting her alarm by reassuring her that he has good intentions and is not the kind of man that she suspects him of being. In lines 22–24 something is said about taking an oath: πί]στις ἔστω τού[του, τὰ]ὀμοσθέντα το[ὅρ]κου πεπιστευ[. Thereafter the couple are reconciled and spend all of each day together, except for such time as is required for Ninus's military duties. This seems to imply that no military campaigns are in progress at the time, and that the scene of the lovers' meeting is at the Assyrian court. In lines 33–35 of this column reference is made to early spring, if the small restoration adopted by all editors is correct, and the Armenians are mentioned in lines 35 and 36. The last two lines of the column, nos. 37 and 38, are missing entirely. Mention of the Armenians here means that the lovers are about to be separated temporarily by the military crisis which is described in cols. 2 and 3, in both of which the text is well preserved, especially so in col. 2. At the beginning of col. 2 (B2) we read (in Gaselee's translation of the unimpaired text): "According to the instructions of his father, Ninus took the whole body of the Greek and Carian allies, seventy thousand chosen Assyrian foot and thirty thousand horse, and a hundred and fifty elephants, and advanced. What he most had to fear were the frosts and snows over the mountain passes; but most unexpectedly a gentle south wind, much more summer-like than the season would warrant, sprang up, both melting the snow and making the air temperate to the travellers beyond all that they could dare to hope. They had more trouble over crossing the rivers than in traversing the high passes . . ." But the army took it all in its stride and "thought that it would be but a slight labour to capture a host of mad Armenians. Ninus invaded the river-country, taking much booty, and built a fortified camp on a piece of flat ground; and there for ten days he rested his army, especially the elephants who were worn out from the journey." This brings us to the end of column 2. What follows in the first 29 lines of col. B3 is a detailed description of the tactical disposition of his forces made by Ninus in preparation for what appears to him to be a difficult and decisive struggle with the Armenians, and the last 9 lines of fragment B, lines 30–38 on the column, read as follows: "And stretching out his hands as if (offering sacrifice, 'This'), he said, 'is the foundation and the critical turning point of my hopes. From this (day) either I shall enter upon some greater career or I shall fall even from the (power that I now possess). For the (war) against the Egyptians (and) my other hostile (expeditions . . .)' " Here fr. B ends. What the last sentence implies is quite uncertain: possibly that the wars against the Egyptians and other nations either have been, or will be, relatively easy triumphs as compared with the Armenian war with which Ninus is now confronted.

Fragment A, as was noted above, has five columns of writing with 38 lines in each column, but so many words and syllables are missing in the first column (A1) that only the last seven lines of it can be restored with any confidence. Something is said about Ninus being greatly in love (σφόδρα ἐρῶν), about his or her hope, about modesty or bashfulness (αἰδώς), about parents, about the postponement (of the marriage, lines 24, 25), and, finally, in lines 32–38, that (neither Ninus nor) the girl dared . . . but both felt confident (about approaching) their aunts rather than (their own) mothers, and that (Ninus, talking with) Der(ceia said) "Mother . . ." The sentence beginning with "Mother" here at the end of A1 is continued without a break in column A2, in which, as in the remaining columns (A3, A4, and A5) very few words or syllables are missing and the exact sense of what is said is seldom if ever in doubt. Ninus continues speaking to his aunt Derceia as follows at the beginning of A2: "It is with my oath kept true [this may well refer to the oath mentioned above in lines 22–24 of B1] that I have come into your sight, and to the embrace of my most charming cousin. This let the gods first of all know, as indeed they do know it, and as I shall doubtless prove by what I am now saying. I have overrun so much territory and have made myself master of so many nations, both those who were subdued by my own spear [including, one would suppose, the nearby Armenians mentioned in B3], and those who pay me homage and bow down to me on account of my father's power, that I could have indulged myself to satiety with every carnal pleasure; and had I done so, perhaps my passion for my cousin would have been less. But now that I have come back (*sc.* from my military conquests) pure and uncorrupted, I am conquered by the god of love and by my age. I am in my 17th year, as you know . . . up to now I have been only a boy, a child; and, if I were still unaware of Aphrodite's power, I should feel happy in my firm strength. But, now that I have been taken prisoner by your daughter, in no shameful fashion but agreeably to the desires of both of you, how long am I to be refused?" . . . "I am old enough to marry," he says in effect, "and how many men have kept themselves unspotted (as I have) even up to their fifteenth year? I am injured by a law that is not a written law but one observed by foolish custom, that [col. A3] among our people virgins usually marry at the age of fifteen" . . . "Let us wait two years, you may say; but suppose we do wait patiently, mother—will Fortune (Τύχη) also wait? I am a mortal man engaged to a mortal maid; and I am exposed not merely to the ordinary hazards of life, such as diseases and the ill Fortune (Τύχη) which often destroys even those who remain peacefully at home by their own firesides; but *sea-voyages are waiting for me* and wars after wars, and I'm not without daring, or such a one as to take refuge in cowardice by way of insuring my safety . . . ."

Ninus continues his plea to the girl's mother, Derceia, by declaring that his marriage to her daughter ought to be hastened by considerations of state (βασιλεία), by their mutual passion for each other, by the unstable and incalculable future that lies ahead of him. "Let also the fact that we are each of us the only offspring of our parents be anticipated and provided for, so that, if Fortune (Τύχη) plans any calamity for us, we may at least leave you some pledge of our affection . . ." A4, lines 5 ff.: "There is nothing shameful in my speaking thus to you as a mother about your daughter's marriage, which has been the object of your vows. I am claiming what you have already promised, and asking that the prayers both of our house and of the entire kingdom may not be postponed to a time when things are no longer in your power to dispose." Ninus ends his plea with these words (A4, line 13) and the text continues as follows: "In saying this to Derceia he anticipated her own desire, and perhaps, if he had delayed a while longer, he would have compelled her to speak first about these matters; but she, after dissembling a bit, promised to plead his cause." The remainder of fr. A describes, in a spirit of heroic idealism, the ineffectual efforts of the 13-year-old girl (Semiramis) to speak out and tell her aunt Thambe, the mother of Ninus, that she is in love and anxious to marry her cousin as soon as possible. That is too much for the little girl's *savoir faire*. She had been brought up in the women's quarters and had never been outside. Throughout the conference she fails to say anything articulate, although she succeeds several times in opening her mouth and looking as if she would say something. She is dumbfounded by conflicting emotions—love for Ninus, fear of being raped by him (so Thambe supposes), and, above all, by a burning sense of shame (αἰδώς) in trying to confess her love or to speak of marriage. Her cheeks become first red from the sense of shame, then pale with fear in trying to say something, and she weeps profusely with broken sobs. This is the *ne plus ultra* of childish embarrassment, unequalled in any other heroine of Greek romance. Thambe is sympathetic, takes the child in her arms and wipes away her tears, saying: "This silence of yours tells me better than any speech could (how you feel). But don't blame my son. He has not ventured upon any improper or unlawful advances against you. Although he has returned to us after many military successes and triumphs, he has not, in the manner of a warrior irresponsible and drunken with power, committed any offense against you; had he done anything of the kind, you would probably not be silent about it now. Is the minimum age fixed by convention too tardy for young people already ripe for marriage? Is my son in too great a hurry? Not even on that account ought you to weep as having suffered any outrageous violence." Etc. So the two sisters (Thambe and Derceia) got together, and Derceia spoke first saying, "It is about important matters . . ." And here fr. A ends.

The marriage of the lovers probably followed soon after the conference mentioned at the end of A5, when the two sisters met to discuss "serious matters"; for the girl's mother, Derceia, had promised Ninus to plead his case for him and it was only the girl's age that was in question. Thambe, the mother of Ninus, could have no objection to her son's marrying a 13-year-old girl, if her mother and the girl were willing, and no mention is made of any need to consult the father of Ninus, the king of Assyria. The matter must have been settled by the royal sisters Derceia and Thambe, and in accord with the desire of the lovers. But great difficulties are involved in assuming, with Weil, Lavagnini, and others, that the lovers appear as man and wife in fr. B1. If that were so, assuming the order AB, the scene described in B1, picturing a squabble, about anything you please, between the married lovers, would be anticlimactic and non-functional in the plot of the romance, as we now see it in the light of fr. C; for there Ninus is shipwrecked and apparently separated or about to be separated from his wife Semiramis. That, following after both B and A, must have been the beginning of their manifold adventures, similar in kind to those described in the later romances. It was only in the course of one of those sea-voyages, mentioned as future in fr. A, that the lovers could be separated and start on their career of adventures in quest of each other. So long as Ninus was fighting on land with immense military forces at his command, as in B2, he could not be defeated or made helpless and separated from his wife, as later on, when shipwrecked, he very well could be and probably was. Because the quarrel or misunderstanding mentioned in B1 in this romance could not have occasioned the disastrous separation of the lovers from each other, as it does in Chariton's romance,[5] the description of it after A and the marriage would be useless and inconsequential; but if we read B before A, then the quarrel, whatever it was, by its outcome serves to reassure the timid little girl, still far from married, that her eager lover is not a reckless libertine of whom she need be afraid. B is functional if read before A, but useless and inconsequential if read as a sequel to A and the marriage.

The words εὐορκήσας ἀφῖγμαι, with which Ninus begins his plea in A2, have reference to an oath which has already been taken in the past. On the assumption that fr. A preceded fr. B, that oath could not be the one mentioned in B1, and the latter would be a useless repetition of one made in a part of the text preceding A. That involves a distinct improbability. Assume on the contrary that B preceded A; in that case the oath mentioned in B1 refers very naturally, in part at least, to the future conduct of Ninus on his extensive military campaigns abroad, which are renewed, if not begun for the first time in B2, and from which he has returned home triumphant and true to his promise of good behavior in A2. This again points to BA as the right order of events.

The priority of B to A, moreover, is implied quite clearly, as it seems to me, by the statement made by Ninus in B3 that his whole career, whether to rise or fall in power, depended on his success in the Armenian war, and the fact that in A he has risen in power. He has returned home triumphantly after having subjected "so many nations." If, after that statement in A, a new hazard is assumed to have arisen in the form of an Armenian revolt in B1, the detailed description of that battle given in B2 and B3 would lead nowhere in the economy of the plot of the romance, since, for the reasons mentioned above, it could not serve to separate the lovers from each other. Coming after A, in which Ninus has already made himself master of many nations, the detailed description of putting down a subsequent revolt would be a back-tracking digression from the forward march of the romance, the substance of which could not be expected to include a full account of every military action that had to be taken by a ruler after he had made himself master of many nations. In fr. A all the military conquests that the author needed to mention or describe for the purpose of his preliminary *Ninopedia* are past. What followed (after the marriage) must have been something that led to the separation of the lovers; and that event would be brought about on one of the naval voyages mentioned by Ninus as a future hazard in A3. "Wars after wars" are also here mentioned as future hazards; but, since the lovers are going to be separated and undergo a series of adverse adventures, those wars would take place, if at all, only when Ninus and Semiramis were reunited and living happily ever after.

Fragment C as edited by M. Norsa consists of one column of 50 lines, each of which contained originally somewhere between 15 and 19 letters. In the first 17 lines only isolated words and phrases can be read, yielding no sure meaning for the context; but the remaining lines, 18–50, are fairly well preserved and admit of translation with a few small restorations.

Line

1]··ἐπ' ἀκτῆς "Ἱππου·[—— on the bank of the Hippos
   ]   περι   (a river in Colchis)?[6]
   ]·δαστε γύναι μοι καλ[
   ]νια καθάπερ ἐδηλ[—— my wife ——?
                        —— just as showed?

5]·νειληφυΐα μετα[——————————————————?
   ]·εισ δ ἐτα[·]·ων τῶν·[one of the companions?
   ]·τον ἐμ··ἐπίκουρ[—— my helper?[7]
   ·]ναύτου καὶ ἐπιστή[μονος   sailor and skillful
   ]κυβερνήτου ου·[pilot

10]α·αλ·οσ ἀσφαλέσ[—— safe ——
   ]οσ πρὸ[[σ]] τῆσ βορει·[σ   who(?) before the transfer
   ]μεταβολῆσ εἰσ τὴν[τῆσ   from the north to the coastal
   Κ]ολχίδοσ ἀκτὴν ἐ[headland of Colchis[8]
   ]········δερ··ο·[

15]ἐκ γὰρ·····ω···[——————————————————
   ]ετω···ανκειμενο[——————————————————
   ]········ουμηκ[——————————————————
   ]ιων καὶ ἄλσος ὑπὲρ[and beyond it a shady grove,
   α]ὐτῆσ σκιερόν·οὗ κατ'[αὐ   from the midst of which

20 τὸ]τὸ μέσον εἰς ῥεῖθρον   a spring sufficient to form an a-
   πάν]υ ἀρκοῦσα πηγή μέ-   bundant stream issued forth and
   χρι] τῆς κυματωγῆσ κα-   broke upon the beach.
   τε]ρρήγνυτο τὸ μὲν οὖν   The ship,
   σ]κάφοσ—οὐ γὰρ ἀγχιβα-   since the water was not deep

25 θῆσ ἦν ἡ ἀκτή—πρόσ τ[ι-   inshore at the foot of the promon-
                        tory,
   σιν ὑφάλοις ταινίαις ἐξ[ο   having grounded on some under-
   κεῖλαν διε[σ]αλεύετο κα[ὶ   water sandbanks, was being
   δ··δ·····[τ]αῖς ἐμβο-   shaken and —— by the on-
   λαῖς κ·····ἀπολλύ   slaughts —— destroyed.

30 μενον οἱ[δὲ δι]έβαινον   But they crossed over im-
   α]ὐτὸν εἰς ἄκρους μαζοὺς   mersed up to their breasts, and
   κλυζόμενοι. καὶ παντα   having saved everything
   τὰ ἐν τῇ νηΐ διασώσαν-   on the ship

τ]ες εἰδρύθησαν ἐπὶ τῆς
35 ἠϊόνος, ἐν μὲν οὖν
τῷ ἀνελπίστῳ πάντ' ἐ[π]ό-
ν]ουν ὑπὲρ τῆς σωτηρ[ί-
α]ς, διασωθέντες δ'ἐπε-
θ]ύμουν θανάτου. καὶ ο[ἱ
40 μὲν ἄλλοι μετριώτε-
ρο]ν τὴν μεταβολὴν
ἔφ]ερον·ὁ δὲ Νίνος ἀ-
θλ]ίως αὐτῆς ἤσθετο. πρὸ
τρι]ῶν μὲν ἡμερῶν ἡγεμὼν
45 το]σαύτης δυνάμεως
ἑτοί]μης ἐπὶ πᾶσαν
τὴν 'Ασ]ίαν στρατεῦσαι
νυνὶ δε——?] πάντοτε
——————————] ναυαγός
50 ἀπαχ]θείσης δορικτή-
του]

they set it down on the
beach. In
this unexpected situation
all their toil was for attaining
safety, but when they had saved
themselves they began to wish
they were dead. The others
endured this reversal of fortune
with greater equanimity, but
Ninus felt very miserable
about it; three days ago he
had been the leader of a mighty
military power capable of
marching against all of Asia,
[but now he was] at all
events —— shipwrecked,
while [his wife?] had been
carried off a captive(?)

Ninus is shipwrecked, but how did it happen? Was the ship driven ashore by a storm, of which no mention is made in our fragment, or had it run aground accidentally during an attempt to land a party on shore? Had there, perhaps, been a naval battle in which the ship carrying Ninus had been overpowered and forced to retreat, and in the course of which battle Semiramis had been taken captive by the enemy? Something like that is positively suggested by the words -θείσης δορικτη-, which are given as one reason why Ninus feels more woeful than his companions; although what these words really meant in the context is nevertheless quite uncertain, and for us unknowable. The possibilities of the general situation herein described are numerous and such as would allow for an immediately preceding action in which Semiramis had been separated from her husband Ninus. That she was so separated somewhere in the narrative of this romance is almost certain from the analogy of other romance-plots and from the representation of Ninus on the mosaics of Antioch gazing forlornly on the picture of a woman.

The trivial, and therefore non-patriotic nature of the Ninus romance, with its unique inventions (its *hapax heuremena*) in contrast with the historical and legendary tradition about the protagonists, comes into clear view when we look at the national saga about Ninus and Semiramis in outline as reported by Diodorus (II 1 ff.). Herein the account given of the military conquests made by Ninus agrees in substance with what is told about them in the extant fragments of the romance; but the characters of Ninus and Semiramis and their actions are here pictured in a very different light, one that is truly Oriental rather than Greek. In the saga the imperial power achieved and exercised by the principals, by hook or crook, stands in the foreground, without any animadversions on what a pretty and conventionally proper pair of lovers Ninus and Semiramis had once been when they were teen-age youngsters. Only an obscure Greek romancer addressing himself primarily to juvenile readers would write in *that* fashion about the national heroes of any country. Nothing of the kind written in an Oriental language exists so far as I know, not even in literature of the Hellenistic age; and the known Orientals who wrote in Greek—Berossus, Manetho, and Josephus—likewise do nothing of the kind in writing patriotically about the history of their respective nations.

In the saga (Diod. II 1, 8), as in the romance (fr. B), the Armenians are mentioned (along with the Medes in Diod. II 1, 10) as the principal adversaries of the Assyrian power;[9] while the conquest of Egypt is mentioned only casually in both accounts (Diod. II 2, 3; romance fr. B3) as one of many conquests made by Ninus. From this it appears that the author of the romance followed the historical tradition in writing about the military successes of Ninus, having found it unnecessary for the purposes of his story either to change it in substance or to leave it out, although he may have passed over a large part of it summarily.

Semiramis has been surely identified, in the contemporary royal correspondence of Assyria, with the Assyrian queen

Sammu-rāmat, the form of whose name, meaning "The goddess Shammu is Exalted," is not Assyrian but Aramaic. She rose in fact from the royal harem (like the Jewess Esther of much later invention) to become the official queen of the short-lived king Shamshi-Adad (823–810 B.C.), and was queen-regent during the first five years of the reign of her son, Adad-Nirari III (809–782). Owing to her prominence as a feminine figure in a world otherwise ruled by men, and to the fact that she was a princess of Aramaic descent, Semiramis made a strong impression upon the memory of the peoples of Syria and Mesopotamia, and in later times was thought of as semi-divine. She was said to have been the daughter of the goddess Derceto of Ascalon,[10] otherwise known as Atargatis, a deity closely akin to Astarte and to Ishtar, the Babylonian goddess of love and war. Like her divine parent Derceto and like Ishtar in the Gilgamish epic, Semiramis in the legend is represented as an amorous and voluptuous woman who kills her numerous lovers as soon as she is through with them, lest she should marry a master, or one who would interfere with her sovereignty.[11] Many marvellous achievements in the way of military conquests and the building of public works, including the founding of Babylon, are ascribed to Semiramis in the account of her given by Diodorus, which comes mainly from Ctesias, a Greek physician who was resident at the court of Persia around 400 B.C. and wrote on the history of Assyria. According to this account, after a reign of 42 years, she disappeared from the earth, taking flight to heaven in the form of a dove. Before she came into power, Semiramis married a man named Onnes, who was governor of Phoenicia under king Ninus of Assyria, and one of his generals. Later when Ninus was having difficulty in capturing the fortified city of Bactra, Semiramis, who had joined her husband Onnes in the besieger's camp, took the city for Ninus by stratagem. Thereupon, Ninus, having become enamored of Semiramis, forced Onnes to give her up and the latter committed suicide.

According to the saga (Diod. II 2, 1), Ninus had spent 17

years in conquering western Asia and Egypt before he met
Semiramis at the siege of Bactra and took her away from her
husband by force, having threatened to blind him if he failed
to hand her over of his own accord. His conduct is that of the
triumphant warrior ruthless in the exercise of his power over
women and other chattels—just the kind of man that he claims
not to be in the Greek romance, where he pleads long and
earnestly with Aunt Dercy for permission to marry her daughter under the most respectable circumstances. In the saga
Ninus keeps a harem, like other Oriental kings, and takes all
the women he wants by force, regardless of how their husbands
or their mothers and aunts feel about it. Nothing heroic or ideal
about that, you may say. True. But it is not inconsistent with
patriotic legends in the Semitic Orient; and it is far from being
so ugly morally as the intensely patriotic story, invented in
Alexandrian times, about Esther and Mordecai at the court of
the Persian king Ahasuerus, so called.

The story of the stratagem by which Semiramis got rid of
her husband Ninus, as reported by historians in the Alexandrian age, is related by Diodorus (II 20, 3–5), Plutarch (*Ama-
torius* 753 D–E), and Aelian (*Var. Hist.* VII, 1). Here we read
that Semiramis coaxed Ninus into letting her rule the empire
in his stead for a period of five days (one day according to
Plutarch), during which time she caused Ninus to be im-
prisoned and put to death, with the result that she herself
became queen of Assyria and ruled for many years afterwards.

Unlike Semiramis, Ninus of the saga is a fictitious character,
named after the city of Nineveh, eponymously, and representing in the composite person of one man the exploits of a long
line of Assyrian kings.

3

The text of the Ninus romance (frs. A and B) as previously
published by Wilcken was edited and translated in 1902 by the
French scholar Henri Weil in his *Études de Littérature et de
Rhythmique Grecques*, under the title "La Ninopédie." Here

Weil called attention for the first time to the fact that our fragmentary romance of Ninus is built on the same structural pattern, so far as we can see, and with the same orientation of subject-matter toward the training and education of an idealized hero from infancy on, as the *Cyropedia* of Xenophon. That was his justification for dubbing the Ninus romance, significantly, a *Ninopedia*. The author himself would probably not have given that title to his romance, because he was posing as an historiographer; but, because he knew that he was lying from the standpoint of an historian, and that his love story would be rated accordingly by those educated men who dominated literary fashion, he would probably have felt honored and reassured to have his composition recognized by scholarly judgment from outside as sanctioned by the classical example set by Xenophon in the *Cyropedia*. If he himself was a liar, when judged by the standard of historiography, so likewise was the respected Xenophon of Athens, whose account of the kings of Media and Persia, and their associates, was not much truer, historically, than his own account of Ninus.

That the earliest romancers thought of themselves as writing in the tradition and manner of Xenophon, as emulators of that classical author, is evident from the fact, noted long ago by Rohde and others, that the name Xenophon served as a *nom de plume* under which unknown authors of romances published their books. Three Xenophons are mentioned in the *Suda* lexicon (Suidas) as authors of erotic romances, as follows in translation:

Xenophon of Antioch, historian (ἱστορικός). *Babyloniaca;* this is erotic (ἐρωτικά).

Xenophon of Ephesus, historian. *Ephesiaca;* this is an erotic narrative in ten books about Habrocomes and Antheia, and about the city of Ephesus and other matters.

Xenophon of Cyprus, historian. *Cypriaca;* this too is a history dealing with erotic themes, concerning Cinyras and Myrrha and Adonis.

From the foregoing citations we see that ethnographical titles on the pattern of *Ephesiaca* and *Babyloniaca* were conventional

in the titling of Greek romances, that the authors professed to
be writing history (of a kind), and were classified as historians
by ancient scholars who had no more exact term for romance
as a literary form. The extant romances of Iamblichus and of
Heliodorus have similar titles, namely *Babyloniaca* and *Aethiopica*. It is only when we have the book itself extant, or someone's description of it, as above, that we can know what such
titles imply about the specific content of a book. What is ethnic
or geographical in it may be the political history of a city or a
country, a geography, or a description of its institutions and
customs, and that is normally the case. But the ethnic element
implied in the historical-looking title may also consist in
nothing more than the nationality of the characters whose
private affairs are related, or of the persons who tell such
stories, as in the case of the *Milesiaca* of Aristides "of Miletus"
(who may well not have been a Milesian), or the Aesopic fables
which are called Carian, Cyprian, Sybarite, or Cilician, etc.,
according to the nationality of the man or woman who is
credited with telling the fable or about whom it is told (Theon,
Progymnasmata 3). The romancer knows well enough that
what he writes is not history. He does not, like Ps.-Callis-
thenes, *intend* to write history, but he is obliged to pose as an
historian as a matter of *décor*, in order to launch his book into
a literary world that would recognize and accept serious narration in prose only in the guise of history, science, or philosophy
—not as *belles lettres*.

Xenophon had many admirers and imitators of one kind or
another in Roman times, besides the romancers, and the influence of his various writings on the literature of that period,
especially on historiography, is manifold.[12] The historian Arrian
modelled much of his own writing on the patterns of Xenophon's books, proudly emulated that author, and was himself
nicknamed Xenophon by his contemporaries.[13] In the time of
Diocletian the epic poet Sotericus, according to Suidas, wrote
an epyllion dealing with the famous love story of Abradates
and Panthia, which had been related at scattered intervals by

Xenophon in the *Cyropedia;*[14] and another version of that romantic love story was written in prose in the second century. Philostratus tells us that Celer, royal secretary under Hadrian, wrote a book about the love of Araspas for Panthia and ascribed it to a rival rhetorician, Dionysius of Miletus, in order to disgrace him. Araspas was the man assigned by Cyrus to guard the beautiful captive Panthia, loyal wife of Abradates in the *Cyropedia*. According to Xenophon's account, he fell madly in love with Panthia and tried to force her to do his will, but Cyrus, after gently reproving him for this conduct (of which Araspas himself was ashamed), sent him abroad on a diplomatic errand in order to put him out of the way of temptation. It is quite possible, and not unlikely, that the affair of Araspas with Panthia as Celer told it was quite different and not so ethically correct as it appears in the *Cyropedia*. Xenophon may have whitewashed the characters and suppressed an earlier form of the story followed by Celer, as he has done with other characters in his ideal picturing of Cyrus and his associates. In any case, Celer's composition must have been an erotic romance in our sense of the term, hence more protracted than in Xenophon, and ascribed as such to Dionysius of Miletus it would have served well enough to spoil the reputation of that rival rhetorician, whether the story of Araspas and Panthia as Celer wrote it was ethically proper as in Xenophon, or otherwise.[15]

Many verbal and stylistic imitations or reminiscences of the *Cyropedia*, and also of the *Anabasis*, are found in the earliest completely extant romance, that of Chariton; enough to show that this author was thoroughly familiar with Xenophon's text and much influenced by his style and thought. One of the best climactic scenes in Chariton's romance, by virtue of its dramatic irony (VII 6, 7–12), is suggested by and imitative of a similar but briefer and less effective scene in the story of Abradates and Panthia (*Cyrop.* V 1, 6), where one of her guardians tries in vain to console the captive Panthia by telling her, after praising her husband's reputation, that Cyrus himself will marry her. In both cases the heroine, on being told that the commander will take her for himself, is greatly disturbed, wails, and tears her garments; but in Chariton's drama the heroine Callirhoe does not know, as the reader does, that the commander into whose power she has fallen is her own beloved husband, Chaereas.[16]

The author of the *Ephesiaca, concerning Anthia and Habrocomes* (so entitled) is given as plain Xenophon in the only manuscript in which this romance has survived, but in the *Suda* as quoted above the name is qualified by the word *Ephesius*, serving to distinguish the author from other romancers named Xenophon. It is possible to assume, with Lavagnini, that the designation of this Xenophon as *Ephesius*, and of the two other Xenophons as "he of Antioch" and "he of Cyprus" respectively, was made by the compiler of the *Suda* lexicon or by someone other than the romancer himself, in order to distinguish one author from another of the same name; but, in light of what has been said above about the historiographical pretense of these romancers with their ethnographical titles, I think it much more probable that the authors themselves claimed to be natives of the city or country to which their heroes and heroines belong, in order to make their "histories" look authoritative. Presumably a native would know whereof he spoke better than an outsider. In an article entitled "La Patria di Senofonte Efesio," first published in 1926, Lavagnini demonstrated, on the basis of a penetrating study of the topographical data given in this romance, compared with what we know from other sources, that the author shows no first-hand acquaintance with the city and its environs as they were in the fifth century and later, and that what he says about the distance of the Artamisium from the city must have been taken verbatim from Herodotus (I, 26), from whom likewise he seems to have taken the names of a number of his odd characters, including Habrocomes.[17]

What we now know to be true in the case of "Xenophon of Ephesus," that he was not (as he claimed) a native of the city which was the home of his hero and heroine, is likewise true, in all probability, of the two other Xenophons mentioned by Suidas as the authors of romantic histories pertaining to Cyprian and to Babylonian affairs respectively. Unlike the elegiac poets, who wrote on themes of the same kind found in antiquarian books recording the obscure mythical or legendary lore of foreign places, these *prose* writers had a cogent reason for posing as native historians of local tradition. C. Helvius Cinna, an Italian who spent nine years in composing a poem on the Cyprian love affairs of Cinyras and Myrrha (in his *Smyrna*), had no need to pretend that he was a native of Cyprus; but the romancer "Xenophon" who wrote in prose on the same subject was more or less bound by literary convention to make that claim, and the fact that he did so, or that someone else did it for him, creates no presumption that he had ever lived on the island of Cyprus. The probability is that he had only read about Cinyras and Myrrha in some handbook of mythological antiquities. And what about "Xenophon of Antioch" with his *Babyloniaca*? It has been plausibly conjectured that the author of the Ninus romance was none other than this "Xenophon" mentioned by Suidas. That is not unlikely, but of course we cannot know. Although *Assyriaca* might seem to be a more appropriate title for the story of Ninus, nevertheless a native of Antioch-on-the-Orontes in Syrian territory could very well speak of Ninus and Semiramis (his heroine whose home was nearby in Palestine) as fellow nationals who had once ruled all of western *Asia*, and could think of Babylonia as the center of their activity. In like manner it appears that Iamblichus, a Syrian who wrote a romance about *Babyloniaca*, professes, implausibly, to have learned the Babylonian language (which in his time was essentially Syriac or Aramaic, not Akkadian) and Babylonian history, authoritatively, from a Babylonian prisoner of war in Syria; so Rohde, *Gr. Rom.*[3], 391. There is no good reason to suppose that the author of the Ninus romance was really a native of Syria; but he would probably have claimed to be such, for the same historiographical reason that the author of *Ephesiaca* pretended to be a native of Ephesus and the author of *Cypriaca* a Cyprian.

Recently mosaics have been found on the floor of a man's house in Antioch-on-the-Orontes picturing scenes from the romances of Ninus and of Metiochus and Parthenope.[18] This shows that Greek romances were read and cherished as *belles lettres* in Syria in the second century after Christ, at least by one man; but that is all that it does show. It has no more bearing on the question of where the Ninus romance came from than it has upon the place of origin of the romance of Metiochus and Parthenope, which was built on a local myth about the founding of Naples, or the fact that the text of both romances as we have them happen to come from manuscripts found in Egypt. Copies of these Greek romances—for Greek they are and not Oriental as concerns their composition and the nature of their ethical idealism—undoubtedly circulated also in Hellenized Syria and were read with appreciation by Syrians; but even that tells us nothing about the presumable nationality of the authors. The puerile romance of Ninus has no patriotic or nationalistic orientation or significance. It relates the private affairs of a pair of teen-age lovers chafing under the restraint of middle-class social conventions, anxious above all else to get married as soon as possible, if only their mothers can arrange it, and to stay married and together, come what may in the political fortunes of Western Asia and Egypt, which will be arranged to suit the convenience of the lovers and of the romance. A Syrian patriot proud of his ancestors' achievements, in rivalry with the claims of other Oriental peoples (as Braun sees it), is the last person whom I, for one, should expect to have written in this fashion about Ninus and Semiramis. It is only those characters that are in any sense Syrian or Assyrian, not what is said about them in this romance; no more than what is said about the Persian Cyrus the Great by Xenophon, or by Scudéry, is Persian in origin or written in Persia. The author of the Ninus romance was probably a foreigner living and writing not in Syria, but in Egypt, and in the Greek rather than in the Semitic literary fashion and tradition.

4

The importance of the fragmentary romance of Ninus as a document of literary history is this, that it shows us just how the first Greek romance must have been composed and put before the reading public under the literary conditions that prevailed in its day, near the end of the Alexandrian age. The first romance to be written necessarily had to appear, like *Ninus*, in the guise of historiography, in spite of its ideal non-historical nature and purpose. This was the case because, before the birth of the novel as an independent form of ideal creative writing, any narrative written in prose, even in *Kunstprosa*, had always come under the banner of informative literature, and it was only as poetry of some kind, chiefly stage drama and epic, that ideal creative fiction (i.e. invention on an historical base), could be sanctioned.

Like Ninus, the first Greek romance must have been modelled structurally on the pattern of Xenophon's *Cyropedia*, because the earliest known romance, that about Ninus and Semiramis, is, as a matter of fact, so constructed, and because the name Xenophon was used as a *nom de plume* by the authors of at least three romances, serving to conceal their real identity. In this connection one must never lose sight of the fact that the romance or novel, wherever or whenever it emerges for the first time on the surface of literature, is always on the defense against the established conventions, and must therefore justify itself in terms of those conventions. In the case of the Greek novel, the precedent established by the classical author Xenophon in writing about the ideal career of Cyrus the Great served to give some respectability to the novelist's product, in spite of the very different kind of ideal values that it purveyed, simply because its outward form was essentially the same as that of a book written by Xenophon. The first Greek romance might have been, but was not, expanded like many later romances on the nuclear basis of an obscure local myth. The fact that it was not built on an obscure myth, but instead around characters famous in ancient Oriental history, is due likewise to the influence of Xenophon, the patron saint of the first romancers, in writing about the ideal behavior of Cyrus as a boy.

How the author of the first Greek romance implemented his purpose, which was to write a dramatic story of love and adventure in prose for the gratification of a reading public, has been told, as Xenophon would say, in the preceding discourse: *en tōi prosthen logōi dedēlōtai*. As for the author's purpose, the immediate creative force that brought the first novel into existence, that too has been mentioned before and is easy to understand, as regards its birth, in the light of the literary and cultural conditions that prevailed in the late second century B.C. At that time there was a much wider reading public, potentially, than there had ever been before, even in the early Alexandrian age; so that the popular entertainment which had previously been given to the public in the form of drama on the stage, and there only occasionally and in the larger cities, could now be supplied for Everyman, even on the farm or in the army, by means of books, and in much greater quantities than was possible on the stage. There, in the time of Terence, the amount of exciting action purveyed, and of the attention given to the love affairs of individuals, together with the complication and the happy solution of their personal problems by the intervention of Tyche, had reached its limit of extension in five-act plays. After that the dominant type of performance in the theaters was a one-act mime, or a pantomime in which the actor "danced" the passionate experiences of mythical characters by means of animated gestures without words— what we would call a ballet.

Thus the capacity of the theater to supply the popular demand for drama of a popular kind in quantity, and for

Everyman, sharply decreased as time went on; but even its five-act play on the stage was not enough in the second century B.C. to supply that demand. Some vehicle in addition to the theater was needed by which to convey drama, and none of the established literary forms could admit it, unless in very small quantities, without injury to itself. Historiography was most susceptible to its encroachment. Polybius in the time of Terence protests against the tendency of authors of historical monographs to distort the meaning of historical events by casting them into the form of sensational tragedies;[19] but later on Cicero (see above, p. 144 f.) recommends this dramatizing of the historical monograph, and it was realized to some extent by Sallust in his *Catiline* and in his *Jugurtha*. Such was the structural pattern of the historical monograph that it could contain a sentimental romance of adventure, featuring the private fortunes of a pair of lovers, as well as the kind of dramatized history that was put into it by such intellectual writers as Xenophon and Sallust. The *content* of the monograph would be determined by the kind of drama that the author wished to exploit, and at this time, near the end of the second century B.C., the Greek world was full of people whose ideals of dramatic value and interest in love affairs were similar to those of Chariton and the author of *Ninus*, but for whom no literature adapted to their taste existed. Under those conditions it was inevitable that someone sooner or later would satisfy the needs of that reading public by inventing the literary form that we have called romance or novel. Nothing else would satisfy the demand among people of small understanding for big drama, drama without limits.

The first romance was deliberately planned and written by an individual author, its inventor. He conceived it on a Tuesday afternoon in July, or some other day or month of the year. It did not come into being by a process of development on the literary plane. What had really developed was the complex cultural outlook, the *Weltanschauung*, of society as a whole in the Alexandrian age, in contrast to what it had been in the age of Pericles. That outlook on the world explains the kinds of literary purposes that the individual writer conceives, but it is the latter always that creates the end-product, the literary composition, and no two compositions can be exactly the same form. Many are very similar to each other owing to the environment of time, place, and social stratum in which they are produced, and these we speak of collectively and descriptively— *universalia post rem*—as a genre or a literary form, in this case romance or novel.

The word "development" implies a steady progression in the same direction, and in the sequence of time, towards a single, preconceived end or object; but there is no such thing in literature, as there is, for example, in the manufacture of passenger automobiles meant for speedy, safe, and comfortable transportation. What was the end toward which the ancient novel moved? Every different novel aimed, necessarily, at a different point on the compass of aesthetic value and orientation. All we can do about tracing the "development" of Greek romance after its birth is to describe each different romance; and, by way of so doing, partially, we may note here a few conspicuous varieties. Some of the romances are more directly under the influence of the founders of the genre than are others of nearly the same age. Thus Chariton's Chaereas only in the last book of his romance becomes, like Cyrus in Xenophon's *Cyropedia* and Ninus in the *Ninopedia* (romance of Ninus), but unlike any hero in the extant later romances, a commanding general who triumphs over the enemy's forces, in this case over the Persians of King Artaxerxes Mnemon. This represents a retreat from the earliest traditional type of novel, not an advance toward a preconveived ideal type, in which the hero's principal virtue, apart from his loyalty, will be his readiness to commit suicide whenever fortune turns against him.

The pseudonymity (or anonymity) under which the earliest romancers concealed their personal identity, to avoid the scorn of those learned academics, was boldly abandoned by Chariton, who tells us just who he was personally; but the pseudonymous

Xenophon of Ephesus, who, in all probability wrote somewhat later than Chariton, has conservatively retained it. If there is any development here, it goes backward rather than forward in the sequence of time. The mentality of one author, which is what creates a romance, does not necessarily march in the same direction as that of another author who precedes or follows him.

Contrary to Rohde's theory, the "sophistic" romances, as we now know, were not the first to appear in the history of the genre. That is because the authors of the earliest romances happened not to be sophisticated or learned men, and did not aim to produce the kind of novel that we have in Iamblichus, Achilles Tatius, and Heliodorus, in which the story of the lovers' adventures is heavily interlarded with learned excursuses on ethnographical or curiously scientific subjects, and with studious displays of rhetorical virtuosity. When sophists stooped to become authors of erotic romances, as Photius implies in speaking of Iamblichus, they imposed their own wares on the originally sentimental story, which had been written by and for the poor-in-spirit, and for naïve readers.

Classified according to its formal structure the *Daphnis and Chloe* of Longus is an *ecphrasis* (the description of a series of painted pictures), and the contemporary *Leucippe and Cleitophon* of Achilles Tatius, like the story of *Manon Lescaut* (below, p. 352), is represented as something told by the protagonist himself speaking in the first person. Is this the result of a development reaching back to *Ninus*? Obviously it is nothing of the kind. It is the arbitrary choice of an individual artist in each case.

5

The transition from poetic fiction to prose fiction in the writing of encomiums of individual men was begun, apparently, by Isocrates in writing about Evagoras, the ruler of Cyprus, who died in 374 B.C.; and the pattern of this encomium in prose (the *Evagoras*) was followed shortly afterwards by Xenophon in his *Agesilaus* and in his *Cyropedia*. In the *Evagoras* (sections 2 and 3) Isocrates deplores the fact that praise adequate to their achievements, and often far more than adequate, has been bestowed by poets upon men who lived, if at all, many centuries before their own time, and that envy has prevented writers from praising men whom they have known as their own contemporaries. On that account, and because men are thereby discouraged from aiming high in public life at the cost of personal sacrifice without any prospect of being rewarded with praise as heroes—for nations have great men only in spite of themselves—Isocrates proceeds to write his encomium of Evagoras. Unlike the *Evagoras*, however, and unlike the Xenophontean *Agesilaus*, the *Cyropedia*, while *formally* influenced by Isocrates, sings the praises of a ruler who lived many generations before the author's own time, becoming hence more fictitious and in a sense more poetic; and such likewise is the case with the *Ninopedia*, the romance of Ninus. In one of its aspects therefore, that namely which concerns the formal pattern of its composition only, Isocrates was the grandfather, as Xenophon was the father, of Greek romance as it appears in *Ninus*. But in another, and more significant aspect, Xenophon in the *Cyropedia*, followed by the author of *Ninus*, was the first to transfer the values and recognized licences of poetic fiction relating to characters far away in time or place to narrative in prose.

Parallel to the extension of encomiastic literature from poetry into prose, of which we have just spoken, is the extension into prose narrative, in the form of ideal romance, of the artistic aims and methods which had previously been recognized as legitimate only in some kind of ideal poetry, chiefly in epic and in classical "tragedy," including the romantic dramas of Euripides, such as the *Helen*, the *Alcestis*, and the *Andromeda*. On this subject we have already dwelt at some length in section 8 of chapter II above.

Another parallel, showing the transfer of poetic aims and values to prose literature in later times, may be seen in the emergence of that studiously cultivated art-prose known as the "Second Sophistic," which was the most dynamic and highly respected form of literature from the beginning of the second century after Christ onward to the end of the fourth. Herein what we have normally is an epideictic oration or essay which relates to little or nothing of consequence or contemporary interest (unless the matter happens to be scientific) but is carved with great care out of mainly archaic (i.e. Attic) materials: out of ancient topics and banalities discussed with subtle reproduction of Attic words, phrases, idiomatic nuances, rhythms, etc. Never mind what is said here, but *how* it is said. Or would you like to learn from the solemn Aelius Aristides, who, given a sense of humor, might better have written the encomium of a fly, as Lucian did, what may be said in praise of each of the twelve gods, or why the Athenians in 414 B.C. ought and ought not to send reinforcements to Sicily? He will inform you of all that eloquently and with elegance.

This prose of Aristides and his fellow sophists is no longer written primarily to instruct, as all serious prose had been in earlier times, but for the purpose of exhibiting much the same kind of verbal virtuosity that we have in the Alexandrian poets, in what has been aptly called their *poèsie pure* or *poèsie verbale*. Hereby think ye on Callimachus his antiquarian novelty, how erudite the man is, he never speaks by the card; on Lycophron labouring in the murk of Alexandra's mystic profesie; on Euphorion, Aratus, and many another architect of Alexandrian verse, some of their poems shaped in the likeness of axes, eggs, or altars. The nature and direction of that obscure poesy is well elucidated, howbeit with unclassical enthusiasm and approval, by B. A. Van Groningen in a recent essay entitled *La poèsie Verbale Grecque: Essai de Mise au Point*.[20] The point that we are making here is this: that, when the verbal poesy of Alexandrian times ceased to be cultivated, it was succeeded by a sophistic prose in which essentially the same kind of poetic and verbal values that had constituted the *raison d'être* of Alexandrian verse were cultivated with equal intensity and even greater indifference to topical subject matter. In other words, pure poesie in verse was succeeded by pure poesie in prose. It is more difficult for us of today to appreciate the verbal beauties which thrilled the connoisseurs of Attic prose in the second century, than it is to understand the virtuosity of the Alexandrian *poésie verbale;* but there can be no doubt—so great was the acclaim given to its practitioners—that this prose was felt to be a very high form of art. Like the Alexandrian poetry, it was esoteric. Lucian on one occasion (Zeuxis 1–2) complains that his audience lately had shown no appreciation at all of his stylistic finesse, his Attic salt, but had been lavish in their praise of the novelty of his ideas and subject-matter. Oh, how fresh and interesting *that* was![21]

Like Lucian, the romancers Apuleius and Iamblichus were also top-notch sophists and very ambitious and successful in the cultivation of fine style; but each of these three, unlike most of their fraternity, found it worth while, for the purpose of entertaining their readers and hearers, to write in their exquisite style about such things as would arouse the interest of ordinary men in their time: comedy with satirical orientation, romance, or paradoxical curiosities.

In the Second Sophistic the strong Greek love of rhythm, harmony, and proportion in verbal expression reaches its final phase and thereafter, in Byzantine times, disappears from Greek literature. With Homer and Sophocles it was instinctively manifested. Homer might be dull now and then in his subject-matter, but neither he nor Sophocles, so it seems, could tolerate a single metrically imperfect line. Their artistic instinct was unerring. But throughout the later Hellenistic period this poetry of form was consciously and studiously exploited by learned men, at first in Alexandrian verse, then later in prose by the Atticists.

On the analogy of the career of verbal poesy, poetic fiction likewise, viewed as subject-matter with all its proprieties and licence of invention as described above, was transferred to prose narrative in the late Alexandrian period and became—the novel.

PART TWO

The Comic Romances

INTRODUCTION
On Ancient Comic
Romances

THE CULTURAL background of the comic romance,
in contrast to that of the serious or ideal romance, was described above (pp. 87 ff.), and the main points there made are
implicit in the literary-historical explanation of the novels of
Petronius, Lucian, and Apuleius which here follows. It was
noted first that comic romances in antiquity were written only
on rare occasions and were not, like the ideal romances,
produced in quantity in response to a popular demand, nor in
accord with any literary fashion commonly recognized as such.
Secondly, there is no connection in literary tradition or practice
between the comic romance and the ideal. Thirdly, comic
romances are written only by highly sophisticated authors
whose adherence to the proprieties of formal literature requires
them to have, or to pretend to have, an ulterior purpose such
as that of satire or of instruction of some kind (philosophic,
scientific, or religious), on the few occasions when they publish
a story of personal adventure which stands by itself and is not
subordinated to a larger whole. For writers in the formal
traditions of literature, as contrasted with the newly-arrived
ideal romancer, a fictitious story in prose, like an Aesopic fable,
can be used legitimately only as an illustration of something,
and for that reason it is normally short and subordinated to a

context. Let it be noted, furthermore, that all the comic romances known to us from antiquity are told in the person of the principal character speaking about his own experience. This is no accident, nor is it due to the author's desire to make his story more vivid or more dramatic. It is because the authors, like Homer who makes Odysseus relate his own incredible adventures, and like the sophists Longus and Achilles Tatius, are deterred by the conventions of historiography from telling an obviously fictitious story on their own authority. For these sophisticated writers of prose, a story of any kind is not conceived as an imaginative work of creative art, like a poem of some kind or a tragedy, or a modern novel, but necessarily as a *history*, the truth of which must be formally vouched for by *someone*; and the author himself cannot assume that responsibility (see Appendix III).

The origins and *raison d'être* of comic romances, whether ancient or modern, have to be explained far less with reference to literary traditions and precedents than to the special purposes of their individual authors. The first mentioned of these two factors is trivial and insignificant, but the latter is decisive. One cannot account for Butler's *Hudibras* by pointing to books like *Don Quixote* and *Gargantua* as forerunners; but it is necessary above all else in this case to know something about Butler himself personally, his times, his politics and religious affiliations, the special circumstances under which he wrote, and the readers for whom his book was intended. The same would be true in the case of Cervantes or Rabelais. So too in antiquity, there is no use in trying to name precedents for the *Satyricon* on the supposition that the author was writing in accord with a definite formal tradition, although he was undoubtedly influenced by the subject matter and stylistic mannerisms of many such traditions; nor does the example of Petronius himself help us in any way to explain the appearance of the *Metamorphoses* of Apuleius or of its Greek original. These are three separate problems which call for three separate explanations. It is not the concept of comic romance as literary form that needs to be explained, for that had always been known in its essence and was easily invented; what we need to explain is why and how that simple form, shaped by the author's purpose, happened to be called into use in this or that isolated instance.

V
Petronius and
His *Satyricon*

1

THE *Satyricon* of Petronius, written in the time of
Nero, is a very unusual kind of book. There seems to be nothing
quite like it in ancient literature. The problem of what its
purpose was, and where it stands in relation to traditional or
recognized forms of writing in antiquity, while fascinating, has
proved to be one of the most baffling problems in literary
history, and no one yet has offered a solution which seems to
be entirely satisfactory, or acceptable to more than a minority
of critics. Those who have tried to tell us what the *Satyricon*
is, after feeling of the subject from various angles, have brought
back reports as different from each other as those of the fabled
six blind men who went to see the elephant.[1] One critic thinks
that the *Satyricon* is very much like a Roman satire, whatever
that may mean in terms of literary form or tradition;[2] another
sees in it a parody on the epic;[3] another a parody on the Greek
erotic romance;[4] another thinks of it as erotic romance in a late
stage of development, no longer ideal and sugary, but turned
to vinegar as it were under the acid conditions of Roman
environment, having acquired thereby a very strong, realistic,
and picaresque flavor;[5] another student of the question is

impressed chiefly by the similarity of the *Satyricon* in spirit and subject matter to the burlesque mimes that were popular on the Roman stage, and there is much of significance in that;[6] another thinks of the so-called Milesian tales as the nearest thing in kind to Petronius' book;[7] and one scholar, looking about for precedents that might have served as models for Petronius, says it is tempting to see a connection between the *Satyricon* and the prologues of Plautine comedy, because those prologues, outlining the action of the play and its background, sometimes run up to 80 or even 152 lines, thus amounting to short realistic stories about everyday people.[8] Here one is led to infer that if the prologues had been twice as long as they are they would have been twice as good as models, and the problem, being one of literary evolution and imitation, would then be twice as near a solution. In any case, these prologues might have furnished Petronius with the basic concept of what a comic story was like, assuming of course that it was possible for him or any writer of the time to be unaware of such elementary things. In this connection I would repeat my own conviction that the form of a literary species, such as the novel, when considered in its external aspects as a pattern, is the least significant thing about it; and that anyone after Homer, if not before, could have written a burlesque novel, if he had had the necessary motive for doing so, without needing any literary precedents to guide him. Such a book, in fact, must have been the mock-heroic epic about *Margites*, the clown who learned many arts and learned them all badly. In early Greek literature that book (a *tour de force* ascribed to Homer) stood out as isolated from literary fashion as does the book of Petronius in Roman literature, and for the same reason. It is only the serious thoughts of men that find expression in regular literary practice and effort, while the mood of parody or burlesque is felt to be so trifling a thing, at least in the minds of the ancients, that it is only under special circumstances of time, place, and authorship that this mood can call forth the effort or inspiration necessary to write a whole book about such things. Books dealing with the history of a nation are serious in almost all cases, but I have seen one called "A Comic History of England." To what tradition of literary practice would one say that such a book belongs? Obviously to no tradition, properly so called; and the same, I think, must be assumed in the case of Petronius' book, seeing that various attempts to establish the existence in Greek literature of a burlesque or realistic novel prior to Petronius have not proved convincing. One of those attempts was my own, published in 1925,[9] in conformity with the offhand opinions of such scholars as Leo and Wilamowitz; but I have since unlearned that way of thinking.

I have not mentioned here *all* the theories put forward to explain the *Satyricon*, only seven of them. Most of these explanations as set forth by their authors are indeed instructive and contain much that is true and important about Petronius' book, but none of them goes deep enough or far enough, and a key is still wanting to unlock the main secret. Professor E. T. Sage, finding the problem insoluble, concluded that Petronius was the creator of a new literary genre, of which the chief and best known example—indeed the only one—is the *Satyricon* of Petronius.[10] When I asked the late Professor Prescott of Chicago what he thought about the *Satyricon*, he replied with an ironical smile that it was what the biologists call a "sport." Webster defines this term as "a sudden, spontaneous deviation or variation from type, a mutation." Excellent. I agree with Prescott, and also with Sage, that the *Satyricon* is in a class by itself and that the word "sport" in biological language well describes it. That at least tends to sterilize the problem and keep off the germs of evolutionary theory; but beyond that it contributes nothing to the solution of the problem, which is: Why did Petronius write such a book; what was the basic form of literature with which he worked, if any, and what was the nature and purpose of his innovations? In attempting to answer these questions, it is important that we have clearly in mind the character and environment of the author personally and the manner and substance of his book, insofar as these can be known to us. Although we cannot be entirely sure of the matter, it is almost certain that the author of the *Satyricon* was identical with the Gaius Petronius concerning whom Tacitus in his *Annals* gives us the following account, after listing him along with numerous other victims of Nero in the year 66 A.D.[11] (John Jackson's translation as quoted by Heseltine in the Loeb *Petronius*; with a few small changes):

2

"Petronius deserves a word in retrospect. He was a man who passed his days in sleep, his nights in the ordinary duties and recreations of life; others had achieved greatness by the sweat of their brows—Petronius idled into fame. Unlike most who squander their substance, he was never regarded as either debauchee or profligate, but rather as one highly skilled in the art of luxurious living. In both word and action he displayed a freedom and a sort of self-abandonment which were welcomed as the marks of a forthright and unsophisticated nature. Yet, in his proconsulship of Bithynia, and later as consul elect, he showed himself an energetic and capable administrator. Then came the relapse; his genuine or affected vices won him admittance into the narrow circle of Nero's intimates, and he became the Arbiter of Elegance, whose sanction alone divested pleasure of vulgarity and luxury of grossness.

"His success aroused the jealousy of Tigellinus against a possible rival—a professor of voluptuousness better equipped than himself. Playing on the emperor's lust for cruelty, to which all other lusts were secondary, he bribed a slave to turn informer, charged Petronius with his friendship for Scaevinus, deprived him of the opportunity of defense, and threw most of his household into prison.

"At that time, it happened, the court had migrated to Campania; and Petronius had reached Cumae, when his detention was ordered. He disdained to await the lingering issue

of hopes and fears; still, he would not take a brusque farewell
of life. An incision was made in his veins; they were bound up
under his directions, and opened again, while he conversed
with his friends—not on themes of grave import nor in the key
of the dying hero. He listened to no discourses on the im-
mortality of the soul [like Cato at Utica] or the dogmas of
philosophy, but to frivolous songs and playful verses. Some of
his slaves tasted of his bounty, others of the whip. He sat down
to dinner, and then drowsed a little; so that death, if com-
pulsory, should at least be natural. Even in his will, he broke
through the routine of suicide, and flattered neither Nero nor
Tigellinus nor any other of the mighty; instead, he described
the emperor's enormities; added a list of his catamites, his
women, and his innovations in lasciviousness; then sealed the
document, sent it to Nero, and broke his signet-ring to prevent
it from being used to endanger others."

Anyone familiar with the *Satyricon* is bound to think of its
author as being just the kind of man that Tacitus here describes. The studied naturalness and simplicity of manner, the
love of style, the voluptuous sensibility, the keen artistic sense
as manifested in many subtle ways, the urbanity, the intellectual gaiety and amorality, and above all the refusal to appear
serious about anything—these qualities of mind and manner
are everywhere evident in the *Satyricon*; and it is hard to
imagine a book better suited than this one was to entertain and
amuse the intimate court circle of Nero, or more likely to have
been written by the man who Tacitus says was head of the
imperial pleasure department.[12]

3

What has come down to us in the manuscripts from the work
of Petronius consists of a number of fragments totaling about
110 octavo pages in Bücheler's closely printed text (6th ed.),
and these include, according to statements made in the manuscripts, all of Bks. XV and XVI, interrupted by many small

gaps, and probably also that part of Bk. XIV which precedes the *Cena Trimalchionis* at Chapter 26.7 on page 18. Estimated on this basis the 15th and 16th books of the original *Satyricon* must have totaled about 96 pages. If then we allow 50 pages for each book, the original work must have extended to 800 pages in the first 16 books, and there may have been other books following the 16th.[13]

The main body of fragments preserved in the manuscripts— as distinguished from those quoted by various authors or handed down by a separate tradition—are of such a nature that they cannot be regarded as "excerpts," the term usually applied to them by editors, but must rather be seen as pieces of salvage from a badly damaged manuscript, representing everything intelligible that some copyist in the ninth century, or earlier, was able to make out from the torn or blotted pages before him, ancient pages which he may have found cast out in some rubbish heap or in a badly neglected library. Much was entirely missing, including apparently the whole of the first 13 books. The biggest gap between the separate fragments corresponded with the major part of the famous banquet of Trimalchio, some 36 pages long in Bücheler's text, which has been elsewhere preserved entire as an excerpt in a separate tradition. Between the other fragments relatively small portions of text have been lost; each fragment taken by itself amounts to one or more complete and intelligible sentences or phrases, showing that the copyist was unwilling to transcribe meaningless words and syllables; there is no discernible principle of selection in these fragments, and no expurgation. Taken together, they provide a loosely continuous narrative, interrupted by gaps which seem not to be wide ones.

4

The title of the book and what it implies has seldom been rightly understood, and the statements about it in our handbooks are very often wrong or misleading. *Satyricon*, with which one understands the noun *libri* or books, is the Greek genitive plural of the adjective σατυρικόs, which is used by Plutarch and by Pliny the Elder, contemporary authors, in the sense of "satyr-like" or "lascivious." [14] A purely grammatical translation, therefore, would be "Books of Satyrlike Things." In relatively late manuscripts, and hence in some modern editions, the unfamiliar Greek word *satiricon*, which belonged in the original title and is attested by our oldest manuscript in the tenth century, was replaced with the familiar Latin word *satirae* meaning "satires"; but these two words are totally different in meaning, and between them in antiquity no connection either etymological or otherwise existed. Logically the title of Petronius' book should be cited in the nominative as *Satyrica*; and this title, being patterned after the formulaic titles of histories and romances such as *Assyriaca*, *Ephesiaca*, *Aethiopica*, etc., means in effect something like "Chapters in the History of the Satyrfolk," or "A Tale from the Land of Lascivia." We may now consider the contents of the book and its nature more closely.

5

The *Satyrica* deals throughout with the adventures of a purely neutral character named Encolpius, as told by himself in the first person. Accompanied by two companions, Giton and Ascyltus, he goes about from place to place aimlessly, driven on by chance circumstances and living by the arts of the parasite. The scene of action in the story as we have it is mainly in a town on the Bay of Naples, probably Cumae or Puteoli, but towards the end it shifts to Croton in southern Italy. An illusion in Sidonius Apollonaris indicates that one of the scenes in the lost part of the book took place at Marseilles in southern France. The characters move about for the most part in very low society amid cheap rooming houses and brothels; and many farcical episodes are motivated by the mock-heroic, homosexual love-affair of Encolpius with the

boy Giton, whose loyalty, as well as that of Encolpius himself, constantly wavers. The leading motif of action is thus
thoroughly anti-heroic, amounting to a gross caricature of real
or serious love. In one passage Encolpius complains in epic
verse—for the narrative often passes from prose to verse—that
he is pursued on land and sea everywhere by the heavy wrath
of Priapus (the homely god of sexuality), just as Odysseus was
pursued by the anger of Poseidon. Ascyltus, who accompanies
the two lovers and shares their fortunes, serves in the main as a
foil to Encolpius, frequently causing him trouble by running
off with Giton. Aside from this central theme many of the
episodes are of a pornographic character involving hetero-
sexual relations, interspersed with numerous short poems form-
ing part of the narrative, all of which poems are clever and
some of them really beautiful in themselves. So much for the
narrative part of the *Satyricon* in general. Into the framework
of this burlesque story, which for all its grossness is extremely
witty and full of very effective comedy, especially in the many
mock-heroic scenes, there is introduced an amazing variety of
first-class poetry, literary and artistic criticism, eloquent declamation, and philosophical reflection upon the tragedy and
comedy of life, or upon the frailty of human nature.

It will be worth while to describe here a few of the episodes
and to illustrate by quotation from Heseltine's excellent translation in the Loeb Library, the nature of some of the author's
criticism and poetry. Our fragments begin with a scene in
which Encolpius and Ascyltus have been listening to a lecture delivered by a professor of rhetoric named Agamemnon.
Encolpius has been commenting spiritedly upon this lecture
and is denouncing the kind of instruction in oratory that
prevails in the schools. In his opinion it is frivolous and
impractical. "These declamations on fanciful themes might be
endured," he says, "if they smoothed the path of aspirants to
oratory. But as it is, the sole result of this bombastic matter
and these loud empty phrases is that a pupil who steps into a
court thinks that he has been carried into another world. I

believe that college makes complete fools of our young men
because they see and hear nothing of ordinary life there. It
is pirates standing in chains on the beach, tyrants pen in
hand ordering sons to cut off their fathers' heads, etc. . . . .
With your permission I must tell you the truth, that you
teachers more than anyone else have been the ruin of true
eloquence . . . . I certainly do not find that Plato or Demosthenes took any course of training of this kind. Great style,
which if I may say so, is also modest style, is never blotchy and
bloated. It rises supreme by virtue of its natural beauty . . . ."
etc. Encolpius continues with a vigorous denunciation of the
modern education, and Agamemnon replies in part as follows:
"Your talk has an uncommon flavor, young man, and what is
most unusual you appreciate good sense. I will not deceive you
by making a mystery of my art. The fact is that the teachers
are not to blame for these exhibitions. They are in a mad-
house and they must gibber. Unless they speak to the taste of
their young masters, they will be left alone in the colleges, as
Cicero remarks . . . . A master of oratory is like a fisherman;
he must put the particular bait on his hook which he knows
will tempt the little fish, or he may sit waiting on the rock with
no hope of a catch. Then what is to be done? It is the parents
who should be blamed for refusing to allow their children to
profit by stern discipline." Agamemnon then proceeds to describe the ideal education of an orator in line with the lofty
standards of Cicero; and in so doing he imitates with good
effect the earnest and ingenuous preaching style of the satirist
Lucilius, beginning in iambic verse and mounting into dactylic
as the tenor of his harangue increases in dramatic intensity and
elevation of mood. Both speeches, that of Encolpius and that
of Agamemnon, are eloquent and forceful on the subject of the
decline of oratory and culture, and what the education of an
orator ought to be; but here as elsewhere the attitude of the
author ostensibly is that of a mimic rather than of a partisan.
He remains ironically aloof and pleads no cause of his own. He
may be, and undoubtedly often is, fully sympathetic with the

substance of what his characters are saying, but in one way or another he manages always to deprecate or disavow the serious assertion of anything. Sometimes he makes fun of the speaker, but in this case it is the earnestness of Agamemnon in his pleading of a noble but lost cause that makes us smile.

Much of the poetry in the *Satyricon*, as well as much fine literary and artistic criticism, is put into the mouth of the poet Eumolpus, who is first introduced in chapter 83 and thereafter becomes a principal actor in the story, taking part in all kinds of scandalous adventures, and sometimes appearing to be half crazy. Encolpius tells of his meeting with Eumolpus as follows:

"I came into a gallery hung with a wonderful collection of various pictures. I saw the works of Zeuxis not yet overcome by the defacement of time, and I studied with a certain ter-rified wonder the rough drawings of Protogenes, which rivalled the truth of Nature herself. But when I came to the work of Apelles the Greek which is called the One-legged [rather, the Monochrome], I positively worshipped it. For the outlines of his figures were defined with such subtle accuracy that you would have declared that he had painted their souls as well. In one the eagle was carrying the Shepherd of Ida on high to heaven, and in another fair Hylas resisted a tormenting Naiad. Apollo passed judgment on his accursed hands, and adorned his unstrung lyre with the newborn flower. I cried out as if I were in a desert, among these faces of mere painted lovers, 'So even the gods feel love.' . . . Suddenly, as I strove thus with the empty air, a white-haired old man came into the gallery. His face was troubled, but there seemed to be the promise of some great thing about him; though he was shabby in ap-pearance, so that it was quite plain by this characteristic that he was a man of letters, of the kind that rich men hate. He came and stood by my side . . . . 'I am a poet,' he said, 'and one, I hope, of no mean imagination, if one can reckon at all by crowns of honour, which influence can set even on unworthy heads. "Why are you so badly dressed, then?" you ask. For that very reason. The worship of genius never made a man rich.'" Here Eumolpus breaks into verse as he becomes more eloquent: "The man who trusts the sea consoles himself with high profits; the man who follows war and the camp is girded with gold; the base flatterer lies drunk on a couch of purple dye; the man who tempts young wives gets money for his sin; eloquence alone shivers in rags and cold, and calls upon a neglected art with unprofitable tongue." In the original:

> Qui pelago credit, magno se faenore tollit;
> qui pugnas et castra petit, praecingitur auro;
> vilis adulator picto iacet ebrius ostro,
> et qui sollicitat nuptas ad praemia peccat;
> sola pruinosis horret facundia pannis
> atque inopi lingua desertas invocat artes.

After some further comment along this line Eumolpus relates as his own experience in Asia a homosexual adventure of such a scandalous nature that I would not venture to translate it; and after listening to this Encolpius continues as follows:

"Encouraged by his conversation, I began to draw on his knowledge about the age of the pictures, and about some of the stories which puzzled me, and at the same time to discuss the decadence of the age, since the fine arts had died, and painting, for instance, had left no trace of its existence behind. 'Love of money began this revolution,' he replied. 'In former ages virtue was still loved for her own sake, the noble arts flourished, and there were the keenest struggles among mankind to prevent anything being long undiscovered which might benefit posterity. So Democritus extracted the juice of every plant on earth and spent his whole life in experiments to discover the virtues of stones and twigs. Eudoxus grew old on the top of a high mountain in order to trace the movements of the stars and the sky, and Chrysippus three times cleared his wits with hellebore to improve his powers of invention. If you turn to sculptors, Lysippus died of starvation as he brooded over the lines of a single statue, and Myron, who almost caught the very soul of men and beasts in bronze, left no heir behind him. But we are besotted with wine and women, and cannot rise to understand even the arts that are developed; we slander the past, and learn and teach nothing but vices. Where is dialectic now, or astronomy? Where is the exquisite way of wisdom? Who has ever been to a temple and made an offering in order to attain to eloquence, or to drink of the waters of philosophy? They do not even ask for good sense or good health, but before they even touch the threshold of the Capitol, one promises an offering if he may bury his rich neighbour, another if he may dig up a hid treasure, another if he may make thirty millions in safety . . . . So there is nothing surprising in the decadence of painting, when all the gods and men think an ingot of gold more beautiful than anything those poor crazy Greeks, Apelles and Phidias, ever did. But I see your whole attention is riveted on that picture, which represents the fall of Troy. Well, I will try and explain the situation in verse.' "

Here follows a poem in tragic meter, 65 lines in length, in which it appears that Petronius was trying to see what he could do with the tragic muse. This effort seems to be fairly successful, though less so, in my opinion, than the long epic poem about the Civil War which he puts into the mouth of Eumolpus later on. Encolpius continues: "Some of the people who were walking in the galleries threw stones at Eumolpus as he recited. He recognized this tribute to his genius, covered his head, and fled out of the temple. I was afraid that he would call me a poet. So I followed him in his flight . . . and as soon as we were out of range and could stop, I said, 'Tell me, cannot you get rid of your disease? You have been in my company less than two hours and you have talked more often like a poet than like a man. I am not surprised that the crowd pursues you with stones. I shall load my pockets with stones too, and whenever you begin to forget yourself I shall let blood from your head.' His expression altered, and he said, 'My dear young friend, I have been blessed like this before today. Whenever I go into the theatre to recite anything, the people's way is to welcome me with this kind of present.' "

Shortly afterwards, on another occasion, Eumolpus exclaims,

"Why, I was nearly flogged while I was washing, because I tried to go round the bathhouse and recite poetry to the people sitting in it; and I was thrown out of the bathroom as if it were the theatre."

It is not long before Eumolpus begins to take a dangerous interest in Giton, and this leads him into tragic conflict with Encolpius. A number of farcical scenes ensue in which the lovers Encolpius and Giton pretend to commit suicide in the tragic manner, and at one point Eumolpus, having gotten into a fight with one of the inmates of the lodging house, is set upon by the rest of them.

"All the household ran up and a crowd of drunken lodgers," says Encolpius. "I had a chance of punishing Eumolpus, so I shut him out and got even with the bully . . . . Meanwhile cooks and lodgers belabored him, now that he was locked out, and one thrust a spit full of hissing meat into his eyes, another took a fork from a dresser and struck a fighting attitude. Above all, a blear-eyed old woman with a very dirty linen wrap round her . . . took the lead, brought up a dog of enormous size on a chain and set him onto Eumolpus . . . . We saw everything through a hole in the folding doors . . . . I put my eyes to the chink and gorged myself on the miseries of Eumolpus like a dainty dish, and approved their prolongation. Then Bergates, the proprietor of the lodging house was disturbed at his dinner, and two chair-men carried him right into the brawl, for he had gouty feet. In a furious, vulgar voice he made a long oration against drunkards and runaway slaves, and then he looked at Eumolpus and said, 'What, most illustrious bard, was it you? Get away quick, you damned slaves, and keep your hands from quarreling.'"

After a while Eumolpus, Encolpius and Giton become reconciled with each other and the event is thus poetically related by Encolpius:

"I burst into tears and begged him to be friends again with me too . . . . 'Only he must remove all irritation from his mind, like a man of true culture and leave no scar. On the wild rough uplands the snow lies late, but when the earth is beautiful under the mastery of the plough, the light frost passes while you speak. Thus anger dwells in our hearts; it takes root in the savage, but glides over the man of learning.' "

Later on Encolpius and Giton, following the lead of Eumolpus, go on board a ship bound for Tarentum, the owner of which, much to the dismay of Encolpius, proves to be an honest man named Lichas, whom he had greatly wronged on a previous occasion, and from whom he and Giton had fled in great fear. Encolpius and his friends try to hide their identity by shaving their heads and eyebrows, painting their faces, and posing as the branded slaves of Eumolpus; but they are discovered after a lot of comical theatrics: a battle then ensues between their faction and the party of Lichas, and in the end a truce is established. Shortly afterwards a great storm arises and the ship founders. Lichas, who seems to be the only respectable character on board, is swept into the sea and drowned, but all the rascals, including Encolpius, Giton, Eumolpus, and a harlot named Tryphaena, manage to get safely ashore. "On the next morning," Encolpius relates, "I suddenly saw a man's body caught in a gentle eddy and carried ashore. I stopped gloomily and, with moist eyes, began to reflect upon the treachery of the sea. 'Maybe,' I cried, 'There is a wife waiting cheerfully at home for this man in a far-off land, or a son or a father, maybe, who know nothing of this storm; he is sure to have left someone behind whom he kissed before he went. So much for mortal men's plans, and the prayers of high ambition. Look how the man floats.' I was still crying over him as a perfect stranger when a wave turned his face towards the shore without a mark upon it and I recognized Lichas, but a while ago so fierce and so relentless, now thrown almost under my feet. Then I could restrain my tears no longer; I beat my breast again and again, and cried, 'Where is your temper and your hot head now? Behold: You are a prey for fish and savage beasts. An hour ago you boasted the strength of your command, and you have not one plank of your great ship to save you. Now let mortal men fill their hearts with proud imaginations if they will. Let misers lay out the gains they win by fraud for a thousand years. Lo! This man but yesterday looked into the accounts of his family property, and even settled in his own mind the very day when he would come home again. Lord, Lord, how far he lies from his consummation! But it is not the waves of the sea alone that thus keep faith with mortal men. The warrior's weapons fail him; another pays his vows to Heaven and his own house falls and buries him in the act. Another slips from his coach and dashes out his eager soul; the glutton chokes at dinner, the sparing man dies of want. Make a fair reckoning, and you find shipwreck everywhere.' "

These are the words of Encolpius, a puppet-actor who can be given any part to play, whether noble or ignoble; but they probably represent at the same time the thought and feeling of the author himself. The same is true of other passages in the *Satyricon*, wherever we meet with a poem, or with an eloquent declamation on some serious topic, such as the decline of art or culture, or the degradation and corruption of present-day society, or the tragic ironies inherent in the lot of mortals. In these utterances the author is putting forth his best artistic efforts, and from them we may judge not only his talent as a poet and critic, which is of a high order, but also the nature of his thought, and his outlook on the world in general. The spirit of Petronius is quite different from that of the Roman satirists, though basically no less elevated, owing to his broad and sympathetic understanding of human nature with all its frailties and its sorrows. But the satirists want to improve the world, or instruct it, or criticize it; while Petronius simply despairs of it. He is resigned to it. All he can make of contemporary society, as he sees it, is either comedy, which is everywhere *ostensibly* the main thing, or else, as we infer from some of the poems and utterances put into the mouths of negative characters, a sadness akin to that of tragedy in the contemplation of humanity in the large, or of the degradation of the society about him. The intention of Horace, in his own famous phrase, was *ridentem dicere verum*—to proclaim the truth, but to do so with a smile; that of Petronius, in his picturing of society, might be described as *vera dicentem ridere*— to get a laugh out of telling the truth, or rather by mimicking it. As for the truth itself, deplorable though it may be, there's no use in getting excited or indignant about it, he implies, because the world is full of human folly and depravity and nothing can be done about it. There is in Petronius a profound but latent pessimism, which springs from the cosmic disillusionment of a man of worldly experience living in a time and place where the degradation of men in society and politics was unusually conspicuous. He seems to be weighed down at times by a sense of weariness with the highly artificial and multifariously corrupt surroundings in which he lived, and to long for a simpler and saner world of honest men, which he can see only in the past, or far away, in a romantic light, and with a melancholy feeling of nostalgia. This is especially evident in some of the short poems which have come down quoted by early writers in the Latin Anthology presumably from the *Satyricon*, where they were probably uttered by such characters as Encolpius or Eumolpus against a background of farce. Since these poems reveal the mind of Petronius in various aspects, it is worth while to quote a few of them, as translated by Heseltine in the Loeb Library volume:

"My little house is covered by a roof that fears no harm, and the grape swollen with wine hangs from the fruitful elm. The boughs yield cherries, the orchards ruddy apples, and the trees sacred to Pallas break under the wealth of their branches. And now where the smooth soil drinks from the runnels of the spring, Corycian kale springs up for me and creeping mallows, and the poppy with promise of untroubled sleep. Moreover, if my pleasure is to lay snares for birds, . . . or draw out the quivering fish on slender line, so much deceit is all that is known to my humble fields. Go, then, and barter the hours of flying life for rich banquets. My prayer is that since at the last the same end waits for me, it may find me here, here call me to account for the time that I have spent.

"O seashore more sweet to me than life! Happy am I who may come at once to the lands I love. O beauteous day! In this country long ago I used to rouse the Naiads with my hands' alternate stroke. Here is the fountain's pool, there the sea washes up its weeds; here is a sure haven for quiet love. I have had life in full; for never can harder fortune take away what was given us in time overpast.

"For sooner will men hold fire in their mouths than keep a secret. Whatever you let escape you in your hall flows forth and beats at city walls in sudden rumours. Nor is the breach of faith the end. The work of betrayal issues forth with increase, and strives to add weight to the report. So was it that the greedy slave, who feared to unlock his knowledge, dug in the ground and betrayed the secret of the king's hidden ears. For the earth brought forth sounds, and the whispering reeds sang how Midas was even such a one as the tell-tale had revealed.

"The sailor, naked from the shipwreck, seeks out a comrade stricken by the same blow to whom he may bewail his fate. The farmer who has lost his crops and the whole year's fruits in the hail, weeps his sad lot on a bosom wounded like his own. Death draws the unhappy together; bereaved parents utter their groans with one voice, and the moment makes them equal. We too will strike the stars with words in unison; the saying is that prayers travel more strongly when united."

6

The *Satyricon* has rightly been called a novel, because it is a long story of personal adventure; but all that one can safely infer from that fact is that Roman literature before Apuleius produced one novel. We cannot point with certainty to the existence of any book of similar scope and character before the time of Petronius either in Greek or in Latin, although it is possible that one or two of a roughly similar nature, about which we know nothing, were written. If so, they too must have been rare birds in the woods of ancient literature and subject to the suspicion of having been hatched in a very special kind of nest. As for Apuleius, in the second century, his comic novel, the *Metamorphoses*, comes from a contemporary Greek original; and after his time no book of a similar nature appears to our knowledge in either Greek or Latin before the Middle Ages. When modern critics speak of such things as the development of prose fiction among the Romans, or the growth of the realistic, comic, or burlesque novel in ancient times, they assume unconsciously (under the influence of their chosen phraseology) the existence of something which cannot be established and very probably did not exist: namely a regular practice, or a definite tradition, in the writing of such books. The first question that needs to be asked is not *how* the ancient burlesque novel developed as a type, a question which begs another question and leads one only into the realm of vague and unsubstantiated hypothesis, but whether it developed at all or not; and the answer to that primary question, in my opinion, must be negative.

The most peculiar thing about the *Satyricon* is the length of the main narrative, which has reached novel proportions in both senses of that word. If it were a short story of the same nature, there would be no problem about where it belonged among literary types, because we know that many such stories of a burlesque or realistic or scandalously erotic nature were in circulation before the time of Petronius, both orally and in writing here and there, but especially on the stage in the form of low, farcical one-act mimes, which were very popular with the crowd of Remus at the theaters. The authors of these mimes, produced in quantity for the entertainment of crowds, were performing a utilitarian or commercial service, in response to a popular demand. They were not writing for literary reputation and it was not a reading public to which they addressed themselves. The libretto of a farcical mime was just about the lowest and least respected form of literature in existence, if indeed you could call it literature at all. Its place was on the stage, and it had to be brief. Hence it is very difficult to see what motive any man of letters could have for prolonging a farce of this kind, as Petronius has done, so far as to make an 800-page book of it. All the literary fashion of antiquity and all its respectability were dead set against such a procedure. The ancient critics had no use for prose fiction merely as entertainment apart from a context, whether it was long or short, comic or serious; and least of all would they have any respect for an author who purveyed it to the reading public in large quantities for its own sake as comedy or sensation, at the cost of a sustained literary effort—*magno conamine nugas*. The mountain labors and gives birth to nonsense. The genius of Petronius was not so ponderous nor so stupid; and he was no ordinary man. If he had wanted to write a book that would appear contemptible in the eyes of the literary world of his day, and one which nobody would take seriously as a literary product, he could not have done better than he did in writing about the farcical adventures of Encolpius and Giton. My thesis is, therefore, that Petronius intended his book to appear in just that light, as something beneath the notice of literary men; and that he had the best of reasons for so doing. Those reasons were special and personal, however, and not such as were prompted by precedent or contemporary literary fashion.

When a certain type of book is produced in quantity, as was the case with the Greek sentimental romances, we have to explain its genesis with reference to the cultural outlook and taste of large numbers of people. But when a book stands forth as something unique and without parallel, such as the *Satyricon*, we must conclude, by the same kind of historical logic, that its appearance is due to an idea or a motive which is as peculiar and individual as the book itself is rare in kind; and when we have explained that motive, we have explained the book.

7

Petronius wrote farce because he did not dare to write anything
else; and he wrote a long farce instead of a short one, in other
words a burlesque novel instead of a mime or a Milesian Tale,
because he needed a large framework, or container, into which
he could pour with some hope of impunity all the wealth of
literary, philosophical, and artistic expression that was welling
up within his fertile genius and demanding an outlet. The
framework into which he put this expression, which represented
in reality his most serious efforts and experiments in the field
of poetry, declamation, and criticism, had to be, at the same
time, a strong shield against the suspicion that he was engaged
in anything other than tomfoolery. In the center of Nero's
court, where destiny had placed him, and in that fierce light
that blazed around the throne of a jealous tyrant, for Petronius
to appear as a serious aspirant to any kind of literary or artistic
distinction was almost equivalent to signing his own death
warrant. All excellence of that kind was vested in the person of
his majesty, the great artifex, who had not yet perished, and
who would not allow any conceivable rival to coexist with him.
The epic poet Lucan was one of his victims, and Seneca was
another. Woe unto the ambitious and those who followed the
path of honest *industria*; it was by *inertia*—idleness, jesting,
triviality—that Petronius came into favor, as Tacitus says; and
it was only through *inertia*, or the pretense of it, that he could
hope to remain. The younger Pliny tells us in one of his letters
(III, 5) that in the last years of Nero's reign his uncle, the
famous naturalist, historian, and polymath, did not dare to
write on any subject other than formal grammar, because "a
despotic rule rendered dangerous every type of study that was
at all independent and lofty." [15] We know from Tacitus as well
as from the *Satyricon* itself that Petronius was by temperament
strongly averse to appearing serious about anything, even at
the moment of his death; and we know from the contents of

his book that he had much to give the world in the form of
serious poetry and criticism. He was compelled by circumstances either to keep quiet and not write anything, thereby
starving his artistic impulses, or, if he was to give expression to
that artistic talent, which he possessed in so large a measure,[16]
it could only be under the cover of a well-wrought disguise. The
farcical story of Encolpius served principally as that disguise,
but it also gave him the welcome opportunity of indulging his
native wit without restraint in the safe and agreeable business
of amusing the emperor and his low-minded associates. Thus
the first and only truly Roman novel was born of necessity and
special circumstances, springing up full grown all at once like
Athena from the head of Zeus. It was merely an accident of
time, place, and individual personality. It had no forebears and
no descendants. As for the influence of satire and other literary
forms and traditions upon the writing of the *Satyricon*, those
are secondary matters having nothing to do with the genesis
or *raison d'être* of the novel as such. Petronius makes use of
various types of subject-matter that were topical or prominent
in such antecedent literary forms as Roman satire, whether
Menippean or Lucilian, mime, and Milesian tale; but these for
him were simply building materials. Like so many bricks, they
tell us nothing about the architectural scheme of the *Satyricon*
as a whole and the purpose that guided the author in the
construction of it.

8

Fundamentally, the nearest thing in kind to the *Satyricon*, in
respect to its *raison d'être* as a form, and to the use of a long
rogue story told in the first person as a means of framing and
communicating a wide variety of serious poetry and eloquent
declamation on diverse philosophical or religious themes, is the
Arabic form of literature known as *maqāmāt* (plural of *maqāma*),
which was invented by Al-Hamadhānī of Ecbatana, d. A.D.
1008, who was known as the Wonder of the Age (*Badī ʿuʾ*

l-Zamān). *Maqāma*, says R. A. Nicholson (*A Literary History of the Arabs*, second edition, Cambridge 1930, p. 328) "is properly 'a place of standing'; hence, an assembly where people stand listening to the speaker, and in particular, an assembly for literary discussion . . . the word in its literary sense is usually translated by 'assembly,' or by the French *séance*." The famous *Assemblies* of Al Ḥarīrī (A.D. 1054–1122), fifty in number, are exactly the same in kind, as regards their structure and the nature of their contents as those of Al Hamadhānī, whose work served as a model for Al Ḥarīrī and whom, in the opinion of the Muslim world, he greatly excelled.[17] In Al Ḥarīrī's book each Assembly is independent of those that precede and follow and stands in the same paratactic relationship to others, unmotivated by any inner logic, as do the successive episodes in the *Satyricon* of Petronius. In each *maqāma* the narrator is the same Al Ḥārith, who speaks in the first person and tells of his aimless wandering from place to place, like Encolpius in the *Satyricon*; and in each place he meets with an unscrupulous rogue and impostor who proves always to be, when his assumed disguise is thrown off, one Abū Zayd of Serūj, closely analogous to the poet Eumolpus in Petronius. It is as if Encolpius, in each succeeding episode of the *Satyricon*, had described his meeting with the rogue Eumolpus and reported his marvelous poetic improvisations, and his eloquent declamations on all kinds of serious subjects, instead of introducing now and then such other declaimers and poetic virtuosos as Agamemnon at the beginning of our fragments. With Petronius the function of the burlesque rogue story is to shield the author against the suspicion of seriously exercising his poetic and artistic talents, as we have seen; but in the *maqāmāt* or *Assemblies* of Al Ḥarīrī the rogueries and impostures of Abū Zayd, which are regarded as of no consequence in themselves, enable him to exhibit his marvelous powers of poetic and declamatory improvisation on the most opposite and mutually exclusive topics and principles. He cannot be sincere but must play the role of a hypocrite and impostor in order to charm his audiences into giving him alms, as they never fail to do; but, once he has received the money, he throws off the mask and turns to such self-indulgence as gives the lie to much that he has proclaimed on opposite themes. In the *Assemblies*, as in the *Satyricon*, the main thing for which the form was invented was the display of poetic talent and eloquent declamation on serious subjects; but the two forms have no historical connection with each other, nor with the Menippean satire. They appear as remarkably similar, but widely separated constellations in the broad heavens of literary history, each invented independently by its author in accordance with his need for framing a variety of artistic displays in the way of poetry and eloquent declamation on ideal themes, not themes of mockery, such as prevail in the Menippean satire.

The Menippean satire, which the erudite Wilhelm Schmid compares with the Arabic *maqāmāt*[18] only because it combines prose and verse, differs profoundly from both the *Satyricon* and the *maqāmāt*, because it is satire. Schmid rightly observes, however, that such a mixing of prose and verse is not Greek but Oriental. It is significant that Menippus himself was a Syrian, and equally so that he was a Cynic who made it his business, in his σπουδαιογέλοιον, to flout all the respected conventions of the Greek world and to counter them with what was closest to elemental human nature and belonged to the folk primatively— in this case the mixture of prose and poetry. That was in defiance of the Greek Academy. In the Semitic world this mixture of prose and poetry was never taboo but was sanctioned in religion by its use in the Old Testament and in the Koran. It appears also in the *Arabian Nights*, although that book did not attain to respectability as literature among the Muslims until less than a century ago.[19] Poetry and prose succeed each other alternately throughout the *Consolation of Philosophy* by Boethius in the sixth century and in the thirteenth-century *chantfable*, *Aucassin et Nicolette*; but neither of these two books bears any resemblance otherwise to either the *maqāmāt* or

Menippean satire, and were uninfluenced by either. They are both spontaneous reversions, made long after the old Graeco-Roman canons of style had ceased to be influential, to what is natural and primitive in any dramatic narrative, the tendency to pass from prose to verse as the mood of the speaker becomes more impassioned and elevated in feeling. This natural tendency is more conspicuous in Lucilian satire as imitated by Petronius in chapter 5 than it is in the Menippean, and more characteristic of the *Satyricon* and of the *maqāmāt*, in the sense that it is declamation rising into verse on a serious subject, instead of mock-heroic verse intended to ridicule something or somebody. Petronius tells us that this, on the part of Lucilius, was a humble and unprententious kind of improvisation.[20] Mock-heroic verse predominates over sober poetical experimentation with Menippus, because his purpose is primarily satirical, and he is intent on raising a laugh as a means of making his criticism effective.[21] Petronius, to be sure, has a fair amount of mock-heroic verse, like Menippus, and he makes much of the sheer comedy in his rogue story throughout, which he enjoys, far more so than the authors of *maqāmāt*, who play it down. Petronius also has satire—what else is the *Cena Trimalchionis?* Or the will of Eumolpus read to the legacy hunters in chapter 141? And he has mime, all kinds of it, and Milesian tale, and parody of epic, and of tragedy, and of the ideal love story. In short, Petronius has just about everything; but his *Satyricon* as a whole cannot be explained in terms of any one of the forms just mentioned, nor any combination of them. It is not seriously emulative of any literary tradition but is shaped by the author's need (peculiar to the special circumstances in which he lived) for a safe place in which to experiment artistically with various types of poetry, rhetorical declamation, and criticism. For this purpose he flouts all recognized literary tradition by choosing as his medium of expression the most contemptible and least respected of all possible literary forms, that namely of a lengthy burlesque novel.

In respect to the underlying purpose of its inventor, the

Satyricon, as we have said, is very similar to the Arabic *maqāmāt*, much more so than to any other known form of literature; but the rogue story, which is common to both forms as a medium for the exploitation of serious poetry and declamation, plays a larger role with Petronius, and one differently oriented.

VI
Lucian's *Metamorphoses*

1

No COMPOSITION entitled *Metamorphoses* is listed among the writings of Lucian either in our manuscripts or in the modern handbooks of literature; but the lost Greek book which served as the source of the Latin *Metamorphoses* of Apuleius bore that title, and I have long been convinced, for reasons which will presently be outlined, that Lucian was the author of that original Μεταμορφώσεις. Its story is known to us from its derivatives. It tells how a young man named Lucius, while prying into the secrets of witchcraft as an earnest student of the subject of metamorphoses, was transformed into an ass and underwent many curious and comic adventures in that shape, until, finally, he was restored to human form by the eating of roses; such was the magical requirement. For convenience in referring to it, this story of Lucius, which is told in the first person, may be called the *Luciad*, without reference to any particular version of it.

2

The original Greek Μεταμορφώσεις was read by the patriarch Photius in the ninth century, who ascribes it to an author otherwise entirely unknown whom he calls Lucius of Patrae.

Photius tells us something about the nature and contents of this lost book and compares it with the extant Λούκιος ἢ Ὄνος of Lucian (henceforth cited as *Onos*), which he reckoned to be an epitome or a syncopated edition of the Μεταμορφώσεις of Lucius. A close-up comparative study of the two extant versions of the *Luciad*, namely the *Metamorphoses* of Apuleius and the Greek *Onos*, has led scholars to the well-founded conclusion, no longer disputed, that each of them is derived independently from the Greek Μεταμορφώσεις mentioned by Photius.[1]

The ascription of this work to an author named Lucius of Patrae is undoubtedly false; because Lucius of Patrae is the name of the protagonist in the story, according to the *Onos* (Lucius of Corinth in Apuleius, who otherwise often changes the names); and this Lucius, speaking in the first person, tells us that he was a "writer of histories and other things" (*Onos* 55), as well as an ass in both the literal and figurative sense of the word. Since no ancient author would write about himself in this way, at least no sophisticated author of an intentionally comic and burlesque story such as the *Luciad*, we are bound to infer that the principal character, Lucius of Patrae, who was only a dramatic fiction, was mistaken for the real author of the book who created him as the butt of his comedy. This confusion of the pretended narrator of the tale with the author himself, whether by Photius or by someone before him, could very easily be made by a hasty or uncritical reader, and the error is one that has often occurred in the history of fiction. St. Augustine made the same kind of mistake about the *Luciad* when, failing to distinguish between Lucius and Apuleius, he stated that Apuleius was changed into an ass, or if not, that he claimed to have been![2] Augustine could believe that Apuleius, his fellow countryman, would make such a claim as a matter of professional pride; because the reputation of Apuleius as a magician and thaumaturge had long been current in North Africa and he, together with Apollonius of Tyana, were regarded by some people, much to the bishop's displeasure, as rivals of Christ. It is because Augustine thinks about miracles very seriously, and in a spirit of belief, that he sees nothing funny about a man's being changed into an ass. What impresses him above all is the miracle *per se*, regardless of its motivation and the manner of its telling; and besides—*O deus meus*—he had no sense of humor. It was in a far different frame of mind, as anyone may see by reading the story in the *Onos*, or even in the mystical Apuleius, that the pagan author of the original *Metamorphoses* approached the subject of magical transformations. His spirit was ironical, and one of fun-making, if not positively satirical; and, whoever he may have been, he was certainly not a credulous miracle seeker named Lucius of Patrae proclaiming his own experiences as a student of magic.

3

The manuscript tradition of the *Onos*, its language and style in detail, and the rich vein of ironical humor with which it sparkles throughout, all point strongly to Lucian as the author of its original, the more so because Lucian is the only man known to us in the second century who wrote artistically in that humorous and satirical spirit. But before we can assign the original *Metamorphoses* to Lucian we must understand, more clearly and definitely than others in the past have understood, what the contents of that lost book must have been, and what its nature was as a whole. This can be inferred with reasonable certainty from a careful study of the two extant derivative versions, in the light of the few objective facts given us by Photius concerning the lost original, and with reference to literary conventions in the time of Apuleius and Lucian. The following is a literal translation of what Photius says about the lost Greek *Metamorphoses* (cod. 129):

Read, the *Metamorphoses* of Lucius of Patrae in several books. The style is lucid and correct, and one of studied charm. The author avoids affectation in the use of words, but makes an extravagant parade of the marvellous in his narrative, and is, one might say, another Lucian. His first two books at any rate are almost transcribed from Lucian's story called *Lucius or the Ass*, or else Lucian has copied from the chapters of Lucius. Indeed, Lucian appears to be the one who has copied, so far as we may guess; for which of the two writers is the older I am not able to learn. Apparently Lucian has thinned out the fuller chapters of Lucius, and, after omitting all that he did not think useful for his own purpose, has moulded the rest into one book, retaining the very words and syntax of the original, and has given the title *Lucius or the Ass* to what was stolen thence. Both books are full of mythical inventions and shameful indecency. But Lucian wrote his book for the purpose of deriding and satirizing Greek superstition, just as in his other works; whereas Lucius is in earnest. He (Lucius) believes in the metamorphoses of men into each other and of animals into men and conversely; and believing this, as well as the other idle talk and nonsense of ancient myths, he committed it to writing and made a book of it.

This testimony by Photius concerning the contents and nature of the lost Greek *Metamorphoses* has been variously interpreted, and has given rise to some strange and, as I believe, completely false inferences on the subject. Those inferences, which were based upon a too narrow and too literal interpretation of Photius' words without regard to the realities of literary history, and shaped, moreover, upon false analogies drawn from the title, had already become dogmas before the time when the interrelationships between the three versions of the *Luciad* became established by comparative study of the two extant versions; and they continued to be propagated afterwards when there was no longer any rational excuse for them. They are still found now and then in the handbooks. But if we agree, as I think we must, that both Apuleius and the author of the Greek *Onos* derived their texts independently from the Greek *Metamorphoses* falsely ascribed to Lucius, then we have some data of primary importance concerning the lost work, in the light of which we must be guided in our interpretation of the noncommittal or ambiguous phraseology of Photius. This makes a lot of difference—all the difference between historical plausibility on the one hand and downright absurdity on the other.

4

Before I wrote on this subject in 1920, it had always been assumed, and perfunctorily stated, that the Greek *Metamorphoses* consisted of a series of different stories, each of which involved a metamorphosis.[3] This belief rested on nothing more than a careless reading of the title as given by Photius (Μεταμορφώσεων λόγοι διάφοροι) interpreted on the false analogy of Ovid's *Metamorphoses* and other books of the same title. But neither the wording of the title, nor anything that Photius says or implies about the book, either requires or makes probable such an interpretation; and if one does interpret the title as referring to a series of different stories about transformations, then the kind of book whose existence in the second century we are thereby forced to assume, becomes, on closer consideration, a monstrosity without parallel in ancient literature. The first story, our *Luciad*, was a burlesque novel at least forty-five pages long, as we can infer with certainty from the extant derivatives. It had nothing to do with ancient mythology or with the kind of myths and sagas which are related in Ovid's *Metamorphoses*. To have added to that burlesque novel about Lucius either other novels, or stories, of a similar character featuring a metamorphosis, or anti-quarian myths like those in Ovid, or any other conceivable kind of metamorphosis story, would have resulted in a combi-nation of materials such as could not be paralleled elsewhere, and would have no conceivable meaning, function, or purpose as a book. The oldest manuscript of the *Onos*, written in the tenth century, contains a subscript at the end stating that the *Onos* is an epitome of the *Metamorphoses* of Lucius, which means of course an epitome of the entire *Metamorphoses*; and Photius himself in another part of his *Bibliotheca* refers to the book of Lucius in such a way as to imply that it was all one continuous story.[4] For these and other reasons which cannot be fully explained here, it is as certain as anything of the kind can be that the lost Greek *Metamorphoses* ascribed to Lucius of Patrae, like the Latin *Metamorphoses* which is derived from it, dealt in the main with only one story, namely that of Lucius changed into an ass.

The next question is, how long was this story, and in how many book divisions was it contained? When we add to the thirty-six-page Greek epitome (i.e., the *Onos*) only those episodes in the Apuleian version which, judging by the context, *must* have belonged in the original *Luciad*, we get a story barely fifty Teubner pages in length;[5] and in the light of this reconstruction, based on a careful comparison of the two derivatives, I conclude that the Greek *Metamorphoses*, like the *True History* of Lucian, probably consisted of only two books; although it could have extended to three if we allow no more than seventeen or eighteen pages to a book. Photius often uses the loose expression "several books" (λόγοι διάφοροι) when he does not know, or does not wish to commit himself concerning the number of books into which a work before him is divided. In such cases, as in this one, the number of book divisions was probably not indicated on the title page, and the patriarch did not take the trouble to thumb through his volume in order to find out just where a particular composition ended. Moreover, since he had already read the same story in Lucian's *Onos*, in the same words and syntax, except for omissions, it is unlikely that he finished reading even the second book, since he considered the story an indecent one, and the author of it a fool.

5

Since the *Luciad*, as represented by the original *Metamorphoses*, was substantially, and to a large extent even verbally, the same story as that preserved in the Lucianic *Onos*, it must have been of the same comic and playfully ironical character. The long-discredited, though occasionally recurring notion that it was a serious or superstitious piece of writing, that it was wonder-

seeking in tone, rather than comic or satirical, or, in short, that
the spirit of the narrative differed in any way from that of the
Luciad in our extant versions, rests entirely upon the misleading statement of Photius that Lucius of Patrae wrote in a
serious vein and believed in the reality of magic transformations. Now Lucius of Patrae was indeed credulous and superstitious; but Lucius of Patrae was not, as Photius supposed,
the author of the Greek *Metamorphoses*; he was merely the
principal character speaking in the first person, a character
intentionally represented as credulous and as a writer, by the
facetious author in the background. In this rôle, Lucius undoubtedly professed his serious belief in magic and magical
transformations quite as explicitly in the Greek *Metamorphoses*
as he does on repeated occasions both in the *Onos* and in
Apuleius. That was part of the fun, and of the satire. Photius
noticed those explicit declarations of faith and curiosity on the
part of Lucius; and it is probable that they were more fully
developed and more conspicuously exhibited in the forefront
of the original story, which he read, than in either of its two
derivatives. The epitomator would naturally leave them out in
the *Onos* because they did not advance the action of the story,
which was probably all that interested him, hence the change
in title; and Apuleius, although he indicates the presence of
conversations relating to magic in two different places where
they are absent in the *Onos*, still does not develop those
conversations, but cuts them short, and possibly alters them,
in order to introduce in their stead some marvelous tales and
anecdotes of his own concerning witchcraft, including the relatively long stories of Aristomenes in Book 1 and of Thelyphron
in Book 2. Photius says that Lucius believed in the metamorphoses of men into each other. This must be a reference to
the Pythagorean doctrine of the transmigration of souls, with
which Lucian has so much fun in his dialogue entitled *The
Cock or the Dream* and elsewhere. Although no mention of this
doctrine is made either in the *Onos* or in Apuleius' version, yet
it is probable that some reference was made to it in the Greek

Metamorphoses, because Photius mentions it first among the articles of Lucius' belief.

Since the *Onos* is a word-for-word reproduction of the lost original, except for omitted material, and since Apuleius is everywhere inserting new material into the framework of the main story, and sometimes alters or expands that story for his own purposes, it is the *Onos* upon which we must principally rely in order to form a just idea concerning the nature of the original *Metamorphoses*.

The keynote of Lucius' character (for unlike Encolpius he has a character) is his περιεργία, his curiosity—the same state of mind that inspired Lucian himself in the *True History*, so he playfully tells us, to sail beyond the Pillars of Hercules on a voyage of exploration into unknown seas. But the curiosity of Lucius is of a particular kind. He is an investigator of magic, and, more especially, of the phenomenon of metamorphosis, as he tells us explicitly again and again. "I was very eager," he says, "to hunt up one of those women who know how to perform magical operations, and to see some marvelous sight, such as a flying man [like the Hyperborean in Lucian's *Lover of Lies* 13], or one being changed into stone." And again he says to the maid Palaestra, whose intimacy he had sought for that purpose: "Dearest, do please show me your mistress in the act of transforming herself, or better still, perform some magic yourself, so I may see one form after another appearing before me." So Lucius is an eager student of metamorphoses; and it is with ironical reference to the subject of metamorphoses in general, and not to separate stories about change, that the book gets its title.[6] This title, understood in the generic sense, implies that the author is telling us about the subject of metamorphoses as exemplified in the case of Lucius. Such was the leading motif of the original *Luciad*.

6

It is in the theater at Thessalonike, on the occasion of a big and varied spectacle, that Lucius the ass, himself one of the principal exhibits, suddenly regains his human form by the eating of roses. Being in danger from the excited crowd, Lucius runs up to the governor of the province, who is present in a front seat, and after telling his story asks to be protected. The following conversation ensues (*Onos* ch. 55): " 'Tell me your name,' says the governor, 'and that of your parents, and your kinsmen, if thou claimest to have any, and your city.' And I said, 'my father . . . .' " Here there is a small break in the text, after which Lucius continues: " 'and my name is Lucius, and my brother's name is Gaius, and our last two names are the same. I am a writer of histories and other things; and he, my brother, is a poet of elegies and a good prophet. Our home is Patrae in Achaea.' When the governor heard this he exclaimed, 'You are the scion of men very dear to me, men who have entertained me as guest in their house and honored me with gifts; and I know very well that, being of that stock, you tell no lies.' Then he jumped up from his seat, threw his arms around me, kissed me a lot, and took me home to his own house." Soon thereafter his brother Gaius arrived bringing him money and other provisions, the governor publicly acquitted him of the charge of being a magician, and the two brothers engaged a ship to take them home, and put their luggage on board. Here the story might well have ended, but the author was not content to take leave in that sober fashion. He adds, on the last page, an episode that is more farcical than anything that precedes. Lucius decides to visit the woman who had been enamored of him when he was an ass, supposing that he would be more attractive to her now that he was a man. At first the woman welcomes him, pleased by the novelty of his transformation; but when she finds that he is only human in a sexual way, she scorns him and reviles him, saying that he has been "metamorphosed from a handsome and useful beast into an ape." "Then she called her servants and ordered them to pick me up and carry me out of the house; and I was shoved outdoors naked and beautifully wreathed and perfumed, and I embraced the naked earth and slept with her that night. As soon as dawn came, I ran naked to the ship and told my brother about my ludicrous experience. Then, when a favorable wind began to blow, we left the city and sailed thence, and in a few days I arrived home. Thereupon I sacrificed to the savior gods and set up thank offerings, for having at long last been rescued (and cured), not from looking into the back end of a dog, as the (medical) proverb has it, but from the curiosity of an ass." [7]

It should be obvious from the passages above quoted, wherein Lucius, the professed student of metamorphoses, is represented as a writer of histories and the brother of a prophet, belonging to a prominent Roman family intimate with the provincial governor, that in the original story there was a positive satirical tendency, even though that tendency was not everywhere in evidence, being overshadowed in most places by preoccupation with the comic narrative.

Nothing could be more surprising or startling to an ancient reader of fiction, especially burlesque fiction, than to find the leading character in a story, he who was the butt of the farce, a Roman of high social standing. All the other heroes and heroines of ancient romance that I can think of, even in Latin literature (apart from the heroic sagas belonging to early Roman history), are either Greek or Oriental, never Roman, and never literary figures like Lucius and his brother Gaius. Whether the satire was directed against a real and particular Roman writer living in Patrae, or whether it was only against superstitious people in general, of which high-born Romans with their credulous attitude towards miracle-lore, and especially Pythagorean lore, were thought of as being typical, is a question which I cannot answer for myself with any strong feeling of conviction. The particularities, painstakingly, but only partially, given about Lucius and his family in the passage above quoted, suggest that the satire was directed against a definite person, and some critics have taken that stand quite positively.[8] I am inclined to doubt, however, that the satire was personal, because there are so few personal allusions and the author shows no hostility to Lucius as an individual man other than what is implied by his naïve curiosity and his belief in metamorphoses. The names Lucius and Gaius seem to be chosen rather for their generic significance than as referring to real and particular persons. Both were used together by the Roman jurists to indicate typical Roman citizens in hypothetical cases, like John Doe, or Smith or Jones in English.[9] In any case it seems certain that the author of our story thought of prominent Romans as being on the whole a credulous lot of men, among whom one would naturally expect to find just such a miracle-monger as Lucius. Otherwise he would not, contrary to all convention in such matters, single out a Roman of high standing as the subject of his sport.

7

Now we happen to know of one Greek writer, a man famous for his satirical wit, whose attitude towards Romans in high place was at times very similar to that which is shown by the author of the lost Greek *Metamorphoses*. That writer is Lucian. In his famous report on Alexander of Abonoteichos, the false prophet who imposed upon the ignorant and superstitious multitudes of Asia Minor with his manifold quackeries and his pretense of being semi-divine and akin to Pythagoras as well as to the god Asclepius, Lucian speaks as follows concerning the enormous success of Alexander's oracles: "Now all this took place within the boundaries of Ionia, Cilicia, Paphlagonia and Galatia. But when the fame of the oracle spread abroad into Italy and fell upon the city of the Romans, every man there tried to get ahead of his neighbor in consulting it. Some went in person, others sent their representatives; and especially prominent in this activity were those Romans who were the most powerful and influential, and who held the highest rank in the city. Foremost and chief among these was Rutillianus. He was a gentleman in most respects, and one who had held many high offices in the government; but, when it came to matters relating to the supernatural, he was mentally quite ill and would believe anything, however outlandish . . . . Being a friend of many important men, he went around telling them what he had heard from his envoys to the oracle, at the same time adding some things of his own. And so it was that he threw the city into a turmoil of excitement, and most of the men about the court were roused and eager to have their own fortunes also told by the oracle." When Rutillianus asked Alexander what teacher he should choose for his young son, the reply was "Pythagoras"; and when the boy died a day or two later, Alexander was greatly embarrassed and knew not what to say to his critics. But Rutillianus—bless his soul (ὁ βέλτιστος)—came gallantly to the aid of Alexander with some sophistry of his own, to explain what the oracle had really meant. It referred to education in the *next* life. "How can we blame Alexander," asks Lucian, "if he chose to work on simpletons of that kind?" One of the questions that Rutillianus put to the oracle was, "Where did my soul come from?" and the answer was, "First you were Achilles, after that you were Menander, next, the man you are now, and hereafter you will be a sunbeam. And you will live one hundred and eighty years." Rutillianus, however, so Lucian informs us, did not wait for the promise of this oracle to be fulfilled, but died at the age of seventy.

It is clear that in Lucian's mind the Roman nobility, as a class, were just the kind of persons who would be most likely to believe in the reality of all kinds of miracles, especially those that involved a change of form or the transmigration of a soul from one body into another. Hence, if Lucian had wanted to write a comical story with a satirical tendency in it, about a credulous student of metamorphoses, it would be very natural for him to choose a Roman of high social position, like Lucius, as his principal character. The *Luciad*, like the passage in the *Alexander* above quoted, shows a satirical attitude on the part of its author towards the credulity of Romans in high places.

8

The *Onos* has come down to us under the name of Lucian in
the oldest and best manuscripts of that author's works, and
Photius in the ninth century read it in such a manuscript. He
tells us that it agreed word for word, except for omissions, with
another Greek book called *Metamorphoses*. This means, so far
as the testimony of tradition goes, either that Lucian stole his
text of the *Onos* from the work of another unknown satirist,
whose way of thinking and writing was very much the same as
his own, or else that he wrote the original *Metamorphoses*, of
which the *Onos* is an epitome or an abridged edition, probably
by a later editor. It has often happened in the transmission of
ancient books, as in the case of Xenophon of Ephesus, or of
Aelian's *Varia Historia*, that what has come down to us under
the author's name is only an abridgement of his original work.
The same must be true in the case of the *Onos*. If this work is
Lucianic, as the tradition says, it must be an abridgement, not
of an unknown writer's composition, but of one written by
Lucian himself, namely the *Metamorphoses*. It is extremely
unlikely that Lucian, who is the most original genius among
the sophistic writers of his age, would have copied out another
man's composition word for word and represented it as his own.
And even if you could imagine him doing such a thing, there
would be the further difficulty of explaining why, in making the
epitome, he concentrated on the bare action and left out just
that kind of thing which was most essential to the satirical
meaning of the book as a whole, namely, the title *Metamorphoses*, the conversation of Lucius with his fellow travelers at
the beginning concerning magic, the banquet at Abroea's house,
where there was further talk of the same kind, and Lucius'
battle with the metamorphosed goatskins on his return home
from that banquet.[10] This is the kind of thing that Lucian with
his satirical turn of mind would be most likely to retain. The

adventure with the goatskins in particular was an important part of the motivation in the original story, and one of the wittiest of all the episodes.

Titles given to books in ancient times are notoriously fluctuating and uncertain. The title or titles under which the original *Luciad* appeared in the time of Photius and before can only be surmised, but the possibilities are numerous. It may have been Λούκιος ἢ περὶ μεταμορφώσεων on the analogy of the *Alcyon* (Ἀλκυὼν ἢ περὶ μεταμορφώσεως), and this might then have been misread as Λουκίου περὶ μ., thereby assigning the authorship to Lucius. Double titles of the kind here assumed for the *Metamorphoses* occur frequently in the writings of Lucian. Other possible titles, from which the authorship of Lucius could have been wrongly inferred, are Λούκιος ἢ μεταμορφώσεις (which seems to me more probable than any of the others in view of the title of the epitome), and Λουκίου μεταμορφώσεις (meaning the transformations undergone by Lucius). The editor of the abbreviated edition, Λούκιος ἢ Ὄνος, substituted the word *Onos* for *Metamorphoses*, probably because he thought that the subject-matter of the book, objectively viewed, was better indicated by that word than by the more abstract title *Metamorphoses*. A very similar substitution, *Asinus aureus*, must have appeared on some manuscripts of the *Metamorphoses* of Apuleius in the time of St. Augustine; for he says that the book was inscribed with that title, and the archetype from which all our manuscripts are derived, an edition made, or critically emended, by one Sallustius at Rome in the year 395, bore the title *Metamorphoses*, taken over by Apuleius from the Greek original. The mistaking of Lucius for the author of the Greek *Metamorphoses* might have been due to a misreading of one of the titles above suggested; but to me it seems more probable that the mistake was made by someone who read the text, narrated by Lucius in the first person, in a manuscript in which the real author's name, Lucian, did not appear on the title page, owing to the fact that the *Metamorphoses* was only one in a series of works by Lucian, perhaps the last, and that

the manuscript contained works by other authors along with
those of Lucian. The reader may not have known where the
writings of Lucian ended and one by another author began.

9

Some critics have taken the view that the manuscript tradition
is wrong, that the *Onos* was ascribed to Lucian only by error,
and that Lucian had nothing to do with the composition of
either the *Onos* or its original. The misapprehensions of these
critics concerning the content and nature of the original
Metamorphoses, which we have attempted to set right, prevented them from assigning *that* work to Lucian; and they
denied Lucianic authorship to the *Onos* itself either because
they could not believe that Lucian would plagiarize another
man's work word for word, or because the style in which the
Onos is written, although Atticistic in the main, is more informal and admits more *koine*, Ionic, and poetic usages in
grammar and vocabulary than do the other writings of Lucian.
These so-called vulgarisms may be due in part to the epitomator; but the principal reason why the *Onos* is not written in
a highly finished Attic style, uniform with that of the philosophical dialogues and the sophistic essays, is that a style of
that kind, which is epideictic, was not appropriate for a comic
prose narrative, or for one that dealt with a trivial, non-
academic theme. That was a matter of convention and literary
tradition, not an indication that the author could not write
good Attic and was therefore someone other than Lucian. Style
must be adapted to subject-matter, even by Lucian. The style
that was traditionally suited to a story such as the *Luciad* was
easy-going and informal, allowing much at times that would be
avoided in the more academic genres in the way of colloquial
usage, poetic or Ionic vocabulary (due partly to tradition,
partly to the mock-heroic spirit of the narrative), non-Attic
words or constructions in everyday use, and paratactic structure. Apuleius called this style the *sermo Milesius*, presumably

because it was characteristic of the *Milesian Tales* of Aristides and Sisenna. For us, it is exemplified, in varying degrees and aspects, by the *Life* and *Fables* of Aesop in their oldest extant recension and, in Latin, by the novels and comic novellas of Petronius and Apuleius. The extent to which non-Attic, poetic, Ionic, or *koine* elements are admitted in this narrative Greek style may vary a great deal with the author and the subject; but the essential thing about it is its informality and its independence of the severe Attic standards which prevailed among ambitious writers of philosophical dialogue, sophistic orations and essays, and sober histories. The traditional background of this novella-style, or *sermo Milesius*, was the Ionic λόγος as it appears in Herodotus. This included, broadly speaking, two kinds of narration: history as an informative record of past events; and the novella or short story of personal experience, which appeared in writing only within the context of a history, but which had been cultivated orally, in all probability, before the time of Herodotus. Both branches of the λόγος originated in, and were shaped by, the Ionic-epic tradition of narrative, which retained many poetic features; but the branch that was history migrated, so to speak, to Athens, where it became thoroughly restylized, after which it was written mainly in the classical Attic dialect or in an approximation to it. Meanwhile the λόγος as novella or fable had no stylistic cultivation in the Attic tradition, because it was normally only part of a context. Its style was shaped chiefly by its context, which was usually Attic and learned in Hellenistic times, and varied with individual writers; but when it appeared as something apart by itself and without a context, as in the *Onos* and in the Aesopic fables in collections, the idea of traditional literary propriety affected it, and novella and fable tended to acquire a style of their own, one which was influenced by that of the Ionic prototype.

It was because they ignored what W. Schmid calls the principle of "mimische Erzählung" in the *Onos*, that is the necessary adaptation of style to subject-matter, that the nineteenth-

century editors of Lucian athetized this composition, along
with many others in the Lucianic corpus, on the ground that
its language was not sufficiently in line with Lucian's Atticism
as they knew it in the dialogues, and in the philosophical and
oratorical essays. But the Lucianic peculiarities of thought
and expression in the *Onos*, as in some other writings of Lucian
that were once branded as spurious but now regarded as
genuine, are so numerous and so striking that no one who
weighs them judiciously can doubt that they originated with
Lucian.[11] Since we cannot assign the epitome to him, that is,
the *Onos*, we are bound to conclude, in consideration both of
the manuscript tradition and the nature of the text, its language
and thought, that the original *Metamorphoses* was written by
Lucian. No other explanation will account for the facts as we
know them today.

10

The contents of the original story as told by Lucian can be
reconstructed in outline with reasonable certainty on the basis
of the *Onos*, supplemented by the substance of certain chapters
in Apuleius. The story was about as follows:

A young Roman of high birth named Lucius makes a journey
to Thessaly, bearing with him a letter of introduction from a
sophist at Patrae to a citizen of Hypata whose name is
Hipparchus. On the way he falls in with some travelling companions whose homes are in Hypata. These men tell him about
the miracles performed by Thessalian witches; and Lucius,
listening eagerly and credulously, declares his belief in the
reality of various kinds of metamorphoses, including the Pythagorean variety, and is fired with enthusiasm at the prospect
of actually seeing something of the kind while in Thessaly. After
arriving in Hypata and spending the night with his host
Hipparchus, he goes about town in search of a witch, at first
without any success. At length he meets with a woman who
recognizes him, speaks to him, telling him that she is Abroea,

an intimate old-time friend of his mother, and invites him to stay at her house. Lucius does not feel free to accept this invitation, and when Abroea learns that he is staying with Hipparchus, she warns him against the wiles of the latter's wife Pamphile (in Apuleius, not named in the *Onos*). "By all means beware of *her*," says Abroea, "for she is a formidable enchantress, who is lustful and sets her eye upon every young man. If one does not yield to her, she avenges herself by the exercise of her magical arts. Ere now she has metamorphosed many persons into beasts, and some she has utterly destroyed." On hearing this Lucius, far from being alarmed, is delighted with the news and hurries home, thinking only of how he may contrive to learn some of Pamphile's secrets, and to see her in action. For this purpose, he decides to make love to Pamphile's maidservant, Palaestra, on the principle that servants always know their master's affairs. And, besides, as the student in *Faust* wisely observes, "the hand that wields the broom on Saturdays will best on Sundays fondle and caress." Lucius thereafter becomes intimate with Palaestra. A few days later he is invited to dinner at Abroea's house. Just what the subject of conversation was on that occasion we cannot be quite sure, since the episode is omitted in the *Onos*; but in Apuleius it turns about the machinations of witches, their lustful propensities, and their habit of transforming themselves and others into various shapes. It is past midnight when Lucius returns home in a somewhat tipsy condition. On approaching the house of his host, he sees three men beating against the door and trying to break in. Believing them to be robbers, Lucius attacks them with his sword, and after a terrific battle slays all three. Being aroused by the tumult, Palaestra lets him in and immediately explains to him what has happened. Those three men were not robbers, nor even human beings, but only goatskins which, by a curious mistake, had been brought to life by Pamphile's arts and were being impelled by magical attraction to come into her presence. Pamphile had taken a fancy to a young Boeotian lad and wanted to fetch him to herself. In order to accomplish this, she needed something that came from his person, such as hair or fingernails. She had sent Palaestra to the barber shop that same afternoon in order to pick up some of the young man's hairs, but Palaestra, being driven away by the suspicious barber, and not daring to return to her mistress empty-handed, had clipped some goat hairs off three wineskins hanging in a shop window and had given these to her mistress in place of the young man's hairs. Pamphile performed her magic operations upon these goat-hairs, with the result that the three goatskins from which they had been taken became animated and were beating against her door just at the time when Lucius happened to come stumbling home. Upon hearing this account of the miracles performed by Pamphile, Lucius becomes more eager than ever to see her in action, and so begs Palaestra to give him the opportunity to do so. He had become so preoccupied with his love affair, as we are told in the *Onos*, that he had almost forgotten the purpose of it, and this incident, omitted in the *Onos*, served to renew and to stimulate his curiosity. A few days later Palaestra announces to him that her mistress, having failed to bring the young Boeotian *to herself*, has decided to take the form of a bird and fly to him; and Lucius is enabled by Palaestra to witness this transformation. Pamphile rubs herself with a certain ointment, utters an incantation, is changed into an *owl* (as Peregrinus, according to a similar jest by Lucian, was changed into a *vulture* at his death), and flies out the window. Thereupon Lucius begs Palaestra to change him into a bird likewise; "for," says Lucius, "I wanted to learn by actual experiment whether, if changed into a bird, I should also have the soul of a bird." Palaestra complies with his wishes, but in her haste gives him the wrong flask of ointment, with the result that Lucius is metamorphosed into an ass instead of into a bird. Palaestra tries to console him by telling him that he has only to eat some roses in order to regain human form. But since there are no roses at hand, Lucius will have to spend the night in the stable with his own horse and another ass; and Palaestra will bring him roses the first thing in the morning.

During the night robbers break into Hipparchus' house and, on leaving, carry away Lucius and the other animals. From that time on Lucius passes into the hands of one master after another and undergoes many comical adventures, until finally he is brought into the theater at Thessalonike, where he is changed back into a man, makes known his identity to the governor of the province by whom he is befriended, and, after the last very farcical adventure, is brought home in the end by his brother Gaius, a poet of elegies and a good soothsayer.

11

Such in broad outline was the story in Lucian's *Metamorphoses*. Its length in all probability was about the same as that of the author's *True History*, although it may have exceeded the latter by as much as eight or ten pages. The *True History* is forty-three pages long in the Teubner text.

Lucian was not the man to write a *long* novel; but there can be no doubt that he was uncommonly fond of telling a witty or a romantic story for the entertainment of his readers, whenever he could do so under the guise of ridiculing superstition or credulity, or of making a serious point or criticism of some kind, so as not to soil his academic gown of respectability by indulgence in mere fiction for its own sake. So long as he has that shield up to ward off the disgrace of seeming to be trivial, he can and does give us all kinds of interesting stories, fascinating either for their wit or only for their novelty. Good taste required him to make his stories short, but Lucian knew well how to interest the average reader of his day and ours, and he is the only educated Greek writer of his time, known to us, who dares to do so. He was the Voltaire of his age; but unlike the great Frenchman who was surrounded by wits similar to his own, he stood alone among his fellow professionals as a man who lived and thought in the present, was aware of it, and had something to say about it. Compared with Lucian, the other sophists of the time, such men as Maximus of Tyre and Aelius

Aristides, have little or nothing in their substance which could interest a reader either of their day or ours. They are essentially word-workers. All their brains and learning are sacrificed on the altar of their style, whereby they try to speak in words and phrases, and to a large extent also on topics, whose currency and reality were four or five hundred years removed from the realities of their own day. Lucian belonged to the guild of these sophists professionally and could do anything they did as well or better than any of them; but he had too much common sense and originality to confine his literary efforts to the empty and arid kind of verbal gesturing which was fashionable with them and their audiences throughout the Roman world. As a sophist, he held his head up, and the artistry of his style was unexcelled; but he saw no harm in speaking about something interesting at the same time, and his mind was such that, unlike the others, he could hardly help doing so. On one occasion he discovered to his surprise and chagrin, so he tells us (*Zeuxis* 1–2), that his audience was so greatly pleased with the novelty of his ideas and the charm of his unusual subject-matter that they had obviously taken no heed of the fine Attic style in which it was presented, the exquisite choice of words, the rhythms, the subtle nuances of thought, and the studied harmony that per-vaded the whole. "I have cast a bag of pearls among them," he says in effect, "and they admire the bag. I give them a little relish in the way of novelty along with a banquet of art, and what they admire and attend to is only the relish."

In the second century after Christ the outlook of men upon the world was profoundly romantic.[12] A spirit of wonder was abroad, a sense of dreamlike unreality. Men lived in the twilight of the ancient culture, oblivious to the present or the future save for the miracles or the revelations, religious or scientific, that might come out of its gathering darkness, gazing in ad-miration upon the past, which they saw through a golden haze without understanding its values, and wandering about, as it were, in a petrified forest filled with the giant figures of classical times. A great fondness for what is strange, or supernatural, or

far-away, or new, or curious, whether in the realm of nature
or of human experience, reveals itself in almost all the thought
and literary expression of the time. We see it in the ambitious
Atticism and archaism of fashionable writers, in the restless
seeking after a spiritual or an ontological revelation in philosophy, religion or magic, in the multiplication of books about
the supposed marvels of nature, in the romances of love and
adventure, and, what concerns us here more especially, in the
folktales of various kinds and tales about the supernatural,
which appear in literature abundantly for the first time, though
under different pretexts, in the writings of Apuleius and Lucian.

It is in the works of these two authors especially that the
groundswell of popular interest in romantic lore and folklore,
mounting in the second century, breaks at last through the
upper crust of a literature that had long kept it hidden, or at
any rate much less in evidence. Within the bounds of the formal, respected literature of antiquity, there was no recognized
place for dramatic prose fiction on its own account; hence that
fiction had to come under the aegis of something else if it was to
be authored by an ambitious or scholarly writer. Lucian
purveys his stories, which he and his readers must have enjoyed
on their own account, in the guise of satire, or the ridiculing of
superstition, or the illustration of a philosophical idea; but
Apuleius, a Roman writer from the province of Africa, is much
less careful about the wearing of the academic gown. His state
of mind is more closely akin to that of the people whom Lucian
ridicules. It is like that of his fellow Romans Pliny and Aulus
Gellius, dwelling in a spirit of admiration or credulity upon the
very things that Lucian makes sport of as frauds or super-
stitions: the long white beard of the philosopher Euphrates,
which is so becoming and so suggestive of wisdom and sanctity
(Pliny, *Ep.* I, 10; cf. Lucian, *The Lover of Lies* 5, and often
elsewhere); how a Pythagorean philosopher laid the ghost in a
haunted house at Corinth (Pliny, *Ep.* VII 27; Lucian, *op. cit.*
31; and if you don't believe it, ask Tibius the janitor if ever you
go to Corinth); and that good and wonderful man, Peregrinus

Proteus (Gellius, *Noct. Act.* XII, 11), whom Lucian denounces as a charlatan and, incidentally, as a patricide. Apuleius tells us outright at the beginning of his *Metamorphoses* that he will charm our ears with a series of stories in the unpretentious Milesian style, if we will but condescend to read his book. He writes subjectively, and the spirit of belief and wonderment and delight in which he tells his strange or miraculous tales is more like that of Lucius the credulous student of metamorphoses than of Lucian the satirist. At times, indeed, he even identifies himself with the character Lucius. But though he lets the bars of formality down thus far, farther than any other educated writer of antiquity whose work has survived to us, yet even so Apuleius has not dared to let his book stand forth before the world as nothing more than fiction for its own sake as entertainment, unredeemed by any show of serious purpose. He had to give it *some* kind of formal ballast, but the satirical orientation of the original *Luciad* was not in his mood. He was not a satirist by temperament in spite of his lively sense of humor and his skill in comedy. Rather he was, fundamentally, a serious-minded mystic and a seeker after hidden things, or a revelation, like the great majority of men in his day whose outlook on the world he reflects more truly than almost any other pagan writer. Hence, in place of the original burlesque ending of the *Luciad*, he substituted in his eleventh book an entirely different kind of ending, which consists in a lofty and elaborate description of the mysteries of Isis, in which it is suggested, though only in passing and by an afterthought, that Isis alone has been able to rescue Lucius from the consequences of his youthful folly and the blind vicissitudes of Fortune. His previous experience, we are led to infer from one or two passages, was only a preparation for his initiation into the mysteries. In reality, however, this eleventh book furnishes no key to the meaning of the *Metamorphoses* as a whole or to the author's purpose in writing it. Like many other additions to, or digressions from, the main story, including the tale of Cupid and Psyche, it is an independent artistic unit by itself, having no real inner connection with the ten books which precede it. The purpose of Apuleius in adding this chapter on the mysteries to the *Metamorphoses* was only to give to that book as a whole the *appearance* of some weight or some serious purpose. Thus the gesture by which the Roman writer seeks to redeem his book from the appearance or the reproach of unbecoming frivolity is contrived only in a mechanical way, by adding something from without, instead of weaving into it and its foundations, as Lucian does, a philosophical or a satirical idea of which the substance is illustrative and to which it is theoretically subordinate.[13]

In conclusion, let us consider once more how fiction is managed in Lucian. His *Toxaris* is taken up mainly with ten different stories of ideal or tragic adventure, each of them relating to the mutual devotion of a pair of friends, five of them featuring Greek characters, the other five Scythian. Each of these stories is a miniature romance in itself, and their value as romantic stories far outweighs the author's pretense that they are told only as illustrations of what friendship amounts to among Greeks and Scythians respectively. Lucian has found a convenient philosophical peg on which to hang a string of interesting stories; but his philosophizing in dialogue form is only a necessary pose with which no sophist could afford to dispense. In the dialogue entitled *The Lover of Lies* Lucian, under the guise of ridiculing superstition, treats his readers to such interesting folktales as that about the magician's apprentice, who got into trouble with his water-carrying stick, about the haunted house at Corinth, and about the sorcerer who rid the countryside of snakes in the manner of the Pied Piper of Hamlin —all the snakes were charmed away except for one old serpent who lagged behind on account of age. The *True History* is primarily a comic romance, in which the satirical tendency, according to Lucian himself in his preface, is a thing of only secondary importance, meant to give some weight to an otherwise too frivolous composition. Lucian's statement, in substance, is as follows: "Just as athletes do not exercise all the time, but consider it important, even for their bodily welfare, to get rest and relaxation at regular intervals, so in the case of those who are concerned with literature, it is fitting that, after prolonged occupation with more serious reading, one should relax his mind and take a vacation. Such a vacation may be be profitable when one reads something that is not merely clever and entertaining, but something which at the same time has a further meaning in it." And here Lucian goes on to explain very briefly the satirical implications of the *True History*. It is exactly in this light that we must view Lucian's purpose in writing the original *Metamorphoses*, wherein there may have been a similar preface; it was a satire on superstition incidentally, but primarily an entertaining story told by the author while on a literary vacation. Lucian is often, as in the *Dialogues of the Gods*, much less concerned with the satirical implications of his work than with its value as comic entertainment or as artistic mime. He claims to have, and does have, much of importance to contribute in the way of ideas and criticism as well as in artistic writing; but, along with all that, he is also, as one of his detractors maliciously observed, "quite serious in the business of raising a laugh"—σπουδαῖος εἰς τὸ γελασθῆναι.[14]

VII
Apuleius and
His *Metamorphoses*

1

Apuleius was born some time near the year A.D. 124 at Madaura, a small city in the Roman province of Africa, corresponding to the modern village of Mdaurush in Algeria. His father was a prominent man and a magistrate in that city, and from him Apuleius received a comfortable inheritance. His career was that of a writer and an itinerant lecturer well known to North African audiences. Although probably of Roman descent, Apuleius is conscious of being a provincial; and the spirit of veneration and wonderment with which he views the glories of Greece and Rome, whether past or present, is perhaps one manifestation of his provincial psychosis. Hadrian looked away from Rome; Apuleius looks toward it from afar. For him already, as for men of later ages and distant lands, Rome is the eternal city, with an air of something mystic about it. "On the day after the Ides of December," he says in one place, " . . . at evening I drew nigh unto that sanctified city (*sacrosanctam istam civitatem accedo*)." [1] And on another occasion when speaking in a famous city, which is not named, but may have been Athens or Rome, he describes his feelings on being there in the following words, which are worth quoting as typical of his copious and pointed oratorical style, as well as of his mystic outlook on the world:

As is customary with religiously-minded wayfarers whenever in their journey along the road they come upon some sacred shrine or place divine, to make a supplication, to place a bit of fruit upon the spot, and to tarry there some while:—so it is with me, now that I have entered this most sacred of cities; I must bespeak your indulgence, and exhibit my eloquence, and inhibit my precipitance. For surely there is nothing that could more justly cause a traveller to linger in reverent meditation [than this city], neither an altar draped with flowers, nor a grotto shaded with boughs, nor an oak tree burdened with horns, nor a beech tree crowned with skins, nor yet a little knoll consecrated with an enclosure, nor a tree trunk made into an image, nor a grassy turf moistened by libations, or a stone annointed with unguent. These are small things, to be sure, venerated by only a few, yet most of those who pass them by do so in ignorance.[2]

Here note the copiousness of expression, the etymological word-play (*lucus—locus sanctus, habenda ratio et inhibenda properatio*), and the typical Apuleian rhythm. The fame of Apuleius flourished in Africa during his lifetime, and he was thought of long afterwords as one of the glories of the province. Statues were set up in his honor at Carthage and at Oea in North Africa, and in other cities abroad. His early education in grammar and elocution was carried on at the nearby city of Carthage, and he later studied at Athens. The range of his intellectual interests was extremely wide, as manifested both in what he wrote and in the numerous arts to which he aspired. Proudly he proclaims to an audience at Carthage, where he was already famous, that he, their own Apuleius, has cultivated each of the nine Muses in turn, if not with equal ability at all events with equality of zeal. The first cup of learning, he tells them in his picturesque, figurative style, "takes one over the elements of reading; the second trains him in the principles of grammar, and the third fortifies him with the eloquence of the orator. Many students imbibe thus far. But I have drunk other cups of knowledge at

Athens: the fancy one of poetry, the limpid one of geometry, the sweet one of music, the austere cup of dialectic, and the nectar-flavored and inexhaustible cup of universal philosophy." [3]

The extant writings of Apuleius include, in addition to the *Metamorphoses*, his defense against the charge of practicing magic, entitled *Apologia*; a collection of excerpts from his public speeches known as the *Florida*; an essay concerning the demon, or guiding spirit, of Socrates, entitled *De deo Socratis*; a popular exposition of the doctrines of Plato called *De dogmate Platonis*; and an essay on the physical world entitled *De Mundo*, which is a translation in the main of an extant Greek book of similar title falsely ascribed to Aristotle. Among the writings of Apuleius which have not come down to us may be mentioned some amatory poems in elegiacs, some playful verses on trifling subjects, including a eulogy of tooth powder, a romance in two or more books entitled *Hermagoras*,[4] numerous public addresses delivered on various occasions, a book on trees, one on agriculture, one on fish; and others dealing with such diverse subjects as proverbs, medicine, arithmetic, music, astronomy and Roman history.[5] Probably some of these were written in Greek, since the author tells us that he spoke and wrote in Greek as well as in Latin; but all his extant works are in Latin.

When Apuleius married a wealthy widow named Pudentilla, her relatives brought a legal action against him on the ground that he had won the lady's consent by the use of magical arts. That he was acquitted at the trial can scarcely be doubted, in view of his confident manner of speaking in the *Apologia*, wherein he shows the accusation to be absurd and unfounded, and welcomes the opportunity of displaying to a well-educated judge the encyclopedic range of his knowledge of obscure subjects, including books on magic; which, like Goethe, he probably examined mainly out of curiosity. But in spite of his legal acquittal and of the facts in the case, the reputation of being a magician clung to Apuleius in the popular imagination long afterwards, and in the fourth century he, along with Apollonius of Tyana, was believed to have been one of the great miracle-workers of the ancient world, comparable to Christ himself. This popular notion was fostered by other of his writings besides the *Apologia*, notably the *Metamorphoses*, which deals to some extent with magic and stories of the super-natural, and by the *De deo Socratis*, wherein the author seeks to prove the existence of demons as lesser divinities, playing the part of intermediaries between gods and men. This book was read in the Middle Ages, when the *Metamorphoses* had been forgotten, with the result that between the fifth and the fifteenth centuries Apuleius was thought of as a magician and an authority on demonology rather than as a romancer.

Yet even the modern reader of the *Metamorphoses* can scarcely help feeling that there is something magical about this author, in the sense that his book is deeply permeated with a spirit of belief in the hidden and marvellous potentialities of nature and human life, and that a kind of alchemy is wrought, as it were, by the very charm of his style, whereby whatever he touches upon, leaden though it may be by nature, is transmuted forthwith into literary gold, illumined with the glamour of poetry or of strange but graphic reality, and spellbinding in its effect upon the reader. Indeed, it is in the realm of style that Apuleius has made his most original contribution to literature; for that style—so highly colored, fanciful, and rococo, so studiously piquant and recherché, and so picturesque, varied, and opulent—is shaped in large measure by his own romantic outlook on the world; whereas the subject-matter of his books is derived in the main from Greek sources, and his knowledge of science and philosophy tends to be as superficial as his interests are wide and scattered. He likes to think of himself as a Platonic philosopher, yet he has no comprehensive grasp of Plato's thought, which he seeks to dish out in packages, and he lacks the temperament necessary for organizing a philosophical system of ideas. He cannot linger long enough on any one thing. He is ever the *desultor litterarum*, to use one of his own figures, leaping from one literary horse to another and admiring his own dexterity in so doing. He is less a thinker than a showman; not a painstaking scholar, but a dilettante and a dandy, who likes to hear himself speak on any subject because he does it so gracefully, so copiously and, to all appearances, so learnedly. For him philosophy is composed of secrets relating to the hidden powers of nature and the spiritual world, and he loves to pose before the public as the high priest and interpreter of things which it is bound to admire but does not understand.

The romantic temperament of Apuleius, and that restless spirit which seems to be in endless quest for a revelation of one kind or another, or for communion with the *anima mundi*, the mystic soul of the world which he found adumbrated in Plato, and impersonated in Isis, may be seen in his religious experience. In the *Apology* (Ch. 55) he tells us that he had been initiated into many religious mysteries, which in his day were relatively new and popular cults, evangelistic and ecumenical in character as compared to the older cults of the city state, and for the most part oriental in origin; and in the eleventh book of the *Metamorphoses*, where he identifies himself almost completely with the protagonist Lucius, he describes his initiation into the mysteries of Isis with an eloquence deeply inspired and made beautiful by the force of a living religion. Here the pantheistic spirit of the second century and of Apuleius himself is brought vividly before us. It will be worth our while to quote a few passages by way of illustrating this mystic spirit, which is one aspect of the romantic Apuleian psychosis.

Lucius, while still an ass and about to pray to Isis for deliverance, relates his experience as follows (Byrne's translation):[6]

I was started from my sleep in sudden dread . . . and there I saw the full orb of the Moon, shining in excess of light and just beginning to emerge from the ocean waves. My heart was opened to read the silent mysteries of the dark night around me. I felt the majestic influence of that great Goddess of the sky, and recognized her providential rule of all the affairs of men. It is not only beasts and cattle who live in her divine light and through the will of her divinity, but inanimate nature is subject to her too. All bodies that exist on earth, in air and sea, now gain as she waxes, now lose their substance as she wanes . . . Then with tears upon my cheeks, I addressed myself in prayer to the most mighty Goddess: O Queen of Heaven, whether thou art Ceres, the great mother of old time who feedest us with thy fruits, who rejoicest in the recovery of thy daughter, and, putting an end to all savage pasture, hast shown us a gentler food, and tillest now the Elusinian glebe; or Venus, the heavenly, thou, who in the first beginnings of all things hast generated love to bind the sexes into one, and, propagating the human race with unceasing offspring, art worshipped now in thy sea-girt shrine of Paphos; . . . Give pause to the cruel mischances I have undergone! . . . Restore me to the Lucius I really am! . . .

It was thus I poured my prayer and raised my wretched plaints, when once more sleep fell on my languid soul . . . I had scarcely closed my eyes, when lo, from the ocean's midst there arose a godlike vision, displaying a face that must surely be venerable to the gods themselves. She seemed to shake the waters gradually from her form, and to rise before my eyes as an apparition of light . . .

Such and so great she was, breathing of all the spices that blow in Araby the blest, and with her heavenly voice she deigned to address me: "See Lucius, I am here. Thy prayers have touched me, me the parent of nature, the mistress of the elements, the first-born of the ages, the highest of the Deities, the Queen of Departed Spirits, the chief of Heavenly Ones, the Gods and Goddesses all united in One Form. I am she who disposes the lightsome mountains of the sky, the healthful breezes of the deep, and the much-mourned silence of the grave, as it pleases my high behest. My name is One, my appearance manifold. In various rites and under many names the whole world pays me homage. . . . I am here in pity of thy lot; I am here to show my favour. Cease then to weep, and still thy lamentations. Soon shall the day of thy salvation dawn through the action of my providence. . . .

"But thou shalt live in blessedness; under my protection thou shalt live gloriously! And when thou hast measured thy allotted course and descendest to the grave, there too, in the hemisphere below the ground, thou shalt behold me as a light amidst the darkness of Acheron and a queen in the palace of the Styx, and thou shalt dwell thyself in Elysian Fields and win my favour by unceasing adoration. . . ."

In describing his actual initiation into the mysteries (XI 23), Lucius says: "I neared the confines of death; I trod the threshold of Proserpina; I was borne through all the elements and returned; in the midst of night I saw the sun beaming in glorious light; I stood before the Gods of heaven and the Gods of the lower world, and adored as I stood close to them. See, I have told thee all, which thou mayest hear, but still be in ignorance of."

The eleventh book of the *Metamorphoses*, from which these eloquent descriptions of religious experience are quoted, tells how the protagonist Lucius becomes a devotee of Isis, regains human form miraculously through her favor, and is initiated, first into the mysteries of that goddess near Corinth, and later into those of Osiris at Rome, where, finally, he enters upon a career as orator and advocate in the Roman forum, with the necessary encouragement of Osiris, and becomes a priest with shaven head in the service of that deity. From beginning to end this last book of the *Metamorphoses* celebrates, in a tone of gravity and high moral seriousness nowhere relaxed, the triumph of revealed religion in a man's life over all other human concerns. It is a personal gospel in which the author intentionally makes it clear to his public that he is testifying on the basis of his own religious experience and conviction; and that "Lucius," hitherto of Corinth but now of Madaura (XI 27), and an advocate in the Roman forum (XI 30), is none other than Apuleius of Madaura, who tells us in the *Apologia* (55, 56) that he had participated in many religious mysteries in Greece, and in the *Florida* (ed. Helm p. 31) that he had carried on his studies (in oratory) at Rome.

2

Structurally considered in relation to the *Metamorphoses* as a whole, Book XI is an artistic unit standing apart by itself in strong contrast to the preceding ten books, with which it is only loosely and outwardly connected, and in which, by con-

trast, the real nature and *raison d'être* of the *Metamorphoses*—
primarily a series of mundane stories exploited on their own
account as such for the reader's entertainment—is to be seen.
The contrast in mood and nature of subject matter between
the last book of the *Metamorphoses* and the ten that precede
it is no sharper than that which marks the transition from one
story or group of stories to another in the first ten books. Love
of variety and the tendency to pass in rapid succession from
the contemplation of one wonderful thing to another, with a
minimum of logical connection, is profoundly characteristic of
Apuleius in all his literary activity. Like the bizarre Hadrian,
whose manysided interests and activities reflect the romantic,
wonder-seeking spirit of the age, Apuleius throughout the first
ten chapters of his story-book is *omnium curiositatum ex-
plorator,*[7] *semper in omnibus varius;*[8] but the last chapter taken
by itself is uninterrupted by digressions of any kind, and occupation with the central theme, the initiations of Lucius and his
consecration as a devotee to the service of Isis and Osiris, is
maintained throughout with intensity. This solemn ending
of the story of Lucius the miracle-seeker, extending through
twenty-five pages of the Teubner text, has been substituted
by Apuleius, with a special purpose of his own, in place of
the original Lucianic ending, which is two pages long in the
Greek and ends with a farcical episode in harmony with the
spirit of the objective, fast-moving narrative that precedes.
What Apuleius has added to the original story, as he found
it in Lucian's relatively short and comic Μεταμορφώσεις, may
be viewed in the light of its aesthetic quality as well as of
its bulk. Owing to the insertion of many kinds of new stories
into the framework of the Greek *Luciad*, and to the expansion
of that basic story itself, the Latin *Metamorphoses* is extended
to almost six times the length of the original on which it was
built.[9] Many of the stories that have been added, because they
are tragic in tone, or superstitious, or otherwise serious and
solemn in the manner of their telling, are incongruous in the
context of the story into which they have been inserted, which

was uniformly ironical, objective, and comic in spirit throughout. This incongruity, which is often praised by critics as an
artistic effect for which the Latin romancer consciously strove
(be that as it may), results from the juxtaposition of new
Apuleian matter beside the monochromatic substance of
Lucian's original.

All the other additions made by Apuleius to the original story
of Lucius are plainly for the purpose of entertaining or amusing
the reader with a good story told for its own sake, or with a
display of rhetorical or dramatic virtuosity on whatever subject; but the last book of the *Metamorphoses* was added for a
very special purpose, quite apart from its interest as an
eloquent description of religious experience, and independently
of any specific statement or hint concerning the moral of the
Metamorphoses as a whole that an imaginative interpreter may
succeed in finding in it.[10] The real purpose, as we have already
explained in the preceding chapter (p. 234), was to redeem his
book from the appearance of complete frivolity. To publish for
sheer entertainment a lengthy work of fiction in the form of
dramatically spun-out witch stories, fairy tales, and tales of
sensational or scandalous adventure, all of which types of
prose narrative were looked upon with disdain by his contemporaries as trivial old wives' tales (*aniles fabulae*), or tales fit
only to be told on the street-corner (*aureae fabulae*), was something that Apuleius really *wanted* to do, but did not *dare* to do,
without qualifying his work in such a way as would leave the
impression that he had, after all, something of serious importance to convey by it, which was instructive, and high-minded,
and thereby worthy of an educated writer. Book XI served
that necessary purpose, but only in a very perfunctory and
superficial fashion. Instead of building into the framework of
his story-book as a whole an ostensible meaning in terms of
satire, philosophical critique, or allegory which would be
evident from start to finish, as is the case in Lucian's novels,
Apuleius is content merely to tack on at the end a piece of
solemn pageantry as ballast to offset the prevailing levity of the

preceding ten books. With his showman's instinct for the value of immediate dramatic effects (which often leads him into self-contradiction elsewhere), he feels that all he needs to do in order to prevent the publication of his old wives' tales from becoming a scandal in the literary world, comparable to that of Aristides' *Milesiaca*, is to make a personal appearance on the stage in the last act, bow deeply and reverently before his audience, and overwhelm them with the magic of his eloquence on a subject of grave and universal import, a subject about which he speaks with earnest conviction and sincerity, but which does not belong with the story of Lucius. Deeply impressed with the solemnity of this final act, his public will go away without thinking about the nature of what went before, and thereby two objects will have been achieved: the author will have delivered, in the form of "Milesian" tales in the first ten chapters, the kind of entertainment with which he knew that his readers would be charmed, in spite of its disrespectability as literature; and, at the same time, his book as a whole will have been redeemed in some measure from the appearance of complete frivolity and from the scorn of his learned contemporaries.[11] It was probably with a similar purpose in mind that the authors of the sophistic romances, Iamblichus, Achilles Tatius, and Heliodorus, weighted their love stories, which were generally considered unworthy of a sophist's pen, with numerous digressions of a learned, informative nature on scientific subjects of one kind or another, or lengthy rhetorical descriptions.

3

In the *Metamorphoses* two opposite forces, one active and aggressive, the other static, are pulling against each other; and those features of the book which are most distinctive and most significant of the precise place which it occupies in the history of prose fiction generally are the results of that conflict. The active force is the striving of the author everywhere to prolong and intensify his stories dramatically; and the static or resistant force is the weight of ancient literary convention in prose narrative, and the organic nature of the ready-made materials with which he works and which he uses as building blocks in the agglutinative structure of new and longer corridors of narrative with more dramatic suspense. In the *Metamorphoses* the narrower limits of extension and dramatic exploitation, within which the short story in ancient prose literature had previously been confined and thereby restricted to summary statement, are being expanded by the explosive force of a literarily new artistic ideal. The Apuleian conception of what a story ideally ought to be, and his striving to bring this about in prose literature, is dynamic and explosive in its effect because this urge is deeply rooted in a popular taste that had long been repressed, and was still being repressed, by the conventions of respectable literature. It is natural to tell a witch story or a fairy tale, or an animal fable, or a story of adventure of any kind, *for its own sake*, and thereby to dwell at length upon the particulars of action and circumstance, and to multiply the actions, regardless of any ulterior meaning or context. Such is and always has been—before, during, and after the reign of classical literature—the spirit and method of the story teller or the epic minstrel on the subliterary plane of oral communication. In classical prose literature, however, which was always *informative* in theory (i.e. historical, philosophic, political, scientific), this *Lust zu fabulieren* was severely restrained, because the story was ancillary to a larger context, and only the sum of its action, not the how of it or the close-up view, was in point. But in spite of this restraint, the natural tendency to tell a story in the epic fashion, like the parallel tendency to make *Kunstprosa* out of informative prose (thereby diverting the writer's aim from the informative matter to the matter of style), was always pressing from the outside against the intellectual barriers inherent in the theory of the prose genres. In the Alexandrian age this pressure, backed by the heavy tide of popular taste for dramatic narrative and action for action's sake, although resisted in formal prose literature, tended nevertheless to warp it and succeeded now and then in distorting history into "romance"; but the tide was too abundant to be held in check by the dikes of the established literary forms, and its overflow consequently had to be channeled into the new and despised form of ideal romance or novel, which was made especially for it on the bottom lands of Hellenistic literature, where it flourished on a low level for three centuries, officially unrecognized by the Academy and too humble even to be mentioned by such classical writers as Cicero, Quintilian, or Lucian. Many obscure Greek authors were writing ideal romances of love and adventure for the populace, or for boys and girls, and probably for money, in the time of Apuleius, in defiance of the intellectual fashion; but no Latin author with literary ambitions would emulate that kind of Greek model, because it was not held in honor. To do so would be to lose that which he, as a Latin writer, wanted most to achieve and what the Greek romancer, often probably anonymous or pseudonymous, and perhaps a commercial writer, cared nothing about —the reputation of being a literary man.

Like the other literary men of his day who are well known to us as rhetoricians and sophists, or for their writing on historical, philosophical, or scientific subjects, Apuleius had no traffic with the ideal romance. In the *Metamorphoses* his concern is principally with the short story or novella—*varias fabulas conseram*—along with the comic romance of Lucius, serving as a framework, which he took over from Lucian. But both these forms of narrative, the short story and the comic romance, had always been admitted into classically oriented literature, though only under special conditions: the comic romance having appeared at rare intervals in the guise of satire or parody, as in the mock-heroic *Margites*, Lucian's *True History*, and his *Metamorphoses*, or to disguise a variety of serious literary experiments, as with Petronius; and the short story or novella had appeared only in a larger context of history, philosophy or science, to which it was formally subordinated.[12] Apuleius is busy breaking down the fences that previously con-

fined the novella in formal literature; and that, as we stated
above, is the most significant thing in his book, as regards its
bearing upon the history of prose fiction on its way from the
classical environment to the medieval and modern. Later on
below we shall exhibit in concrete detail the process by which
Apuleius expands the ancient novella in his striving to prolong
it dramatically with more action and more suspense, and so to
make of it what it was in the Middle Ages and in modern times,
and what it always had been in folklore and epic, but had
never been in classical prose literature: a story dramatically
told at length for its own sake as entertainment, not as information or for the purpose of illustrating something else.

4

The "short story" as we know it today is shaped by artistic
aims and principles that were brought into literary *prose* and
freely exploited for the first time by Apuleius in the *Metamorphoses*. Before that—and long afterward in the formal literature
of ancient and Byzantine times—the short story in prose was
controlled and qualified more or less by the standards of the
informative genres (historiography, science, pseudo-science,
paradoxography, philosophy), if it was serious or ideal in kind.
If it was farcical, burlesque, naughty, or satirical, it was controlled by the classical conventions of comic literature wherein,
as in the Old Comedy, Petronius, and Lucian, the action is
described as farce objectively, unmorally, and summarily, and
the actors, who are usually abstract type-characters, are hardly
more than puppets. No interest is shown by the classical author
in their individual personalities or their inner emotions (as in
Cervantes and Fielding), and what they do is not told as a
means of illustrating their characters, their significantly human
virtues or failings, with which the reader is expected to sympa-
thize, or the principles of conduct by which they are guided—as
is the case in ideal epic and dramatic literature—but, instead,
objectively on its own account as ludicrous or sensational

action. The story as a whole is put forth as a jest for the amusement of sophisticated wits in the Dionysiac (rather than the Apolline) spirit of Old Comedy, usually with a satirical implication or in tones of mockery. In respect to its objectivity and the premium put on action *per se*, with the consequent neglect of character, this kind of story retains the fundamental features of the oral folktale, from which the matter itself is usually taken, and to that extent it is, in a sense, subliterary; for all literary fiction outside of comedy tends to put ethical character and human nature as such in the foreground, with the action ancillary thereto, while comedy proper and comic stories in the classical tradition, being conceived only as jests, are conventionally not used as media for the artistic portrayal of those positive human values, as they are or tend to be in Apuleius. The literary virtuosity of Aristophanic comedy lies in its lyrics, which are poetry, and much interest attaches to the political and satirical ideas that the play promulgates; but the rest is farce in the grand manner, and to some extent pure folklore or invention in the style of folklore, *Märchenkomödie* according to Zielinski, *Weltvernichtungsidee* as Heine called it. It is not, like epic and tragedy, or as in *Don Quixote* or Fielding's *Joseph Andrews*, what may be called a study or an artistic portrayal of human nature in its various aspects, intended to arouse one's sympathetic reflections upon the values or the morphology of man's inner life and character.

Now all that we have been saying about the externality and objectivity of comic narrative and drama in the classical tradition is characteristic of the story of Lucius as originally told by Lucian; but Apuleius in retelling and expanding the same story has greatly qualified it. Just how he has qualified it becomes abundantly evident when one compares, scene by scene, the narrative in the Greek original, as represented by the Lucianic *Onos*, with the corresponding Apuleian version of the same events. Such a comparison of the *Metamorphoses* with its Greek original throughout has been made, in painstaking detail and with illuminating results, by Paul Junghanns in a monograph entitled *Die Erzählungstechnik von Apuleius' Metamor-phosen und ihrer Vorlage*.[13] Some concrete illustrations of the innovations made by Apuleius in his exploitation of the comic novella, and the artistic aims and principles by which these changes are motivated, will be noted below in connection with certain parts of the *Metamorphoses* which we shall describe in detail. Meanwhile, stated abstractly, the changes that Apuleius has introduced in retelling the objectively comic story of Lucius, and other similar stories inserted into its framework, are somewhat as follows. The tone in which the story is told is often much more serious, more moral, and more sympathetic with the thoughts and emotions of the actors, however superstitious or credulous these may be, than in the Greek original. Indeed the author frequently ascribes what are obviously his own feelings and judgments—moral, philosophical, artistic, and religious— to Lucius and at times, as notably in Book XI, actually identi-fies himself with the protagonist Lucius. Magic and super-natural phenomena, moreover, are described by the Latin author sympathetically from the viewpoint of the credulous believer in a spirit of awe and wonder, instead of being exhibited objectively and ironically in a spirit of burlesque, as in Lucian's satires. Here the method of Apuleius in dealing with stories of the supernatural differs from that of the Greek author in much the same way, incidentally, as the method of Pliny (*Ep.* VII 27) differs from that of Lucian (*Philopseudes* 31) in telling the story of the haunted house at Athens: the action in outline of the story is the same with both authors, but the Roman Pliny tells it seriously as a miracle that he thinks may be true, while Lucian treats it as farce in a spirit of ridicule. Another in-novation which Apuleius makes in his exploitation of the comic novella consists in the lifelike portrayal of character and emotion for its own interest as a principal exhibit in many kinds of persons. Not content with describing outward actions in the objective manner of the Greek original, he makes many changes and additions of his own which serve to illustrate and to bring

vividly before us the inner thoughts and feelings of his characters, some of whom have no necessary function in the plot of
the main story but are introduced for the sake of their picturesque value.[14] Like Euripides and the modern novelists, but
unlike his predecessors in the telling of comic stories, Apuleius
is studiously interested in human nature as such, in what
Balzac calls the *comédie humaine*, and much of his artistic
effort is directed to presenting it in various aspects as vividly
and dramatically as possible. Viewed broadly against the
background of ancient literary history, what Apuleius has done
in effect is to transfer to the comic novella the artistic aims and
values of fiction which had long been confined to the essentially
serious or ideal literary genres, such as epic and tragedy and
poetry of various kinds. Insofar as we know, this had not
happened before with the comic novella in prose, because it
had never been cultivated as an independent literary form,
having appeared only rarely in a context of some kind; but it
had happened in a general way, and very conspicuously, in the
history of ancient stage comedy. Old Comedy in the Dionysiac
tradition of farce gave place in the fourth century to the New
Comedy, rightly so called, of Menander and his colleagues;
wherein the farcical element, though retained in part, is subordinated and overshadowed by the serious, ideal purpose,
made fashionable by Euripides, as by Moliére, Shakespeare and
Balzac in modern times, of dramatizing human nature, human
character, and typical human problems of ethical choice and
conduct, as an artistic end in itself. The New Comedy is the
comédie humaine in Balzac's sense of that term; and it was
"new" in the fourth century because the ideal aims and values
of Euripidean drama had been imposed, by popular taste, upon
its original character as farce, or substituted therefor. In the
history of the modern novel, at its beginning, a close parallel to
the kind of innovation made by Apuleius in dealing with his
comic narrative may be seen in Fielding's *Joseph Andrews* and
Tom Jones, as discussed earlier.

5

We have considered the qualitative changes that Apuleius made in retelling the fundamentally comic stories that he took from Greek sources; but we must not overlook the many serious or ideal stories which he has introduced into the *Metamorphoses* and which, as a class broadly conceived, have a very different background in ancient literary convention. These stories in the serious or ideal mood differ from one another: they include the beautiful fairy tale of Cupid and Psyche in *Met.* IV 28–VI 24 (50 pages), which is called a "Milesian" tale because it is an *anilis fabula,* although not in the comic tradition, the tragic story of Charite and Tlepolemus in VIII 1–14 (10 pages), that of the three poor man's sons in IX 35–38, and such sensational stories of crime and atrocity as that of the vengeful stepmother in X 2–12 (8 pages), and that about the multiple crimes of the condemned woman in X 23–28 (5 pages). Before Apuleius such stories as these would have appeared in prose literature (other than the romances) only in an historiographical or a scientific context, and in summary outline. Their length and the limited extent to which they were dramatized in the telling, if at all, would be normally what it is in the paradoxographers, or the mythographers, or Plutarch, or in the collection of thirty-six stories of tragic love excerpted from local histories or summed up from the poets, which was compiled by Parthenius of Nicaea, one of Vergil's teachers, as raw material for the use of his friend, the Roman elegiac poet Cornelius Gallus. On the basis of those documentary outlines of the careers of historical or mythical lovers, Gallus would compose narratives dramatically prolonged with much character analysis and a lively portrayal of the thoughts and emotions of the characters. Ovid does this, for example, with the story of Scylla in his *Metamorphoses* (8.6 ff.) and so Parthenius himself had done;[15] but all this would be *poetry* in the form and tradition of epic or elegy, not prose. Where Apuleius found the outlines of his tragic or ideal stories, whether in poetic versions, in collections like that of Parthenius, in historiography, or in folklore, we do not know; but the artistic aims and methods that he follows in filling in the outlines so as to produce a dramatic story in the modern conception of that term—as opposed to an abstract summation of events—are essentially the same as those followed by the poets, except for musical and verbal effects; and the fact that this is done by Apuleius for the first time, so far as we know, *in prose*, marks a new stage in the history of prose fiction in Graeco-Roman antiquity.

Personal experience in an historiographical context (or in any kind of writing that is governed by the informative theory of ancient prose), is necessarily brief and summary, because the subject with which the author is principally concerned is either a wide field of events in which one man's or woman's actions are only a part—and usually a small part—or an historical idea, or a general principle, of which the individual's biography, or action, viewed in its totality, is not told on its own account as pathos but as an illustration, or for the sake of its historical or scientific meaning. Here the reader is not invited to linger over the emotions elicited by particular acts or situations, or over the scenic background. It is the author's conscious purpose in writing, what he aims to do, that determines what an account of personal experience will be. In the hands of a writer whose primary purpose is to entertain the reader with a story dramatically told for its own sake, as with Apuleius and many medieval writers, a narration that was originally only a skeleton outline of events in an historiographical, philosophic, or scientific context, is padded and prolonged with the addition of many dramatic details and often with new episodes added either within or beyond the original framework of events. The later history of the Aesopic fables affords many illustrations of this, and other examples may be seen in the medieval epics or romances that are built on the basis of ancient historiographical or biographical texts.[16] The process by which Apuleius expands and dramatizes stories previously written only in summary outlines and abstractly often involves the addition of one or more originally independent stories as further episodes in the story with which he begins. This multiplies the amount of sheer action in the story, but tends to minimize the logical inner connection between one episode and another, so that each stands out by itself, more or less, in paratactic relation to what precedes.

Up to this point we have been stating in general terms what innovations Apuleius has made in the telling of his stories, their significance and place in the history of prose fiction, and something about the mechanical methods employed by the author in prolonging his stories. It remains to illustrate these matters concretely by means of typical examples chosen from the text of the *Metamorphoses*. We begin with the description and illustration of a certain feature of the Apuleian narrative which reveals the author's neglect of logical sequence and is profoundly characteristic of his desultory psychosis throughout the *Metamorphoses*.[17]

6

Preoccupation with the scene immediately before him often leads Apuleius as narrator into self-contradiction or logical absurdity, at times even within the limits of a short space of text. He thinks of one thing at a time in its close-up aspect, ever intent on his showmanship, passing rapidly from one exhibit to another. In so doing he often forgets or ignores as inconsequential something that he had said before about a character or a situation, which contradicts what he is now saying, or he disregards the logical requirements of the situation within which a witticism or a sensational act is suddenly projected.

In *Met.* II 26, when a group of angry servants make a sudden attack on the character Thelyphron, the latter, speaking in the first person, tells us that the servants "picked up weapons of every kind and went after me; one punched my cheeks with his fist, another dug his elbows into my shoulder blades, another battered my ribs with the palms of his hands, they kicked me, they pulled my hair, and tore my clothes." Now a reader may not notice the incongruity involved in picking up weapons for the purpose of making an attack, then attacking in every possible way except by the use of those weapons; but for an author to narrate an action with such complete disregard of logical sequence is very unusual. And yet it is characteristic of Apuleius. He will say whatever occurs to him at the moment as being dramatic or picturesque, and in the next moment he will forget it in his preoccupation with some other fancy.

When, in *Met.* III 12, a male servant brings Lucius an invitation to dinner from his elderly kinswoman Byrrhena, verbally delivered, Lucius is made to reply as if he were speaking to Byrrhena herself, instead of to her servant: "How happy I should be to comply with your request, mother, if only honour would permit me to do so. But my host Milo . . . " Here the probability is that Apuleius has simply forgotten the person to whom Lucius is represented as speaking directly; but if one assumes, as some editors do, that these words of Lucius are dictated to the servant as a reply which he intends the servant to report literally to Byrrhena, in that case the failure of the author to tell us so explicitly is no less the result of an absent-minded disregard of plausibility in the circumstances in which Lucius speaks.[18]

The mock-heroic exploits of the robber chieftains Lamachus and Alcimus, which, as related by one of their company (*Met.* IV, 9–12), ended in both cases with the death of the hero in a ludicrous situation, are said to take place in "Seven-gated Thebes"; but, before the robbers move on to Plataea in the direction of the sea for their next campaign, we are told that they buried the bodies first of Lamachus then later of Alcimus in the sea! Since Thebes is far from the sea in any direction, the robbers could not have buried their companions in that element if they were operating at Thebes; but they may well have done so in some pre-Apuleian form of the story in which the scene of their activity was located somewhere on the coast. The contradiction on the part of Apuleius seems to have resulted from his locating the action at "Seven-gated Thebes," for paratragic effect, while retaining from an earlier form of the story, through inadvertence, the statement that the robbers buried their dead companions in the sea.

According to the original story as told by both Apuleius (*Met.* IV 8) and Lucian (*Onos* 21), concerning the arrival of a second band of robbers in the cave, there to join the first band who had carried off Lucius the ass in their robbery of Milo's house in Thessaly, this second band had returned from their foray heavily laden with costly spoils of every kind. At this point the author of the original Greek story says no more about the doings of the robbers on this night, except to remark that they celebrated the occasion with a big banquet at which there was a great deal of talk (λόγος πολύς). Apuleius, however, taking his cue from this statement in his Greek original, inserts here three mock-heroic stories of brigandage told one after the other by one of the robbers of the second band, who admits implicitly the charge made by one of his rivals that his own company has had no success, and proceeds to relate, as their complete and immediate experiences, the adventures ending in the deaths of Lamachus, Alcimus, and Thrasyleon, all of which result in comparative failure and so contradict the statement made above by both Lucian and Apuleius, according to which this second band of robbers had returned triumphantly from their expedition with an unusually large amount of valuable spoil.[19]

In another episode (*Met.* IX 41–42), which is told differently and logically in the Greek epitome (*Onos* 45), Apuleius shows a troop of public officers, policemen, and magistrates searching every angle of a private house without being able to find Lucius the ass who was loose in an upstairs room. After that, Lucius, being curious about the noisy crowd in front of the house, peeps his head out of the window to see what is going on. In the Greek original the crowd of course sees the ass's head, and the author remarks playfully, but very appropriately, that this was the origin of the well-known proverb "from the peep of an ass." But in Apuleius the crowd, strange to say, does not see the ass himself but only his shadow; and this clumsy alteration of the original story enables the Roman author to explain *two* proverbs instead of one, namely "from the peep of an ass" and "about the shadow of an ass"; although the latter proverb involves a totally different idea and cannot, like the other, be plausibly explained in any such way.[20] Again in the Greek original of this passage, there is only one search of the house by the public officers and that, taking place after Lucius had put his head out the window, was immediately successful. Before that the officers had ordered everyone out of the house and questioned them concerning the whereabouts of Lucius and his master; and the inmates had denied that either one was inside. In Apuleius there are two searches of the house instead of one; but the first is only a rash anticipation of the second, resulting, as we see, in a high degree of logical absurdity. Apuleius was so absorbed with the immediate mental picture of a group of magistrates and policemen in action, that he could neither keep them out of the house before the ass was seen, as he should have done, nor refrain from exaggerating the thoroughness of their unsuccessful search.

When Lucius the ass is put to work in a flour mill for the *second* time, according to both versions (*Met.* IX 11, *Onos* 42), Apuleius makes him say that he knew how to grind because he had seen such mills in operation when he was a man; but the author of the Greek original had explained this familiarity with mills much more appropriately and wittily as due to sad experience: "I knew well enough how to grind, having suffered from so doing many a time in the past, but (on this occasion) I pretended not to know." The reference here is to the experience of Lucius as recorded in *Onos* 28 and *Met.* VII 15, where he was put to work in a mill by the herdsman's wife. Apuleius has momentarily forgotten all about this previous experience of Lucius in the mill, which he himself had described in *Met.* VII 15, when he explains, in IX 11, why Lucius knew how to grind.

The passages which we have described above show how negligent Apuleius can be of the context within which he introduces an action, and how completely oblivious he sometimes is of the most elementary considerations of logic, sequence, and probability, even within the limits of a very short space of text. Since that is so, it is all the more to be expected that he will neglect to harmonize discordant and contradictory elements when those elements are more widely separated, and especially when they come from originally independent stories where they had a different function and a different orientation of their own. Further examples of this will be noted in the three composite stories which we shall now undertake to analyze from the point of view of their mechanical structure (sections 7-9 below): the stories told by Aristomenes and by Telyphron in Books I and II respectively, and that about the Risus festival in Book III, which is artificially tacked onto the original Greek story concerning the adventure of Lucius with the animated goatskins. The strange conflicts in motivation, and the absence of natural sequence, which we find in these composite narratives, made up of two or more originally independent stories, go far to explain the dreamland atmosphere of mystery and unreality which pervades much of the *Metamorphoses* in the first four books, and is not inherent in the romantic or miraculous nature of the subject matter itself, nor in the writer's artistic aim. No folktales that I have ever read or heard relating supernatural events, however paratactic or agglutinative their structure may be, have this puzzling contradictory quality which, in Apuleius, results accidentally from the artificial combination of one originally independent story with another and the author's failure to trim and shape his building blocks in such a way that they fit harmoniously into the new structure.

7

Aristomenes is one of the travelling companions of Lucius on the road to Thessaly. The story that he tells (*Met.* I 5–19) describes what happened to his friend Socrates and himself at the hands of Thessalian witches during an earlier visit that he had made to Hypata. It was a terrible experience, enough to convince anyone that there was scarcely any limit to the miracles that those wicked witches could perform by means of their magic arts. The story as Apuleius tells it contains a series of very puzzling contradictions and violations of plausibility, all of which belong together and have been caused by the badly managed insertion of a farcical story about a lover's suicide in the middle of the sensational witch story with which the author began. To make this clear, I shall first outline the story as I think it must have been in the unknown written source which Apuleius was using; after that I shall point out how Apuleius has altered the original story of Aristomenes in the process of inserting another story from a different source, discordantly, within its framework.[21]

Aristomenes, a merchant travelling through Thessaly puts up at the town of Hypata one evening and, on going to the public baths, finds there his old friend Socrates, whom he has not seen for many months. Socrates is in a pitiful condition, emaciated, dirty, ragged, and penniless—as the saying goes, down and out completely. Aristomenes does everything he can to resuscitate his friend and to cheer him up. He takes him to his own room in a local inn, where Socrates tells him how he had been reduced to his present condition. While travelling on the road he had been robbed by brigands of everything he possessed, and after that he had fallen into the power of a sorceress named Meroe, who kept an inn. Meroe treated him with kindness at first, in the midst of his distress; but soon made him her lover, and thereafter her abject slave. Says Socrates: "I contracted this old woman as a sort of disease; I gave her the very clothes which the good robbers had allowed me to keep, and also the small earnings I gained as a common porter, as long as I had the strength." When Aristomenes shows some skepticism about the magical powers of Meroe, Socrates relates a series of marvellous exploits that she had performed, such as changing a man into a frog or a goat, and transporting a house and all its foundations a hundred miles away to the top of a rugged mountain overnight. Aristomenes is much impressed and says, "My dear Socrates, what you tell me is wonderful and no less terrifying. You have filled me with anxiety of no small order, not to say alarm, lest your old woman, making use of her divine power, learn what we have been talking about. Let us go to bed early and get our sleep, so that even before the sun rises, we may get away from here as far as possible." Note that this is Aristomenes who wants to leave the inn before daybreak, in order to get away from the witches. Immediately after this, Socrates falls into a sound sleep; but Aristomenes remains awake until well after midnight. He is just about to go to sleep when two witches enter the room, one of whom is Meroe. The scene as described by Apuleius is wonderful, being both terrible and comic, but too long to report here. Meroe stands by Socrates, who remains unconscious throughout, buries a sword in his throat, reaches her forearm into the hole, and plucks out his heart without spilling a drop of blood, catching it in a basin. Then her companion, Panthia, stuffs up the hole in Socrates' neck with a sponge, exclaiming "Ho there, sponge, born in the ocean, see that thou cross no river."

Up to this point Apuleius has followed the outlines of the original story faithfully in all its essentials; but what he tells us next about the actions of Aristomenes, including his attempt to commit suicide, is an interpolation of his own, which I shall explain later. Meanwhile, to go on with the original story, this is what must have happened. As soon as the witches left the room, Aristomenes sought to verify his astounding impressions, to find out whether or not Socrates was really dead, and whether he himself had only been dreaming about those witches. Accordingly, he went up to Socrates, found him asleep and aroused him only with difficulty from a deep lethargy. Relieved to find his companion still alive and apparently un-harmed, yet more fearful than ever about the witches, Aristom-enes urged Socrates to get up and leave the inn with him immediately, as he had proposed that they do on the evening before. But Socrates, still half asleep and not worried about the witches, because he had remained entirely unaware of their visit, refused to get up and said, "What do you mean by pro-posing to travel forth at this time of night? Don't you know (as I do by experience) that the roads are infested by robbers? You may be willing to risk your own life, but I'm not going to risk mine just to accommodate you." And with these words, which are retained in Apuleius, but put into the mouth of the wrong speaker, namely an interpolated janitor, of whom we shall speak below, Socrates went back to sleep; and Aristom-enes, having nothing else to do, at last went to sleep himself. Aristomenes was still snoring when Socrates, shortly before sunrise, woke up and, seeking to arouse his companion, cried out "Where are you now, you who were in such a grand hurry to leave in the dead of the night and are now snoring wrapped up there in the bedclothes?" So the original story. In Apuleius, however, these words also have been transferred from the mouth of Socrates, where they certainly belonged, to that of the interpolated janitor, where they make no plausible sense. From this point on, which marks the end of his interpolated story about the attempted suicide of Aristomenes, Apuleius adheres to the original story with which he began. Aristomenes leaves the inn in company with Socrates and, since his com-panion seems to be well and unharmed, concludes that what he had seen in the night was only a bad dream. Socrates re-marks that he too had had a nightmare in which he dreamed that his throat was cut and his heart pulled out. "Even now," he says, "I feel a pain in my throat, and a kind of faintness all over." Presently the two companions prepare to eat breakfast on the banks of a stream; and when Socrates attempts to drink from it the sponge suddenly comes out of his neck and he falls dead.

Such in outline was the original story. Now let us see how Apuleius has altered it. His innovations begin at the point when the witches leave the room, and are chiefly the insertion of a new comic episode, namely an unsuccessful attempt by Aristomenes to hang himself, together with certain changes and additions to the original story which were necessary for the purpose of motivating this suicide. Contrary to natural probability, Aristomenes in Apuleius' version is represented as being so terrified with the thought that he will be accused of murdering Socrates, and condemned on circumstantial evidence, that he does not even look to see whether Socrates is dead or not, but tries to leave the inn immediately.[22] In order to drive him to suicide, Apuleius brings in a janitor who refuses to open the outside door; and this janitor, described as more than half asleep, remonstrates with Aristomenes in the same words that Socrates had used in the original story in refusing to set out with him on the road at night. "Travel at night is very dangerous," says the janitor, "and even if *you* are desperate enough to take the chance, I'm not going to risk *my* life to please you." This is unintelligible nonsense in the mouth of the janitor, since he would not be risking anything, but Apuleius makes him add, "Besides, how do I know you haven't murdered your companion, and are now trying to run away?" On hearing this Aristomenes concludes that he is doomed to die on the gallows and returns to his room resolved on suicide. He prefers to kill himself for certain, rather than to take a chance on being unjustly put to death by the law. "Fortune," he says, "supplied me with no death-dealing weapon but the bed, and I addressed myself to it with these words: 'Now, now, thou bed dearest to my heart, thou who hast endured so many hardships together with me, thou conscious arbiter of the deeds done by night, the only witness of my innocence whom I can summon into court, supply me now with the weapon needed for my salvation, as I hasten to join the dead below.' And as I spoke I proceeded to undo the cord that was plaited beneath it. I threw one end of the cord over a beam that projected from the window-frame into the room and fastened it there [here note the *window*], then I mounted the bed and on that fatal height arranged a noose and put my head through the halter. But as I kicked away the support beneath me with one foot, the rotten old cord suddenly broke into two pieces. Down I tumbled in a heap on Socrates, who was lying beneath me, and rolled around on the ground with him. And, behold, at that very moment the janitor rushed in vociferating loudly: 'Where are you, who were in such a great hurry to leave in the dead of night and are now snoring wrapped up in the bedclothes?' " These words, which were originally spoken by Socrates to Aristomenes in the morning before the latter was awake, are totally inapplicable to the situation which Apuleius is describing, since neither Aristomenes nor Socrates is asleep or wrapped up in bedclothes. Moreover, Apuleius, feeling self-conscious about the falsity of his janitor's action, makes it worse by trying to give it some function in the story and some plausible motivation; for he makes Socrates say that it was the janitor's loud shouting that woke him up (instead of Aristomenes falling on him and knocking him out of bed), and that he, Socrates, supposed that the janitor had broken into the room with an uproar for the purpose of stealing something: "People who stay at inns," he said, "have good reason to hate the proprietors. I was dead in the depths of sleep and this busybody comes rushing in at the wrong time—in the hopes of stealing something, I suppose—and wakes me up with his loud shouting." The real reason why Apuleius brought his janitor in at this point was in order that he might bear witness to the innocence of Aristomenes, by being on hand when Socrates woke up alive, and might hear Aristomenes exclaim triumphantly, as he does, "Behold my trusty janitor, the comrade whom you falsely said I murdered during the night." Apart from this trifle, the janitor has no function in the story as a whole other than to motivate the attempted suicide of Aristomenes by cutting off his escape from the inn, for which purpose he had been brought in for the first time by Apuleius himself. As for the suicide act in itself, considering the words in which it is described, not even that fits into the context which Apuleius has made for it; because it is not the suicide of a man cut off from escape by imprisonment, but a lover's suicide, belonging to a familiar burlesque pattern. The window accidentally mentioned in this scene would mean nothing to a despondent lover, but to Aristomenes it was salvation itself, or at least the hope of it which could not be overlooked; and the bed to which he addresses his farewell apostrophe is no ordinary transient's bed in an inn occupied only once for a few hours by a single person, but a lover's bed which has long been with him and has witnessed a great deal of his own erotic experience. Thus the episode of the suicide was not made to go with the story of Aristomenes; and the insertion of it by Apuleius is responsible for many puzzling contradictions in the narrative. No doubt an uncritical reader may overlook these contradictions, although editors and commentators have called attention to them without explaining them; but I think that any reader must admit that, for the reasons indicated, the story as a whole makes a very strange impression quite apart from the nature of its subject-matter.

8

Even more strange in its effect upon the reader is the story told by Thelyphron in Book II 21–30, which consists of three originally independent stories woven into one cleverly, and with a great deal of dramatic effect, to be sure, but with very superficial and unreal motivation, accompanied by many puzzling inconsistencies in the sequence of events.[23] To state the matter summarily, the story in question is made up of two mutually contradictory witch stories (parts 1 and 3) joined together in the middle by a third, originally independent, story about the resurrection of a dead man by an Egyptian priest for the purpose of testifying in a murder trial. Many readers find this composite story charming, I suspect, for the very reason that they cannot understand just what goes on in it and are agreeably mystified by its atmosphere of surrealism. This queer romantic effect, if we may call it that, results from the artificial sewing together of originally independent tales; but the composite narrative as a whole, in spite of its conspicuously disruptive sutures, is much richer in suspense and dramatic surprise than was any one of its component parts.

In the first component part (II 21–26) Thelyphron tells very dramatically how he, a Milesian travelling in Thessaly, was hired by a widow at Larissa to guard the dead body of her husband overnight against the depredations of witches. The exact nature of this undertaking, its dangers, and the responsibility resting upon the watcher are explained to him very definitely and with much emphasis in chapter 22. Here we learn that it is necessary for him who keeps watch to be extremely wakeful and alert; for the witches, intent on slicing off facial appendages from the corpse for use in their magical operations, are in the habit of entering the closed room by transforming themselves into small animals. The penalty that the watcher must pay in case he fails to protect the corpse is very explicit and severe: "And ah, yes!—what I'd almost forgotten to say—any watchman who fails to restore the corpse in the morning intact and unimpaired will be compelled to replace everything that is found to be missing from the corpse by cuttings from his own face." Thelyphron accepts the proposition with this understanding, and with boastful confidence. "You're talking nonsense," he says to the widow's agent, when the latter cautions him about keeping a strict watch over the corpse: "In me you see a man of iron, who doesn't sleep, one with sharper vision than Lynceus himself, or Argus, eyes all over." Thereupon he is escorted to the house of mourning, where he finds the widow of the dead man weeping in a dark inner room, entirely alone. Her grief is obviously genuine and unaffected. She leads Thelyphron into another room where the body of her husband lies, then she calls in seven witnesses to testify to the perfect condition of the corpse, saying: "Behold, the nose is intact, the eyes uninjured, the ears safe, the lips untouched, the chin solid." This is officially recorded in writing by an attendant scribe and sealed by the witnesses. The whole scene emphasizes anew the solemnity and the legality of the contract by which Thelyphron is bound. While on watch during the night he is put to sleep in spite of himself by a witch who enters the room in the form of a weasel. When morning comes, the widow enters hastily, accompanied by her seven witnesses, and anxiously begins to scrutinize the body, prepared, to all appearances, to cut off from Thelyphron any features that are found to be missing from her dead husband's face. This is the climax toward which we have been led very clearly from the beginning, amid many ironical nuances; and there can be no doubt, I think, that at this point in the original story which Apuleius was following Thelyphron's nose and ears were cut off, according to the terms of his contract, in order to replace the corresponding parts that the witches had taken from the dead man's body. Precisely this ending of the original story is echoed in the words with which Apuleius closes his episode, although he has altered, in what immediately precedes, the motivation for that outcome: "Thus in the manner of the proud Pentheus or of Orpheus, lacerated and pulled to pieces (*laceratus atque discerptus*) I was thrust forth from the house." (II 26).

Thelyphron's vigil, ending with his mutilation in accord with the terms of his contract, is a complete and well-rounded story in itself; and, as one may see from the manner in which Apuleius tells it, a story full of ironical amusement and rich in its dramatic possibilities. We do not know where Apuleius found this story; but as a one-act mime on the Roman stage, similar in kind to many burlesque episodes in Petronius and in Apuleius himself, it was bound to make a hit with any theatrical audience: Enter Thelyphron overflowing with confidence and braggadocio, pooh-poohing the herald's solemn and ominous warning, and boasting of his wakefulness—more keen-sighted than Lynceus or Argus, and all eyes; Thelyphron in the house of mourning, where the atmosphere is elaborately pictured as solemn and funereal, asking for plenty of wine and good food with which to make his vigil a pleasant one and hearing from the grief-stricken widow, in effect, "What do you think you came here for, a banquet?"; Thelyphron on guard, the gradual coming on of darkness and night (*ecce crepusculum et nox provecta et nox altior et dein concubia altiora et iam nox intempesta*), his rapidly mounting fear, the sudden appearance in the room of a little weasel that gazes at him with such a piercing look of self-assurance and impudence as to quite unnerve him, causing him to exclaim with more bravado than he feels: "Get away, you dirty little beast, go join your kind in the back yard before you feel the might of my arm. Be gone!"; Thelyphron falling suddenly into a deep sleep and snoring loudly, all but dead himself and "in need of a watchman on his own account"; daybreak, Thelyphron awakes and is terrified on realizing what has happened; enter the widow with her seven witnesses; the nose and ears of the dead man are found to be missing; Thelyphron's ears and nose are cut off to replace them, he is thrown out of the house mutilated, and down goes the curtain . . . . The show is over, ended with theatrical finality, and the audience is satisfied.

But Apuleius was not satisfied. He wanted to prolong the suspense as much as possible, to multiply the elements of surprise, and to bring in more and more action. For this purpose he adds two more originally independent stories represented as continuation of the adventures of Thelyphron, the widow, and her dead husband; but, in order to achieve this prolongation of the story and of the suspense, it was necessary for him to postpone the climax of Thelyphron's adventure, which came originally in his source at the end of the first witch story as described above. This he does by changing the ending of the first story. To the great surprise of the reader, as well as of

Thelyphron himself, the dead man's body in the morning is
found to be intact and unimpaired, in spite of the fact that
the witches had entered the room and had had easy access to
it; and Thelyphron, his vigil having been successful, is warmly
thanked by the widow for his services and paid in gold coin.
Apuleius might well have ended the episode of Thelyphron's
vigil right here, for the time being, by letting him depart from
the widow's house peacefully and with no more ado; because
the final outcome of Thelyphron's encounter with the witches,
which he intended to bring in later on as a new surprise at the
very end, was thus successfully avoided and postponed at this
point, and nothing more than Thelyphron's departure from the
house was needed for transition to the following story about
the dead man's resurrection. But Apuleius the showman could
not forget nor forego the highly theatrical manner of exit with
which the original story of the vigil had ended—Thelyphron
with his nose and ears cut off thrown bodily out of the house;
and, in order to preserve something of that impressive finale
in his own altered version of the story he invents a new and
very poorly motivated incident; "Since you have served us so
well in this," says the widow in parting, "we shall account you
henceforth as one of our own family." To which Thelyphron
replies in all innocence, "Nay, lady, consider me as one of your
servants, and whenever you have need of my services, you can
trust me to carry out your orders." "I had scarcely spoken
when the servants, cursing me for the outrageously evil omen,
picked up weapons of every kind and attacked me. One
punched my cheeks with his fist, another dug his elbows into
my shoulder blades . . . and thus in the manner of the proud
Pentheus, or of Orpheus, lacerated and torn apart, I was
thrown out of the house." The evil omen that the widow's servants resented so instantaneously and so furiously seems to
have been the insinuation, unintentional on Thelyphron's part,
that their mistress was likely to have other dead husbands in
the future. But such reckoning is surely farfetched and not
plausible in the circumstances. It seems unlikely that the

widow would allow her servants thus to chastise her benefactor, to whom she was feeling grateful, for so slight a matter,
or that they would presume to do so without her consent.
Apuleius is here hinting, very slyly as usual, by way of foreshadowing, that the widow was a murderess, the role that he
intends to give to her in the following story about the resurrection of the dead husband, in order to connect that new and
alien story with the story of Thelyphron and the (innocent)
widow by representing both widows as the same person. But
the occasion alleged for Thelyphron's rough treatment by the
servants in any case is quite inadequate and unpersuasive. If
I am not mistaken, Apuleius shows himself conscious of the
falsity of this motivation when he makes Thelyphron reassure
himself (and the reader) as follows after leaving the house: "On
recalling my unlucky and imprudent remark, alas, too late, I
confessed to myself that I deserved even more blows than I had
received." Here it seems that Apuleius, who is always self-
conscious, is trying to persuade himself against his own better
sense that Thelyphron really deserved his maltreatment, or
that his well-meaning words were the real cause of it.[24]

Thelyphron next proceeds to tell us (II 27–30) what happened when he came into the forum of the city and mingled
with the crowd there:[25] "The dead man was now brought forth
in procession after he had been mourned for and summoned by
name, and, according to the custom of the country, the funeral
procession was a public one and went through the market place,
as he was one of the nobles. Behold, an old man, whose grief
was expressed by the tears he shed and the amount of gray hair
he pulled out, came up beside the body and, laying hold of the
bier with both hands, addressed the people in a loud voice,
interrupted every now and then by sobs: 'I call upon your
good faith, O citizens,' he said, 'and upon your devotion to the
public weal. Come to the aid of your fellow townsman who has
been murdered, and punish that criminal and wicked woman
for this worst of all crimes. She it is, and no one else, who has
killed with poison this young man, my sister's son, for the sake

of an adulterer and to gain an inheritance!' " The effect of this
speech, Thelyphron relates, was to inflame the crowd against
the widow as a murderess. "They call for fire, they shout for
stones . . . but with well-rehearsed tears, she (the widow)
called on all the divinities as religiously as she could and
denied having committed such a crime. 'Well then,' said the
old man, 'let us leave the decision of truth to Divine Providence. Here is Zachlas the Egyptian, a prophet of the first
rank, who has already agreed with me for a considerable reward to recall the spirit for a time from the grave, and to
animate that corpse by a return from the realms of death.'
And as he spoke he led a man into the midst who was dressed
in linen garments, with his feet shod in palm leaf and his head
completely shaved.

"He kissed the prophet's hands for a long time and even
laid hold of his knees. 'Have pity on me, O priest;' he said,
'have pity on me by the stars of heaven and by the gods below,
by the elements of nature and the silence of the night, by the
Coptic dikes and by the risings of the Nile, by the mysteries
of Memphis and the rattles of Pharos! Grant a brief use of the
sunshine and infuse a little light into eyes that are closed forever! We do not fail in resignation or deny the earth her due:
we only pray for a brief moment of life, in order to obtain the
consolation of revenge.'

"Thus was the prophet made propitious, and upon the face
of the corpse he placed a certain herb, and another upon the
breast. Then turning towards the East in silent prayer to the
rising glory of the sun, he became the central figure of an im-
posing scene, which attuned the sentiments of the crowd to the
great miracle that was about to be wrought.

"I mingle with the people and take my stand near the bier
itself on a stone raised a little above the level, observing everything with a curious gaze. And now the chest of the corpse rises
and expands; its veins pulsate as in health; it is filled with the
breath of life; the body rises up; and the young man speaks:
'Oh, why do you bring me back to play a moment's part in

life, when I have drunk my draught of Lethe and am floating now upon the Stygian lake? Cease thou, I pray thee, cease, and allow me back to my repose!'

"Such were the words that the body was heard to speak! But, quoth the prophet with rising emotion: 'Nay, tell thy whole story to the people, and reveal the mystery of thy death! Dost thou forget that my prayers can rouse the Furies? That they can bring tortures to thy wearied frame?'

"Straightway the one upon the bier makes answer, and addresses the people with a hollow groan: 'I was carried off by the wicked arts of my bride, condemned to a poisoned cup, and gave up my marriage-bed warm to an adulterer.' "

Hereupon the widow bandies words with her dead husband in denial of his accusations. The populace seethes with excitement, carried to opposite extremes of opinion. "Some say that the villainous female should at once be buried alive with her husband's body; others, that no credence should be given to the lies of a corpse.

But this contention was set at rest by the following words of the young husband . . . 'I shall give you, ah, yes, I shall give you a clear proof of the inviolable truth! I shall lay my finger on something that has never before come to the knowledge of man!' Then, pointing at me in the crowd, he said: 'When this most sagacious of watchmen was holding sleepless vigil by my body, the old witches hovered over my remains with their enchantments, and many a form they assumed for their purpose in vain. At last they injected a cloud of sleep into the room, and when he was buried in profound repose they did not cease calling me by name, till my senseless frame and limbs, chilled in death, endeavoured to respond to the magic by ineffective movements. Hereupon this man, who was of course alive and only in the death of sleep, rose up mechanically to answer to the name, which happens to be his name as well as mine. He walked forward of his own accord like a lifeless shade to the doors of the chamber; and, though they were carefully bolted, still, through a crevice that was there, his nose first of all, and then his ears, were cut off, and so he was mutilated in my place. And to complete their illusion, they fixed wax models of the ears they had cut off with the greatest exactitude to the proper spot, and the same with regard to his nose. There stands the poor fellow with the reward he has gained, not for his diligence, but for the maiming he has received!'

"Terrified at what he said, I begin to tempt Fortune. I put my hand up to my nose and take hold of it; it comes off! I handle my ears; down they fall! The fingers of all are pointed at me; I am a butt for the nods and winks of every one present; laughter begins to bubble up, and I save myself, tripping over the bystanders' feet as I run, with a cold sweat pouring down my body. I was unable afterwards, in my ridiculous, mutilated condition, to return to my ancestral home, and I have had to train my hair in long bands on each side to conceal my wounded ear-holes; while, as for my nasal deformity, I have had to contrive a decent covering for it by the linen arrangement you see there glued tightly over it."

What the resurrected dead man tells the crowd concerning what happened to Thelyphron at the hands of the witches is brought in with great dramatic effect, and in that respect is successful as storytelling. But, logically considered, this stunning denouement is contradictory both to the story of the resurrection and to that about Thelyphron's vigil as told by Apuleius in the beginning (II 25–26); and it is just these contradictions that reveal the tripartite nature of the Apuleian story as a whole and the mechanical methods by which the author has woven three originally independent and diverse stories into one.

The dead man was brought to life momentarily for the purpose of testifying concerning the cause of his own death, on the natural assumption that what he had to say about that would prove the case. He would surely know who, if anyone, had killed him, and he could have no object in telling a death-dealing lie about his wife's guilt, if he knew her to be innocent. As soon as his testimony has been given, to the effect that his wife was guilty, the story of the resurrection has reached its natural and logical conclusion. What follows in Apuleius as ostensible but sham proof of the dead man's veracity in testifying against his wife, namely that he can show you—very impressively—what happened to Thelyphron, is irrelevant and anticlimactic to the murder story and has value only as an introduction to the new and contradictory story about the doings of the witches which the dead man here tells, and with which the Apuleian story of Thelyphron comes to its end.

In the story told by the dead man the witches were unable to enter the room even after the watchman, Thelyphron, had been put to sleep. Instead, they summoned the dead man to the door by the magic power of his name, and when Thelyphron was the first to respond, because his name was the same as the dead man's and he was alive, they cut off *his* nose and ears, by mistake, from the outside through a chink in the door. By contrast, in the first story about Thelyphron's vigil as told by Apuleius (II 25), a witch actually entered the room in the form of a weasel, and that means that the witches had easy access to the corpse *inside* the room. Under those conditions they would not cut off Thelyphron's nose and ears but those of the dead man, there would be no summoning of the man by name, and the mutilation of the corpse would take place inside the room and not on the outside. In that first story about the vigil Thelyphron must have suffered his mutilation at the hands of the widow's servants for having failed to keep the witches away from the corpse; and of that original ending, suppressed by Apuleius, many indications still remain, as we have seen, even in the story as Apuleius tells it.

9

The famous story told by Apuleius about the battle of Lucius with the three magically animated goatskins (wine-skins), which he mistook for robbers trying to break into his host's house (*Met.* II 32 and III 15–18), was certainly part of the original *Luciad* as told in the Greek Μεταμορφώσεις, although it is omitted in the epitome (the Lucianic *Onos*). But the episode describing the carnival of the great god Laughter (*Risus*) in *Met.* III 1–11, and everything in the text that points forward or backward to that charming episode is Apuleian addition; whereby a new and very dramatic story has been inserted into the original story about the fight with the goatskins, not without puzzling contradictions in the motivation which betray the fact that it has been interpolated by the Roman author.[26] For the purpose of making it clear to the reader how Apuleius has joined these two originally separate stories together into one, I shall begin by describing first of all the course of events as it must have been, in outline, in the Greek original, that is, in the lost *Metamorphoses* of Lucian, which was the principal source followed by Apuleius in his own *Metamorphoses*.

Reconstructed on the basis of its two independent derivatives, the Lucianic *Onos*, an epitome of the Greek Μεταμορφώσεις, and the Apuleian *Metamorphoses*, an expansion, the original story about the slaying of the animated goatskins was somewhat as follows, within the context of Lucius' stay at Hypata:

Lucius, in the course of his eager investigation of Thessalian magic and of metamorphoses in particular, learns from his kinswoman Byrrhena (= Abroea in *Onos* 4), by way of warning (*Onos* 4, *Met.* II 5), that the wife of his host Milo (= Hipparchus in *Onos* 4), appropriately named Pamphile in Apuleius, is a mighty sorceress capable of performing all kinds of miracles and metamorphoses in the pursuance of her lust, and that she makes love to every handsome young man that she sees. "And if anyone fails to yield to her desire," says Byrrhena, "she moves against him by means of her magic arts. Before now she has changed many men into animals and some she has quite destroyed." (*Onos* 4, *Met.* II 5). On hearing this, Lucius, far from being alarmed by Byrrhena's warning, is delighted to learn that what he had long been searching for was at home with him in Milo's house in the person of his wife Pamphile.

He hurries home, resolving on the way to make love to the maid Fotis (= Palaestra in the *Onos*), in order to learn from her the secrets of her mistress Pamphile, and to see the latter in the act of performing some miracle (*Onos* 5, *Met.* II 6). Here follows in both versions (*Onos* 6–10, *Met.* II 7–17), but interrupted by digressions in *Met.* II 8–9 and 11–14, a relatively long description of Lucius' erotic encounter with Fotis, ending with the statement that several nights were spent in this luxurious fashion. At this point the author of the Greek epitome makes Lucius say, at the beginning of *Onos* 11, that he was so preoccupied with his erotic pleasures that he forgot about other matters until, suddenly, he happened to remember the purpose for which he had made love to Fotis in the beginning, and thereupon asked her to show him her mistress in the act of performing magic or of transforming herself: δεῖξόν μοι μαγγανεύουσαν ἢ μεταμορφουμένην τὴν δέσποιναν. The transition here is noticeably abrupt and poorly motivated; which suggests that the epitomator has left out an important motivating episode, that namely about Lucius' battle with the animated goatskins, which is retained by Apuleius in a passage later on (*Met.* II 32). What follows in the remainder of chapter 11 in the *Onos*, consisting of a dialogue between Lucius and Fotis on the subject of Pamphile's magic, beginning with the words "Show me" (δεῖξόν μοι, etc. as quoted above) and ending with a promise by Fotis that she will show Lucius her mistress in the act of transforming herself whenever an opportunity arises—all this, which must be reckoned as belonging in the original *Luciad*, is reproduced in substance by Apuleius at a later point in his own narrative, namely in *Met.* III 19–20, immediately following the explanation given by Fotis of how the three goatskins which Lucius had mistaken for robbers breaking into Milo's house and had killed, had been brought to life accidentally by Pamphile's magic. It was that marvelous adventure with the goatskins and the explanation of how it came about that revived and stimulated Lucius' curiosity about magic, reminded him of his original purpose in making love to the maid Fotis, and induced him forthwith to beg of her that she show him her mistress in the act of transforming herself. It was on his return home from a dinner party at Byrrhena's house after midnight that Lucius battled with the goatskins at Milo's door, according to the well-motivated account given by Apuleius; but all this, including the description of the entertainment and conversation at Byrrhena's house, has been omitted in the Greek epitome (*Onos* 11 *ad init.*), passed over in a single transitional sentence: "Finally it occurred to me to investigate those things on account of which I was engaged in these (erotic) struggles" (καί ποτε ἐπὶ νοῦν μοι ἦλθε τὸ μαθεῖν ὧν ἕνεκα ἤθλουν). It is probable that the description given in the original Greek Μεταμορφώσεις of Byrrhena's banquet, at which Lucius was present, included some conversation on the subject of witchcraft, but we have no clue to indicate precisely what this conversation was. It certainly did not contain Thelyphron's story as given by Apuleius (*Met.* II 21–30), which is a long digression from the main story, alien in kind to the style and method of the original *Luciad*.

After his battle with the animated goatskins, which he mistook for robbers on his return to Milo's house late at night, Lucius was met at the threshold by Fotis, "who was aroused by the tumultuous battle and threw open the doors, through which I crept in, all out of breath and sweating profusely, after fighting three robbers in the manner of Hercules at the slaying of Geryon" (*Met.* II 32). At this point the original story is interrupted by Apuleius for the purpose of tacking on his own story about the festival of Risus, which required the passage of another full day before Lucius could learn from Fotis, as he does in *Met.* III 13–18, how the goatskins had been brought to life by Pamphile's magic operations, and were beating against her door just at the time when he happened to return home, intoxicated, from Byrrhena's party. In the Greek original this explanation by Fotis was made, naturally, as soon as Lucius was alone in the house with her, immediately after his slaying of the goatskins; but in Apuleius it is postponed, very implausibly, until the following night after the Risus festival, although there is not a word in Fotis' explanation about the Risus festival, at which Lucius had been made the butt of public laughter, nor about the instigators of it. Instead, it all relates to Pamphile's operations and the collaboration of Fotis, as must have been the case in the Greek original, and Fotis blames herself for all that had happened. Her mistress Pamphile had recently set her affections on a young Boeotian, and, on the afternoon preceding Lucius' nocturnal fight with the goatskins, had ordered Fotis to gather some of the young man's hairs at the barbershop, in order that she might force him, by means of magic, to come to her in person. Fotis, however, being driven away by the barber and not daring to return to her mistress empty-handed, gathered some hairs clipped from three goatskins, which were on sale as wine-bags in a nearby shop, and gave these to her mistress in place of the young man's hair. In order to perform her magic operations on the hairs it was necessary for Pamphile to wait until after sundown, and meanwhile she was extremely eager and impatient for the coming of night: "I heard her *this evening*," says Fotis (*Met.* III 16), "with these very ears of mine I heard her threatening that, unless the sun went down more quickly and gave place to night for the practice of her magic allurements, she would hide it in a cloud and darken it forever!"

Since the words *audivi vesperi*, quoted above in translation, are spoken at night after Fotis has put her mistress to bed (*Met.* III 13), they can mean only *this* evening; which was the evening *before* the nocturnal combat of Lucius with the goatskins animated by Pamphile's magic, *not* the evening following the Risus festival twenty-four hours later, as Apuleius elsewhere represents the matter in order to make room for his interpolated episode. Now on the day of the Risus festival, when Apuleius was obliged to represent this conversation with Fotis as taking place, Pamphile's magical operation on the hairs, intended to bring the young man perforce to her door, had already failed and she had no other tangible object on which to exert her magic. She would not then be eager and impatient for the coming of night, and if she threatened anyone on that day it would not be the sun for lingering but Fotis for having given her the wrong hairs. It is therefore an oversight on the part of Apuleius, due to incautious adherence to either the phraseology or the thought of the Greek original, when he lets Fotis say that Pamphile threatened the sun "this evening"; such a statement could be made only in a context in which there was no Risus festival, as there was none in the original *Luciad*.

A few days after the night on which Lucius learned from Fotis how Pamphile's magic had brought the goatskins to her door by mistake, in place of the young Boeotian, Fotis comes to Lucius with the exciting news that Pamphile is now about to transform herself into a bird and fly to her loved one (*Onos* 12, *Met.* III 21), because, as Apuleius tells us, her various attempts to bring the young man to herself had all failed. Soon afterwards Lucius is enabled by Fotis to see Pamphile change herself into a bird; and when Fotis tries to do the same for Lucius at his own request, she applies the wrong ointment by mistake and transforms him into an ass instead of into a bird.

The story of Lucius' encounter with the goatskins on his return from a dinner party at the house of his kinswoman Byrrhena, as told by Apuleius but omitted in the Greek epitome (*Onos* 11), is not likely to have been absent in the original Greek *Luciad*, for the following reasons. It is not a digression from the main story but an integral part of Lucius' experience with Pamphile's magic and his eager investigation of metamorphoses, which is the central theme of the *Luciad* at the beginning in both extant versions. It is the basis on which the story of the Risus festival, a public performance planned in advance, was founded, but it is ill-suited for that purpose because it was an unforeseeable *accident* that took place late at night in private surroundings; Apuleius must have found this story about Pamphile's magic already told in his Greek original, otherwise he would not have chosen it as the basis for his

Risus festival. Its occurrence served to explain the suddenly renewed and greatly stimulated curiosity of Lucius about Pamphile's magic, which his love affair with Fotis had caused him temporarily to forget, and which is unmotivated in the Greek epitome (*Onos* 11). And finally, it tells us why Pamphile found it necessary to transform herself into a bird and fly to her loved one; she did so because she had failed in an attempt to bring the young man by magic to her own door.

If the adventure with the animated goatskins as told by Apuleius was part of the original story of Lucius, it follows that the episode of the Risus festival was not such but rather an Apuleian invention, because it is logically incompatible with the story of the goatskins. It was after midnight (*fere iam tertia vigilia*, *Met.* III 3) when Lucius slew the goatskins which had been brought to life by Pamphile accidentally; and it was shortly after sunrise, according to Apuleius (III 1–2) that many thousands of citizens, all of them laughing in anticipation of the mock trial that they knew was about to take place, thronged around Lucius in the public square after his arrest by the magistrates on a charge of triple murder. This implies, what is scarcely credible, that plans for the mock trial had been made by the magistrates, and the entire populace notified of it, in the interval between midnight and sunrise. Apuleius does not tell us this explicitly, but it follows of necessity, from the sequence of events in his narrative, as the only possible explanation of how the Risus festival could have been managed. That explanation, however implausible in the nature of things, and in the absence of any explicit reference to it, is at least humanly *possible*; but what Apuleius himself suggests concerning the instigation of the mock trial, deliberately but by means only of dark hints and ironical foreshadowing in *Met.* II 31 and III 12, is simply *not possible*, namely that Byrrhena and her friends knew on the preceding evening what was going to happen to Lucius at the Risus festival on the following day and had taken some part in the planning of it.[27] No one, not even Pamphile herself or Fotis, much less Byrrhena and others,

could possibly have foreseen that Lucius would slay three animated goatskins on his return to Milo's house late at night.
Any plans made for the mock trial at the Risus festival would
therefore have to be made after that accidental encounter with
the goatskins, not before.

The falsity of Apuleius' motivation for the Risus festival is
in itself an indication that he has interpolated that episode
into the original story of Lucius' adventures at Hypata; and
so too are the implausibilities, already mentioned, which are
occasioned by the postponement of Fotis' explanation until the
night after the mock trial, and the fact that in that explanation
not a word is said about the mock trial (Risus festival) or the
instigators of it. It is contrary to probability in the realm of
human nature that Lucius, after his exciting battle with the
goatskins, which he believed to be robbers, should go to sleep
immediately afterwards, as soon as Fotis, aroused by the tumult, had opened the doors and let him into the house (*Met.*
II 32). In those circumstances, the most natural thing to follow
was the conversation with Fotis in which she explained to
Lucius what had just happened and her own part in it; and
Apuleius, by his own inadvertence in allowing Fotis to say in
effect that Pamphile performed her magic operation on the
goathairs "this evening," betrays his awareness of the fact
that, in the Greek *Luciad* which he was following, and which
in many places he translates almost literally,[28] this explanation by Fotis was made on the night when Lucius fought with
the goatskins at Milo's door. After learning from Fotis that
the three men whom he thought he had killed were only goatskins, Lucius could not have been made an April-fool victim
at a solemn mock-trial for murder on the next day and there
could have been no Risus festival featured by such ceremonies
as Apuleius describes.[29]

10

The three composite stories which we have analyzed above are
meant to illustrate in detail certain features of the Apuleian

narrative which are profoundly characteristic of the author, and which explain, incidentally and among other things, the unique atmosphere of mystery and surrealism that pervades the first three books of the *Metamorphoses*. That mysterious, unworldly effect, in a degree which is elsewhere unparalleled in narrative literature of the West, as far as I know, results from artificially joining together two or more originally independent stories in such a way that elements appropriate to only one or another of the original stories are left standing in the new composite structure, where they are either meaningless or contradictory and lead into blind alleys of motivation. Like other Roman authors who work with Greek originals, Apuleius strives constantly to add something new to a subject matter which he has borrowed and which had already been shaped organically by some other writer. In so doing, and in combining source materials, he retains carelessly, under the dramatic impulse of the moment, instead of eliminating carefully, some of the building blocks used by the original architects which at best are non-functional in his own new and larger structure, and often interfere with it and make it look queer. The reader is consequently puzzled at times to understand just what is going on and what the meaning may be of this or that incident or speech in relation to the larger context of the story as a whole. He looks instinctively but in vain for organic connections between things which the author has not given him, or, if so, falsely and unconvincingly, and which he can find for himself only by the exercise of a very free and hazy imagination. Nevertheless, in spite of its contradictions, the composite Apuleian narrative as a whole is much richer in suspense and dramatic surprise than was any one of its component parts, and that is what the author intended.

The principal aims of Apuleius in retelling a Greek story, and in adding to it, or in making one story out of two or more shorter ones, are to prolong the suspense, add to the amount of action, and to the number of surprises for the reader, and fill out with picturesque and dramatic details that which the

Greek author had told in more summary and abstract terms for the sake only of its total meaning, with little or no effort having been made to dramatize the story or to entertain the reader in the process of telling it.[30] The general effect of these Apuleian innovations, the illustration of which, if complete, would require an entire book on the subject, is to create a new kind of story which is more in accord with the modern conception of what a short story artistically told for its own sake as entertainment should be.

So much for the structural features of the Apuleian story and the aesthetic effects that they produce. More important, for the realization of where Apuleius with his *Metamorphoses* stands in the history of prose fiction, is the fact that he has superimposed upon a basically comic, picaresque or satirical narrative, which was something cold and impersonal, the warm ideal values of sympathetic character portrayal which had previously been exploited only in poetry—except insofar as they had spilled over occasionally into historiography and other prose forms wherein they were contraband elements, as in Herodotus (cf. p. 251 above). Consider that what Apuleius did in the second century was precisely the same kind of thing, fundamentally, that Cervantes did later in *Don Quixote*, that Fielding did in *Joseph Andrews* and the Abbé Prévost in *Manon Lescaut*.[31] It is the fusion in those books of two originally separate traditions each with its own proprieties and conventions, the one essentially comic, picaresque or satirical, the other ideal and poetic, that made the potentialities of the novel what they are today, and what they were likewise in Greek literature at the end of the second century.

APPENDICES

APPENDICES

APPENDIX I
The Pseudo-Clementine Romance

THE ROMANCE of Ps.-Clement, which has a very complicated history, has come down to us in two principal texts, as follows:

1. The Latin version called *Recognitiones* made by Rufinus near the end of the fourth century on the basis of a Greek text that bore the title Ἀναγνώσεις or Ἀναγνωρισμοί. The earlier form from which the latter in turn was derived may be designated *R*.

2. A Greek text which is entitled *Homilies* by modern editors, but which has come down under the title Κλήμεντος τοῦ Πέτρου ἐπιδημιῶν κηρυγμάτων ἐπιτομή. The original form of the text from which these extant *Homilies*, twenty in number, were derived is designated *H*.

Texts and English translations of the Latin *Recognitiones* and of the Greek *Homilies* are mentioned below in the Bibliography. Here we may add that the Greek text of the *Homilies* edited by A. R. M. Dressel in 1853 at Göttingen is reproduced in Migne's *Patrol. Gr.*, Vol. II cols. 19–468. Both texts, *R* and *H*, include, within the report of twenty homilies delivered by Peter, the story told by Clement of how the members of his family (father, mother, identical twin brothers named Faustinus and Faustinianus, and Clement himself) were separated from each other and, after long travels around the shores of the eastern Mediterranean, were finally reunited and recognized each other on the island of Arados in the company of Peter. Both texts, *R* and *H*, give the same story—which was derived from a pre-Christian Greek romance built on a structural pattern similar to that of *Apollonius Prince of Tyre* and to the plot of Plautus' *Menaechini* —with only small variations; but the two versions vary widely from each other in the sermons reported, i.e. the homilies of Peter. The texts *R* and *H* are derived independently from a common source, which was probably entitled Περίοδοι Πέτρου (*Peregrinations of Peter*), but the two traditions were conflated with each other in the *Homilies* (see p. ix in B. Rehm's ed., *Die Pseudoklementinen* I, *Homilien* [Berlin, 1953]). The common source of *H* and *R* is dated to the second century by O. Cullmann in his book on *Le Problème Littéraire et Historique du Roman Pseudo-Clementine* (Paris, 1930). Between the common source of *R* and *H* and the Latin *Recognitiones* of Rufinus there must have intervened, as indicated above, a text called 'Αναγνώσεις or 'Αναγνωρισμοί, which was so entitled by an editor who thought of Clement's story about the reunion of his family as the principal or most characteristic feature of the homilies called Πέτρου Περίοδοι from which his own text was copied or adapted. That was a natural thing for a later redactor to do in revising or abbreviating a text which was weighted with theological or abstract philosophical matter. Much as he may have favored the theology, as a Christian ought to, still he was more impressed by the romantic narrative, and for that reason put it in his title. The romance as such is better preserved in the *Recognitiones* than in the *Homilies* (Cullmann, p. 63); and in the *Homilies* the sermons of Peter are preserved more faithfully than they are in the *Recognitiones* (Cullmann, p. 70).

The entire romance of Clement and his family is related in *Homilies* XII 8–XIV on pp. 177–211 of Rehm's text, and in the *Recognitiones* in *Homilies* VII 8–38 and IX 32–37 (= J. P. Migne, *Patrologia Graeco-Latina* I [Paris, 1857], cols. 1358–1371 and 1417–19). Thus we see that the romance itself takes up only a small amount of text, relatively, in a lengthy book composed of twenty sermons by St. Peter, as reported by Clement. It is preceded by an introduction consisting largely of homily no. I, in which Clement tells how he came to leave Rome and to join the congregation of St. Peter in Palestine, and is followed by six more homilies (nos. XV–XX) in 69 pages.

The story: Clement, son of Faustus and Mattidia, high-born Romans, had two older brothers named Faustinus and Faustinianus, respectively, who were identical twins. Of these older brothers, and of his mother, Clement had only the dimmest recollection. He was told by his father that his mother had dreamed that, unless she left Rome with her twin sons and stayed away twelve years, she and they would perish by a miserable death. Acting on this prophetic warning, Faustus, Clement's father, put his wife Mattidia with her twin sons on a ship bound for Athens, that they might be educated there, but he kept Clement at home with himself. When a year had gone by Faustus sent messengers with money and provisions for his wife and children at Athens, instructed to inquire and report on how they were getting along; but the messengers never returned. In the third year he sent other envoys with provisions and similar instructions, and these, returning in the fourth year, reported that they had not found either the mother or her sons, Clement's brothers, that they had never been in Athens, nor could any traces be found of those who had accompanied them. On hearing this the father, in deep dejection and hardly knowing where to turn next, went down to the port and there made inquiry of many persons who had been shipwrecked within the last four years, to learn whether any of them had seen the body of a woman floating on the sea with her two children; but he could learn nothing. After that he had left Clement at Rome, then twelve years old, and had set forth on shipboard in search of his wife and children. Since that time, twenty years ago, Clement had received no letter from his father, he tells Peter, and did not know whether he was living or dead. He supposed that his father was dead, either from grief or from shipwreck. Peter condoles with Clement on the loss of his father, and briefly sermonizes about it. When he had finished speaking one of the company proposed that they should all cross over to the island of Arados near by, in order to see there some famous columns of vines. To this Peter consented; but on reaching the island, instead of going inland with the others to see the sights, he remained behind near the harbor, where his attention had been attracted by an old woman sitting in front of a door and begging food from passers-by. Peter asked her why she had stooped so low as to be begging instead of working for her living with the hands that God had given her. She answered with a sigh, "Would that I had hands capable of doing work!" All she had now was the semblance of hands; her hands were really dead, because she had gnawed them so fiercely in the agony of her grief. Had she been stouthearted instead of weak, she says, she would before now have thrown herself off a cliff or into the sea, and so ended her suffering. When Peter tells her that suicide is wrong and would be punished after death, the old woman says she wishes she could be persuaded that there is life beyond death; if so, she would be glad to die and face punishment for the sake of meeting with her dear ones there if only for an hour. Peter then asks her to tell him what has happened to her, promising in return to convince her that there is life after death. She consents and tells what her life has been. She was the offspring of highborn parents in a certain city. She had married a nobleman to whom she had borne twin sons at first and later a third son. When it happened that her husband's brother made unwelcome advances to her, in order not to be false to her husband by yielding, nor, by telling him about the matter, to bring on quarreling between the brothers, she decided to leave home with her twin sons and live abroad for a while, until her brother-in-law should forget his evil passion for her. For the purpose of obtaining her husband's consent, she falsely pretended to have had a dream in which she had been warned that, unless she left home with her twin sons, she and her husband and children would perish miserably. Persuaded by this story her husband had put her with her sons on a ship bound for Athens; but she had been shipwrecked, separated from her twin sons without knowing what had become of them, and driven ashore on this island of Arados. Here she had been befriended by some poor women and, in particular, by the old woman in whose house she was now staying, before the latter had become a hopeless paralytic unable to move from her bed. This woman too had lost her young husband on the sea. She was begging for her disabled friend as well as for herself. Peter then asked her where she came from and the names of her sons, and she sought to withhold the truth about herself by saying that her home had been in Ephesus, and she gave him false names in place of the real names of her three sons. Peter told her that there was a young man among his followers who was a Roman citizen, and related to her what this young man had told him about his mother; that she had dreamed that she must leave home in order to save her family from destruction, that she had acted accordingly by taking a ship for Athens in company with her twin sons, leaving himself, a younger son, behind with his father in Rome, and that he, Peter's young follower, did not know what had become of his mother, his father, or his two older brothers, but supposed they had perished on the sea. On hearing this from Peter, the old woman was greatly excited and almost fainted from joy, knowing, as Peter now did, that she had found her youngest son. She begged Peter to take her to the young man immediately. "First tell me his name," said Peter, "otherwise you shall not see him." "I'm the young man's mother," she said. "But what is his name?" "His name is Clement," she replied. "Yes," said Peter, "that is his name. He is the young man who was speaking with me here a little while ago. I told him to wait for me at the ship." Peter then leads the old woman to the ship and there, after some hesitation and doubt on the part of Clement, mother and son recognize each other amid great rejoicing on all sides. Peter miraculously cures the paralytic woman, who was brought to him on her bed, and likewise Mattidia's hands. Thereafter the whole party crossed over to Antarados on the mainland and from there they journey northward along the coast, bound for Antioch, where Peter planned to stay for some time preaching. On the way Clement's mother asks him about his father, Faustus, and Clement tells her that he had left Rome twenty years ago in search of her and his twin sons, and had never returned or been heard from since then. Mattidia weeps bitterly on learning that her husband too has been lost and has probably perished on the sea. When the party arrives at Laodicea they are met at the city gates by two of Peter's ardent followers, Nicetas and Aquila, who are wealthy and prosperous citizens of the city and who welcome Peter and his company to their homes. They ask who the woman is that they are bringing with them. Clement answers that it is his own long lost mother whom he has just now found with Peter's help, and Peter then proceeds to relate everything that Mattidia had told him about the circumstances of her leaving Rome, the names of her children, and her misfortunes abroad. On hearing this, Nicetas and Aquila are astounded: "Is this the truth or only a dream? We are Faustinus and Faustinianus!" A joyful reunion with their mother and Clement follows soon afterwards at the home of one of the twins. Faustinus (Nicetas) explains that he and his twin brother had assumed the false names Nicetas and Aquila after their capture by pirates—not for any useful purpose or advantage to themselves here mentioned, but because, as the reader of romances should know, the author wanted to get his protagonists into more trouble by their telling of lies about themselves, thereby thickening the plot of their adventures. After the shipwreck Faustinus and Faustinianus, separated from their mother, were captured by pirates and taken to Caesarea on the coast of Palestine, where they were sold to a Jewish

woman named Justa. This woman, a Christian proselyte, had brought
them up as though they were her own children. They had religious
faith from childhood; but "we were given also a thorough education
in Greek philosophy," says Faustinus, "in order that we might
convict the Gentiles of their error by means of dialectic."

While this conversation was going on, Peter, who had not yet
joined the company but had remained behind in the city, entered and
explained why he was late. He had been waylaid by an old laboring
man who was a confirmed astrologist, believing that a man's or a
woman's fortune in life was predetermined by the conjunction of
stars at one's birth, and that there was no God or Providence in the
guidance of human affairs; he wanted to convince Peter of his error.
Peter had argued with this old man and a crowd had gathered around
them to listen. In order to prove his point the old man had told about
the experience of a Roman citizen and his wife with whom he was
closely acquainted and whose horoscopes he knew. Their fortunes in
the end proved to be exactly what the stars had forecast. It was fated
that his friend's wife, the old man said, was to be an adulteress falling
in love with her own servants, and to perish with them far from home
on the sea; and so it came about that she fell in love with one of her
servants—no fault of hers—and, having run away with him, shared
his bed, and perished with him on the sea. At this point Peter had
begun to cross-examine the old man: "How do *you* know that, after
fleeing into foreign parts, she married the servant, or that, after she
had married him, she perished?" "I know the truth about her accurately, not that she married the servant, for at the time I did not
know of my own knowledge even that she had fallen in love with him,
but after she went away her husband's brother told me everything
about her and her love affairs. He was a pious man and had resisted
her erotic advances, because he could not think of defiling his brother's
bed. On being repulsed by her brother-in-law she feared him and, in
order to leave Rome with her husband's consent, she told him that
she had been warned in a dream that, unless she did so in company
with her twin sons, the whole family would perish by a miserable
death. Persuaded by this story, her husband had put her on board a
ship bound for Athens with her twin sons, who were to be educated
there, sending with them servants and provisions necessary for their
journey. He kept his third son, the youngest, with himself at Rome.
Afterwards he went abroad in search of his wife and children, taking

me along with him as a friend, but our search was in vain. We ended up in Selencia, where, after a few days, he died brokenhearted. After that I came to this neighborhood and earned my living by manual labor." When he heard this story from the old man, Peter knew that he was lying and that he himself was the Roman whose wife had deserted him along with her twin sons. Peter had questioned the old man about himself and his family as follows: What was his name? He answered "Faustus." The names of his twin sons? "Faustinus and Faustinianus." Of his third son? "Clement." And his wife's name? "Mattidia." Peter had not yet told the old man that his family had been found, but he was now telling them, the mother and her sons, that their father had survived and was living nearby; and soon afterwards Faustus himself entered the room and the whole family was thus joyfully reunited.

Much of what is told about Clement and his family in these Christian homilies is non-functional, superfluous, or even contradictory in the context in which it stands; from which fact one must infer that the whole matter has been taken from an outside source, presumably for the purpose (seen in the title *Recognitiones*) of making the lengthy sermons on theological doctrine more attractive. This is demonstrated in clear detail by Miss Trenkner on pp. 101 f. of her *Greek Novella* (Cambridge University Press, 1958). In view of the nature of the subject matter and the irrelevance of parts of it to the Clementine context, scholars who have made a close-up study of the problem are generally agreed that the source from which the romance of Clement was taken was a pagan Greek romance antedating the second century; so Rohde, *Gr. Rom.*[3] p. 507; Cullmann, pp. 140 f.; W. Heintze, *Der Clemensroman und seine griech. Quellen* (= *Texte und Untersuchungen* 40.2 [Leipzig, 1914]; Christ-Schmid-Stählin, *Gesch. d. Gr. Litt.*[6] (1924), II, 1210; W. Bousset in *Theol. Literaturzeitung* 40 (1915), 296, who, in agreement with Heintze, sees among the sources, in addition to the old Greek romance, a Jewish apologetical disputation on mythology, providence, and astrological fatalism.

Another pagan text, one verbally imitated by Clement in the first homily, where he describes his intention, later abandoned, of hiring an Egyptian magician to call up a dead man who may inform him about the fate of the soul after death and the nature of the universe, is extant in the introduction of an astrological book written in the early second century by one Harpocration, who tells us that he was an Alexandrian grammarian and who may therefore have been the author of the well-known *Vocabulary of the Ten Orators*. In his astrological book (ed. P. Boudreaux in *Cat. Codd. Astrol. Gr.* VIII 3, [Bruxelles, 1912], 132 ff.) this Harpocration describes in serious vein an Egyptian *nekyomanteia* which appears to have been a principal source alike for Lucian in his satirical dialogue of that title and for Clemens in his preface to the homilies of Peter. For a full account of these texts and their interrelationship, see the article by Franz Boll entitled "Das Eingangstück der Ps.-Klementinen" in *Ztschr. für die Neutestamentliche Wiss.* 17 (1916), 139–148.

Two of the component parts of the pagan romance which was taken over into the Clementine *Homilies*, later called *Recognitions*, are attested in pre-Christian literature. One of these is the basic frame-story of a woman who, like Mattidia, leaves home and travels in order to avoid attempts made by a close relative upon her virtue, or against her marital fidelity, after which she is driven by Fortune "all around the shores of Syria, Phoenicia, and Judaea." This, as I have explained in *Aesopica* I, pp. 19–20, was told as a fable by Aesop to the Delphians in ch. 141 of the *Life of Aesop* (Vita G), which itself was written not later than the first century after Christ. The other component part of the romance, to which we referred, concerned the adventures of the twin sons of the woman in exile above mentioned, how they were separated from each other in the course of their travels, and how one twin was mistaken for the other by the other's intimate associates. This tale, typified by the plot of the *Menaechmi* of Plautus, appears in many variant forms both written and oral throughout the ages. That it was taken into the Clementine *Homilies*, or the *Peregrinations of Peter*, from an outside written source is evident from the fact that the mention of the twins Faustinus and Faustinianus, and their great similarity to each other, leads to nothing in the Christian context since these twins are not, as elsewhere, separated in their travels or mistaken one for the other.

The story of the *Recognitions* incorporated in the Clementine *Homilies* had a long history and passed into many variant forms, both written and oral, mainly under the influence of the Clementine texts, both in western Europe and in the Muslim world of the Near East. The most complete account of these later versions is given by W. Bousset in a monograph entitled "Die Geschichte eines Wiedererkennungsmärchens" on pp. 469–551 of *Nachrichten von der königlichen*

Gesellschaft der Wissenschaft zu Göttingen, Philol.-hist. Klasse (1916).
On the Arabic versions see further the important article by Gustave
von Grunebaum entitled "Greek Form Elements in the Arabian
Nights," in *JAOS* 62 (1942), 382.

APPENDIX II
The Latin Romance
Apollonius of Tyre

Apollonius Prince of Tyre is the title of a Latin romance, the earliest form of which, free of later interpolations, can be dated with confidence on the basis of its abundant numismatic terminology and calculations to the third century after Christ. Many complex problems of interpretation and of literary and folkloristic tradition, in part unsolved or insolvable, arise in connection with the study of this unique book; whether one looks to its wide propagation in medieval and early modern times, its multifarious influence on other famous stories, and its entanglement with traditions stemming from the Ps.-Clementine *Recognitiones*, or whether one inquires into the nature of its composition, the sources of its narrative material, and the question of whether or not or in what sense it is a translation of a Greek original.[1] Three aspects of this Apollonius romance, viewed

[1] A lucid and comprehensive survey of our data on this book, the problems connected with it, and the critical bibliography up to 1914, is given by Schanz in Schanz-Hosius-Krüger, *Geschichte der römischen Litteratur*, IV 2 (1920), pp. 87–92 (art. 1043). The lengthy book by Elimar Klebs entitled *Die Erzählung von Apollonius aus Tyrus* (Berlin, 1899) deals exhaustively with the manuscript tradition (pp. 1–294), with the nature of the romance and its place in ancient literary history (pp. 295–322), and with its medieval and early modern derivatives in the direct line (325–528). The best edition of the text is that of A. Riese in the Teubner series (Leipzig, 1893), but a new edition based on the researches of Klebs has long been needed. Two studies to which reference will be made below may be cited here: one is an article

in broad perspective, are dealt with in the following pages: (1) its narrative substance in outline; (2) the presumable sources or models, Greek and Latin, which were used in its composition; (3) the mechanical methods of combination and the disregard for natural sequence and motivation shown by the Latin author in putting together episodes that had been shaped in other contexts, and the significance of this. The narrative substance of *Appolonius*, in contrast with that of the extant Greek romances, is so similar in kind to that of the Ps.-Clementine romance that the title *Recognitiones* would apply almost as well to the one as to the other. In both plots the various members of a family are separated and lost to each other for many years by misadventures on the sea; in both the separation of father and mother from their children, as well as the husband from his wife, is featured; and the means by which the recognitions finally take place are the same in both stories and quite different from the means employed in the other extant romances, that is, one member of the family is recognized and made known as such to the other, hitherto a stranger, by hearing the life-story of the other told by himself or herself, or by a third person. Indeed the similarity of *Apollonius of Tyre* to the Ps.-Clementine romance, in respect to a number of its essential motifs, is such that we may well believe that the author of *Apollonius*, in composing his romance, was directly influenced by an earlier form of the Ps.-Clementine story, or by the same source on which the latter was built. In the outline which follows below, the substance of the Apollonius-romance is divided into sections arbitrarily numbered for the sake of convenience in referring to them later on; and, for similar reasons, some of the sections are followed by critical notes in which attention is called to peculiarities of sequence and motivation, that these may be clearly seen in their context.

1 (ch. 1–6)

In the city of Antioch there was a certain king named Antiochus whose wife had died leaving him a very beautiful young daughter.

by P. H. Goepp entitled "The Narrative Material of *Apollonius of Tyre*" in *ELH, A Journal of English Literary History*, 5 (1938), 150–172; the other is A. H. Krappe's article "Euripides' *Alcmaeon* and the Apollonius Romance" in *Class. Quarterly* 18 (1924), 57–58.

Many suitors came to seek her in marriage, offering large dowries. While her father was considering to which one of the suitors he would give his daughter, he fell madly in love with her himself, and after trying in vain to subdue his evil passion, one morning at dawn he entered her bedroom and raped her. Soon afterwards her nurse came in and found her in great distress, dissolved in tears and horror, and thinking of killing herself. On learning what had happened, her nurse tried to soothe her and, to prevent her suicide, urged her to accept her father's will, impious though it was. Thereafter Antiochus enjoyed his daughter as wife in the privacy of his own house, posing as a pious father before the public and careful to conceal his crime from the knowledge of outsiders. In order to rid himself of the suitors he proposed a riddle for them to solve, with the stipulation that any suitor who succeeded in solving it correctly would be given his daughter in marriage, but anyone who failed to solve it would be beheaded. Many suitors of royal blood from nearby lands tried in vain to solve the riddle and were beheaded, and, *whenever anyone by his shrewdness did succeed in solving the riddle correctly, his head was chopped off nevertheless by the king's orders* and was hung up with the heads of other suitors on the gate of the palace, on the charge of Antiochus that his solution of the riddle was incorrect. Undeterred by these cruelties, a very rich young man from Tyre named Apollonius came by sea to Antioch and, going into the presence of Antiochus, greeted him and asked him for the hand of his daughter in marriage, saying that he himself was of royal lineage. Looking angrily at the young man, Antiochus said "You know, I suppose, the conditions of this marriage?" "I know them," Apollonius replied, "I saw them on the gate of the palace." "Well then," said Antiochus, "this is the riddle:

> "I am borne along by crime.
> I devour my mother's flesh.
> I seek my brother, the husband
> of my mother, the son of my
> wife. I do not find him."

Apollonius went away and, after a period of deliberation, returned to the king and announced that he had found the solution of the riddle: "As for being borne along by crime, look to yourself; and as for devouring a mother's flesh, consider your daughter." When the king perceived that Apollonius had found the solution to his riddle, he said; "You're wrong, young man, there's no truth in what you say. You deserve to be beheaded, but *I give you a respite of thirty days* in which to reconsider the problem. When you have returned with the right solution, you will receive my daughter in marriage." Greatly disturbed at this, Apollonius boarded his ship and returned to his native Tyre. After his departure Antiochus sent his trusted servant, Thaliarchus, to Tyre with orders to seek out some enemy of Apollonius who could be hired to kill him. Meanwhile, Apollonius, on arriving home in Tyre, looked into all the books written about such problems by the philosophers and Chaldaeans by way of checking his own solution. Then, having found that the answer he had given was correct according to the books, he understood that Antiochus intended to seek him out and kill him at all costs. He must flee from Tyre. So, accompanied by a few of his most trustworthy servants, he went secretly on board a ship, taking with him a great quantity of gold and silver and costly raiment, and in the dead of night fared forth on the high seas.

Antiochus had two purposes by which his action was motivated; one was to prevent outsiders from knowing anything about his incestuous relations with his daughter; the other, more urgent, was to rid himself of every suitor for his daughter's hand, not merely by discouraging a suitor and making it very hard for him to win a contest, as in other myths of this kind where the suitor has a sporting chance (e.g. Pelops vs. Oenomaus, Oedipus vs. Sphinx, Hippomenes vs. Atalanta, etc.), but by making sure that every suitor lost his life, whatever the pretext for killing him might have to be. After making it clear that these in fact were the purposes by which Antiochus was inspired, the author of the romance represents him as acting in a way that tends to nullify and defeat both of those purposes.

The riddle that Antiochus puts before the suitors was such as to advertise his own guilt. Some of the suitors at least understood it and, if so, there was danger of its being let out to others before the suitor was killed. Why should Antiochus, intent on *his* business, take such an unnecessary risk? It is not understandable why *he* should choose to do so. Why, then, does the author of the story choose the riddle about incest as the problem—one of many possible in the circumstances—which Antiochus is said to have put before the suitors for solution? *That* is understandable: the author's mind was preoccupied and absorbed, temporarily, with the subject of incest *per se*, which was outstanding in his story of Antiochus and his daughter. This reminded him of a very interesting riddle which he had read or heard about *in some other context*, where it may or may not have been used, but probably was not, as a problem for suitors to solve. In telling us about this riddle the author ignores the requirements of the new context into which he has imported it and in which it does not belong. That is thoroughly characteristic of this Latin author's method of composition, as we shall see below; and it is also typical of Apuleius, in respect to that author's frequent disregard of natural sequence, resulting from the importation of alien matter into a story in which it does not fit, as we have seen above in chapter vii.

Before Apollonius appeared on the scene Antiochus had beheaded every suitor who had tried to solve his riddle, on the charge that the solution given was wrong, even in cases when he knew it to be right. Thus the dice were so heavily loaded by Antiochus that the suitor had not the slightest chance of succeeding; heads I win, tails you lose! But this Roman game is badly interrupted in the case of Apollonius, who, after failing to solve the riddle, according to Antiochus, is given a respite of thirty days in which to try again, and during that time he is allowed to go free wherever he pleases out of the king's reach. Would the crafty Antiochus turn about and become so stupid as to suppose that Apollonius would ever return to Antioch of his own accord, when he knew very well that if he did so he would be killed? The author tells us (ch. 6) that Apollonius understood, after his first experience, that Antiochus intended to kill him, and Antiochus must have known that Apollonius knew what his intention was. And, again, how could Antiochus, acting in his own interest, afford to let Apollonius go free on this occasion when later on, as we shall see, he uses all the resources of his great kingdom to hunt down the fugitive Apollonius and kill him? Obviously Antiochus could not have acted so foolishly under the circumstances given us. Why, then, is he represented as doing so? Here again the author has brought into the story of Antiochus an episode that does not belong in it and could not have been in it originally. Where did he find the pattern of that episode? Probably not in any folktale relating to a contest, because in such tales a competitor is very rarely, if ever, given a second chance gratuitously by his opponent. We must conclude, therefore, that the Latin author introduced this self-defeating action on the part of Antiochus for no other purpose than to motivate the travels and adventures of Apollonius in exile, disregarding, as before, the requirements of the context into which he has brought it.

2 (ch. 7–10)

On the day after his departure the citizens of Tyre looked in vain for their beloved prince, Apollonius; and when he could nowhere be found, there was public mourning on his account throughout the city for a long time. Meanwhile Thaliarchus the king's steward arrived from Antioch and, finding the city in mourning, inquired of a boy on the street what the cause of it was. He was told that the people of Tyre were mourning for the disappearance of their ruler Apollonius a few days after his return from Antioch. On hearing this, Thaliarchus returned immediately to Antioch and reported what he thought would be very good news to Antiochus: that "Apollonius, fearing the power of your kingdom, has fled from Tyre and is nowhere to be found." To this Antiochus replied: "He can flee, but he will not be able to escape." Then he published an edict in which he offered a reward of 100 talents to anyone who would bring him Apollonius alive, and 200 talents for his severed head. For such a compensation not only the enemies of Apollonius but even some of his friends might be expected to turn him in if they could, or kill him. Thereafter Apollonius was hunted throughout the lands, in the forests, and on the mountains, but could not be found. Then Antiochus fitted out squadrons of ships to pursue the young man on the seas, and while he was making these preparations Apollonius in his flight arrived at Tarsus. There, as he walked about on the shore, he met with a fellow citizen named Hellanicus, who had himself just arrived from Tyre. This Hellanicus, a poor man and a plebeian, told Apollonius, by way of warning, about his being proscribed by Antiochus and the rewards that had been offered for his capture, dead or alive. When Apollonius asked him why Antiochus wanted to kill him, Hellanicus replied: "Because you have sought to be to his daughter what he is." This implies that all Tyre knew about the incest that Antiochus had tried to conceal (!) in his riddle, although we are not told how the Tyrians learned about it. Apollonius then offered Hellanicus 100 talents as the price for not betraying him, but Hellanicus would not accept it; he was a real friend to Apollonius, and his friendship was not to be bought. After that Apollonius met on the shore another man whom he knew and whose name was Stranguillio. In reply to this man's queries, Apollonius told him that he had been proscribed by Antiochus and that he wished to hide himself in their city of Tarsus. Stranguillio informed him that the people of Tarsus could not support him owing to their poverty and the fact that they were suffering terribly from a great famine. Apollonius then promised to relieve the famine by giving the people of Tarsus 100,000 pecks of grain, on condition that they would conceal his flight among them. Stranguillio gladly agreed to this on behalf of his fellow citizens, and the two men entered the city. Apollonius then mounted a platform in the forum where everybody could see him and announced to the people that he would give them for a very small price 100,000 pecks of grain (which he had brought on his ship from Tyre) in exchange for refuge; and when they joyfully agreed to those terms he remitted the cost. In gratitude for this favor, the people of Tarsus set up a bronze statue in his honor in the public square with this inscription: THE CITY OF TARSUS HAS GIVEN THIS MONUMENT TO APOL-LONIUS OF TYRE FOR HAVING RELIEVED ITS FAMINE.

The internal contradictions *within* the story of Antiochus and Apollonius, and its inorganic composition, which were described above after section **1**, are almost enough in themselves to show that this episode as a whole was the invention of a Latin author who com-bines and contaminates his sources or his narrative models, whether written or oral, in the same manner as does Apuleius here and there and as do the Latin dramatists Plautus and Terence. *Contaminatio* is a peculiarly Latin literary phenomenon. Its presence in Greek literature after Homer, including the Greek romances, can be only rarely if ever detected; but there is no virtue in denying its existence in any one case, as Unitarians have done, when they find it standing out like a sore thumb in the second book of the *Iliad*. Only "disinte-grating criticism" can reveal the truth about the carelessly mechani-cal methods of composition actually employed by Apuleius and the unknown Latin author of *Apollonius*.

The Antiochus-story as a whole, with which the romance begins, serves to motivate the travels of Apollonius in exile, but in a round-about and unnatural way. It remains to consider what changes the author has made in the pattern of the folktale involving incest upon which his story about Antiochus and his daughter was based, or by which it was inspired.

The most essential feature, outstanding in almost any folktale about incest or enforced adultery, or the threat of it, is what happens to the unwilling victim of such action, whether a woman or a man, or what he or she does about it. This is the case in a wide variety of ancient myths, among which may be mentioned that of Oedipus striving to avoid incest with his mother; that about Niobe and what she suffered for refusing to have incestuous relations with her father Assaon, as recorded by Parthenius in no. 33; that about Periander, what he did and suffered when he discovered to his dismay that the woman with whom he had been sleeping was his own mother, who had substituted herself for another (Parthenius no. 17); that about Smyrna, what befell her in consequence of having shared her father's bed without his knowledge or consent for twelve nights, and what her father did about it, as told by Apollodorus, III 14, 4 (see Frazer in the Loeb Library edition, vol. II p. 87); the variant myths about

Caunus and his sister Byblis as recorded by Parthenius in no. 11: one, that Caunus, because he was unable to rid himself of his passion for Byblis, left home and travelled far away from his native land, where he founded a city; the other, that he left home and travelled in order to avoid the incestuous passion of Byblis, who thereafter killed herself; the myth about Mattidia in the Ps.-Clementine *Recognitiones*, who went into exile with two of her children and travelled around the eastern shores of the Mediterranean in order to avoid the adulterous attentions of her husband's brother; and the prototype of that story in the *Life of Aesop*.

The direction and result of the story of Antiochus as told by the author of *Apollonius*, is, like that of the last three folktales mentioned above, to force *someone* into exile far from home; but nothing is said in the Latin romance about what the unwilling victim of the incestuous aggressor suffered, or did by way of revenge, which is related in all the similar stories that we know, and was to be expected here. From all this it appears that the author of *Apollonius* must have made one radical change in the terms of the original myth about incest, whatever it was, whether written or oral, upon the basis of which his own story of Antiochus was fashioned: he substituted a suitor (Apollonius) in place of one of the parties to incest (the daughter of Antiochus) as the victim of the aggressor's persecution. This he did for the purpose of motivating the travels of his hero Apollonius, whose adventures were shaped by him on the model of other sources, both Greek and Latin; and, in so doing, the fate of Antiochus' daughter was necessarily, but conspicuously, ignored.

The story about the incest of Antiochus with his daughter was undoubtedly suggested to our author by the famous and scandalous love of Antiochus I (324–262 B.C.) for his stepmother Stratonice, the wife of his father Seleucus I, the story of which is told at length by Lucian in his *Syrian Goddess* (ch. 17–18) and by Plutarch in his *Life of Demetrius* (ch. 38). The young Antiochus fell ill and seemed about to die from a strange malady which his father did not understand, but which a physician diagnosed as love-sickness, and, on further investigation, discovered that the object of the young man's love was his father's wife Stratonice. The physician assumed that Seleucus, the father, would be unwilling to give up Stratonice to his son, even though he was very anxious about his son's safety. So, in order to test his sentiment, he told Seleucus that his son's malady could not be cured, because it was love for his, the physician's wife, and he would never surrender her. Seleucus thought that he ought to do so, to insure the prince's recovery; and the physician then asked him whether he would be willing to do as much for his own son's sake, if the latter were in love with his wife Stratonice; and when Seleucus declared that in that case he would sacrifice his wife for his son, the physician told him the truth. Because Seleucus had meant what he said, he gave up Stratonice to his son for wife, and, migrating eastward, settled in the city of Seleucia on the Tigris. Thereafter Seleucus ruled in Seleucia and Antiochus in Antioch-on-the-Orontes.

With this well-known story in mind, the author of *Apollonius* must have thought of Antiochus as one who joined in illegitimate love with a kinswoman, and for that reason it was easy for him to imagine and represent Antiochus as guilty of incest with his daughter instead of with his stepmother. He did so because that would serve his purpose, which was to motivate the enforced exile and persecution of his young hero, a suitor, much better than would the story about Antiochus and Stratonice.

3 (ch. 11–14)

After hiding in celebrity at Tarsus for a few months or days (*sic*), Apollonius, at the instigation of Stranguillio and his wife Dionysias, set sail for Pentapolis in Cyrenaica, with the intention of concealing himself there. On the way a great storm arose, which is described in hexameter verses imitative of Vergil in *Aeneid* I., and Apollonius, who alone survived the wreck, was cast up on the shore at Apollonia, one of the group of five cities near Cyrene collectively called Pentapolis. There he was given shelter and befriended by a poor fisherman who gave him half of his own cloak and advised him to enter the city, where he might find some wealthy man of noble rank like himself, one who would be better able to help him. "And if you fail to find such a man," he added, "come back here and toil with me as a fisherman; we can both live in poverty. But I ask of you that, if ever by good fortune you are restored to your own kindred and kingdom, you will not be unmindful of my poverty and my tribulation." To which Apollonius replied, "If I fail to remember you, then may I suffer shipwreck a second time and not be able to find any such friend as you have been to me!" On entering the city Apollonius came to the gymnasium, where he found a great crowd of men exercising and bathing but saw no one of his own rank. Soon afterwards, however, a nobleman entered the gymnasium accompanied by a large retinue, who proved to be Archestrates, the king of the city. Apollonius managed to win his favor by playing ball with him, in which he showed great skill, and by massaging him after the game. After he had left the gymnasium, Archestrates, having learned that this man whose skill he admired was a shipwrecked stranger, sent his servant back to invite Apollonius to dinner. Apollonius accepted the

invitation; but at the dinner he ate nothing and looked very sorrow-
ful. One of the king's friends accused him of being envious of his
master's wealth, but Archestrates defended him because he understood just how the shipwrecked Apollonius felt, and he urged him to
eat and rejoice and hope for better fortune.

4 (15–18)

Just then the king's daughter, a beautiful young maiden sparkling
with gold, entered the room and, after saluting her father with a kiss,
proceeded to greet his guests in the same way. When she came to
Apollonius she asked her father who this young man was who reclined
in a place of honor at the banquet, and why he seemed so sad. The
king told her that he was a shipwrecked man whom he had met at
the gymnasium. He had liked him and invited him to dinner, but did
not know who he was. She would do well to learn all about him and
try to bring him cheer. In reply to her gracious inquiries, Apollonius
told the princess who he was and all that had happened to him, after
which he began to weep. The princess, who is unnamed in the original
text, sought to cheer the young man by playing for him on the lyre,
and, when she had finished, everyone present praised her performance
except Apollonius, who said as politely as he could that she needed
more instruction, and he begged to be allowed to demonstrate what
lyre-playing should be. This he did, and the company was so fascinated by his playing that they could believe he was Apollo in person.
The princess, daughter of King Archestrates, thereupon fell in love
with Apollonius. First she persuaded her father to allow her to bestow
rich presents on their guest; and, accordingly, with his hearty consent,
she gave him 200 talents in gold, 40 talents in silver, 20 servants and
a great abundance of clothing. Everybody praised the princess'
liberality. When the banquet was over Apollonius thanked his hosts
and prepared to leave with his cargo of presents; but the princess,
mindful of the fact that he had nowhere to go, and tormented with
the prospect of not seeing him whom she loved any more, had her
father provide a villa for him where he could live in safety. But still
she was restless and unsatisfied. In the middle of the night she went
to her father and begged him to appoint Apollonius as her teacher,
that she might be with him much of the time and profit by his great
skill in the arts. And the king gladly made that arrangement. After

that, the princess became seriously ill of a malady which the doctors could not diagnose, because it was love-sickness.

Whoever it was who invented the story of Apollonius as told in the preceding sections 3 and 4, whether he was a Greek author or a Roman, must have been familiar with a pre-existing story which was the same in its essential outlines as the story of Aeneas told by Vergil in Books I and IV of the *Aeneid*: A prince or famous hero who is shipwrecked on the northern coast of Africa near a famous city, Cyrene or Carthage, with the loss of all his companions in a storm at sea, is first befriended, then loved and married, by the queen or princess of the city. Either the story of Aeneas and Dido or some other story shaped along the same lines would probably have been known to a Greek author who is assumed to have been the inventor of the romance about Apollonius, which is known to us only in a Latin text. There is however no need to make that assumption, because no Greek romance with the same general content is known to have existed, and a Latin writer could have created it just as well or even better than a Greek writer, considering its manifold Latin precedents in Vergil and Roman comedy. Surely the burden of proof must rest with those who assume a Greek original about which nothing is known. In order to make way for that thesis a lot of special pleading is necessary such as is not likely to convince one who has studied the nature of Latin translations or adaptations of Greek texts. The Latin text of the episode of Apollonius at Cyrene contains many obvious imitations in hexameter verse of Vergil's description of the storm in *Aeneid* I (ch. 11), quotations of *Aeneid* IV in the description of the princess' oncoming love (ch. 18), and from *Aeneid* II 3 in reference to the sorrows of Apollonius.[2] These verbal imitations and quotations of Vergil, accompanied by four or five others from Ovid's *Metamorphoses*, are not likely to be translations or adaptations or illustrations of the substance of a Greek narrative, because they are too numerous and because the substance itself seems to be founded on, or shaped by Latin authors. Petronius quotes six verses or parts of verses from Vergil's *Aeneid* in four different passages of the *Satyricon*, but in contexts which nobody believes or can believe to have been based on Greek originals; they are parts of an original Latin composition. Apuleius in those parts of his *Metamorphoses* which have substantial equivalents in the text of the Greek *Luciad* (Lucian's *Onos*) adds no quotations or verbal reminiscences of the Roman poets; and the absence of such is what one would expect in a Latin writer translating or freely interpreting a Greek original. In the light of these

[2] The details of this, and of the author's verbal imitations of Ovid's *Metamorphoses*, are described by Klebs on pp. 283–287. The quotations from *Aeneid* IV in ch. 18 include *regina . . . iam dudum saucia cura; nec . . . membris dat cura quietem*; and *credit genus esse deorum*.

considerations it seems to me very probable that the quotations from the *Aeneid* in the episode of Apollonius at Cyrene were introduced by the author of the original romance and that, consequently, that author, the inventor, was a Latin writer and not a Greek.

5 (ch. 19–21)

A few days later the king walked out hand in hand with Apollonius towards the public square, and on the way three noble young men, scholastics who had long been suitors for his daughter's hand, met him and saluted him with one voice. The king, on seeing them, smiled slyly and said to them, "What's the meaning of this, that you greet me all at once in a chorus?" One of them answered, "We have been seeking your daughter in marriage and you make us weary by putting us off so frequently. That's why today we have come here together. Choose from among us the one whom you wish to have for son-in-law." The king said, "This is not a suitable time for you to be intruding upon me, because my daughter is busy with her studies, and she's so much in love with *them* that she's now lying ill in bed. However, lest I seem to be putting you off any longer, write your names on a tablet, each of you, with the amount of dowry that you bring. Then I will send the letter itself (tablet) to my daughter, and she will choose the one she wants for husband." So the three young men wrote their names on the tablet and the amount of their dowries. The king took the tablet and, having sealed it with his ring, turned to Apollonius and said, "Here, Professor, in addition to the insult that you're getting, take this letter and carry it to your pupil. That is the place where you are wanted." Apollonius took the letter and, hastening back to the royal residence, entered the bedroom and delivered it. The princess recognized her father's seal and said to her loved one, "Oh, my teacher, what's the meaning of this, that you have entered my bedroom all alone by yourself?" Apollonius said, "Mistress, although you are not yet a wife (*mulier*) you are suffering from a lying-in! Come, take this letter from your father and read the names of your three suitors." The girl opened the letter and on reading it failed to find in it the name of the one she loved. Then she looked at Apollonius and said, "Professor Apollonius, aren't you sorry that I'm going to be married?" "On the contrary," said Apollonius, "I congratulate you, that you have received such a good education from me in these studies that you are now ready to marry the man whom your heart desires." The girl answered, "Master, if you were in love, you would be sorry." Then she wrote something on the tablet, sealed it with her own ring, and handed it to the young man. Apollonius carried it back to the forum and gave it to the king, who opened it and read what his daughter had written: "Best of fathers, since by your kind indulgence you permit me to speak out, I want that man for my husband who was shipwrecked and lost his patrimony." After reading this the king, not knowing whom she meant by the shipwrecked man, turned to the three young men who had written their names on the tablet and asked, "Which one of you has suffered shipwreck?" One of them, whose name was Busybody (*Ardalio*—cf. Phaedrus II 5), said, "I." Another said to him, "Keep still, damn you. I know you. You're a schoolmate of mine and you've never been outside the gates of this city. So how could you have suffered shipwreck?" When the king could not discover which one of the suitors had suffered shipwreck, he turned to Apollonius and said, "Master Apollonius, take this tablet and read it. You may be able to understand what it means and what I have failed to find in it, since you were present (with her when she wrote it)." Apollonius read the letter and blushed when he perceived that the princess was in love with himself. The king then led him aside from the three young men and inquired, "How about it, Master Apollonius, did you find the shipwrecked man?" "Yes," said Apollonius, "if you will permit me to say so, I have found him." The king saw that his face was red with blushing as he said this and so understood his meaning. He was glad about it and said, "What my daughter desires is what I too desire." Then he looked at the three young men and said, "Surely I told you that you intruded upon me at an unsuitable time. Go now, and when the time comes for it I'll send for you." And so he dismissed them.

Goepp (pp. 157 f.), who sees the foregoing episode in much the same light that I do, comments as follows: "The whole episode of the suitors is remarkable in several ways. It provides the only comedy in the romance [not the *only* comedy—see below in section 8 on ch. 34–35], and probably the best narrative. But it is also the most puzzling, despite the fact that compared to the story as a whole it is related with unusually detailed vividness. This naturalness is not enough to blind the reader to the essential artificiality, even absurdity, of the circumstances. Why does the king hold audience with the noble suitors out in the street in such an undignified, insulting fashion? Why does he suggest the extraordinary and cumbersome procedure of writing letters to someone a few yards away? Why, above all, does he send the letters by Apollonius, causing the princess to exclaim, quite understandably, 'Master, why do you come alone into my chamber?' For all we are told to the contrary, the king is merely indulging a taste for whimsy in all this, but it is likely, also, that the author is here following, in his own fashion and with some alteration, a course of events already determined for him."

Indeed there are many indications that the course of events described in this episode was shaped originally for a different context and background, that, namely, of a scene on the stage in a comedy or a mime. For the episode as a whole is otiose and non-functional in the context of the romance, where it does nothing to advance the action or to resolve the preceding situation; and some of its details are so ill-fitted to the surrounding circumstances that they puzzle the reader and leave him in doubt as to just what the joke is, or why there should be any joke in this place. What does King Archestrates mean by saying to Apollonius (ch. 19) that he has received an insult? We have to suppose, in the circumstances, that this refers to the rude competition of the suitors with Apollonius as a rival and a favored lover of the princess, and that the king knows that his daughter is in love with Apollonius, as he very well ought to have known from observing her conduct at home; but all this is contradicted near the end of the episode, where the king is represented as not knowing who was meant by the shipwrecked man, although he knew that Apollonius was such a man (ch. 16), and as not suspecting that his daughter was in love with Apollonius, or he with her. And why is it that Apollonius is here represented, unlike any other lover in an ideal romance, as being indifferent and not positively in love with the young woman who loves him so ardently? He politely consents to marry her at the king's request in a spirit of resignation, expressed in the words "If such is the will of God, and your desire, so be it." I shall be glad to accommodate you! Surely this scene was meant for comedy, not for a serious romance. The reason why the conversation with the suitors takes place on the street instead of in the palace, and that letters are sent back and forth between the king and his daughter, who is only a few rods away, is that the scene was intended originally for representation on a stage, where everything had to be pictured on the outside of a house, in a street or a public square. Finally, why should Apollonius, if he respected the king's daughter, and thought seriously of her, be so indelicate as to tell her in jest that she seemed to be pregnant while still unmarried? That is fit for a comedy, but it looks strange in a story of ideal love such as is expected in this romance.

6 (ch. 22–25)

After the letter-writing farce that had taken place in the street nearby, King Archestrates entered the royal residence with his prospective son-in-law, now no longer a stranger guest. Inside, he left Apollonius for a time and conversed privately with his daughter in her room. She told her father frankly, amid tears, that she was deeply in love with Apollonius and begged him to allow her to marry him. King Archestrates very gladly consented and, returning to Apollonius, begged him to accept his daughter in marriage. To this Apollonius replied, "If such is your will, and the will of God, so be it." After that the wedding took place in the midst of royal splendor, gaiety, and rejoicing on all sides. The pair loved each other intensely. When his bride was *six months* pregnant, Apollonius chanced to be walking with her one day on the shore when he saw a fine-looking ship that had just put in from Tyre. In conversation with the pilot Apollonius told him that he himself was a native of Tyre, and the pilot then asked whether he happened to know the prince of Tyre whose name was Apollonius. "As well as I know myself," said Apollonius. "Then," said the pilot, "whenever you see him, bid him rejoice, because that cruelest of kings, Antiochus, while lying with his daughter, was struck down by a thunder bolt and all his wealth and his kingdom are being held for King Apollonius, his successor." On learning this, Apollonius sought permission of his wife to go to Antioch and Tyre (the author forgets to mention either city as his destination) in order to take over his kingdom; but his wife begged him not to leave her alone at such a time but to allow her to go with him on the voyage. She also besought and obtained permission from her father to go, and he fitted out a ship for the purpose. On board he put his daughter's nurse Lycoris and a skilled obstetrician, after which he kissed his daughter and son-in-law good-bye, wishing them a prosperous voyage, and returned to the palace. Apollonius went on board with a large retinue of servants and abundant supplies and they set sail with a favorable breeze. After a few days on the sea, they were detained by adverse winds, and during that time, in the *ninth month* of her pregnancy, the princess gave birth to her child; but soon afterwards, having fainted from the clotting of blood, she became lifeless to all appearances and was believed to be dead. Apollonius grieved madly over the loss of his precious wife, whom he loved so dearly. The ship's pilot, although he sympathized with Apollonius, insisted that his wife should be buried at sea, because it was not safe for the ship to transport a corpse. Accordingly, the body of the young mother was set adrift in a chest made large and tight for the purpose. The chest was adorned with royal insignia, and 20,000 sesterces in gold were placed at the head of the body. After weeping over the body of his wife, Apollonius ordered that his newborn child should be nursed with great care, that he might have some solace in his great misfortune and that he might bring a granddaughter to King Archestrates in place of his daughter.

In the foregoing section the author makes contradictory statements concerning the duration of the princess' pregnancy: he tells us that she was six months pregnant when she went to sea (ch. 24), that the ship had been gone from port only a few days when she gave birth to her child, and that that was in the ninth month of her pregnancy. This shows a disregard of context on the part of the author which again reminds us of Apuleius.

Why Apollonius should inherit the kingdom of Antiochus is an unexplained mystery; this may have belonged originally in a story which the author has altered or entirely omitted.

7 (ch. 26–28)

Three days later the chest containing the wife's body drifted ashore at Ephesus near the residence of a certain physician, who happened at the time to be walking along the shore in company with his students. He discovered the chest and had it brought at once to his house. On opening it, he saw a beautiful young woman regally clothed, with twenty gold pieces lying at her head and a letter begging whoever found the coffin to give honorable burial to the dear dead, whose "departure has left us in tears and bitter sorrow." The physician gave orders for the body to be buried according to these directions; but one of his students, an apprentice gifted with greater genius than his master, discovered signs of life in the body and, by skillful treatment, restored the young woman to full consciousness. Then the princess, wife of Apollonius, told her whole story, and the physician adopted her as his own daughter; and when she begged him to protect her, he secluded her among the priestesses of Diana at Ephesus. This episode is unfolded in dramatic detail with very good effect.

Meanwhile Apollonius, with his newborn babe, changed the course of his voyage and went to Tarsus; where he put his child, with her nurse Lycoris, in the care of his old friends Stranguillio and Dionysias, to whom he told all that had happened to him and his wife after his arrival at Pentapolis. He begged this friendly couple to bring up his child as one of their own until she was of marriageable age, and to name her Tarsia. He said that on account of his wife's death he did not want to take over the kingdom (sc. of Tyre and Antioch) which was being held for him; that he was unwilling to return to his father-in-law, King Archestrates, whose daughter he had lost at sea; and that he intended to become a merchant. He left much money and costly raiment with her foster parents for the upbringing of his child Tarsia, and he declared that he would not cut his hair or fingernails until he bestowed his daughter in marriage. Stranguillio and his wife were deeply impressed by this solemn oath and promised to educate Tarsia and to take the best of care of her until he should return. Then Apollonius boarded a ship and set sail on the high seas, until he came to the distant and unfamiliar regions of Egypt. Later on we learn that his sojourn as merchant in Egypt lasted fourteen years, but nothing is said about his experience there.

Why does Apollonius go to Tarsus with his newborn child, there to leave her in the care of foster parents for fourteen years, instead of going home with her to Tyre, where he would be welcome as king of the city and would be able to attend personally to his daughter's upbringing, and to have her with him in his own home? And why should he, a king and a man of great wealth and popularity at home in Tyre, choose to live the private life of a merchant wandering about for fourteen years in a strange land separated from his daughter and his old friends? This makes no sense from the standpoint of the hero's personal interest and motives. Hence, the only possible explanation for this representation of events in the romance is the author's desire to tell the story about the attempted murder of Tarsia by her foster parent Dionysias which he brings in later for its own sake as an interesting tragic episode, in spite of the fact that it does not fit into the preceding context of the romance but clashes with it. The probable source upon which the whole story about Tarsia and her fate was modelled, namely the lost *Alcmaeon* of Euripides, will be discussed below.

8 (ch. 29–36)

Tarsia was well cared for by her foster parents, with the aid of her beloved nurse Lycoris, and was educated along with the couple's own daughter, named Philomusia, until she was fourteen years old. At that time her nurse, being sick and on the point of death, told Tarsia all about herself and who her real parents were, and advised her what to do in case her foster parents should bring any injury upon her: she should appeal to the citizens of Tarsus by embracing the statue of her father Apollonius in the forum and declaring that she was that man's daughter, and they would vindicate her. The nurse died in Tarsia's arms, and afterwards Tarsia, such was her noble character, stopped every day on her way back from school at the tomb of her nurse to pray for her and to invoke the departed spirits of her parents. One day, on the occasion of a festival, Dionysias was walking on the crowded streets in company with her daughter Philomusia and Tarsia. When she saw that all the people admired the beauty of Tarsia with her fine jewels, and commented on the ugly appearance of her own daughter, she became furiously jealous and resolved to do away with Tarsia and to bestow her jewels on Philomusia, reckoning that Apollonius would not return because he had not been heard from for fourteen years. Accordingly, she forced her steward Theophilus by means of threats and bribery, much against his own will, to agree to stab Tarsia on her way home from school and to throw her body into the sea. The steward seized Tarsia at her nurse's tomb, but before killing her, allowed her to say her prayers. While she was doing so, pirates suddenly intervened and carried her off on the sea. The steward thanked God that he had not had to kill the innocent Tarsia; but when he returned and reported to his mistress Dionysias that the deed had been done, she called him a murderer and gave him no reward. She told her husband, Stranguillio, *who was horrified to learn of it*, all that had been done, and she made him put on mourning with herself to conceal the crime. She then announced to the people the sad death of her ward, as due to a fatal sickness, and the citizens, mindful of the benefactions of her father Apollonius, set up an inscription in bronze in honor of Tarsia.

Meanwhile (ch. 33) the pirates, on arriving at Mytilene, proceeded to sell the girl Tarsia at auction. A procurer who wanted the girl for his brothel managed to outbid a wealthy nobleman named Athenagoras, who was the ruler of Mytilene, and who wanted Tarsia for himself. This scene is described at length in dramatic detail and with comic effect. Having failed to buy the girl, the enamoured Athenagoras entered the brothel "with veiled head" and presented himself as her first customer. But Tarsia prevailed upon him to spare her virginity by telling him all her tragic story, and he, out of sympathy, gave her 40 gold pieces with which to satisfy her master, the bawd. Tarsia, weeping profusely, thanked him for his kindness. As he was leaving the brothel, Athenagoras met at the door one of his young colleagues who was about to enter and who said to him, "How did you make out with the new one, Athenagoras?" "It couldn't be any better," he answered, "it was good to the point of tears!" Then he stepped aside, and when his friend had gone in he waited and listened outside the door, to learn how he would fare. The young man asked Tarsia how much the man who had just left had given her and she told him the amount, ⅖ of a pound. "Oh damn him," says he, "how stingy! What would it have mattered to him, so rich a man as he is, to have given you a full pound? I want you to know that I'm better than that. Here, take this full pound in gold." Athenagoras, standing outside the door, remarked, "The more you give her, the more you'll have to weep for." Then the girl fell at his feet, told him all about her misfortune, and implored him to refrain from violating her virginity. The young man agreed to do so, saying, "Arise, mistress. I too am human, and subject to the accidents of fortune." And the girl said, "I thank you very much for your virtuous consideration." When the young man came out, he found Athenagoras laughing and said to him, "You're a great man, seeing that you didn't have anyone on whom to bestow your tears!" Then the two men agreed not to reveal their secret to anyone else, and waited at the door of the brothel to watch others come and go. While they waited behind the door, with a hidden view of what transpired inside, a number of other prospective customers entered, each one of whom gave Tarsia a single gold piece and came out weeping. After that the girl gave all the money she had acquired to her master, the bawd, saying, "Behold the price of my virginity." He approved of this and congratulated her; but on the next day, after giving him a similar sum of money, she told him that she had collected the money as before by means of her tears and supplications, and that she was still a virgin. On hearing this, the procurer was angry, scolded his steward for such negligence, and ordered him to go in himself and deflower Tarsia. But this steward proved to be as kindhearted and sympathetic as the other men who had visited Tarsia; so he refrained from violating her, and when she proposed to make money for her master by means of public concerts as a musician, he allowed her to do so, and the concerts proved to be popular and a great financial success. Athenagoras, mindful of Tarsia's virginity and of her noble birth and character, guarded her as if she were his only child, by giving the steward much money and commending him.

In Section 9 as outlined below Apollonius finds his long-lost daughter Tarsia at Mytilene, and later, in section 10, he recovers his wife in the temple of Diana at Ephesus. The literary source upon which in outline the whole story of Tarsia and her fate seems to have been modelled is the lost *Alcmaeon* of Euripides, as explained by A. H. Krappe in a short article on the subject in the *Classical Quarterly* 18 (1924), 57–58. The narrative substance of that play is outlined by Apollodorus (III 7; see Nauck's *Trag. Graec. Fragmenta* pp. 479 ff.) as follows (Frazer's translation in the Loeb Library edition): "Euripides says that in the time of his madness Alcmaeon begot two children, Amphilochus and a daughter Tisiphone, . . . and that he brought the babes to Corinth and gave them to Creon, king of Corinth, to bring up; and that on account of her extraordinary comeliness Tisiphone was sold as a slave by Creon's spouse, who feared that Creon might make her his wedded wife. But *Alcmaeon* bought her and kept her as a handmaid, not knowing that she was his daughter; and coming to Corinth to get back his children he recovered his son also." In comparing this, the plot of the Euripidean *Alcmaeon*, with the story of Tarsia, Krappe defines the chief difference as follows: "(1) In Euripides the father loses and recovers his daughter and his son, in the romance his daughter and his wife. (2) In Euripides the jealous wife fears the heroine may deprive her of her husband, in the romance she is jealous of the adopted daughter because she is more beautiful than her own child. (3) Euripides says nothing about the pirates or the brothel; the jealous wife of the foster father sells her directly as a slave and the girl's own father buys her without knowing her . . ."

Concerning these differences: (1) Before he came to telling of Tarsia's experience and her eventual recovery by her father, the author of the romance had made it clear that Apollonius had no son, and that he had lost his wife; for that reason he could not follow the Euripidean story about the loss and recovery of a son, but was obliged to speak only about the recovery by Apollonius of his daughter and his wife. (2) As the romancer saw it, Tarsia at the age of fourteen was more likely to be regarded by the jealous foster mother, Dionysias, as a rival to her own daughter than to herself as the wife of Stranguillio. The mainspring of the foster parent's hatred for her ward was jealousy in both cases, one case suggested the other, and there was no need for the author of the romance to follow the Euripidean story slavishly in such a matter, which for him was inconsequential. (3) Pirates, and virgins in brothels, could not be put on the Euripidean stage, but such machines were grist for the romancer's mill, and he liked them so well that he interpolated one of them, taken from a comic source, into the middle of his story of Tarsia. Creon's wife in the play of Euripides would have no difficulty in selling her ward into slavery, thereby getting rid of her and making it possible for her father Alcmaeon to recover her later on; but Dionysias in the romance could not sell Tarsia as a slave in the city of Tarsus, because everyone there knew who she was and held her and her father in high esteem. Hence the foster parent in the romance is represented as planning to murder her ward secretly in order to be rid of her; and, in order to make it possible for her to be recovered by her father later, it was necessary to save her by the interference of pirates.

The most significant aspect of the episode of Tarsia in the brothel, as regards the probable source on which it was modelled, is its outright comic nature, broad farce of the kind that one thinks of as typically Plautine and Roman. This is recognized by Klebs (*Die Erzählung von Apollonius aus Tyrus*, pp. 305 f.), who cites similar scenes and verbal motifs in Roman comedy; but, so strong and lasting is the impression made upon the reader by the tragic coloring of the preceding narrative, that one can easily overlook the farcical nature of this brothel-scene, obvious though it must be to an unpreconditioned mind. Even Goepp failed to note the comedy here, although he was on the lookout for incongruities in the romance, and there is no suggestion of it in Miss Haight's sober summary of the episode. In the outline given above I have sought to bring this quality more vividly before the reader by describing or translating the details of it.

A very similar story, but a serious one, about a girl who claimed to have kept her virginity in a brothel by the same means that Tarsia employed, was a well known subject for debate in the Roman schools of rhetoric, as told and argued about in Seneca's *Controversiae* (I 2), and discussed by Klebs in this connection. The theme is as follows: A girl who seeks to qualify as a Vestal virgin had been carried off by pirates and sold in a strange city to a procurer, who put her in his brothel. She was given a small bedroom with a price tag for her services marked on the door outside. Many men came to visit her as a prostitute, but they all came away as from a priestess. For she so stirred their emotion by means of her tears and the rehearsal of her painful misfortunes that every one of them out of respect gave her of his own accord more money with which to preserve her virginity than the violation of it would have cost him.

The author of *Apollonius* must have been familiar with the story about the girl in the brothel which is discussed in Seneca's *Controversia* as outlined above; but, in addition to that, it is probable that he was acquainted with the same or a very similar story in the form in which it had been staged in some Roman comedy or mime. Or, if this story had not already been put on the stage, our Latin author may himself have given it the *theatrical* form which it has in his romance and which it would have in a mime or a stage comedy, on the familiar analogy of what he had read or seen on the Roman stage. Listening on the outside of a closed door or peeking in through a crack, to see or hear what goes on inside, was a stock device in the mime, good examples of which recur in Petronius. Nothing of the kind can be found or is to be expected in a serious Greek romance. Anthia in Xenophon of Ephesus (V 7) is made to stand in front of the brothel beautifully dressed with a price tag on the door above her head; a large crowd of would-be customers, attracted by her beauty then gathers around her, and Anthia escapes from them all without being violated by pretending to fall down in an epileptic fit. Later, when she explained to the whore-master that she had been afflicted with this strange malady ever since childhood, he believed her, treated her kindly (as no *leno* on the Roman stage would do), and decided to sell her in the slave market. Here there is no going in and out of the brothel, one man at a time, which makes possible the comedy in *Apollonius*; instead the tone and coloring of the whole episode is in the tragic mood, as it would be, I think, in any ideal Greek romance.

The following obscurities and contradictions, which puzzle the reader in the story about Tarsia, are noted by Klebs on p. 308: Why is it that, after Tarsia has been showered with gold in the brothel, neither she herself nor Athenagoras, her lover, who was a very rich man and the ruler of the city, buys her freedom outright from the keeper of the brothel? Athenagoras could easily have done so, either with or without that owner's consent. He could also have bought her from the slave dealer in the first place by outbidding the procurer. His action throughout is not prompted by his own interest as a lover, nor by the interest of Tarsia; it has been so represented by the author for no other purpose than to make possible the comic scenes, first the rival bidding at the auction, then later the scene at the door of the brothel. Here the author has treated the reader to some very good and very broad comedy in the Plautine manner, the kind of horseplay that we think of as characteristically Roman rather than Greek; but in so doing he has neglected to provide any plausible motivation for the actions of his characters, thereby leaving the reader to wonder about it.

Finally, the worst deficiency of this kind, according to Klebs, and one that neither of us can explain, is "die ganz unklare Stellung, die der Pflegevater (Stranguillio) zu Tarsias geplanter Ermordung eingenommen hat." See the fuller analysis of these inconsistencies made by Klebs on pp. 33–35 of his book. Near the end of ch. 32 Stranguillio learns for the first time, from the confession of his wife Dionysias, that she has murdered Tarsia out of jealousy, what her calculations were about the safety of so doing (the likelihood that Apollonius would never return), and how she planned to conceal the crime.

"When Stranguillio heard this he was dumfounded and said to his wife, 'Equidem, da mihi vestes lugubres ut lugeam me, qui talem sum sortitus sceleratam coniugem. Heu mihi! pro dolor, quid faciam, quid agam de patre eius, cum primo eum suscepissem, cum civitatem istam a morte et periculo famis liberavit, meo suasu egressus est civitatem . . . . Heu mihi, caecatus sum! lugeam me et innocentem virginem, qui iunctus sum ad pessimam venenosamque serpentem et iniquam coniugem.' And, raising his eyes to heaven, he said, 'deus, tu scis quia purus sum a sanguine Tarsiae, et requiras et vindices illam in Dionysiade!' " After that Dionysias clothed herself and her daughter in mourning garb, wept false tears, and, summoning all the citizens of Tarsus, told them that Tarsia had died of a stomach ailment and induced them to set up a statue in her memory. In all this Stranguillio takes no part. But later, in ch. 37, Stranguillio sees Apollonius, on his return to Tarsus, approaching in the distance and hurries home to report this to his wife, saying, "Surely, you told me that Apollonius had perished in a shipwreck; but, behold, here he is coming back to claim his daughter. What are we going to say to her father about his child, whose foster parents we have been?" On hearing this, the wicked woman trembled in her whole body and said, "Pity us. I confess to you, husband, that on account of love for our own daughter, I destroyed the child who was not ours. So now put on garments of mourning, let us shed false tears, and say that she died of a stomach disease. Anyone who sees us in this garb will believe us." While this conversation was still going on Apollonius entered the house of Stranguillio, and after hearing from Dionysias that his daughter Tarsia had died of desease, went away in deep sorrow. Klebs believes that it was here, in ch. 37, that Stranguillio, in the original form of the romance, first learned that his wife had killed Tarsia; and after that there was nothing that he could do other than join with his wife in pretending that Tarsia's death had been caused by sickness. Near the end of the romance (ch. 50) when Apollonius comes back to Tarsus with his daughter for the purpose of punishing the foster parents, Tarsia assumes that Stranguillio was as guilty as his wife and allows both of them to be stoned to death by the people. In the original form of the romance, according to Klebs, Stranguillio was everywhere represented as being innocent of complicity in his wife's crime, and unaware of it before Apollonius returned; and the long passage in ch. 32, containing the confession of Dionysias that she had killed Tarsia, and her husband's denunciation of his wife for her crime, was probably interpolated by an ancient reviser of the text in order to correct the impression made in other places that Stranguillio was guilty, but without taking the trouble to revise ch. 37 accordingly. In any case, the substance of ch. 37 conspicuously contradicts that of ch. 32. It should be noted, however, that this contradiction, unlike the others that have been explained above, was not brought about by the author himself in the course of combining conflicting episodes, but is due to the revision and interpolation of his original text on the part of ancient editors.

9 (ch. 37–47)

Meanwhile Apollonius, after fourteen years' absence in Egypt, returned to the city of Tarsus and was told by his false friends Stranguillio and Dionysias that his daughter Tarsia had fallen sick and died. By way of proving their good faith they gave him all of Tarsia's jewels and showed him the monument set up by the people in her honor. Apollonius, brokenhearted, returned to his ship and hid himself in the darkness of the hold while it sailed out for Tyre; but unfavorable winds forced the crew to put in at Mytilene. There Apollonius, because the festival of Neptune was in progress, gave ten gold pieces to each of the crew with which to enjoy the celebration, but he himself remained in mourning in the depths of the ship's hold, after giving orders that he was not to be summoned by anyone. He threatened to break the legs of any sailor who should disturb him, so they all feared to approach him. While the sailors were feasting on the deck above, Athenagoras, who had been walking on the shore, went aboard and mingled with them. On his asking who the owner of the ship was, they said that he was a man who was mourning for the loss of his wife and daughter and was lying in the hold of the ship. Athenagoras then offered the pilot two gold pieces if he would go down and tell the owner of the ship that he, Athenagoras the ruler of the city, wanted to see him on deck. "Get somebody else to go," said the pilot. "I couldn't buy four legs for two pieces of gold. He warned us that anyone who called him would have his legs broken." "That was for you sailors," said Athenagoras, "not for me, whom he does not know. I'll go down to him myself. What's his name?" "Apollonius." Athenagoras remembered that the girl Tarsia in the brothel had told him that her father's name was Apollonius, and so he suspected that this man might be her father. After trying in vain to cheer him and induce him to come up from the hold, Athenagoras sent for Tarsia and commissioned her to bring such comfort as she could to the owner of the ship, who lay in the dark mourning for his wife and daughter. Tarsia came and by her tactful approach succeeded in getting some attention. She sang him a little song in which she outlined her own misfortunes in verse, but Apollonius was too

intent on his personal sorrow to realize that what she related applied
to his own daughter Tarsia. He thanked the girl courteously, gave
her 200 gold pieces and sent her away. Afterwards Athenagoras
promised her 400 *aurei* if she would go back, return the 200 *aurei* to
Apollonius, and beg him to let her talk with him, since she came,
not to make money but to cure him of his grief. This new appeal
softened the resistance of Apollonius so that he let her stay awhile.
She then proceeded to divert his mind and to amuse him by proposing
a number of riddles, each of which Apollonius promptly solved. Then
he told her to go away; and when she, nevertheless, tried to lead him
by the hand up to the light, he struck her so that she fell down and
blood gushed from her nostrils. As she sat there bemoaning this new
cruelty of fortune, she once again related the misfortunes that had
befallen her, but this time in much greater detail, beginning with her
birth at sea and ending with mention of what she had suffered at the
hands of Stranguillio and Dionysias, and her sale to the keeper of a
brothel at Mytilene. On hearing this, Apollonius recognized his
daughter, threw his arms around her weeping for joy, and exclaimed,
"You are my only hope, the light of my eyes. Now may this city
perish!" Athenagoras on hearing these words, hurried back to the
city and warned the people to save themselves by punishing the
keeper of the brothel; and, acting on this advice, the people ordered
the bawd to be burned to death. Apollonius, on coming into the
forum, made an eloquent speech of thanks to the people of Mytilene
for having kept his daughter unharmed, and he gave them publicly
in cash 700 talents with which to rebuild their fortifications. In gratitude the citizens set up a group of statues with an inscription in
honor of Apollonius and Tarsia. A few days later Tarsia was married
to Athenagoras, the ruler of the city, amid rejoicing on all sides.

10 (ch. 48–52)

Thereafter Apollonius, with his daughter and son-in-law, set sail for
his native land, intending to stop at Tarsus on the way; but a dream
came to him in the night directing him to go first to Ephesus, there
to enter the temple of Diana with his daughter and son-in-law and
to relate in order all the misfortunes that he had suffered since youth.
After that he was to go to Tarsus and avenge the wrong done to his
daughter. Apollonius followed these instructions throughout. On

arriving at the temple of Diana at Ephesus he stood before the statue of the goddess in the presence of the chief priestess (who, as the reader knows, was his own long-lost wife) and told the whole story about himself and his experience since leaving Antioch. Thereupon the priestess recognized him and cried out, "I am your wife, the daughter of King Archestrates," and fell into his arms. "And where is my daughter?" "Here," said Apollonius, presenting Tarsia; and the joy of their reunion was completed. All Ephesus rejoiced in the good fortune of their priestess and bid her a fond farewell when she sailed away with her husband, her daughter and her son-in-law.

Thereafter Apollonius, taking with him an army of his own, came with his daughter and her husband to the city of Tarsus; where, on entering the forum, he summoned Stranguillio and Dionysias and revealed to the people their crime through Tarsia and the testimony of their steward, Theophilus. Tarsia spared Theophilus, because he had been reluctant to kill her and had allowed her time in which to pray; but she seems not to have known that Stranguillio was still more innocent, and so allowed him, along with his wife, the wicked Dionysias, to be stoned to death by the angry people of Tarsus.

Apollonius remained in Tarsus fifteen days, after which he sailed for Pentapolis in Cyrenaica, where he showed to his father-in-law, King Archestrates, his long-lost daughter, and his granddaughter Tarsia, with her husband. They lived happily with the old king for a year. Then he died, after bequeathing half his kingdom to Apollonius and half to his daughter. One day while walking on the shore Apollonius saw the old fisherman who had befriended him when he was a shipwrecked stranger and had shared his own cloak with him. He had the old man brought into his presence at the palace and, after reminding him of who he himself was, and how grateful he and his wife felt for the help he had once given him, he presented him with 200,000 sesterces in gold, along with many servants and much clothing, and made him his comrade for life. He also rewarded Hellenicus the Tyrian citizen who had aided him at Tarsus when King Antiochus was pursuing him, and who had now come to Cyrene to claim the benefactions that Apollonius had promised him in case he should regain his kingdom. Soon after that his wife bore him a son whom he appointed king in place of his grandfather Archestrates. Apollonius lived with his wife seventy-four years in peace and happiness, ruling over Antioch and Tyre until they died. He wrote a full account of his fortunes and those of his family, in two volumes (i.e., copies), one of which he deposited in the temple of Diana of the Ephesians, the other in his own library.

The statement that Apollonius had deposited in the temple of Diana at Ephesus an account of his own experiences written by himself, was probably made by the author of the romance, although it is not found in all the best manuscripts. By this statement the author meant to imply that his romance was founded on, or identical with, an historiographical document of the highest authority, which might presumably be found in the temple at Ephesus or which had survived from the private library of Apollonius himself. Such was the pretense, needed by a sophistic writer, for the purpose of sanctioning and of giving some *décor* to his ideal prose fiction.

There is nothing in the contents of the romance of *Apollonius of Tyre* to justify the assumption, made by Rohde and others, that it is either a translation or a free adaptation on the whole of a Greek romance. There is nothing peculiarly Greek about it, either in the language and style or in the narrative substance, but it contains much that is specifically Roman, in respect both to its stylistic mannerisms and thought and to the literary sources on which certain of its episodes are shaped and worded—much more than can be found, for example, in the very free translation by Apuleius of the Greek story of Lucius in his *Metamorphoses*.

The nature of the several episodes in a romance is no indication that the majority of them came from a literary form called romance. Indeed, they might all have been suggested by, or taken from various literary or oral sources other than romances, or some of them from romances and as many others from other kinds of books. Many episodes in the Greek romances are modelled on or suggested by historical events or old myths. The first Greek romancer did not get his substance from predecessors in the same genre; and if a later practitioner imitated or took over an episode or two, or a stock motif, from a predecessor's romance, it was not the whole romance that he took over or imitated, nor any large part of it. Why should not a Latin writer follow the same method of composition in making up a romance of his own? What need is there to suppose that a romance written in Latin is necessarily a translation or an imitation throughout of a particular Greek romance? There is, I submit, no need at all for drawing such a conclusion from the nature of the episodes in *Apollonius*. The stock materials of Greek romance—superlatively beautiful youngsters, who sometimes proudly resist Eros at first but later yield and suffer for it, the meeting or reunion of lovers in temples or religious ceremonies, shipwrecks, pirates in action carrying away the lovers and selling them, travel all around the shores of the eastern Mediterranean, heroines forced into brothels but keeping their chastity, jealous wives or stepmothers plotting cruelly against hero or heroine, burial alive in a sepulchre, or *Scheintod* of some kind, imprisonment or attempted crucifixion or slaughter by an enemy with narrow escapes, oracles and dreams guiding the wandering hero in his quest, the recognition of hero and heroine or of the various members of a family after a long period of separation—no one of these story-motifs belongs exclusively to the form romance, or is confined to that form in ancient literature. Any one of them, and sometimes a group of them together could be found by a writer who wanted to use them here or there in many kinds of literature both Greek and Roman, seen in plays on the stage, or heard about in orally circulated tales or in events of real life that had actually happened. The sources used by the author of *Apollonius* in shaping his episodes, insofar as these can be identified with any degree of probability, include the story about Antiochus and Stratonice (above, sec. 2), which could have come to his knowledge from either a Greek or a Latin book; Vergil's *Aeneid*, Bks. I, II and IV (sec. 4); some stage comedy picturing the importunities of suitors in the street (sec. 5); the lost *Alcmaeon* of Euripides or some Greek or Roman summary account of its plot (sec. 8); a theme discussed in the Roman schools of rhetoric as described in Seneca's *Controversiae* (I 2); and (or) a scene on the stage in a mime or comedy (sec. 8).

In *Apollonius* the new tendencies in the shaping of Latin prose fiction, which first appeared in Apuleius, as defined above in Ch. VII, are extended along their own lines in the direction of medieval Latin and Oriental, but not of Byzantine, prose fiction.[3] The Latin romance

---

[3] Fiction in Byzantine prose, unlike medieval prose fiction in the West, or in the Muslim world of the Near and Middle East, remains static and unchanged in substance, which is all copied, with only slight verbal variations or internal rearrangements, either from ancient Greek texts and their ancient variant forms, or from the archetype of a medieval Greek translation of an Oriental book, such as *Kalilah and Dimnah* or *Sindbad*. This medieval Greek fiction in prose retains the organic structure characteristic of all post-classical Greek narratives, in contrast with the inorganic and agglutinative tendencies in composition which appear in the earliest Latin literature and become more

of *Apollonius* in the third century, in other words, is a natural
development, within the Roman milieu, from the kind of Latin fiction
that appears in the *Metamorphoses* of Apuleius in the second century.
It is such as might well be foreseen by one who understood the nature
of the Apuleian innovations, their direction, and the agglutinative
and inorganic methods of composition employed by that second-
century Latin sophist.

Apuleius brings large quantities of seriously oriented folktales into
the framework of the burlesque Greek story of Lucius, including the
witch story of Aristomenes (*Met.* I 5–20), the resurrection of a dead
man by an Egyptian priest (*Met.* II 27–29),[4] the fairy tale of Cupid
and Psyche (*Met.* IV 28–VI 24), the vengeance taken by Charite on
the murderer of her husband, a tragic story (*Met.* VIII 1–14; cf.
Walter Anderson in *Philologus* 69 [1909], p. 537); the encounter with
a man-eating dragon who had lured his victim into a hidden place
by appearing in the form of an old man in distress and in need of
help to rescue his child (*Met.* VIII 19–21); the tragic story, as Apuleius
calls it[5] about the wicked stepmother who made love to her stepson
and tried to poison him when he resisted her advances (*Met.* X 2–12);
and various other stories of sensational crime; all of which are folktales told in a genuine spirit of belief or superstitious awe or sympathy, with no overtones of comedy or satire in them. Apart from this
importation of serious folktales as wholes into the framework of the
originally burlesque and objectively ironical Greek story of Lucius,
Apuleius has told much of that comic story itself subjectively in a
serious and sympathetic vein, outlining in sharp and picturesque
profiles a wide variety of characters major and minor, who cross the

---

pronounced and more frequent in late antiquity and the Middle Ages. What
corresponds in medieval Greek fiction to that really *popular* kind of narrative
seen in the West and in the Muslim East, is always written or recited in
verse. We see it first in the tenth-century Byzantine epic of *Digenes Akrites*
and later on in great quantities; and the first appearance in a Greek form of
Apollonius of Tyre was necessarily in Byzantine verse, not in prose. On the
structural features of popular medieval prose fiction in the Latin West, and
in the Muslim East, consider the examples cited in note 16 on chap. VII below.

[4] On this see the article by S. Morenz entitled "Totenaussagen im Dienste
des Rechtes, ein ägyptisches Element in Hellenismus und Spätantike" in
Würzburger Jahrbücher für die Altertumswissenschaft III (1948), 290–300.

[5] *Met.* X 2: *iam ergo, lector optime, scito te tragoediam, non fabulam legere et
a socco ad coturnum ascendere.*

path of Lucius, and many of whom, especially women, he has himself introduced for the first time. These characters in Apuleius are no longer viewed as puppets, as they would be in Lucian, but as interesting human beings worth picturing for what they are ethically, and for the pathos of their experience. Still another innovation on the part of Apuleius in retelling comic stories consisted in lengthening them by the addition of many concrete details and incidents and in prolonging the suspense of the narrative, looking forward evermore to a dramatic climax instead of relating it summarily in the relatively abstract style of the Greek comic romance or novella. In other words, Apuleius has brought the qualities and proprieties of serious ideal fiction in large measure into basically comic fiction. All this, including the added stories above mentioned, shows that Apuleius *wanted* to write ideal prose fiction in the likeness, fundamentally, of the Greek romance or the modern novel. That was in the *popular* spirit of his age, something oncoming and dynamic; but he himself, as a famed intellectual writer and philosopher, was still too much under the restraint of classical tradition and fashion to go all the way out in the writing of serious prose fiction, as he might have wished to do, and as the *anonymous* Latin author of *Apollonius* ventured to do in the following century. Even that third-century writer seems, by way of self-defense, not to have put his own name on his romance, although the force of classical tradition in his time had probably weakened to some extent in comparison with what it had been in the time of Apuleius.

The exploitation of fairy-tale lore of all kinds, told in the naïve wonder seeking spirit, and with such details and exaggerations as are characteristic of folktales generally, as opposed to formal literary fictions, appears for the first time in the fundamentally comic romances of Petronius and of Apuleius, and much more abundantly in the latter than in the former. In the third-century romance of *Apollonius* this exploitation of the substance and spirit of pure folklore, pointing in the direction of medieval-Latin romance, is more pronounced and intensified, than in Apuleius, being an extension along the same lines of the materials and tendencies begun by Apuleius.

Much has already been said about the inorganic and agglutinative methods of composition employed by Apuleius, and by the author of *Apollonius*, in joining one originally independent story with another, and the absence of plausible motivation which often results from those mechanical methods. For convenience, all this may be called, now that we have explained what it is, *contaminatio;* and *contaminatio*, as everyone knows, is much more frequently met with in Latin literature than in Greek. That is another reason for concluding, as I do, along with Klebs, Goepp, and others, that the romance *Apollonius of Tyre* is the creation of a Latin author, the only one of its kind in antiquity.

APPENDIX III
The Ego-Narrative in Comic Stories

Before the birth of the modern novel any narrative was judged primarily by the standard of historical or scientific truth; and the outcome of that first judgment determined in the case of any particular narrative what the form of its telling would be, whether in the third person or in the first, and how it would be looked upon aesthetically, whether as sober history in a very broad sense, with or without fictitious additions in poetry, or as outright falsehood in prose, whether intentional or not, or as *comedy*.

In narrating the adventures of the ancient hero of saga, Odysseus, Homer was at liberty, as a tragic poet would also be, by virtue of a well-recognized poetic license, to invent new episodes of his own which had not come down to him in the (presumably) historical saga; hence he *might* have related on his own authority in the third person all the yarns that Odysseus tells in the first person about himself to the Phaeacians. But Homer will not venture so far into pure fiction as to do that. He is restrained from doing so by his strong Greek sense, not of history, but of moderation and reality; a feeling of restraint about the recording of miracles, which is conspicuously absent in most other epics of popular origin. Homer, poet though he was, felt the responsibility of an historian when it came to telling about the visit to Hades and the encounters of Odysseus with the Cyclops and Circe. For that reason, and because he nevertheless wants his audience to enjoy hearing those yarns, he makes Odysseus himself responsible for the telling of them. Nobody could refute what Odysseus had said about himself and his own experiences, and if he was a shameless liar no one would be injured or embarrassed in consequence of that guilt; but anyone could challenge or refute and embarrass Homer, had he told the same things about Odysseus.

This, the rationale of Homer's procedure in the *Odyssey*, explains why so many fictitious but seriously intended narratives in antiquity, or narratives suspected of being such, are told ostensibly by someone other than the author himself. And, since it is usually more convenient for an author to introduce that someone else speaking in the first person, we have accordingly more fictions told in the first person than in the third. The introduction of a sponsor for a fictitious story who speaks in the third person is not so easily arranged. Still, Longus, in the age of *ecphrasis*, did it by bringing in an interpreter to tell us the story of *Daphnis and Chloe*; and Theopompus introduced Silenus, none other, to tell us and King Midas all about the land of Merope (chap. ii, n. 22). Lucian at the beginning of his *True History*, after mentioning the pseudo-scientific writings of Ctesias about the wonders of India, and of Iambulus about the miracles that he personally had met with on a voyage into far-off seas, goes on to say that many other writers, besides these two, had written up fictitious accounts of what purported to be their own travels in strange lands, and that the founder of this tribe of literary liars, and the one who taught them such nonsense, was none other than Homer's Odysseus, telling fables about himself to the Phaeacians, as if he thought they were simpletons. The writers here mentioned by Lucian, and all their kind, wrote in a serious vein in the hope of being believed. Nothing that they recorded was meant to be laughable or ridiculous, and it might be in part positively tragic in tone or awe-inspiring, as is true of what Odysseus relates about his own adventures in the *Odyssey*. Because they published their accounts of wonderful phenomena in the guise of true history or science, and because what they wrote looked like mere fiction, these serious authors felt obliged to guard themselves somehow against being refuted and publicly exposed as liars; and it was for that reason that they wrote in the first person about what they had themselves seen or suffered in faraway lands. Under those circumstances noone could check up on the truth or falsehood of their assertions, because nobody had been present with the author on the scene. Such was the origin of the ego-narrative as a literary form. It began with the purveyors of wonder-stories told in serious mood; but afterwards it was extended to comic narratives.

When *comic* writing takes the form of a long narrative there is no need of pretending that what is related is true, and no need therefore on that account of employing the ego-narrative. Instead, the author may narrate objectively the ludicrous actions of imaginary characters, as is the case in the mock-heroic *Margites* and in the *Battle of the Frogs and Mice*. These poems are parodies of the old epic, and as such they naturally follow the structural pattern of the epics which they mimic. But parody of another type of narrative was not a necessary feature of a comic romance or short story. Some of the farcical scenes in Petronius are related objectively by Encolpius, who speaks in the first person as protagonist throughout the *Satyricon*; from which we see that Petronius, the real author, might well have related the entire substance of his comic romance objectively in the third person, without putting the narration of it into the mouth of an imaginary character such as Encolpius, without, in other words, using what we are calling the ego-narrative. Since statements of truth are not required or expected in comedy, as they are in sober history, the author of a comic story could relate with impunity on his own authority, as it were, anything he pleased about the doings of a fictitious third person; but he could not tell the story about himself, as a serious writer might do, without writing himself down as a *Pechvogel*, or as a clown or a fool of some kind.

Thus it appears that the authors of comic romances, and also of short comic stories, had a choice of three patterns of narrative that could be employed. All three are used as a matter of fact, but the ego-narrative predominates, especially in the long narratives published separately and called romances. Among these only two of those known to us are parodies written in the third person; while the others, four in number, are in the form of ego-narrative: the *Satyricon* of Petronius, Lucian's lost *Metamorphoses* and its epitome entitled *Lucius or the Ass*, Lucian's *True History*, and the *Metamorphoses* of Apuleius. Likewise many short stories of comic effect, relating to witches, ghosts, or other supernatural and incredible phenomena, are introduced into the books above mentioned and others, told in the first person as their own experiences by subordinate characters who are laughed at by others and by the reader for the telling of them, but who declare on oath that what they say is absolutely true.

Typical of these short ego-narratives is the werewolf story told by
the superstitious Niceros in Petronius (61–62), the story told by
Trimalchio about his encounter with witches (63), the witch stories
told by Aristomenes and by Thelyphron respectively in Books I and
II of the Apuleian *Metamorphoses* (cf. chap. vii above, secs. 7 and 8).

Lucian's *True History* is a mocking parody, not of the old epics,
but of a kind of prose book of which many were written and circulated
in the Hellenistic age—specifically, travelogues in which the authors,
writing in the first person for the reasons mentioned above, described
the wonderful things which they had seen with their own eyes, not
heard from others, on their own travels, and the incredible things
that had befallen them, things to which only the author himself and
a crowd of dog-headed anthropoids in Bengal (Ctesias), or women
with ass's legs (*Ver. Hist.* II 46), could bear witness.

Parody of those seriously intended travelogues, which were written
in the first person, explains very obviously why Lucian in the *True
History* employs the ego-narrative; but the same explanation *mutatis
mutandis*, if not quite so obvious, is valid for all the other comic and
miraculous narratives written in the first person which were mentioned above, be they long or short, in a context or published independently in separate books. All those stories are comic mimicries of
stories which had been told seriously as miracle-lore; many of them
only orally, and one of them, presumably (the comic story of Lucius
the Ass), in the third person rather than in the first. The use of the
ego-narrative in the *Luciad* of Lucian and Apuleius, and in Petronius,
was determined by the fashion that prevailed elsewhere in comic or
burlesque stories, instead of by the pattern of narrative found in
a particular form of literature or folktale. What Lucian in the *Luciad*
imitated by way of parody and satire was most probably a folktale
told in the third person; and what Petronius mimics for comedy's
sake in the *Satyricon* is no one kind of book but serious or heroic
actions of any kind, wherever they may have been found in antecedent
literature—in epic poetry and tragic drama, in homely folktales, and
in mimes which were themselves comic and current on the Roman
stage.

In summary: Comic stories are very often mimicries of stories
written or told orally in a serious, wonder-seeking, or heroic mood
(cf. the robber stories in Apuleius); such wonder-stories were most
commonly written or told in the first person; the author of the comic

story or romance in literature follows by way of mimicry what was the *prevailing fashion* in those wonder-stories; hence his use of the ego-narrative. The highly amusing effect of self-irony, produced by letting a protagonist describe with feeling his own humiliations or misfortunes, is an additional reason why the author of a comic story, such as that of Lucius, should employ the ego-narrative in preference to some other form.

NOTES TO CHAPTER I

Greek Romance and the Problem of Forms and Origins

Pages 3–43

[1] Prose fiction when it first appears in literature, and indeed for long afterward, is regarded with disdain by educated people on the accepted level of taste and fashion, chiefly because they have been accustomed to find spiritual beauty and meaning only in *poetic* fiction (epic and drama), and because prose fiction in the beginning, before it comes to be written by authors of cultivated understanding, is nearly always jejune in that respect, as it was in Greek antiquity. In his volume of Sather Lectures, entitled *From Homer to Menander: Forces in Greek Poetic Fiction* (Berkeley, 1951), p. 7, Professor L. A. Post describes the homely and despised successor to poetic fiction, the Greek romance, fairly well, observing by way of illustration that in the early nineteenth century "the blue-stocking Hannah More read the narrative *poems* of Walter Scott but refused to waste time on most of his novels." The distinguished writer on American literature, Fred Lewis Pattee, in his autobiography entitled *Penn State Yankee* (State College, Pa., 1953) testifies as follows: "As a boy I was warned against dime novels, love stories, and all other fiction. 'You admit that what's told in that novel never *really* happened,' my father would say. 'Yes,' I would reply, 'but . . .' 'Then it's a *lie*. Why read lies when you can read history and biography? Love stories! Pshaw!' Never in his life did he read a novel." In ages when the novel is young, narrative in prose, if not subjective, is assumed to be history and is judged by that standard. If what it relates is true and matter of fact it has the virtue of being informative, but if not it is worthless; because, unlike poetry, it is not recognized as creative art.

Concerning the humble status of prose fiction and the disdain with which it was regarded until recently by intellectuals in the Muslim world, see our note 19 in chapter v concerning the *Arabian Nights*. Pearl Buck in her book on *The Chinese Novel* (New York, Longmans, 1939) writes that the noveo in China was never an art and was never so considered; that no Chinese novelist thought of himself as an artist; that literature as an art was the exclusive property of scholars; and that the learned Chinese critics and encyclopedists as late as 1772, in enumerating the kinds of writing which compose the whole of literature, make no mention of the novel, which had flourished on a sub-literary level for centuries among the common people. The status of the novel in modern Greek literature at the beginning was very similar; see A. Mirambel's article, "Le roman neogrec et la langue litteraire en Grèce," in *Bulletin de l'Association Guillaume Budè*, Paris, Les Belles Lettres, March, 1951, p. 63.

[2] The fundamental principles by which I have been guided in explaining what literary forms are, and how they originate, have come to me slowly in the course of much thinking about the matter directly. I am not aware of

having been influenced by recent literature on the theory of literary forms, except for the writings of Croce, G. Lukács (*Die Theorie des Romans*, Berlin, 1920), and R. K. Hack (below, note 11) especially. Now that I have begun to read more in the field of general literary theory, I am pleased to discover, on looking into an excellent and comprehensive book on the subject (R. Wellek and A. Warren, *Theory of Literature*[2] [New York, 1948]), that my positive views are shared to some extent by literary critics of recent times, and that many of these critics have rejected, as I do, the old concepts of literary history which were shaped on the analogy of biological evolution.

[3] Anyone who thinks or writes about the origins of literary forms would do well to ponder carefully what Wellek and Warren (pp. 267 f.) have to say about the descent of literary genres on the analogy of biological evolution as represented by Brunetière's theory. This is a subject to which I shall return near the end of this chapter (p. 37) in the critique of Ludvíkovsky's theory of how the Greek romance originated.

[4] I refrain from naming the author of this statement because he is a scholar whom I admire and whose important contributions to our subject are elsewhere mentioned in this book. Besides, he is only one of three or four scholars who have expressed the same idea. It would be difficult to cite any writer on subjects of this kind in connection with the Greek romance who does not speak of development on the surface of literature, or who ventures to explain precisely what he means by development.

[5] B. Croce, *Estetica*, 9th ed. (Bari, 1950), p. 149.

[6] I have stated this general principle more fully in connection with the history of Aesopic fables in my article "Fable" in *Studium Generale* XII (1959), 17. It is a corollary to the principle of the medieval Nominalist, *universalia post rem;* as opposed to that of the Realist which derives from Plato and Aristotle: *universalia ante rem* with Plato, *universalia in re* with Aristotle.

[7] The elder Seneca's *Controversiae* in ten books, of which only an abridgment has come down to us, consist of seventy-four themes briefly stated, followed by lengthy accounts of how the legal, ethical, and social problems posed by them were argued pro or con by famous orators. These themes, which are well described and illustrated at length by Miss Haight on pp. 125–150 of her *Essays on Ancient Fiction* (New York, 1936), involve sensational stories of adventure and dire hazard, which are very similar in their substance and motifs to episodes in the Greek romances—stories about piracy, enforced prostitution, and poisoning; about the crimes of fiercely jealous women in family relations; or, as Encolpius on the first page of Petronius asserts, stories about "pirates standing in chains on the beach, about tyrants, pen in hand, ordering sons to cut off their fathers' heads, and oracles in time of pestilence demanding the blood of three or more virgins." A *controversia* often cited as typical of the species, I 6 in Seneca's text, relates to a young man who had been carried off by pirates and whose father refused to ransom him. The daughter of the pirate chieftain, having fallen in love with the young captive, told him that she would help him to escape if he would marry her. The pair managed to escape and the young man kept

his word, but his father, because he had found a desirable match for his son in a rich orphan girl, ordered him to divorce the pirate's daughter and marry the heiress. The son refused to do so, and his father disowned him. Which course of action was right, the father's or the son's? The father's action could be justified on the ground of social position, that of the son on the ground of gratitude and honor. Incidentally, Mlle. de Scudéry used the plot of this story in her romance entitled *Ibrahim ou l'illustre Bassa* in four volumes. Seneca told it in six lines. What were the intermediate steps of development between Seneca and Scudéry?

In a book entitled *Les Déclamations et les Déclamateurs d'après Sénèque le père* (Lille, 1902, p. 130) H. Bornecque shows himself to be as good an historian as Scudéry, when he declares that in these *Controversiae*, worked over in the rhetorical schools, we have the first drafts of a new literary genre, the romance. That cannot be true in the sense that romance as a literary form grew out of the *controversia* in the course of rhetorical practice. The purpose for which the sensational themes of the *controversiae* were invented, and in which the characters have no proper names and no alleged connection with history, local myth, or legend, was to inspire eloquent pleading on the part of students and teachers by giving them something interesting and provocative to orate about. The purpose that inspired the writing of romances was nothing more than to entertain the reader by picturing the passions and thrilling adventures of a pair of lovers; and the names of these lovers, at least that of one of them, are always those of characters in a local myth or legend, however obscure they may be. As there can be no genetic relationship between one purpose and another purpose, so there can be no genetic relationship between romance and *controversia*. And, if such a relationship were to be assumed, it would not be possible to explain in any plausible way why the earliest Greek romances deal with named characters belonging to local myths or historical legends, while the nameless characters of the *controversiae* have no such connections. The narrative in the *controversia* is told in the barest possible outline: the longest (VII 5) takes up only 11 lines on the printed octavo page, the next longest (III 8) $7\frac{1}{2}$ lines, and the great majority are told in from 1–5 lines each. How could these skeleton stories possibly have been developed by the rhetoricians into prolonged dramatic narratives, when all their exercise, all their effort, and all their oratory, at times extending to 10 or 15 pages, is devoted to pleading the cases of characters in the story, and there is no practice at all in the telling of the story? If it is only subject matter that gives birth to a new form, such literary biologists as Brunetière, Bornecque, Rohde, and Thiele might better have told us that the first drafts of the novel were made in the prologues of New Comedy, or in the *Odyssey*.

Bornecque's theory, according to which romance originated in the schools of rhetoric, repeats the fundamental error in method made by Erwin Rohde in his *Der Griechische Roman* (3rd ed., Leipzig, 1914). Rohde supposed, on the basis of a dating of the extant romances, which has since been disproved and completely reversed by evidence from the papyri, that the oldest of the romances were the most sophistic and the most rhetorical, and that the romance as a form was, generally speaking, a product of the so-called Second Sophistic in the second century after Christ. At the beginning of his book (p. 3) Rohde poses a rhetorical question, "Did it (the romance) come into the world grey-haired from birth, like Hesiod's Graiae?" And the answer that he gives us in effect later on (p. 269) amounts to an affirmation of just that, although he does not say so explicitly. It is enough to convince almost any literary critic of the present day that Rohde's theory is nonsense, merely to tell what it is. Rohde saw in the typical sophistic romance a mechanical combination of two disparate elements, the love element and the element of travel in strange lands. He has much to say (pp. 262–264) about this strange *Verbindung*. The man who first achieved it was the inventor (*Erfinder*) of the Greek romance and marked out the lines followed by his successors in the genre. Who could this man have been? We are kept in suspense up to p. 269, where we learn that the inventor was Antonius Diogenes with his aretalogy (so called nowadays) entitled *On the Wonders beyond Thule*, in which one Deinias is said to have fallen in love with Derkyllis, a Tyrian girl in Thule, and the latter tells him what had befallen herself and her brother in endless travels and tribulations before she and Deinias got to know each other in Thule. Not much love here. But Photius (cod. 166) noticed this combination of love and travel and, in his offhand remarks, said much the same thing about its significance as a prototype of the later romances that Rohde does. This theory was later espoused by J. E. F. Manso in his *Vermischte Schriften* (Leipzig, 1801), II, 201–320 on the romance, and by Rudolf Nicolai in a programm entitled *Über Enstehung und Wesen des griech. Romans* (reviewed by Hercher in *Jahrb. f. class. Phil.* 77 [1858]) written in 1854.

[8] Brunetière in his *L'Evolution des Genres*, Paris, 1898, p. 13, in connection with the history of the French novel: "Vous verrez là, comment . . . *un Genre se forme du débris de plusieurs autres.*" This characterization of the romance as a collection of the "*débris*" of other forms is repeated by C. B. Gulick in his article on "The Origin of the Novel" in *Harvard Graduate's Magazine* 33 (1924) 205.

[9] Aristotle's too-great fondness for strictly organic structure and complexity of plot, parts of tragedy which he saw in the *Oedipus* of Sophocles, appear to have blinded him to characteristic qualities of Greek tragedy which the modern reader admires and which must have been enjoyed by spectators in the fifth century B.C. So, for example, he says nothing about irony, which results from the antithetical style (λέξις ἀντικειμένη) in the plays of Aeschylus as well as in those of Sophocles, because he admires the organic style (λέξις ὑπεστραμμένη) which dominated post-Socratic thinking in the fourth century. He is in that environment of thought, and he cannot see back beyond it. He does not understand the fifth century. He has very little to say, moreover, and nothing significant, about the virtue and effect of the tragedy as a whole, which is not just the sum of its parts separately considered, as he seems to imply. Instead, he looks at the parts of a tragedy in the way that one might look at a machine, without knowing or caring what the purpose was for which the machine was devised or the product that it turned out. An excellent critique of Aristotle's mechanical methods in dealing with literature

is given us by L. A. Post in the ninth chapter of *From Homer to Menander* (see above, note 1).

¹⁰ Cicero, *De Nat. Deorum* I 10: *Obest plerumque iis qui discere volunt auctoritas eorum qui se docere profitentur.*

¹¹ Roy Kenneth Hack, "The Doctrine of Literary Forms," *Harvard Studies in Classical Philology* 27 (1916), 1–64. The sentence quoted above is on page 43. Hack's essay is a beautiful exposition of the thinking of Plato and Aristotle on literature, and of the influence exerted by their doctrines on later criticism, with which I find myself in complete agreement. Speaking of Plato's theory of imitation on page 43 f. he says truly that it "was employed by Plato to accomplish a special purpose, to achieve the ruin of poetry and art . . . Plato longed for this disastrous consummation because his scheme of the universe was incomplete, because he attempted to make the world wholly scientific and sought to exclude from it all creative activity. This error of Plato was rapidly transformed into a definite system of aesthetics and of criticism; and it has profoundly influenced all men and all things which have since come into contact with it, be they little or great, Horace or Aristotle, the Alexandrian grammarians or the mediaeval scholastics, Scaliger, Boileau, Pope, or Taine and Brunetière and Norden."

¹² As H. D. F. Kitto rightly observes in his *Greek Tragedy*, 3d ed. (New York, 1961), 403: "There is no such thing as a typical Greek play; the form was something created anew and differently year by year, play by play, by dramatic poets of genius."

¹³ The problem, to what form the epyllion belongs and what constitutes it, is discussed by Walter Allen, Jr. in *TAPhA* 71 (1940), 1–26, who notes that there has been no success on the part of critics in ascribing common literary characteristics to the poems usually classed as epyllia. As concerns Horace's *Ars Poetica*, Hack (p. 14) shows how two different students of the problem, Eduard Norden and O. Weissenfels, both of them committed to the biological and prescriptive conception of literary form stemming from Aristotle, arrive at opposite conclusions concerning the "form" to which the *Ars Poetica* belongs. Both assume that it is the *form* that determines the content; but Norden insists that the *Ars Poetica* is an εἰσαγωγή (a manual of an art or discipline) written in strict accordance with a fixed rhetorical scheme, while Weissenfels maintains that the same work is an epistle, that all epistles are written in a loose conversational style, and therefore that the *Ars Poetica* is written in a loose conversational style.

¹⁴ The fact that the numerous biographies written by the Peripatetic Satyrus near the end of the third century B.C. were cast in the form of dialogues—at least such was the case with the *Lives* of the three great Attic tragedians which were contained in the sixth book of the entire compilation— was revealed, much to our surprise, by the recent recovery of a substantial fragment of his Βίος Εὐριπίδου in no. 1176 of the *Oxyrhynchus Papyri* (Oxford, 1912), vol. 9. Much has been written by scholars about these biographies of Satyrus; see the article on Satyrus by A. Gudeman in *RE*, Second Series (1923), II, 228–235.

[15] So much has been written by philosophers and sociologists concerning the contrasted types of society called "open" and "closed" respectively that there is perhaps little need of explaining what these terms mean, except by way of reminding our readers of what their bearing is on the history of the novel. H. Bergson has much to say on this important subject by way of defining it in chap. iv of his book *Les deux sources de la morale et de la religion*, 12th ed. (Paris, 1932). In European history the *closed* societies of which we speak are composed of men living in the Homeric age, in the city-states of Greece down to the end of the fifth century, under Christendom internationally established, and the city-states of Renaissance and early modern times, as in France under the rule of Louis XIV—periods in which the direction of men's thinking is centripetal, instead of being centrifugal and chaotic, as in an *open* society like that of the present. In the *closed* society custom and fixed beliefs about human values and mankind's relation to the beyond are the guides to life and to men's choice of action, instead of philosophy as with the Socratic dialecticians in an *open* society. Men living in a *closed* society, men of faith and fixed beliefs, like Homer and Sophocles, know the answers to life's problems, however tentative, vague or mystical these answers may be; but they know no "problems," whereas everything in the advanced *open* society of today tends to be seen as a problem which only the god Science can be expected to solve. The closed society wants a fence around its world, so to speak, lest it be engulfed and lost in the infinity that lies outside; it insists on order in things, on nature to advantage dressed as in the gardens of Versailles, on proportion instead of chaotic confusion and vastness. Saint-Évremond in the time of Louis XIV writes an essay *Sur le Mot Vaste*, describing its ugly connotation. For him the word implies limitless extension, emptiness, and absence of order or proportion in things. Like some others of his time, he found the Homeric epics *vaste* in the sense that their structure is not organic but admits of indefinite extension in the multiplication of episodes. "Proportionateness," as Nietzsche says (*Beyond Good and Evil* p. 150 in Helen Zimmern's translation, New York: Modern Library, n.d.), is strange to us of the open society. "Let us confess it to ourselves; our itching is really the itching for the infinite, the immeasurable. Like the rider on his forward panting horse, we let the reins fall before the infinite, we modern men, we semi-barbarians, and are only in our highest bliss when we—are in most danger." Catiline's mind seemed *vastus* even to his contemporary Sallust, but in the wide-open society of today, which worships bigness, the English word *vast* is a term of praise. As Homer was *vaste* to Saint-Évremond, and in a lesser degree even to Aristotle, so Balzac with his *Comédie Humaine* seemed *vaste* and ugly to Taine, although the latter was a contemporary. Father Hennepin in the seventeenth century, who was presumably the first European to visit Niagara Falls, described the waters as "falling from a horrible precipice, foaming and boiling in the most hideous manner imaginable, and making an outrageous and dismal roaring more terrible than that of thunder." Who would wish to put a thing so disorderly and so vast into a painting? Certainly not Claude de Lorraine or any of his contemporaries. Their feeling for

Niagara was like that of Aeschylus for the Scythian Caucasus—a horrible place in a world of barbarism.

There is something vast, I fear, in the foregoing note (as there is in the novel). It might not have been so extended, had it been written in the environment of a closed society.

[16] The first and the last of the apocryphal *Acts* here mentioned are very well summarized and described by Miss Haight on pages 48–80 of her *More Essays on Greek Romances* (New York, 1945). For a comprehensive description and analysis of all these *Acts*, see Rosa Söder's *Die Apokryphen Geschichten und die romanhafte Literatur der Antike* (Stuttgart, 1932).

[17] K. Kerényi in his cloudy book on *Die griechisch-orientalische Romanliteratur in religionsgeschichtlicher Beleuctung* (Tübingen, 1927); R. Merkelbach, *Roman und Mysterium in der Antike* (München-Berlin, 1962); Altheim in *Literatur und Gesellschaft im ausgehenden Altertum* (Halle, 1948: I 30 ff.). This is all nonsense to me; as it is to A. D. Nock in reviewing Kerényi (*Gnomon* [1928], pp. 485 ff.), to Morton Smith in his review of Merkelbach (*Classical World* [1964], p. 378), and to H. Wagenvoort in *Bibliotheca Orientalia* XXII (1965) 102 ff.

[18] See Martin Braun's important and interesting study, *History and Romance in Graeco-Oriental Fiction* (Oxford, 1938), with a preface by Arnold Toynbee. Braun describes the little-known national hero legends which were brought into being by tensions between Greeks and Orientals in the Hellenistic period, and also between the Oriental nations themselves, stemming from old rivalries that had been suppressed by the Persian rule. Here we read about the "romance" of Sesonchosis, the early Egyptian hero; of Moses, propagated by the Jews; of Ninus and Semiramis, of Nectanebus the last of the Pharaohs, who was said to have been the real father of Alexander the Great—all patriotic hero legends built up in rivalry against the claims of alien or enemy powers.

[19] See Appendices I and II below for a brief account of these two romances in their ancient setting. I call them "non-erotic" only in the sense that they do not, like the other ideal romances, center entirely about the adventures of a pair of young lovers but about the reunion, after long separation, of various lost members of a family, including father and mother and brothers and sisters as well as husband and wife.

[20] For adverse criticism of Brunetière's theory of literary genres, in agreement with my own views, see Wellek and Warren, pp. 246 ff. They remark that it is generally agreed among literary theorists of today that "Brunetière did a disservice to 'genology' by his quasi-biological theory of evolution," and they show how his theory about the birth, prime, and death of genres in the history of French literature does not fit the realities.

[21] In his review of Miss Haight's *More Essays on Greek Romances* (*AJPh* 57 [1936], p. 188) Warren Blake comments wisely as follows (in terms of Calderini's dubious definition of Greek romance) concerning the real nature of the *Acts of Alexander* by Ps.-Callisthenes: "It is certainly adventurous and 'partly inspired by fact,' but the central theme of love is missing, and the 'fact,' i.e. the history, which is merely the *décor* of a true romance, is here

the chief interest, designed with all its 'romanticism' primarily to stimulate national pride, and not 'for the amusement of the public.' "

[22] *Der Griechische Roman*[3], p. 27.

[23] *Le Origini del Romanzo Greco* (Pisa, 1921), p. 20.

The Form Romance in Historical Perspective

Pages 44–95

[1] Concerning the medieval Greek romances of chivalry, see below, p. 103 f. with note 9 on chap. iii.

[2] An important variety of epic not yet mentioned is what may be called martyr-epic, the dominant form in the age of Christian asceticism; for which see below in chap. iii, p. 101 f. H. Delehaye in *Les Passions des Martyrs et les Genres Littéraires* (Bruxelles, 1921), p. 317: "Il existe parmi les passions des martyrs de veritables romans d'aventures, des romans idylliques, des romans didactiques, aisément reconnaissables."

[3] See the important article on this subject by James A. Notopoulos entitled "The Generic and Oral Composition in Homer," *TAPhA* 81 (1950), 28 ff. Notopoulos shows how "the generic typology found alike in Homer and early Greek art is but the cognate expression of a creative mind which shows in its creation a similar generic, formulaic, and schematic refraction of the world of man and of nature."

[4] Here I am quoting in part what I said in my article "Literature in the Second Century," *Class. Jour.* 50 (1955), 295. See also the excellent chapter on "The Tragic Fallacy" by Joseph Wood Krutch in his volume of essays entitled *The Modern Temper* (New York, 1929). Krutch states clearly and forcefully the sense in which and the reason why Shakespearean tragedy (or Sophoclean) is impossible of creation today. We may indeed appreciate it and enjoy it, as Vergil and his contemporaries appreciated Homer, but we cannot produce it because our own outlook on man is so different. It is no longer a dynamic form of literature and was not such in the Hellenistic world.

[5] René Le Bossu, *Traité du Poeme Épique* (Paris, 1675), II, 166, as quoted and discussed by W. P. Ker in *Epic and Romance* (London: Macmillan, 1922) pp. 33f.

[6] Concerning the decline of drama in England in the early eighteenth century, George Sampson in *The Concise Cambridge History of English Literature* (Cambridge Univ. Press, 1946), p. 513, sums up the matter as follows: "The theater was steadily losing its power as a serious criticism of life, and lost it entirely when the Licensing Act of 1737 established a censorship of plays. Fielding the suppressed playwright became Fielding the unsuppressed novelist. The supremacy in creative entertainment passed from the acted dramas to prose fiction."

[7] On Balzac, his vastness and the cultural outlook of his time and place, see H. Taine's illuminating essay on pp. 1–94 of his *Nouveaux Essais de Critique et d'Histoire* 9th ed. (Paris, 1909).

[8] Oswald Spengler, *The Decline of the West*, translated by C. F. Atkinson (New York: Alfred A. Knopf, 1937), II, 93.

[9] Aptly so designated by George Sampson on p. 502 of *The Concise Cambridge History of English Literature*, after the title of a book by Defoe.

[10] See below, p. 350 n. 15.

[11] The reason for the use of the ego-narrative in ancient fiction, whether serious or comic, is explained in Appendix III.

[12] Theon, *Progymnasmata* 3, in Spengel's *Rhetores Graeci* II (Leipzig: Teubner, 1853) 74 f. Cf. W. Schmid in Christ-Schmid, *Gr. Lit*[6]. I pp. 516–517, where he comments on the use of this device by Xenophon in the *Cyropedia*. One might suppose that this historiographical matter of form would be familiar to any classical scholar, but many have missed it. The erudite Schmid himself seems not to realize fully what it is, when he implies that it indicates the use of an oral source (which may be the case sometimes, but is not necessarily or always so); and the rationale of its use in Horace and other Roman poets is a mystery to H. Tescari, who writes about it in the *Giornale Italiano di Filologia* 4 (1951), 6–7 under the title "De quaestiuncula quadam insulsissima quam saepius mihi posui." I am bound to admire Senor Tescari's intellectual honesty more than his understanding of ancient style, which is not yet quite out of fashion in this matter except in novel and drama. Whether a poet or prose writer chooses to introduce a story in any particular case on his own authority in the "nominative," or whether he prefers to introduce it in the "accusative" by such words as *ferunt, dicitur* etc., depends upon how he feels about the historicity of the event, whether he believes it to be true, or whether he suspects it of being fictitious or untrue.

[13] *Oration* XXI, 11, ed. G. de Budé (Leipzig, 1919), II, 337.

[14] At the end of his story (*Orat.* VII 81 [Budé I, 260]) Dio assures his audience that it was not because he wanted to indulge in idle talk that he had told them all about his sojourn in Euboea, as some of them might suspect, but for the purpose of setting before them an example of how poor people can live and prosper, which was the theme that he meant to deal with from the beginning.

[15] See Rohde, *Gr. Rom.*[3], p. 376, with notes 1 and 3, where numerous examples of this terminology are cited.

[16] Fr. 442, cited and discussed by Rohde, *Gr. Rom.*[3], p. 104, note 2.

[17] *Gr. Rom.*[3], p. 265: "Von der Novella war wohl eine organische Erweiterung zum bürgerlichen Romane nicht zu erwarten, da ein solches Wachstum, wie es scheint, durch die genau umgrenzte Natur der Novellendichtung überhaupt ausgeschlossen ist."

Rohde's view on this matter is sharply opposed by R. Helm (*Der Antike Roman*, Berlin, 1948, p. 8) who thinks it useless and misguided to attempt to distinguish between novella and romance, which differ from each other only in the matter of relative length, not in the nature of their substance or manner of telling. He rightly observes that a novella—and he might well have said *any* novella—can be made into a romance if an author chooses to extend it and publish it separately, or to publish it separately without even extending it. In that last point lies the secret of the whole matter, the thing that marks all the essential difference between a novella and a romance in terms of literary form and practice. Helm seems not to have been fully aware of this principle as such, for he does not state it explicitly. It is clearly implied, however, by the illustration that he chooses for the purpose of showing that there need be no difference at all in either length or substance between a "novella" and a "romance"; for he says rightly that, if the tale of Cupid and Psyche did not stand in the context of the far-ranging romance about Lucius, but instead had been published and transmitted apart by itself, we should naturally and properly call it a "romance." We call it a novella instead of a romance because, like all the other relatively short stories in ancient literature, it is only part of a larger context.

[18] Since it was always subordinated to a larger context, the ancient novella had no independent development of its own. Its varied morphology depends upon the varying nature of the context in which it is used and of which it is a subordinated part. In Herodotus the Ionian novella, so called, is history in theory and therefore attached to a well-known historical person or place; but in any kind of comic writing, as in Aristophanes or Petronius, or Apuleius, the protagonists are either unnamed or fictitiously named. Failure to understand this fundamental truth about the literary history of the novella leads W. Aly to state (*RE* XVII [1936] col. 1178 in the article on *Novelle*), correctly in fact but on a false theory of development, that the stories told in the *Milesiaca* of Aristides were, in all probability, "no longer bound up with great historical names, as they had been in the old Ionic novella"; and, on the same false assumption of development within the form, Wilamowitz declares (*Aristot. und Athen*, II p. 32) that "our scanty evidence does not allow us to see whether the *decisive step* [in the history of the Milesian novella], that is, the *abandonment* of mythological names, was made by Aristides; at any rate this took place soon after, otherwise Petronius' Woman of Ephesus would have the name of a princess of the seventh or sixth century." The unnamed widow of Ephesus is not a princess of the sixth or seventh century for the same reason that Lysistrata in Aristophanes is not such, nor Margites (Odysseus in reverse) a figure of saga. All these are unhistorical because they belong to comedy; but if the stories about them were to be told in an historiographical context, the characters themselves would bear the names of presumably historical persons, no less in the latest of the Byzantine historians than in Herodotus himself. Between the novella in Ionian historiography and the novella in the comic books of Petronius and Apuleius there is no traditional or causal connection, such as Wilamowitz and Aly assume, and no development from one to the other. As historiography never develops into comedy, so the Ionian novella does not develop into the Petronian or Apuleian.

[19] On the lengthy folktales of adventure that were used for plots in some plays of the Middle and New Comedy, and their oral and written circulation elsewhere throughout the later ages, see the learned and interesting chapter in Miss Trenkner's *The Greek Novella in the Classical Period* (Cambridge, 1958), pp. 89–146, especially the sections on the *Rudens* of Plautus (95 f.), the *Menaechmi* (99 ff.), and *Miles Gloriosus* (131 f.). See also R. Reitzenstein in *Eros und Psyche* (Heidelberg, 1914), pp. 29 ff., who comments on the use of well-known folktales in the epigram.

[20] For the identity of the numerous folktales alluded to as familiar or exploited in Greek literature and myth, see H. J. Rose, *Handbook of Greek Mythology*, pp. 286–304; T. Zielinski, *Die Märchenkomödie in Athen* (St. Petersburg, 1885); O. Crusius, "Märchenreminiscenzen in antiken Sprichwort" in *Versammlung deut. Philologen und Schulmänner* (Dessau, 1884); W. Wienert, *Die Typen der Griechisch-römischen Fabel* (Helsinki, 1925 [= F F. Com. No. 56]); W. R. Halliday, *Indo-European Folktales and Greek Legend* (Cambridge, 1933); and my review of Miss Trenkner's book in *AJPh* 81 (1960), 442–447. We all remember the fairy tale told about Gyges and his magic ring in Plato's *Republic* by way of illustrating a philosophical point.

[21] Concerning *Manon Lescaut* by the Abbé Prévost, which is analogous to Fielding's *Joseph Andrews* in that it imposes ideal values of pathos and sympathy upon a basically picaresque novel, see below, p. 352, n. 21.

[22] A full account of these geographical utopias is given by Rohde in *Gr. Rom.*[3], pp. 183–308. One specimen may be outlined here by way of illustration. Theopompus, an historian of the fourth century B.C., had given, in his *Philippica*, undoubtedly with philosophical intent, a long description of the wonderful land of Meropis, which purported to be what the demigod Silenus had once revealed to King Midas when the latter had caught him by making him drunk. This land of Meropis, according to Silenus in Theopompus, was a huge continent standing entirely apart from Europe, Asia, and Africa, which, he said, were mere islands in the sea. Indeed Meropis was out of this world in more senses than one. On that continent men were twice as large of stature as among us, and lived twice as long. There were many large cities in the land, many different ways of life among the peoples, and the laws in force among them differed greatly from those observed by us. Silenus went on to say that there were two principal cities in the land, of which one was called the City of War (Warburg), a hell of a place, and the other the City of Piety. The inhabitants of Warburg, some two million in number, had subdued many of their neighbors and ruled over many cities. Once they made an expedition to the Hyperboreans on the outskirts of the Eurasian hemisphere; but when they learned that these miserable Scyths were supposed, even by Greeks, to be the happiest of men, they turned back in contempt, deeming it not worth while to explore any further. Those who dwelt in the City of Piety were righteous men, among whom the gods themselves were pleased to sojourn now and then. They passed their lives in peace and in the enjoyment of natural wealth. Earth of her own accord bestowed on them her bounties without the need to toil with ploughing and sewing. They lived in perfect health, free from all disease, and they died at last in the midst of laughter and enjoyment. Far away on the borders of this land of Meropis was a place called No Return. It was like a chasm, over which hung always a reddish cloud, unvisited by either day or night. Nearby flowed two rivers, one called the river of Joy, the other the river of Grief. On the banks of the latter grew trees, of whose fruit whoso did taste began to melt away in tears until, after a long period of weeping, his body was reduced to naught, and he died. But whoso ate of the fruit of the trees that grew beside the river of Joy forthwith forgot his former passions and became thereafter gradually

younger, returning first, if he were old, to manhood's prime, then to adolescence, then to childhood and infancy, after which he ceased to exist. So much for the land of Meropis, as related on the authority of Silenus in Theopompus, according to Aelian, *Varia Historia* III 18; see also Mueller, *Fragmenta Historicorum Graecorum* I, pp. 289–291.

[23] The latest attempt to reconstruct the content of the *Margites* in part, taking into account a few papyrus fragments (*Oxy. Pap.* vol. 22, no. 2309), is by Hermann Langerbeck in *Harvard Studies in Classical Philology* 63 (1958), 33–63, entitled "*Margites;* Versuch einer Beschreibung und Rekonstruktion."

[24] Photius, *Bibl.*, cod. 130.

Chariton and the Nature of Greek Romance

Pages 96–148

[1] Article "Chariton" in *RE* III 2 (1899), 2168 ff. In his *Anhang* to the third edition of Rohde's *Griechischer Roman* (Leipzig, 1914), p. 610, Schmid states that Chariton's romance is to be dated, at the latest, near the end of the first century A.D., and, in his *Gr. Litt.*[6] II (1924), p. 808, he states, with reference to his previous writings on the subject (1899, 1901, and 1904) that the lifetime of Chariton must be put "spätestens in das 2. Jr. n. Chr."

Three fragments of Chariton's *Chaereas and Callirhoe*, written on three different papyri, have been dated palaeographically by their respective editors to the second or early third century after Christ. From this fact we may infer with certainty that the text of the romance was in existence and being widely read before the close of the second century; but the date of the writing on these papyri, whatever it may be exactly in each case, gives us only a *terminus ante quem* in the second century, while the dating of the composition of the romance itself can be reckoned more closely only on the basis of other and less objective criteria, such as those by which Schmid was guided.

Papyrus Fayûm 1, edited by Grenfell and Hunt (*Fayûm Towns and their Papyri* [London, 1900]) was dated by the editors to the second century. In the expert opinion of E. G. Turner, whose letter on the subject is quoted by R. Petri (*Über den Roman des Chariton* [Meisenheim am Glan, 1963], p. 47) the writing on this papyrus might be as early as A.D. 150 or as late as 250, but is more probably to be dated some time between 175 and 225. It contains fragments of the text from IV 2,5–IV 3,2.

Papyrus Oxyrhynchus no. 1019 (*Oxyrhynchus Papyri*, ed. B. P. Grenfell and A. S. Hunt, London, Egypt Exploration Fund, vol. VIII, 1910) was dated by the editors in the second or early third century. Turner allows that the writing could be as late as 250, but is inclined to date it rather toward the end of the second century. It contains fragments of Chariton's text between II 3,5 and II 4,2.

Papyrus Michaelides no. 1 (published by D. S. Crawford in *Papyri Michaelidae*, Aberdeen: Univ. Press, 1955) is assigned to the mid-second century by the editor and likewise by Turner. It contains fragments of the text extending from II 11,5 to the end of Bk. II.

My own conviction, that Chariton lived and wrote before the end of the first century after Christ, is based partly on the fact that historical persons and events are much more prominent in his book than in any extant romance known to have been written in the second century or later, partly on the considerations of language and style mentioned by Schmid as preatticistic, and partly on the consideration of certain other features of style and thought which are conspicuous in Chariton's composition but absent in literature of the second century. Here I think primarily of what may be called Chariton's *classical* style of composition, as manifested in the economy and organic structure of his prose drama as explained below (pp. 142 f.), in his effective use of dramatic irony in the manner of the old Attic tragedians (a feature listed as "primitive" by Schmid, *Gr. Litt.*[6] II 809), and in his appreciation of and ability to imitate Thucydidean irony; all of which, together with other significant aspects of Chariton's classic style, are described in my article on Chariton in *AJPh* 51 (1930) 99–134. Broadly speaking, these classical features of mind and style, which one looks for in vain in second-century literature, are too numerous and too indicative of a vigorous and healthy moral outlook on the world to be explained as the idiosyncrasies of an individual living in the tired age of the Antonines, in which the world of classical values is seen far off in a mystic twilight without being understood. For reasons of this kind I suspect that Chariton wrote in the early part of the first century rather than later; I do not think that his romance could have been written as late as the age of Hadrian.

[2] Today this manuscript is known as cod. Laurentianus Conv. Soppressi no. 627. Before its transfer to the Laurentian Library in the early nineteenth century it was no. 2728 (*olim* 94) in the Florentine monastery known as the Abbazia (Badia) Fiorentina. It is often called the Casinensis, not that it is known ever to have been at Monte Cassino, but because the Florentine monastery was founded by the Benedictine monks (*fratres Casinenses*) of Monte Cassino. Our manuscript came into the Badia Fiorentina as one of a number of MSS bequesthed to that monastery by Antonio Corbinelli in 1425, according to Rudolf Blum in his *La Biblioteca della Badia Fiorentina* (Città del Vaticano, 1951), pp. 43, 77, 116, and 160. The fact that this manuscript was written near Melitene on the border of Syria and Armenia is indicated by the mention of a certain "Demetrius of Melitene" as one of the scribes in a subscript at the end; and by the fact, which I shall explain in a forthcoming article (to be published in a *Festschrift* for Franz Dölger), that parts of this particular Greek manuscript were translated into Armenian in a collection of medieval Armenian fables ascribed to Vardan.

For detailed information about the contents of the unique Laurentian codex (Conv. Soppr. 627; for which I use the symbol Ca in the *Fables* of Aesop but W in the *Life*), and about the numerous copies, collations, and studies made of it by scholars previous to 1726 when its text of Xenophon's *Ephesiaca* was first printed by Antonio Cocchia at London, see the following publications: H. Rostagno's catalogue in *Studi Ital. di Fil. Class.* I (1893) 172 f.; the prefaces, respectively, of D'Orville's edition of Chariton (1750); of W. E. Blake's edition of the same author (Oxford, 1938); Aristide Calderini's *Le Avventure di Cherea e Calliroe* (Torino, 1913), pp. 215–219, where a full account is given also of early modern translations and editions; G. Dalmeyda's edition of Xenophon of Ephesus (Paris, 1926) pp. xxxiii ff.; and Fr. Furia's introduction to his *Fabulae Aesopicae* (Leipzig, 1810), pp. xxx–xxxvii. In addition, some other noteworthy facts have recently been called to my attention by Professor Aubrey Diller, concerning the familiarity shown by scholars of the fifteenth and sixteenth centuries with the romances of Xenophon of Ephesus and of Chariton. I am also indebted to Professor Diller for the reference made above to Blum's book on the library of the Badia Fiorentina. In what follows brief mention is made of only the more important facts concerning the use made of our MS subsequent to its arrival in Florence in 1425: Angelo Poliziano in ch. 11 of his *Miscellanea* (1489) quotes at length from Xenophon's *Ephesiaca* (Diller). Codex Holkhamicus 278, written in the fifteenth or early sixteenth century, contains the text of the *Life* and *Fables* of Aesop transcribed from the Laurentian codex; cf. B. E. Perry, *Studies in the Text-History of the Life and Fables of Aesop* (Haverford, Pa., 1936), p. 71, note 1. Cod. Add. 10378 in the British Museum, dated as of the sixteenth century, contains the text of Xenophon's *Ephesiaca* (Diller). H. Stephanus discusses the romances of Chariton and of Xenophon of Ephesus in the Prolegomena of his *Xenophontis Opera Omnia* published in 1561; and a collation by Stephanus of the text of Achilles Tatius in the Laurentian codex is extant in one of the Old Royal MSS in the British Museum catalogue as 16.D.XVIII (Diller). In 1700 Antonio Maria Salvini made a transcript of the text of Xenophon, which is now on fols. 51–82 of cod. Riccardianus 1172.1 (see Vitelli in *Stud. ital. di Fil. Class.* II [1894], 540), and which was later used by Antonio Cocchia as the basis of his printed edition. Salvini also made a transcript of Chariton's text, which is now in Venice (cod. Marc. Classe VIII no. 16, see p. 142 in Mioni's recent catalogue [Venice, 1960]); and this, together with another apograph made by Cocchia, served as the bases on which D'Orville's *editio princeps* of Chariton was made in 1750.

Xenophon of Ephesus is commonly dated some time in the second century (so Rohde, W. Schmid, Sinko, Weinreich, and others), and that much, although vague, is the most that can be inferred with safety from such internal evidence as we have. The mention of an *Eirenarch* of Cilicia in II 13 and III 11 (ὁ τῆς εἰρήνης τῆς ἐν κιλικίᾳ προεστώς) indicates that the romance must have been written after the reign of Trajan, since the office of *Eirenarch* is not known to have been in existence before the time of Hadrian (A.D. 117–138). The famous temple of Artemis at Ephesus, around which the action in the romance is centered in the beginning, was destroyed by the Goths in A.D. 263; and, because the author shows no awareness of that historical event, it has been commonly inferred that he wrote before that time. This, however, is not a necessary inference nor a reliable *terminus-ante-quem* for the composition of the romance. The author, a novelist writing about the Artemisium at Ephesus as it had been in ancient times, would have no occasion to mention its destruction in his own time even if he had seen it or known of it. Only the fame of the temple would have concerned him, and that did not die in A.D. 263. As we have pointed out below (p. 358, n. 17), on the basis of Lavagnini's study, the author of this romance was indebted to Herodotus for what he says about the topography of Ephesus and its Artemisium, as well as for the names of many of his characters, including Habrocomes. If it is true, as we have good reason to believe (below pp. 170 ff.), that "Xenophon of Ephesus" is only a pseudonym, then it follows that the author, in adopting that practice of anonymity, still feels bound by the example of the earliest romancers, who likewise called themselves Xenophons. That practice had already been boldly abandoned by Chariton and none of his successors in the writing of romances except this "Xenophon of Ephesus" is known to have revived it. Iamblichus, Longus, and Achilles Tatius in the second century and Heliodorus in the third all use their own names, feeling no need for anonymity. The resort to anonymity on the part of the author of the *Ephesiaca* would therefore tend to indicate that he wrote in the early part of the second century rather than later. The absence of certain sophistic qualities in this romance has led the majority of critics to classify it as a relatively early specimen of the genre, more closely analogous to Chariton's romance than to the so-called sophistic romances of a later time.

It is stated in the *Suda* lexicon that the romance ascribed to Xenophon of Ephesus was contained in ten books; but the text that has come down to us is only five books in length and in it the narrative seems abnormally syncopated, bare, and hurried in relation to the large number of episodes that are told in rapid succession without being naturally developed. With these facts in view Rohde concluded that what we have is very probably only an epitome of the original romance; and later, in 1892, Karl Bürger (*Hermes* 27, 36–67) demonstrated convincingly, in a close-up study of the internal evidence, that such indeed is the case. In consequence of the epitomator's operation, much of the original motivation and literary virtuosity of this romance is obscured by lacunas in the narration which puzzle the modern reader and make it impossible to estimate accurately or with confidence the real nature of the original.

[3] Three of these are listed above in note 1 as having been dated by their editors in the second or early third century A.D. The other fragment, called the codex Thebanus, was a palimpsest on parchment datable to the sixth or seventh century, which was identified and published by Ulrich Wilcken in the *Archiv für Papyrusforschung* I (1901), 227–272, but was subsequently destroyed in a fire on the docks at Hamburg; cf. Blake's edition of Chariton, pp. x–xi.

[4] Migne, *Patr. Gr.* 116, pp. 93 ff., from the *Acta Sanctorum* for Nov. 5. According to this martyrology Leucippe and Clitophon were pagans living at Emesa in Syria. Leucippe as it happened was sterile and on that account she and her husband were very unhappy. A monk named Onufrius, fleeing from persecution, is given shelter by Leucippe, converts her to Christianity, and baptizes her; after which her prayers for offspring are answered and she becomes pregnant. Then Leucippe, with the aid of Onufrius, converts and baptizes her husband Clitophon. Their son, who is named Galaktion, is as beautiful to look upon as his father had been. He marries an equally beautiful young woman named Episteme who is a pagan. He converts her to Christian asceticism, and thereafter the two, while living apart, suffer a glorious martyrdom in the persecution.

In an article entitled "Die griechischen Romane und das Christentum," in *Philologus* 93 (1938), 274, H. Dörrie cites the foregoing martyr-story in support of his belief that the only thing that can account for the survival and wide propagation of the romances of Achilles Tatius and Heliodorus in the Christian ages, to the exclusion of other pagan romances, was the belief

that the authors or their *dramatis personae* were Christians. Chap. 5 in
H. Delehaye's *Sanctus* (Brussels, 1927) gives us an interesting and authoritative account of "saints who never existed." A certain St.
Epicharis, whose
martyrdom at Rome under Diocletian is briefly related in the *Menologium*
of Basil (Migne, *Patr. Gr.* 117, p. 73 c, and in the *Acta Sanctorum* for Sept.
27), may very well be, as A. D. Nock has suggested (*Jour. of Theol. Studies*
27 [1926], 409 f.), a Christianized projection of the heroic Epicharis who had
taken part in the Pisonian conspiracy against Nero and whose martyr-like
endurance of torture in defiance of the inquisitors is described by Tacitus in
the *Annals* (XV 57).

⁵ See the text of St. John Damascene's *Barlaam and Joasaph* edited with
a critical introduction and translation by G. R. Woodward and H. Mattingly
in the Loeb Library (London, 1937); and Fr. Dölger, *Der Barlaam Roman,
ein Werk des H. Johannes des Damaskos* (= *Studia Patristica et Byzantina* 1)
(Ettal, 1953).

⁶ These twelfth-century romances are described by Krumbacher in *Byz.
Litt.*² pp. 751 (Prodromus), 763 (Nicetas), 764 f. (Eustathius); and, at greater
length, by Rohde in *Gr. Rom.*³ pp. 556–61 (Eustathius), 562–65 (Prodromus),
and 565–67 (Nicetas). The texts of all three romances are published in the
second volume of Hercher's *Scriptores Erotici Graeci* (Leipzig, 1859).

A very good summary and critique of the romance by Eustathius entitled
Hysmene and Hymenias (11 books in prose) will be found in Dunlop-Wilson,
History of Prose Fiction I 77–80. Rohde (p. 539) says of this romance that
it is "nothing more than a caricature of the narrative of Achilles Tatius."
The title given by Theodorus Prodromus to his romance, which is imitative
of Heliodorus, is *The Adventures of Rodanthe and Dosicles* (τὰ κατὰ 'Ροδάνθην
καὶ Δοσικλέα). This consists of 4614 iambic trimeters divided into 9 books.
Nicetas Eugenianus, studiously imitating Prodromus, whose romance for
him is a classic, writes about *The Adventures of Drosilla and Charicles* in
9 books containing 3641 trimeter verses. Concerning the romance written in
15-syllable political verse by Constantine Manasses in 9 books about
Aristander and Callithea, which is not entirely preserved, see Krumbacher,
p. 377, and Rohde, p. 567. Text in Hercher's *Script. Erot. Gr.* vol. II.

⁷ See Krumbacher, *Byz. Litt.*², 827–832; and John Maurogordato's *Digenes
Akrites*, edited with an introduction, translation and commentary (Oxford,
1956).

⁸ For a list of passages in which the written form of *Digenes Akritas* is only
a versification of the text of Achilles Tatius, see O. Schissel von Fleschenberg
in *Neophilologus* XXVII (1941–2), 143–145.

⁹ An interesting and comprehensive description of these Byzantine romances of chivalry, of their cultural background, substance, and sources so
far as these can be known, is given by Krumbacher in *Byz. Litt.*² (1897),
pp. 854–872.

In connection with both the western European romances of chivalry and
with the Byzantine, I would suggest that the Greek sources which influenced
them here and there, insofar as they were written sources rather than oral,
did not come from formal Byzantine prose literature which remained limited

and static in relation to ancient or Oriental texts, but, more likely, from ancient romances which—like Chariton's in Asia and the oldest *Life of Aesop* (Vita G) in southern Italy—had not survived in Byzantium and on the mainland of Greece. Other sources may have been Greek books of fiction or fable-collections written in western Asia under the domination of the Muslim world of ideas and fashions, including *inter alia* certain Greek imitations of *Kalilah* and *Dimnah* mentioned by the Arabs, which were enriched with new narrative substance of popular Asiatic origin. On this see my article entitled "Some Traces of Lost Medieval Story-Books," in *Humaniora* (Essays in Literature, Folklore and Bibliography honoring Archer Taylor, 1960), pp. 150–160; and, supplementary thereto, "Two Fables Recovered" in *Byz. Ztschr.* 54 (1961), 4–14. Rohde in *Gr. Rom.*³ pp. 572 ff. conjectured brilliantly, and with much well-reasoned probability, that Boccaccio's story of Galeso (Cimon) and Efigenia (*Decam.* V 1) came to him, directly or indirectly, from an ancient Greek romance which is now no longer extant, and which was probably entitled *Cypriaca*. Boccaccio tells us at the beginning that he read this story "aforetime in the ancient histories of the Cypriots." Concerning the historiographical pretense implicit in such ethnological titles, which were very common in ancient romances, see further what we have noted below in chap. iv, pp. 167 f. Boccaccio's story is one of love and manifold adventure on land and sea amid piratical actions, hostile intrigues and imprisonment; all the names, some of them specifically Dorian, and all the places mentioned, islands in the eastern Mediterranean, are Greek; and repeated mention is made, as in Greek romances, of the action of adverse Fortune (Tyche).

[10] *Beyond Good and Evil*, no. 168 on p. 90 in Helen Zimmern's translation (New York, Modern Library, n.d.).

[11] On comedy in Achilles Tatius see S. L. Wolff's *Greek Romances in Elizabethan Fiction*, New York, 1912, pp. 157 and 160 f.; and D. B. Durham's "Parody in Achilles Tatius," *CPh* 33 (1938), 1–18.

[12] Before the discovery of any papyrus fragments of his romance, Achilles Tatius was dated conjecturally by Rohde in the mid-fifth century after Christ (*Gr. Rom.*³ pp. 501 ff.). The first papyrus fragment to be published was the Oxyrrynchus papyrus no. 1250 in 1914, which was dated palaeographically by the editors in the early fourth century. Thereafter on the basis of various internal evidence adduced by Lehmann, Boll, and Kerényi, which is briefly summarized by Th. Sinko in *Eos* 41 (1940–1946), 40 f., the dating of Achilles was pushed back to the third, then to the late second century. In 1950 another papyrus fragment was published by W. Schubart, who ascribed the writing on it to the third century at the latest. The main facts about this papyrus, now lost, are stated by E. Vilborg on p. xvi of his recent critical edition (Göteborg, 1955), along with an up-to-date account of two other fragments on papyrus. One of these two, Oxy. Pap. 1250 of the early fourth century, was mentioned above; the other is a papyrus at Milan published by A. Vogliano in *Stud. Ital. di Fil. Class.* 15 (1938), and the writing on this papyrus is assigned with confidence by both Vogliano and Schubart, who examined it independently, to the second century after Christ. See Vilborg

pp. xvi f. From this it appears that Achilles wrote his romance hardly later than the middle of the second century.

[13] The dating of Heliodorus in the mid-third century, on the basis of internal evidence described by Rohde (*Gr. Rom.*³, 462 ff. [and also in the 1st edition, 1876]) and later supplemented by K. Münscher (*RE* VIII 1913, 20 ff.) and others, has been approved by the great majority of scholars who have studied the matter and written about it in recent times. These include R. M. Rattenbury in the Budé edition of Heliodorus (Paris, 1935), pp. xi–xv; Fr. Altheim, article "Helios und Heliodoros von Emesa" in *Albae Vigiliae* 12 (Amsterdam, 1942: repeated in the author's *Literatur und Gesellschaft* I, [Halle-Saale, 1948], 93–124); Th. Sinko in *Eos* 41 (1940–1946), 43; V. Hefti in *Zur Erzählungstechnik in Heliodors Aethiopica* (Vienna, 1950), p. 53 with note 450; and O. Weinreich in *Der Griechische Liebesroman* (Zürich, 1962) pp. 32–40. Rohde (p. 496) suggested the reign of Aurelian (270–275) as the most probable date for our author; but an earlier date, some time between 220 and 240, in or shortly before or after the reign of Severus Alexander (222–235) is favored by Münscher, Rattenbury, Altheim, and Weinreich. It was during those years, in the successive reigns of Elagabalus and Severus, both of whom like Heliodorus were natives of Emesa, that the cult of Helios the sun-god in Syria was at the peak of its influence, and the predominance of that religious cult in the structure of the *Aethiopica* is the principal, but by no means the only reason for dating it in the third century. At the end of his romance Heliodorus himself tells us that he was a native of Emesa and a descendant of the sun-god Helios (τῶν ἀφ' 'Ηλίου γένος). Rattenbury called attention to the significant fact that no Greek romance is known to have been written as late as the fourth century, which would indicate that the genre itself was *épuisé* by that time, and Altheim adduces historical evidence to show that the romance must be dated in the third century. The description of the siege of Syene by Hydaspes in *Aeth.* IX 3 ff. bears such a close resemblance to what Julian in his rhetorical panegyric of the emperor Constantius (*Or.* 1 and 3) says about the siege of Nisibis by Sapor in A.D. 350, that it must be admitted that one of the two authors has been influenced in part by the other. Van der Valk in *Mnemosyne* IX (1940), 97–100, and A. Colonna in *Athenaeum* 28 (1950), 82 ff. and elsewhere, have maintained that Heliodorus depended on Julian and must therefore be dated in the second half of the fourth century; but Weinreich has demonstrated convincingly on the basis of data which were overlooked by Van der Valk, that Julian, who had read Greek romances (*Ep.* 89, p. 141, Bidez), is more likely to have been debtor to Heliodorus and other writers than Heliodorus to Julian. The passages cited by Van der Valk in the two authors tend to show only that Julian had read Heliodorus.

[14] Some noteworthy specimens of these Christian myths are mentioned above, n. 4, in connection with Achilles Tatius, who was also said to have been a bishop—God only knew where—in spite of the fact that there was nothing at all Christian in his way of writing and thinking, and no bishop by the name of Achilles Tatius was otherwise known.

[15] The chronological sequence of the extant romances is somewhat as follows, allowing for exceptions in the cases of closely contemporary productions, where the priority of one to another cannot be known. References in parentheses refer to places in this book where the dating of a romance is discussed:

1. *Ninus*, *ca.* 100 B.C. (chap. iv, sec. 2).
2. Greek prototype of the *Recognitiones* of Ps.-Clement (Appendix I).
3. Chariton, first century after Christ (n. 1 above).
4. Xenophon of Ephesus, early second century (n. 2 above).

SOPHISTIC ROMANCES

5. (6)? Iamblichus, *ca.* A.D. 165 (n. 21 below).
6. (5?) Longus, late second century (n. 17 below).
7. Achilles Tatius, mid-second century (n. 12 above).
8. Heliodorus, first half of third century (n. 13 above).

IDEAL LATIN ROMANCE

9. *Apollonius of Tyre*, third century after Christ (Appendix II).

We see from this that the Greek romance was at the peak of its propagation in the second century. Besides the four romances mentioned above as having been written in that century or earlier, we have fragments of three others copied on papyrus which can be dated palaeographically in the second century: fragments of the so-called Calligone romance, of the romance of Metiochus and Parthenope (cf. below, p. 359), and the Herpyllis fragment. See Zimmermann, *Griechische Roman-Papyri*, Heidelberg, 1936.

[16] Theon, *Progym.* 3. See above, p. 68, where this matter of technique has been discussed more fully.

[17] With one unimportant exception (Psellus, *De operat. Daemonum*, cited by Christ-Schmid, *Gr. Litt.*[6] II 824), no ancient or medieval writer, insofar as we know, not even Suidas, makes mention of this Longus or of his romance *Daphnis and Chloe*; no papyrus fragments of it have yet been found; and we would not have known the book at all, or the name of its author, had it not survived by a lucky chance in a few medieval manuscripts. The approximate time in which it was written can be reckoned therefore only on the basis of internal criteria—linguistic usage, content, rhetorical mannerism, and the age to which the kind of painting described in the author's *ecphrasis* belongs. All these criteria lead, in my opinion, to the conclusion that Longus must have lived on the island of Lesbos in the second half of the second century; and that is the conclusion reached by the majority of critics in recent years, although not all of them have made use of all the available criteria. These data are much too long and complex to admit of being reviewed here in their entirety; but two new points, recently discussed by O. Schönberger in the introduction to his edition of Longus (Berlin, 1960), pp. 1–3 and by Weinreich in *Der Griechische Liebesroman* (Zürich, Artemus Verlag, 1962), pp. 18–19, are deserving of special emphasis in this connection.

The first point is that the cognomen Longus belonged to a distinguished family at Mytilene on the island of Lesbos, which had taken its gentile name, Pompeius, from its patron Pompey the Great, as attested in several inscriptions, most notably *IG* XII 2, 88, and that a consul of the year A.D. 49 whose name was Pompeius Longus (*Prosop. Imper. R.* III p. 67) may have come from the same family. All this was noted by C. Cichorius on pp. 321 and 323 of his *Römische Studien* (Leipzig, 1922), in connection with which he suggested that the romancer and sophist Longus may also have been a descendant of that Mytilenean family. The close familiarity with the island of Lesbos shown by Longus in his romance, and his obvious fondness for its rural scenery, tend strongly to confirm our belief that he was indeed a native of that island, as he himself implies when he tells us that it was there, in a grove of the Nymphs, that he saw the picture which he professes to describe with the aid of a local interpreter. Since Lesbos, unlike Sicily, was never famed as a land of shepherds, there seems to be no special reason why the author of *Daphnis and Chloe* should have chosen it as the homeland of his shepherds, unless it was on account of the idyllic rural landscapes which he had seen on Lesbos and the types of which were favorite objects of contemplation in second-century literature and art.

The second point is that the type of picture described by Longus in his romance can be dated fairly well by reference to the history of wall-painting in Roman imperial times. This point, which was first made by Weinreich in the appendix to a German translation of Heliodorus by R. Reymer (Zürich, 1950, pp. 323–379), is briefly restated on p. 19 of his *Griechischer Liebesroman*. The evidence is to be found in Fritz Wirth's *Römische Wandmalerei* (Berlin, 1934), in which the successive styles of wall-painting in vogue from the destruction of Pompeii in A.D. 79 to the end of the third century are described and illustrated. From this it appears that rural landscapes of the kind described by Longus were in fashion only in the middle of the second century (*ca.* 130–160) in a style of painting which Wirth calls the "Philhellenic" and which extends by his reckoning from A.D. 100–160. See especially *Tafeln* 17 and 18. In literature verbal pictures of rural landscapes, of the life of rustics and shepherds and their love affairs, are numerous throughout the second century and the first quarter of the third, as seen in Dio Chrysostom's idyllic description of the Euboean hunters (*ca.* A.D. 100), in Lucian, Alciphron, Aelian, and Philostratus in his *Imagines*; but after that such pictures are not seen in extant wall-paintings and in literature are rare or different in perspective, as with Himerius in the fourth century, whose writing although poetic, is on mythological themes.

[18] There is no antiquarianism in creative Greek literature, as there is none in medieval literature or in Shakespeare. Convention required that the subject of a drama or an epic should be taken from sagas or myths relating to men and events in a distant past; but the conditions of life and thought in which the actors move about, and by which they are motivated and emoted, whether physical, moral, legal, political, social, or domestic, are those of the writer's own time, and properly so. Classical literature is never antiquarian in matters of detail; it sees man as fundamentally the same today as he

always has been. This has often been noted by students of literature and much might be quoted on the subject. Spengler summed it up briefly in these words: "In the Classical world-consciousness all Past was absorbed in the instant Present" (*Decline of the West* in the translation by C. F. Atkinson, [New York, Alfred A. Knopf, 1937] I p. 103).

19 See note 18 above.

20 See Appendix III on the rationale of the ego-narrative.

21 Essentially the same kind of innovation as that made by Fielding, in bringing the warm ideal values of sympathetic character-portrayal into what was otherwise a comic and satirical narrative in the classical tradition, had been made by the Abbé Prévost in his *Manon Lescaut*, which was published in 1731 and is a genuine novel in our sense of the term. In this novel, as in Achilles Tatius, the author introduces us to a young man, one Chevalier des Grieux, who tells him, speaking in the first person, the tragic story of his foolish and frequently frustrated, but unquenchable and undying love for a *fille de joie* named Manon Lescaut. Manon throughout the story seems to love the young man, in her way, and favors him so long as it is convenient for her to do so; but in order to get out of trouble or to avoid the discomforts of poverty, she frequently sells her favors to high bidders, thereby cruelly betraying the lover who adores her. In the end, however, she clings to him with a true and selfless love, bravely resisting the efforts of powerful men to take her away from the lover who has pursued her overseas from Paris to the wilds of Louisiana. Likewise the lover, M. des Grieux, after the death of Manon and while he is still young, becomes a deeply religious man, having arrived at the haven of peace at last by the grace of God, after all his mental agonies. By birth and early training he had been, and remained fundamentally throughout, a gentleman of honorable principles and good instincts; but his passion for Manon was so overpowering that, regardless of ethical principles and common sense, he would do anything he found it necessary to do, however foolish, dishonest or criminal, in order to attain his love in a world in which almost every man in power was venal and corrupt. Viewed outwardly from the standpoint of common sense and moral principles, the conduct of the young lover is that of a fool and a rogue in the cynical picaresque tradition; but inwardly, as regards the spirit in which the story is told, there is nothing coldly comic or scornful about it, no mockery or satire, and nothing to laugh at, but rather a deep feeling of pity for the frailties of human kind.

As in Fielding and in Prévost, so likewise in Apuleius, the potentialities of prose fiction were greatly increased in the direction of the modern novel by the introduction of ideal values into what had previously been purely comic stories written in a spirit of burlesque. This will be explained below in chap. vii, sec. 4.

22 The dating of Iamblichus in the third quarter of the second century has never been in question. He himself in his romance, as reported by Photius, had stated explicitly that he lived in the time of Marcus Aurelius and Lucius Verus, when the Arsacid Soämus was king of Armenia under the Romans, and that he had accurately foretold the outcome of the Parthian War (A.D.

161–165). See Rohde, pp. 388 ff., for a clear account of all that we know about the person of Iamblichus and his work.

[23] In his *Erotica Pathemata* no. 11, Parthenius in the course of outlining the story of Byblis and Caunus quotes six lines from his own poem on the subject and ten lines from a poem by the Alexandrian Nicaenetus, both in hexameter verse. For the text of Parthenius with notes and translation, see Gaselee in the Loeb edition of *Daphnis and Chloe* (London, Heinemann, 1935), pp. 293 ff. The story was also told, somewhat on the pattern of Mattidia's experience in the Ps.-Clementine *Recognitiones*, by Conon in his *Narrationes* as summarized by Photius in cod. 186 (Migne, *Patrol. Gr.* 103, p. 548). On Cinna's *Smyrna*, see Schanz in *Röm. Lit.*³ II 1 pp. 85 ff.

[24] The first of Theron's men to look into the sepulchre sees the living Callirhoe, takes her to be a ghost, is frightened, and retreats in panic haste. Theron laughs at him; but, finding that his other men are equally afraid, he himself enters and discovers the true situation.

A remarkable parallel to this story appeared in a United Press dispatch from Bucharest which I clipped from a local newspaper some time around the year 1935, as follows: "Josefine Nagy, wife of a wealthy farmer was buried Tuesday in the village cemetery of Trenteamare, central Transylvania, according to the story as it was told here. Wednesday night, three grave-robbers went to the cemetery, dug up the coffin and prepared to loot the grave. They opened the casket and were horrified when the "corpse" moved. Josefine Nagy was alive. She arose, murmured 'Where am I' and stepped out of the coffin. One of the robbers fainted. The others fled. Josefine walked to her home, where her husband and family kept her out in the cold until they were convinced she was not a ghost. Farmer Nagy helped police look for the robbers today. He did not want to punish them, but to 'pay them for bringing Josefine back to me.'" The police ought to have gone after the undertakers.

[25] Many specific instances of this are cited and explained in my long note on the subject in *AJPh* 51 (1930), 100–103. As I remarked there (p. 101), the violence done to Callirhoe by her jealous husband (Chariton I 4, 12) may have been due in the first place to a recollection of the assault made by soldiers upon that daughter of Hermocrates who had married Dionysius the Elder, and who was reported to have died of her injuries (Plut. *Dion* 3; *Diod.* III, 112). In this connection I should have noted also, as Martin Braun points out (*Hist. and Romances in Graeco-Oriental Lit.*, p. 11, n. 1), that the kind of assault made by Chaereas, kicking his wife apparently to death when she was pregnant, had been told also of Cambyses by Herodotus (III 32), to whom Chariton was indebted for other matters. Further, Braun cites the suggestion made to him by M. P. Charlesworth that this Herodotean motif had taken on fresh topicality in Chariton's time from the fact that the same story had been told about Nero's treatment of Poppaea (Suet. *Nero* 35; Tacitus *Ann.* XVI 5).

[26] *Mnemosyne* 1901, p. 98.

[27] Since this description of *narratio quae versatur in personis* would apply

very well to the Greek romance as we know it, the thesis was put forth by
G. Thiele in 1890, and later accepted by others, that Cicero in this passage
was thinking of the Greek romance. But there is no indication that he was
aware of the Greek romance, which he does not mention, and everything in
the context of what he says, and his illustrations, seem to point in the opposite
direction. See the article on this subject by K. Barwick in *Hermes* 63 (1928),
entitled "Die Gliederung der Narratio in der rhetorischen Theorie und ihre
Bedeutung für die Geschichte des antiken Romans." Barwick shows that the
rhetorical theories of Cicero and others about *narratio* were made with no
reference to Greek romance.

[28] Cicero, *Ad Fam.* II 12. Cf. *Brutus* 11, where Cicero agrees with the statement made by Atticus that *"concessum est rhetoribus ementire in historiis, ut
aliquid dicere possint argutius."* In *De Oratore* II 36 he says in effect that the
nature of history is such that only an orator can do justice to it, by way of
bringing out its dramatic values and the importance of its lessons. Concerning the tendency on the part of writers before Cicero to dramatize history,
and the opposition to it by Polybius more in theory than in practice, see
the second part of P. Scheller's dissertation *De Hellenistica Historiae Con-
scribendae Arte* (Leipzig, 1911), and B. L. Ullman's "History and Tragedy"
in *TAPhA* 73 (1942), 25–53.

[29] Ingomar Düring, *Chion of Heraclea, A Novel in Letters*, edited with introduction and commentary (Göteborg, 1951). Historically, this Chion of
Heraclea was a devoted follower of Plato and a martyr to the cause of
freedom in his native city. His kinsman Clearchus, who had also been a
member of the Platonic school, became tyrant of Heraclea and ruled viciously
over that city for twelve years. In 352 B.C. Chion with the aid of a band of
conspirators assassinated Clearchus and was himself thereafter put to death
by the tyrant's followers (Memnon's *Hist. of Heraclea* in Müller's *Frag. Hist.
Gr.* III Paris, 1849, p. 527). Mr. Düring's novel, if such it can be called,
consists of seventeen letters composed by an unknown writer in the first or
second century after Christ (Hercher, *Epist. Graec.*, Paris, 1873, pp. 194–206)
and ascribed to Chion. Fourteen of these letters purport to be written by
Chion to his father, and of the others one is to his friend Bion, one to Clearchus (to put him off his guard), and the last to Plato. In these letters Chion
gives an autobiographical account of himself, his thoughts and activities,
and his association with prominent men, including Xenophon and Plato, for
a few years preceding his return to Heraclea. He announces his intention to
kill the tyrant Clearchus in letters to his father, and in the last letter, addressed to Plato, he says that he expects to die for his deed but that he takes
pride in becoming a martyr in the cause of freedom.

NOTES TO CHAPTER IV

The Origin of the Ideal Greek Romance

Pages 149–180

[1] See *L'Achilleide Byzantine* edited with introduction and notes by D. C. Hesseling (Amsterdam, 1919); and Krumbacher, *Byz. Litt.*[2] 848 f. The circumstances surrounding the death of Achilles in this Byzantine romance are derived from the brief account given by the matter-of-fact historian Dictys Cretensis in his *Ephemeris Belli Troiani* (IV 11), which is closely parallel to what is reported by Dares Phrygius in his *De Excidio Troiae Historia* (ch. 34).

Many stories very briefly told in one form or another about the love affairs of Achilles in his youth, both before and after he went to Troy, matched with a Deidamia on the island of Scyros, with Polyxena or Briseis at Troy, and with others elsewhere including even Helen and Medea, were current in Hellenistic times; and some of these had been mentioned in their bare and unsentimental outlines even in Homer and the epic cycle. Cf. Rohde, *Gr. Rom.*[3], 110.

The existence before the time of Statius of a Greek *Achilleis* now lost, which described the career of Achilles from the cradle to the grave, the education of Achilles so to speak, is convincingly deduced by Kurt Weitzmann on pages 165–168 and 192 f. of his *Greek Mythology in Byzantine Art* (Princeton, 1951). Here Weitzmann shows on the basis of various sculptured monuments surviving from antiquity (see figures 14–16, Achilles with Chiron), compared with similar representations in illuminated Greek manuscripts and on ivory caskets of medieval make (figs. 12–13, 205–206, 208, 210), that the ancient Greek *Achilleis*, which was presumably the principal source used by Statius in his Latin *Achilleis*, was illustrated with a picture cycle, and that this was the source from which the medieval pictures were derived. There is no evidence however that the substance or text of the Byzantine *Achilleis* was influenced in any way by its ancient counterpart, the source of Statius. Weitzmann's argument for the existence of a Greek *Achilleis* in the late Alexandrian age is corroborated to some extent by the currency at that time of books on the structural pattern of the *Ninopedia* or romance of Ninus, describing the youth and early education of the hero.

The *Roman de Troie*, composed by Benoit de Sainte-More in some 30,000 verses *ca.* A.D. 1160 on the slender basis of Dares and Dictys, contains many new episodes and combinations of episodes, including the famous story of Troilus and Cressida, which are nowhere attested before he wrote and are in all probability the inventions of Benoit himself. Cf. Gaston Paris, *La Littérature française au moyen âge*, Paris, 1888, pp. 76 f. Benoit's original romance became enormously popular shortly after it appeared and was worked over by many writers, translators, or abbreviators, from Boccaccio on through Chaucer, Lydgate, and Shakespeare.

[2] *Hermes* 28, (1893), 184. "Nicht einmal das Verhältniss der beiden Frag-

mente zu einander lässt sich mit Sicherheit bestimmen . . . So bescheide ich Mich mit einem *non liquet*."

3 R. Jeništová, "The Novel about Ninus," in *Listy Filologicke* ns. I (1953), 30–54 and 210–228, written in Czech with summaries in Russian and in English. I have not yet seen the author's summary of this article, because it is not accessible to me at present; I refer to the short résumé of it given in *L'Année Philologique*, XXIV (1954), 122.

4 Lehmann-Haupt, in his article on Semiramis in W. H. Roscher's *Lexikon der griechischen und römischen Mythologie* IV, Leipzig, 1909–1915, p. 701, calls attention to the significant fact that the designation of Semiramis only as κόρη (the maiden) here in the romance, derives from the use and connotation of the word "Maiden" in the first syllable of many place-names, very anciently so called, in Armenia and adjacent regions of the old Assyrian empire; and that the saga about Semiramis as given by Ctesias-Diodorus states that she built many cities, fortifications and other public works all over the empire with phenomenal speed: "Nun begegnet man—zunächst nach des Verfassers eigenen Beobachtungen, in Azärbaidyan und in den persisch-türkischen Grenzgebirgen—wiederholt der Bezeichnung *Kizkal* 'ah, 'die Mädchenburg,' für uralte Anlagen, Ortschaften und exponierten Punkten, Burgen u. dgl., und regelmässig wird dabei erklärt, dass die Stätte von einem Mädchen in einer Nacht erbaut worden sei." After the time of Semiramis these places were thought of as having been built by her, in the belief that she, the great Queen of Assyria, was "The Maiden."

5 In Chariton (see above, p. 126) the lovers are married at the start; but the rejected suitors, maliciously plotting against Chaereas, succeed in making him believe, by means of false representations, that his wife Callirhoe has been caught in the act of adultery. This leads to her apparent death and separation from her husband. Nothing of this kind could possibly have resulted from the domestic quarrel described in fr. B1 of the Ninus romance.

6 Norsa (p. 86) comments as follows on the meaning of this line: "Verosimilmente non sarà Κτησίππου, nè ἐπ ακτῆς ἵππου ('cavalleria'), ma piuttosto ἐπ' ἀκτῆς Ἵππου, dato che ὁ Ἵππος (Ἵππης) ποταμός secondo Arriano *Per.* 10.2; 11, 4 e 5, è fiume della Colchide (cfr. r. 13) che sbocca nel mare. (Secondo altre fonti è affluente del Phasis).

7 Norsa, p. 86: "Si può leggere δ' ἑταίρων τὸν π[ισ] τὸτ] ατον ἐμοὶ ἐπίκουρ[ον] [τοῦ] ναύτου καὶ ἐπιστή [μο νος] κυβερνήτου, etc."

8 Wilcken, quoted by Norsa, proposed the reading πρὸ τῆς βορεία[s] μεταβολῆς in lines 11–12.

9 This is historically true. Much is said about the wars with Armenia as a powerful rival of Assyria in the time of Sargon (722–705 B.C.) in the contemporary royal correspondence; see letters 3–14 in R. Pfeiffer's *State Letters of Assyria*, transliterated and translated, (New Haven, 1935) Cf. Lehmann-Haupt, *op. cit.* (above, n. 4) pp. 687 ff.

It is stated in the saga (Diod. II 2, 1) that Ninus spent 17 years in achieving his conquest of western Asia; the statement in the romance that he was only 17 years old at that time looks like a verbal echo of the saga.

10 Derceia in the romance is Derketo humanized, and Derketo at Ascalon

was the name of the great Syrian goddess worshipped elsewhere in Syria as
Atargatis. According to the long account given by Diodorus (II 4, from
Ctesias), this deity fell violently in love with a young Syrian, by whom she
bore an illegitimate daughter afterwards named Semiramis. Being ashamed
of her sin Derketo did away with the young Syrian, her mate, and exposed
her child in a deserted place, where the child was found and reared by
shepherds. Afterwards the child was adopted by a local citizen, one Simma,
who gave her the name Semiramis. When Semiramis was old enough to
marry, being a very beautiful young woman, she became the wife of Onnes
the governor of Syria under Ninus. Onnes took her to the Assyrian court
where he was held in high honor and served as one of Ninus's generals in the
campaign against Bactria. When Ninus on that occasion became enamoured
of Semiramis, he forced her husband Onnes to hand her over to himself.

11 Dante thinks of Semiramis in terms of the ancient saga about her as a
very licentious woman. *Inferno* V 22 ff. in Cary's translation:

> "The first
> 'Mong those, of whom thou question'st", he replied,
> "O'er many tongues was empress. She in vice
> Of luxury was so shameless that she made
> Liking be lawful by promulg'd decree,
> To clear the blame she had herself incurr'd.
> This is Semiramis, of whom 'tis writ,
> That she succeeded Ninus her espoused;
> And held the land, which now the Soldan rules."

12 For a comprehensive account of Xenophon's influence on later writers
see K. Münscher, *Xenophon in der griechisch-römischen Literatur: Philologus*,
Supplementband XIII, Heft II, (Leipzig, 1930).

13 For the details see Christ-Schmid, *Gesch. d. Griech. Litt.*[6] II, 746 ff.

14 In the Cyropedia IV 6, 11; V 1, 2-18; VI 1, 31-51; VI 4, 2-11; VII 3,
2-16. The story is told in outline dramatically and very attractively, without
interruptions, by Miss Haight in her *Essays on Ancient Fiction*, pp. 22-28.
Miss Haight rightly says of this story that it is "one of the most perfect
romances found in classical writings." I would add that it is not only the
best but the only ideal romance, as concerns its substance, written in prose
by a classical author. Note, however, that the ending is not a happy one, as
in all the later extant romances, but tragic; and that this classical "romance"
does not stand by itself independently but is subordinated to a larger context.
For that reason it is not a romance in the generic sense in which we have
defined that term.

15 Philostratus in *Vitae Sophistarum* I 22, 3 (ed. Kayser, p. 37) says that
Dionysius, whose fine style he greatly admires, was highly honored and sub-
sidized by Hadrian, had travelled and lectured in many cities, and had never
incurred any censure for his personal behavior in love affairs, or for licentious-
ness in such matters. Besides, anyone who knows his rhetoric well can see
that the style of writing in the romance attributed to Dionysius is much
inferior to that of anything written by the latter. So it was not Dionysius

who wrote the romance of Araspas but his ever jealous rival, Celer. Celer was good as a royal secretary *ab epistolis*, but in declamation he was mediocre. The story of Araspas and Panthia as told by Xenophon may be read in the *Cyropedia* V 1, 2 f.; VI 1, 31 ff.; and VI 3, 14.

[16] Other ideas drawn by Chariton from the *Cyropedia* are his likening of kings to the queen bee in a swarm (II 3, 10 = *Cyrop.* V 1, 24), and the description of the method of assembling the Persian military forces said to have been instituted by Cyrus the Great. From the *Anabasis* Chariton has taken at the beginning of Bk. V and of Bk. VIII, the familiar formula ὡς μὲν . . . ἐν τῷ πρόσθεν λόγῳ δεδήλωται, which Xenophon uses at the beginning of several books by way of summarizing retrospectively what has been narrated in the preceding book or books.

[17] Lavagnini's article is included in his *Studi sul Romanzo Greco* (Firenze, 1950), pp. 145–156. In addition to Habrocomes, the hero of the romance, Lavagnini (p. 156) calls attention to four other characters in Xenophon's romance who are named after prominent men or women mentioned by Herodotus: Ὑπεράνθης (Xen. III 2 and 3), who is the brother of Ἀβροκόμης and son of Darius in Hdt. VII 224; Κυνώ (Xen. III 12), who is the wife of the herdsman who reared Cyrus as a foundling babe in Hdt. I 110, and whose real name in the Median language was Σπακώ (= Bitch = Gr. Κυνώ, a name nowhere else attested in Greek); Μοῖρις (II 5 and 11), from an Egyptian king of that name mentioned by Hdt. (II 13 and 101); Ψάμμις (III, 11), also named after an Egyptian king mentioned by Hdt. (II 159–161).

I have noted several verbal echoes of Herodotus in Xenophon's romance, the most obvious of which relates to the wonderful beauty of Habrocomes in I 1: γίνεται παῖς Ἀβροκόμης μέγα τι χρῆμα κάλλους. Cf. Hdt. I 36: ὑὸς χρῆμα γίνεται μέγα.

[18] Much has already been written about these mosaics since they were first uncovered by a Princeton archaeological expedition in 1936; but the best account of them in brief compass is the article by Doro Levi entitled "The Novel of Ninus and Semiramis," published in *Proceedings of the American Philosophical Society*, 87 (1944), 420–428. The same writer has since then published a definitive edition of the entire material in two volumes entitled *Antioch Mosaic Pavements* (Princeton, 1947).

Photographic reproductions of these two mosaics, found on the pavements of adjacent rooms in the so-called "House of the Man of Letters," may be seen in Lavagnini's easily accessible *Studi sul Romanzo Greco* (Firenze, 1950). The first (following the Preface on p. xvii) shows Ninus, unidentified by name, lying on a couch and gazing sadly on the picture of a girl held in his outstretched right hand; the second shows Parthenope and Metiochus alone without background, both identified by name on the painting, gracefully posed facing each other. Parthenope, her hand outstretched towards Metiochus, seems to be pleading with him in animated fashion, while Metiochus looks hesitant and doubtful but attentive. This interpretation of the lovers' emotions as seen in the picture is prompted by what we know of the romance itself from papyrus fragments of it; see, for the text of the three fragments, Franz Zimmermann's *Griechische Roman-Papyri*, pp. 52–63. A confession on the part of Parthenope that she, hitherto scornful of Love, was now overcome by love for Metiochus, who was himself still indifferent if not hostile to Eros, was the central turning point in the whole romance. Hence the representation of that moment was well chosen by the artist as an illustration of the book.

In broad outline the story of Metiochus and Parthenope as we see it in the papyrus fragments of the romance, and from other sources, is this: Parthenope, elsewhere known as the siren who gave her name to Naples as its patron saint, "was wooed by many men, but she persisted in her maidenhood. Then she fell in love with the Phrygian Metiochus. She cut her hair and, condemning herself to ugliness, went to Campania to live." So Eustathius commenting on the *Periegesis* of the geographer Dionysius. In the romance Parthenope's purpose in disfiguring herself was probably in order to facilitate her elopement with Metiochus, by freeing herself either from the power of her father and suitors at home or from that of others by whom she had been taken captive after leaving home. In the first fragment, which dramatizes a philosophical dispute on the subject of love, Metiochus shows himself disdainful of Eros and ridicules his supposed dignity and power; and Parthenope who is present agrees with him. This indicates that both protagonists are bound subsequently to be humbled by Eros and to fall violently in love; and that in fact is seen to have happened already before the action which is described in the second fragment, the scene of which, apparently, is in the neighborhood of the Thracian Chersonese. Therein certain persons are pleading for the marriage of Metiochus to Parthenope before the latter's father, a king, who remains implacably opposed to it. The third fragment shows Parthenope on the island of Corcyra separated from her lover Metiochus, with whom she had apparently eloped, and at the disposal of a powerful master who is about to sell her. On the whole, the greater part of this romance must have related the adverse adventures of the lovers, including separation from each other on their way from Phrygia to Campania, and that is on the pattern of the usual Greek romance.

In like fashion the core of the Ninus romance in all probability consisted of the adventures undergone by Ninus and Semiramis after being separated, as we infer from the new fragment C, which was not known to Levi or other commentators on the mosaics. Ninus, unnamed, lying on a couch and looking at the portrait of a girl on the mosaic from Antioch is identified as Ninus by name on a very similar mosaic found nearby at Alexandretta in Syria; for which see D. Levi, *op. cit.* (1944), pp. 427 f., with figures 3 and 4 on p. 423. In the light of fragment C there can no longer be any doubt that both mosaics represent Ninus gazing with longing on the picture of his beloved Semiramis, from whom he has been forcefully separated. Two scenes of a similar nature are described in Chariton's romance: in the first, at the end of Bk. I (see above, p. 129) the heroine Callirhoe apostrophizes her absent husband Chaereas while gazing at his picture engraved on her ring and kissing it; and in a later passage (II 11, 1–3) the same Callirhoe, now pregnant by Chaereas from whom she has been separated, presses his picture to her abdomen and converses with him and with the unborn child on the question of what is best for her to do in the interest of all three.

[19] This subject has been discussed above in chap. iii sec. 8.

[20] *Mededelingen der Koninklijke Nederlandse Akad. van Wetenschappen. Afd. Letterkunde* (Amsterdam, 1953).

[21] "They said a lot to that effect," Lucian continues, "because they were obviously charmed by what they had heard . . . . But for my part, I must confess, their praise bothered me not a little, and, when they had gone away and I was alone, I thought to myself: So then, this is the only thing that is charming in my speeches, that they do not deal with the usual subjects or such as are commonly written about by others of my profession. When it comes to the presence of beautiful words composed in line with the ancient standards, to subtle turns of thought, to Attic charm, or harmony in the structure, and artistic skill governing the composition throughout—forsooth those things must be absent from my composition, otherwise they would not pass them by without mention and praise only what is new and strange in the subject I choose to speak about." Etc. Lucian goes on to say that he has been disillusioned with his audiences; they had shown no taste for the main banquet of art that he had given them, but praised him only for what he meant to be an added relish.

NOTES TO CHAPTER V

Petronius and his *Satyricon*

Pages 186–210

[1] See John Saxe's lively poetical version of what purports to be a Hindu fable entitled "The Blind Men and the Elephant" in *The Poetical Works of John Godfrey Saxe* (Boston, 1892), pp. 111 f. Each of the blind men feels of a different part of the animal's anatomy and reports accordingly: the elephant is very much like a wall, if you feel of its side; like a tree, if you feel of its leg; like a rope, if you feel of the tail, etc.

> "And so these men of Indostan
> Disputed loud and long,
> Each in his own opinion
> Exceeding stiff and strong,
> Though each was partly in the right,
> And all were in the wrong."

[2] The view that the *Satyricon* is a Menippean satire somehow expanded into a romance has been held by a number of famous scholars: E. Rohde in *Der Griechische Roman*³, p. 267; O. Ribbeck in *Römische Dichtung*², III, Stuttgart, 1892, 150; W. Schmid in *Neue Jahrb. f. d. klass. Alt.* XIII (1904), 476; R. Hirzel in *Der Dialog* II, Leipzig, 1895, 37; and J. Geffcken in *Neue Jahrb. f. d. klass. Alt.* XXVII (1911), 485. The presumable connection of the *Satyricon* with Roman satire generally is ably discussed by E. T. Sage on pp. 199–203 of his annotated text of the *Satyricon* (New York and London, 1929). There is no question that the *Satyricon* contains satire and deals with topics commonly treated in Roman satire, such as the banquet; and that fact, together with the consideration of its loose structure, has led some scholars to suppose that it was written as a whole in the tradition of satire.

[3] E. Klebs in *Philologus* 47 (1889), 623–635.

[4] Richard Heinze, "Petron und der griechische Roman" in *Hermes* 34 (1899), 494–519. Cf. Schanz, *Röm. Litt.*³ II 2, p. 125.

[5] C. W. Mendell, "Petronius and the Greek Romance" *CPh* 12 (1917), 158–172.

[6] M. Rosenblüth, *Beiträge zur Quellenkunde von Petrons Satiren*, (Kiel, 1909: diss.); cf. K. Preston, "Some Sources of Comic Effect in Petronius," *CPh* 10 (1915), 260–269.

[7] Cf. B. E. Perry in the article "Petronius and the Comic Romance" in *CPh* 20 (1925), 39–49. By "Milesian tale" inquirers in this field have understood the unmoral or immoral kind of story which is typified in spirit by the tales of adulterous intrigue in Apuleius; although, in principle, such a story was not always or necessarily erotic in substance. Lucian's *Onos* is not so in the main, nor are other conceivable varieties of rogue story in which the unprincipled cleverness of the protagonist in action is the essence of the tale.

We are not here concerned with the insoluble problem of just what the scandalous *Milesiaka* of Aristides was in regard to its length and structure, and the literary sanction or *décor* under which it was put forth as a book. As science broadly conceived, perhaps? As ethnography? As dialogue illustrating a philosophical principle, like Lucian's *Toxaris* on friendship? *Chi lo sa?* That problem was discussed above in section 11 of chap. ii, *q.v.* Those who have sought to explain the *Satyricon* in terms of Milesian tale have assumed such an extension or development of it as would amount to a comic, realistic romance of roguery in existence before Petronius, which would then have served as a precedent to guide Petronius in writing his *Satyricon*. This was formerly my own view of the matter, but on deeper reflection in recent years I have renounced it. It has been held, however, in slightly differing forms by the following scholars in the past: K. Bürger in *Hermes* 27 (1892), 345–358 ("Die antike Roman vor Petron") and in *Studien zur Geschichte des griech. Romans*, I Teil: *Der Lukiosroman und seine litteraturgeschichtliche Bedeutung* (Blankenburg, 1902); O. Schissel von Fleschenberg, *Entwicklungsgeschichte des griech. Romans* (Halle, 1913) 3 ff. (cf. Perry, *Petronius and the Comic Romance*, p. 41, n. 1); Fr. Leo in *Die Kultur der Gegenwart*, Teil I, Abt. 8 (Leipzig, 1912), who remarks (p. 459) that "Die Form des Schelmenromans, die das Bach hatte, war gewiss in den Unterschichten der griechischen Litteratur vorhanden; was solche Produktion wert ist, das hängt ganz von der Persönlichkeit ab, die das Ihrige in die Form hineinlegt." Wilamowitz (*Die Kultur der Gegenwart* I.8, 190) is of the same opinion. Leo's qualifying observation that everything depends upon the personality of the individual author is profoundly true; it means that, if a comic romance of roguery existed before Petronius in Greek, its appearance would have to be explained in terms of its author's individual peculiarity, and in that respect would simply duplicate the problem of the *Satyricon*. Neither author's work could be explained as due to precedent or to literary tradition.

[8] F. F. Abbott on p. 266 of his article "The Origin of the Realistic Romance among the Romans" in *CPh* 6 (1911). This is only one among a number of possible lines of descent mentioned by Abbott. It is not a proposition that he himself approved.

[9] See n. 7 above.

[10] Sage in his annotated text of the *Satyricon*, pp. xiv ff. I have described what seems to be the total result of Sage's heavy speculation; but his struggle with the problem is befuddled with misleading conceptions of "development," intermediate steps and stages, and the gradual transition from one purpose on the part of an author to a different purpose, which is meaningless. On p. xiv, however, he states explicitly that "so far as our knowledge goes, Petronius had no real predecessor." Likewise Abbott, after reviewing many possible lines of descent for the *Satyricon* in his interesting article on the subject (*CPh* 6, p. 270), wisely concludes as follows: "Whether the one or the other of these explanations of its origin recommends itself to us as probable or not, it is interesting to note, as we leave the subject, that, so far as our present information goes, the realistic romance seems to have been the invention of Petronius." I feel sure that it *was* the outright invention of

Petronius. It remains to explain *why* he invented it; and that, as I have undertaken to show in this chapter on the subject, can be readily understood in the light of the author's personality and the peculiar conditions in which he lived and wrote at the court of Nero.

¹¹ The dating of the *Satyricon* in the time of Nero has recently been challenged and denied very vigorously, but on the basis of very negative data (howbeit with a great display of erudition well calculated to bluff the unwary), by Enzo V. Marmorale, who used to know better (see his *Petronio*, Napoli, 1936, and my favorable review of it in *CPh* 33, 327 ff.). In his *La Questione Petroniana* (Bari, 1948), and in other writings, Marmorale now maintains that the *Satyricon* was written at some time not long after A.D. 180. Much of his argument turns about the contention that certain neologisms in vocabulary, orthography, inflection, and grammar, cannot be earlier in origin than the late second century, because they are unattested before that time in either literature or inscriptions, as if either of those linguistic documents provided a safe criterion by which to date the origin of vulgar or colloquial linguistic phenomena. Reckoning on that basis, one would have to conclude that the Pompeian wall inscriptions, which antedate the year A.D. 79 and show many linguistic neologisms comparable in kind to vulgar or colloquial expressions and vocabulary in the *Satyricon*, did not come into use anywhere until a hundred or two hundred years after A.D. 79. There is some difference, in the matter of linguistic formality, between the inscriptions in the *CIL*, mainly official public documents, and the unofficial scribblings on walls of privies and brothels at Pompeii.

Marmorale's dating of the *Satyricon* is clearly disproved, in my opinion, by each of two different studies which were published after the appearance of his book and the substance of which Marmorale himself either did not consider at all or tried in vain to refute. One of these two close-up studies was made by Gilbert Bagnani on pages 14–24 of his book entitled *Arbiter of Elegance: A Study of the Life and Works of Petronius* (Toronto, 1954). This penetrating exposition derives its strength from an intimate knowledge of Roman legal history and inscriptional evidence, not hitherto brought to bear in this connection, and is well and sympathetically summed up by H. C. Schnur in his review in *Classical Weekly* 48 (1955), 135 f. The other learned study, to which I have referred, is one published by H. T. Rowell in *TAPhA* 89 (1958), 14–24 (*sic*) under the title "The Gladiator Petraites and the Date of the *Satyricon*," which is built on abundant epigraphical and archaeological evidence and by itself proves, as I think, that the *Satyricon* must have been written in the time of Nero. Bagnani demonstrates that what Echion says about Glyco's treatment of his steward in *Sat.* 45.7–8 must have been written prior to both the *Lex Petronia de adulterii iudicio* and the *Lex Petronia de servis;* that the former of these laws can be dated in A.D. 61, proposed by the consul P. Petronius Turpilianus, and that the latter was post-Claudian and enacted under Nero, "probably by Petronius Turpilianus in A.D. 61, possibly by Petronius Arbiter, or by T. Petronius Niger between A.D. 60 and the end of the reign." Rowell shows convincingly in his fascinating article that the gladiatorial fights of Petraites, whose name often appears as Tetraites, either by orthographical error or as a nickname (four-time winner), and who is regularly paired in Pompeian inscriptions and on a series of glass cups with a gladiator named Prudens, were famous and much talked about by the crowd of Remus in the time of Nero; and this means, unmistakably, that when Trimalchio (*Sat.* 52.2) boasts of having silver cups picturing the fights of Petraites, and when he orders all the fights of Petraites to be depicted on his tomb (71.6), he is speaking in the age of Nero, and not in the time of Commodus, when the several gladiatorial pairs mentioned in Pompeian inscriptions and on glass cups, as popular heroes, were antiquities no longer talked about or even remembered in sporting circles.

Withoug mentioning L. Friedländer himself, who had argued the case persuasively in the second edition of his *Cena Trimalchionis* (Leipzig, 1906), Marmorale (*Questione*, pp. 70–71) denies the identity of the Apelles mentioned by the singer Plocamus in 64.4 as his only rival in singing when he himself was a boy, with the famous tragic actor named Apelles who was flogged by Caligula according to Suetonius (*Cal.* 33), on the ground that Plocamus refers to a comic actor (which is not a necessary inference here), and that the inflection Apelles-*etis* for Apelles-*is* is not elsewhere attested before the third century. And as for Menecrates—whose tunes Trimalchio drunkenly murders in the bath (73.3), and who is said by Suetonius (*Nero* 30) to have been a *citharoedus* greatly favored by Nero along with the gladiator Spiculus (the latter is mentioned in a Pompeian inscription as *Neronianus*)— Marmorale chooses to believe that this cannot be the Menecrates drunkenly imitated by Trimalchio, because he is not said to have been a musical composer. But a *citharoedus* normally sang an accompaniment to his guitar, and who can say whether or not this Menecrates composed his own accompanying songs, or that Trimalchio in his drunken state would take pains to discriminate between an original composer and a citharist who made a popular hit by singing the songs composed by someone else? Marmorale's special pleading on this point is well refuted by A. Maiuri in *La Parola del Passato* 3 (1948), 101–128; and indeed, if scholarly opinion is to be admitted in the balances, those who have opposed Marmorale's dating and who uphold the Neronian dating of the *Satyricon*, are much more numerous than those who agree with Marmorale. His opponents include E. Paratore (*Paideia* 3 [1948], 261–271), whom he had repeatedly scolded for not sharing his own view on the date of the *Satyricon*; R. Browning in *Classical Review* (1949), pp. 12–14; J. Whatmough in *CPh* 44 (1949), 273 f., who remarks that "it is impossible to take seriously" Marmorale's discussion of the "predecessors" of Petronius, including Juvenal and Apuleius; and P. Grenade in *Revue des Études Anc.* (1948), 282–287.

[12] The position of Petronius as *Arbiter Elegantiae* at Nero's court may or may not have been an official one. A passage in Suetonius (*Tib.* 42) tells us that *Tiberius novum denique officium instituit a voluptatibus, praeposito equite Romano T. Caesonio Prisco.*

[13] It is stated in cod. A, the MS found at Trau in Dalmatia in 1650, that its contents, which consist of the fragments preserved in the ninth-century cod. Bernensis of the so-called O family, and in addition the *Cena Trimal-*

chionis, are taken from Bks. XV and XVI. The fragments preserved in the O family include most of those which precede the *Cena* at 26.7, one fragment belonging in ch. 55 in the *Cena*, and a series of fragments following the *Cena* and ending with one corresponding to 137.9–10. Bücheler (ed. maior 1862) cites a statement in an old lexicon from Fleury that ch. 89 containing the poem on the fall of Troy is from Bk. XV. From this it appears that Bk. XV alone contained considerably more than what is in the *Cena*, and if so the average book-length of the *Satyricon* may be reckoned at 50 pages or more. For further details, see Sage, p. 201 of his edition, who thinks that the division between Bks. XV and XVI may be reasonably placed either at the end of 91 or at the end of 99; and that, in the light of a passage in Fulgentius (*Myth.* 3.8, see Bücheler's frag. VII with notation), Bk. XIV ended with 26.7, just at the beginning of the *Cena*, in spite of the statement made in A.

¹⁴ Pliny the Elder speaks of *saturica signa* in the sense of statues of Priapus (*N.H.* xix, 50), and of *saturicos motus* applied to certain birds (*ib.* x, 138); Plutarch applies the word to men who resemble satyrs, either outwardly (*Cato* 7) or in respect to conduct (*Galba* 16, *Pericles* 13); and Lucian (*Bacch.* 5) refers to κώμοις γυναικείοις καὶ σκιρτήμασι σατυρικοῖς. The meaning "satirical" appears to have originated much later with grammarians who associated Roman satire with Greek satyr-drama; so Lydus, *De Mag.* 41, and the scholiast on Juvenal I 168.

¹⁵ Tacitus (*Ann.* XV 49) says that Lucan had joined the Pisonian conspiracy against Nero, but adds that he was moved to do so by a private grievance, "because Nero out of vain rivalry had tried to suppress the good reputation of his poetry and had forbidden him to display it publicly." Of Seneca, Tacitus tells us in *Ann.* XV 56 that Nero had done everything he could to put him down, and in an earlier passage of the *Annals* (XIV 52) he says that Seneca's enemies brought the charge against him that he was claiming for himself alone the reputation for eloquence and was very active in composing poetry after Nero himself had set his heart on it. In *Ann.* XV 71 it is stated that Nero banished the young Verginius Flavus, whose talent in oratory is praised by Quintilian (*Inst.* VII 4, 40), because of his bright reputation as a teacher of young men. In *Ann.* XVI 29 we are told that Montanus, an honorable young man and no writer of libelous verse, was banished (by Nero) only because he had displayed his poetic talent. In *Agricola* 6 Tacitus says that Agricola was well aware of the nature of the times under Nero, *quibus inertia pro sapientia fuit.*

¹⁶ Petronius, in my opinion, comes close to being the best poet of the first century, or in any case the most versatile. It is difficult for me to understand how anyone can assign such vigorous, irreligious poetry to a Roman writer of the late second century, as Marmorale does on the basis of his mechanical manipulation of negative evidence. I feel quite sure that nothing like the writing of Petronius could have been produced by a Roman in the age of the Antonines. Cf. my article on "Literature in the Second Century" in *Class. Jour.* 50 (1955), 295–298; and, for a thorough and sympathetic study of the poetry in the *Satyricon*, the monograph by H. Stubbe entitled "Die Verseinlagen im Petron," *Philologus*, Supplementbd. 25 (1933).

[17] On the *maqāmāt* in general, and their authors, see the excellent accounts given by Nicholson on pp. 327–329 and by G. E. von Grunebaum in his *Medieval Islam* (2d ed., Chicago, 1953), pp. 288 f. See also, for the direct influence of the *maqāmāt* in shaping the fourteenth-century Spanish novel *Libro de buen Amor*, Maria Rosa Lida de Malkiel in *Two Spanish Masterpieces* (= *Illinois Studies in Language and Literature*, vol. 49 [Urbana, 1961]), pp. 20–22. Al Hamadhani's *Maqāmāt* have been translated by W. J. Prendergast (Madras, 1915). The classic translation of Al Harīrī's *Assemblies*, Vol. I with very learned Introduction and Notes, is that by Thomas Chenery (London, 1867) (= Orient. Trans. Fund, New Series III, 1898), which was completed after the translator's death by F. Steingass: Vol. II, containing the last 24 *Assemblies*, in the same translation series, published by the Royal Asiatic Society in 1898. Nicholson (p. 331) cites the following adverse criticism of the *maqāmāt* made by a writer of about A.D. 1300 in the course of praising his own work, a popular history entitled *al-Fakhrī:*

"And, again, it is more profitable than the *Maqāmāt* on which men have set their hearts, and which they eagerly commit to memory; because the reader derives no benefit from *Maqāmāt* except familiarity with elegant composition and knowledge of the rules of verse and prose. Undoubtedly they contain maxims and ingenious devices and experiences; but all this has a debasing effect on the mind, for it is founded on begging and sponging and disgraceful scheming to acquire a few paltry pence. Therefore, if they do good in one direction, they do harm in another; and this point has been noticed by some critics of the *Maqāmāt* of Harīrī and Badī 'u' l-Zamān."

[18] Christ-Schmid, *Gr. Litt.*[6], II p. 89.
[19] Cf. G. E. von Grunebaum, *Medieval Islam*,[2] p. 288. Nabia Abbott, writing on "A Ninth-Century Fragment of the Thousand Nights" in the *Journal of Near Eastern Studies* VIII (1949), after citing a number of derogatory comments by Muslim writers concerning *khurāfāt* (silly fictions), describes the attitude of learned Muslims toward the *Arabian Nights* (*Alf Lailah*) and its Persian source, the *Hazār Afsāna*, as follows (pp. 157 f.):

"There is, of course, no question of their widespread and increasing popularity from the ninth century on, but generally on the level of folktales that were considered good enough media for the amusement and instruction of the ignorant and frivolous and of women and children, but seldom considered sufficiently dignified for the serious attention of reputable littérateurs and scholars. . . . And since all these elements [of pure fiction] were to be found in the *Alf Lailah*, this representative collection par excellence went merrily rolling along all over the Moslem world, flourishing in its anonymity, cherished by the common man, and ignored by the highbrow, down almost to our own times."

[20] Agamemnon in *Satyricon* ch. 4 says: *Sed ne me putes improbasse schedium Lucilianae humilitatis, quod sentio et ipse carmine effingam*. Concerning what he calls Prosimetrum, as a spontaneous and natural form of narrative expression from India to Ireland, see the significant article by O. Immisch entitled "Über eine volkstümliche Darstellungsform in der Antiken Litera-

tur" in *Neue Jahrbücher für das Klass. Altertum* 47 (1921), 409–421. Immisch has the right idea, but the perspective of his article is obscured by the introduction of dubiously relevant matter. An excellent statement of the matter in brief is made by F. F. Abbott on p. 269 of his article on "The Realistic Romance among the Romans" in *CPh* 6 (1911), which I venture to quote in part: "A little thought suggests that it is not an unnatural medium of expression. A change from prose to verse or from one form of verse to another suggests a change in the emotional condition of a speaker or writer. We see that clearly enough illustrated in tragedy or comedy . . . if we should arrange the commoner Latin verses in a sequence according to the emotional effects which they produced, at the bottom of the series would stand the iambic senarius. Above that would come trochaic verse, and we should rise to higher planes of exaltation as we read the anapaestic, or cretic or bacchiac. The greater part of life is commonplace. Consequently the common medium for conversation or for the narrative in a composition like comedy made up entirely of verse is the senarius. Now this form of verse in its simple, almost natural, quantitative arrangement is very close to prose, and it would be a short step to substitute prose for it as the basis of the story, interspersing verse here and there to secure variety, or when the emotions were called into play, just as lyric verses are interpolated in the iambic narrative."

[21] All the speeches in verse in Lucian's Menippean dialogues are mockheroic, with satirical implications. In the Menippean satire ascribed to Seneca, known as the *Apocolocyntosis* or *Ludus de Morte Claudii*, which is a bitter personal satire ridiculing Claudius throughout, only a few lines describing the time of day in epic verse might be regarded as sober artistic experiments. The rest, especially the anapaests in ch. 12 and the hexameters at the end, are mock-heroic and denunciatory.

The epic descriptions of sunrise and sunset have invited much parody in both ancient and modern times, and a very extensive and interesting collection might be made of such parodies. Note the following as typical:

Butler's *Hudibras*, Part II, Canto 2, 29–34:
> The sun had long since, in the lap
> Of Thetis, taken out his nap,
> And, like a lobster boiled, the morn
> From black to red began to turn,
> When Hudibras . . .

Fielding's *Joseph Andrews*, Book I, ch. 8:

Now the rake Hesperus had called for his breeches, and, having well rubbed his drowsy eyes, prepared to dress himself for all night; by whose example his brother rakes on earth likewise leave those beds in which they had slept away the day. Now Thetis, the good housewife, began to put on the pot, in order to regale the good man Phoebus after his daily labours were over. In vulgar language, it was in the evening when Joseph attended his lady's orders.

Lucian's *Metamorphoses*

Pages 211–235

¹ See *Diss.* pp. 1–12 for an analysis of the controversy concerning these relationships and a summary of the decisive critical work done by K. Bürger in his dissertation *De Lucio Patrensi* (Berlin, 1887), supplemented by that of M. Rothstein in his *Quaestiones Lucianeae* (Berlin, 1888), 129 ff. See also Schanz-Hosius *Röm. Litt.*³ III 107 f., and P. Vallette in the Preface to the Budé edition of the *Metamorphoses* of Apuleius by Robertson and Vallette (Paris, 1940).

² Augustine, *De Civit. Dei* XVIII 18: *sicut Apuleius, in libris quos Asini aurei titulo inscripsit, sibi ipsi accidisse ut, accepto veneno, humano animo permanente, asinus fieret, aut indicavit aut finxit.* On Augustine's belief in the reality of pagan miracles performed by the aid of demons, and his view of Apuleius as a magician, see the interesting account given by Elizabeth Hazelton Haight in *Apuleius and His Influence* (New York, 1927), pp. 97–101.

³ On the content of the lost Μεταμορφώσεις, see *Diss.* Ch. III, pp. 21–31, where all the relevant data are reviewed and the conclusion established that the lost book must have contained only the story of Lucius and such metamorphoses as he himself was represented as experiencing or seeing.

⁴ In codex 166, where he is describing the long story of travel in strange lands entitled *On the Wonders beyond Thule* in 24 books by Antonius Diogenes. Photius, like Rohde, thinks of this book as a prototype of such later romances as those of Iamblichus, Achilles Tatius, and Heliodorus, because it combines two "elements," travel and love, which Rohde later discovered in them; although the "love element" in Antonius seems to have been rather cool and quite incidental in comparison with the long yarns which each lover had to spin out about where he or she had travelled, including a voyage to Hades. But the main point that I am here making is that Photius in this passage (cod. 166) compares the book of Lucius (τοῦ περὶ μεταμορφώσεων Λουκίου) with the *True History* of Lucian on the one hand and with the erotic romances on the other, all of which are single stories, while excluding from the comparison the composite collection of paradoxical stories by Damascius, which he has mentioned at the beginning of his comment on Diogenes, and which he describes in another place, cod. 130. In *Diss.* pp. 25 f. the text of Photius is quoted at length and its implications more fully explained.

⁵ Estimation of the length of the original Greek *Luciad* depends upon how much of the Apuleian narrative with the digressions or extensions which are not in the *Onos* epitome is assigned to the original, in addition to what we have in the *Onos* itself. A. Goldbacher, who was the first in modern times to make a really close-up comparative study of the two texts (*Zeitschrift für die oesterreich. Gymnasien* 23 [1872], 323–341 and 403–421), and whose conclu-

sion concerning the relationships anticipated that of Bürger and later students, assigned much more of the Apuleian narrative to the original *Luciad* than did Bürger (*De Lucio Patrensi*, p. 58). Rothstein (*Quaestiones Lucianeae*, pp. 137 f.) would assign somewhat less of Apuleius to the original Greek version than Bürger; and Paul Junghanns, whose comparative study is more elaborate and detailed than that of any of his predecessors, estimates that the *Onos*, contained on 35 Teubner pages, is no more than five Teubner pages shorter than the original from which it comes: see page 118 in Junghanns' study, *Die Erzählungs-technik von Apuleius' Metamorphosen und ihrer Vorlage*, in *Philologus*, Supplementbd. XXIV, Heft 1 (1932). Today, in consideration of what must be added to the *Onos* to complete the story that it implies, I would say that the *Luciad* in the Greek Μεταμορφώσεις, from which it comes, may have been fifty pages long; but in 1920 (cf. *Diss.* pp. 24 and 31), before I had pondered the Apuleian text so long and so closely in comparison with the *Onos*, I made what I now consider a mistake in allowing 75 or 80 pages as the length of the Lucianic Μεταμορφώσεις.

[6] This is explained at length in my article entitled "The significance of the Title in Apuleius' *Metamorphoses*," *CPh* 18 (1923), 229–238.

[7] For the meaning of the medical proverb, ἐκ κυνὸς πρωκτοῦ, see Junghanns, *Die Erzählungs-technik von Apuleius' Metamorphosen*, p. 36, n. 1, who explains it for the first time with reference to Aristophanes, *Eccl.* 255, and the scholiast on *Acharn.* 863: κομμάτιόν ἐστιν ἀπὸ παροιμίας ἣν τοῖς ὀφθαλμιῶσιν ἔλεγον · ἐς πρωκτὸν κυνὸς βλέπε.

[8] So E. Schwartz in his *Fünf Vorträge über den griech. Roman* (Berlin, 1896), p. 135, whose opinion is shared by Schanz, *Röm. Litt.*[2] III p. 111, and originally by Bürger (*Die Lucio Patrensi*, p. 59), who later, however, changed his mind. Schwartz, *loc. cit.*, says "Es liegt auf der Hand dass der ganze Roman eine dem Cervantes Ehre machende Satire auf die mit der Pythagoräischen Seelenwanderungslehre zusammenhängenden Zaubergeschichten ist, und zwar zielt die Satire auf einen ganz bestimmten Schriftsteller."

[9] Plutarch, *Aetia Rom.* 30, 271e, speaking of the Roman marriage ceremony, says τοῖς δ'ὀνόμασι τούτοις ἄλλως κέχρηνται κοινοῖς οὖσιν, ὥσπερ οἱ νομικοὶ Γάιον Σήιων καὶ Λούκιον Τίτιον · · · παραλαμβάνουσι. There are said to be many examples of this in the *Digest*. This Roman legal practice of using the names Gaius and Lucius to typify Roman citizens was familiar also to the Jewish Rabbis in the East, according to an interesting article by S. Lieberman in the *Annuaire de l'Institut de Philologie et d'Histoire Orientales et Slaves* IX (1949), 409–421. Lieberman quotes a passage in the Palestinian Talmud (Terumoth X 7, 47n) as follows: "And as for those letters of divorce, are not Gaius and Lucius signed in them?"

[10] This episode relating to the magically animated wineskins is described and analyzed below in sec. 9 of chap. vii.

[11] Concerning the linguistic peculiarities of Lucian found in the *Onos*, the most extensive study is that of V. Neukamm in a dissertation entitled *De Luciano Asini Auctore* (Leipzig, 1914), approved by W. Schmid, *Gr. Litt.*[6] II 737. Numerous other Lucianic peculiarities of phraseology, thought, and

style, which are not in Neukamm, are cited on pp. 71–72 of *Diss.* and in my article entitled "On the Authenticity of Lucius sive Asinus," in *CPh* 21 (1926), 225–234.

[12] See my short paper on "Literature in the Second Century," *Classical Journal* 10 (1955), 295–298.

[13] What is said above concerning the method of Apuleius in purveying prose fiction anticipates what I shall have to say later on in chap. vii, sec. 2, concerning the function of Bk. XI in the Apuleian economy. But I see no harm in this kind of repetition, and it makes for clarity in both places. The method of Apuleius needs to be stated in this context for the sake of its enlightening contrast with that of Lucian.

[14] Eunapius, *Vit. Soph.*, p. 454 in Dübner's edition (Paris, 1878).

NOTES TO CHAPTER VII

Apuleius and His *Metamorphoses*
Pages 236-282

[1] *Met.* XI 26.

[2] *Florida* 1.

[3] *Florida* 20.

[4] Five short fragments of this romance are quoted by the grammarian Priscian, and one other by Fulgentius. For these, see the fragments of Apuleius newly collected in the *Index Apuleianus* of Oldfather, Canter, and Perry (Middletown, Conn., 1934), pp. ix f. From the nature of the actions described, the fact that some of the lines quoted seem to be in meter, and that the name Hermagoras suggests a (travelling) rhetorician, analogous to Agamemnon, I have conjectured that the *Hermagoras* was influenced by the example of Petronius, in that it contained a burlesque narrative interspersed with verse and rhetorical declamation. See my review of the data in a short article entitled "On Apuleius' *Hermagoras*," *AJPh* 48 (1927), 263–266.

[5] For the lost writings of Apuleius see the exhaustive account given by Schanz-Hosius in *Röm. Litt.*[3] III, 125–132, where all the relevant testimony is cited.

[6] *The Golden Ass of Apuleius*, translated with Introduction and Notes by Francis D. Byrne (London: The Imperial Press 1904). Byrne's translation of Apuleius is in many places more felicitous than any other in English with which I am acquainted. It maintains a high degree of accuracy throughout, although, like all the other translations, it fails here and there to convey the exact meaning of the Latin text and needs to be corrected. The best French translation is that of Paul Vallette in the Budè text edited by Robertson and Vallette (Paris, 1940–1945); see my lengthy review of this in *CPh* 43 (1948), 192–199.

[7] Said of Hadrian by Tertullian in *Apology* 5.

[8] *Semper-varius* from Spartianus, *Vita Hadriani* 14. The phrase here quoted is preceded in Spartianus by the following characterization of Hadrian: *idem severus laetus, comis gravis, lascivus cunctator, tenax liberalis, simulator simplex, severus clemens, et semper* . . . .

[9] See note 5 on chap. vi above for the probable length of the Greek original, not more than 50 Teubner pages. The Apuleian *Metamorphoses* is about 290 pages long in Helm's text and contains many obvious digressions, along with other stories that are very loosely or artificially connected with the career of Lucius. See the list of 17 *Einlagen* given by Schanz-Hosius, *Röm. Litt.*[3] III, pp. 108 f., which is very well reckoned, but not complete. Problems arise whether many shorter extensions of the narrative are also Apuleian additions, and the probability is, in most cases, that they are.

[10] Conscientious regard for motivation in the sequence of events or of statements (i.e. *Motivzwang*) is seldom present in the *Metamorphoses*, as

Paul Junghanns, *Die Erzählungs-technik von Apuleius' Metamorphosen und ihrer Vorlage, Philologus*, Supplementbd. XXIV, Heft 1 (1932), well observes (p. 89): "Motivzwang spielt bei Apuleius eine geringe Rolle; nur die allernötigsten Einrenkungen [bone-settings] des Handlungsverlaufes werden vorgenommen. Solange andere plausible Erklärungen von Änderungen äusserer Handlungsmotive möglich sind, wird man keinen 'Motivzwang' annehmen." The foregoing statement was made by Junghanns in the course of refuting a misapprehension of my own concerning the operation of *Motivzwang* in a certain passage, and he was entirely right in so correcting me. It is only slowly, and by virtue of long and close familiarity with the unlooked-for methods of Apuleius the showman, that one comes fully to realize how desultory his procedure everywhere is. Once this is realized, however, it becomes impossible to accept or to take seriously any of the numerous theories about the meaning or purpose of the *Metamorphoses* as a whole which have been deduced, on the false assumption of *Motivzwang*, from the allegorical hinting in Bk. XI, or from the story of Cupid and Psyche which happens to come in the middle of the work as a whole. The desultory method of Apuleius and his disregard of logical sequence are likewise conspicuous in his *Apologia*, as the foremost student of that book in recent years, Paul Vallette in his *L'Apologie d'Apulée* (Paris, 1908), pp. 157 and 181, did not fail to observe. Vallette says that for Apuleius "Toute prétexte est bon pour sortir de la question; il s'engage en des sentiers de traverse; il vagabonde; L'*Apologie* est faite d'un assemblage disparate de morceaux rattachés entre eux par un lien plus artificiel que réel; ce que lui manque le plus, c'est l'unité . . . à tout moment il semble oublier qu'il parle pour prouver et pour convaincre; il raconte, il cause, il s'amuse à tout autre chose qu'à la gaguere; l'anecdote n'est pas un moyen, elle est le but."

Apuleius would not write or plan an extensive book for the sake of illustrating any moral or any one idea. For a dozen or more interpretations of the *Metamorphoses* which mistakenly assume that the author would, or even could, so plan his work, see the theories listed by Lehnert in Bursian's *Jahresbericht* CLXXV, 35 ff., together with what I have said on the subject on p. 242 of my article "An Interpretation of Apuleius' *Metamorphoses*" in *TAPhA* 57 (1926).

[11] In spite of his attempt in Bk. XI to cover up his literary exploitation of "Milesian tales" on their own account, of which Cupid and Psyche is one (see my review of the Budé edition in *CPh* 43), the fellow countrymen of Apuleius in Africa had no difficulty in seeing through his disguise, and were shocked by the triviality of his performance. So Macrobius (probably Macrobius Theodosius) in his *Commentary* on Cicero's *Somnium Scipionis* (1.2.8) speaks of "argumenta fictis casibus amatorum referta, quibus vel multum se Arbiter exercuit vel Apuleiun nonnumquam lusisse miramur." In his *Vita Clodii Albini* (ch. 12) Julius Capitolinus states that Albinus, an African, was said by some to have composed "Milesias quarum fama non ignobilis habetur, quamvis mediocriter scriptae sint"; and, a few lines farther on, a letter written to the Senate by Septimius Severus complaining about Albinus is quoted, in which Severus says, "maior fuit dolor quod illum pro

litterato laudandum plerique duxistis, cum ille neniis quibusdam anilibus occupatus inter Milesias Punicas Apulei sui et ludicra litteraria consenesceret."

[12] Concerning the *Milesiaca* of Aristides of Miletus, the problem of what its structure and contents were, and what it purported to be as literature, see note 7 on chap. v above and section 11 of chap. ii.

[13] In *Philologus*, Supplementbd. XXIV, Heft 1 (1932).

[14] What I am saying here is well stated by Junghanns (*Die Efzählungstechnik*, p. 33) as follows: "lebendige, drastische Herausarbeitung seelischer Dinge ist ein Hauptcharakterzug apuleianischer Darstellung. Mimik und Gesten, Redeweise und Seufzer: alles dient der Verdeutlichung des Seelenlebens. Apuleius will nicht nur äusseres Geschehen erzählen, sondern das äussere als Ausdruck der inneren, das innere als Folge des äusseren darstellen—beides steht in engster Verbindung; alles soll Farbe gewinnen, eigenes Leben atmen; der ganze Mensch soll dem Leser gleichsam gegenwärtig sein."

[15] For a full account of the elegiac poetry of Parthenius himself, as well as the outlines of tragic love affairs in prose which he collected as raw material for poetic exploitation by Cornelius Gallus, entitled Ἐρωτικὰ παθήματα, see Christ-Schmid, *Gr. Litt.*[6] II 322 ff. The Greek text of the Ἐρωτικὰ π. is printed in the first volume of the Teubner edition of *Erotici Scriptores Graeci*, ed. R. Hercher, Leipzig, 1858.

[16] For example, among the so-called *fabulae extravagantes*, first published by Steinhöwel at Ulm in 1476, that about the Wolf as Fisherman (Perry, *Aes.* no. 698) consists of two successive episodes which are elsewhere told separately (*Aes.* 625 and 585) but are here combined into one story dealing with the adventures of the same wolf; and, in the following fable, that about the Wolf's Misfortunes (*Aes.* 699), the initial frame story, which is not elsewhere preserved as such, is filled in with four successive episodes describing the wolf's misfortunes, each of which appears elsewhere as a separate fable. This agglutinative process, by which an originally short story is built up into a small animal epic, is characteristic of what often happens in animal tales when they pass from the restrictive environment of classical literature, where they are subordinated to the illustration of a point, into oral circulation as folktales, where they become *stories* dramatically spun out for their own interest as such, just as they had been told, presumably, before they were pressed into the service of ancient literature as Aesopic fables, or as historically oriented myths. How man's years beyond thirty were borrowed successively from horse, ox, and dog, in order to explain aetiologically man's temperament in middle life and old age, is told summarily in only 14 lines in the ancient Greek fable (*Aes.* 105 and Babrius 74); but the same story as told dramatically in M. Gaster's *Rumanian Bird and Beast Stories* (London, 1915), with no new episodes or substance, extends through three pages (336–338) of colorful narrative filled in with lively dialogue and descriptive details.

The romantic Greek *Life of Secundus*, written by an unknown author in the late second century, is about six pages long in the manuscript (cod. Vat. Reginensis gr. 10) and contains within its framework a series of twenty questions asked by the emperor Hadrian of Secundus and answered by him in writing. But the Arabic translation which was made on the basis of this Greek text in the tenth century is about three times as long as the original; because the Arab author, like Apuleius, is bent on making an interesting story full of action and picturesque detail out of what was originally only a summary account of events in the philosopher's life, which led to his defiant encounter with Hadrian and what he wrote in reply to the latter's questions. Here the expansion of the original story is effected by the addition of much dialogue, soliloquy, and circumstantial detail near the beginning; by the interpolation of a story taken from the *Book of Sindbad*, which is told by Secundus to Hadrian and thereafter explained with regard to its symbolical meaning in detail; and by the addition of 33 questions with their answers, the last of which, a long account of the growth of the human foetus, is taken from the preface of the book of *Kalilah wa Dimnah*. For the Arabic *Secundus* and its Greek original, both in translation, see my recent edition of all the versions in *Secundus the Silent Philosopher*: Amer. Philol. Assn. Monograph XXII (1964).

Similar expansions of the original Persian story of *Sindbad and the Seven Wise Masters* in the course of its propagation among Arabic and Persian authors from the ninth to the fourteenth centuries, are described on pp. 66–72 of my *Origin of the Book of Sindbad* (Berlin, 1960, reprinted from *Fabula* III [1959]). Here, as often in Apuleius (see my article, "Some Aspects of the Literary Art of Apuleius," *TAPhA* 54, [1923], 214–217), the narrative is lengthened by the interpolation of incidents which are anticipations in their make-up of incidents that belong later on in the story, although the latter are retained.

[17] Many examples of this and other characteristic features of Apuleian narrative thought and style are given in my article "Some Aspects of the Literary Art of Apuleius . . . ," pp. 196–227 (see n. 16 above).

[18] The passage translated in part above follows immediately after the modest reply made by Lucius to the magistrates of Hypata, who, in order to console him for the part he had played at the festival of Risus, had proposed to set up statues in his honour. The text of the passage in full reads as follows: *et ecce quidam intro currens famulus: "rogat te," ait, "tua parens Byrrhena et convivii, cui te sero desponderas, iam adpropinquantis admonet." ad haec ego formidans et procul perhorrescens etiam ipsam domum eius, "quam vellem," inquam, "parens, iussis tuis obsequium commodare, si per fidem liceret id facere. hospes enim meus Milo . . . ."*

[19] A full account of these robber stories and the contradictions that Apuleius has made in telling them will be found on pp. 218–220 of my article, "Some Aspects of the Literary Art of Apuleius. . . ." (See n. 16 above.)

[20] This proverb, to dispute about the shadow of an ass, as to whether the rights to the shadow on a hot day are rented with the ass, or are retained by the owner, is always represented as a story told to an unattentive Athenian audience by Demosthenes for the purpose of showing them that they were more interested in fables and curious trifles than in the important matters on which he was addressing them. The story is told by Zenobius (VI 28) in

the *Corpus Paroem. Gr.* I pp. 169 f. and, in different words, by Plutarch in *Vit. Decem. Ofat.* 848a under Demosthenes. The text last mentioned is that which appears as fable no. 466 in my *Aesopica.*

²¹ See my detailed analysis of the composite story of Aristomenes published in *CPh* 24 (1929), 394–400 under the title "On Apuleius' *Metamorphoses* I 14–17." From the folktales of medieval and modern times W. Klinger in *Philologus* 66 (1907), 342–345 called attention to four stories about the visitation of witches which closely resemble the witch story told by Aristomenes, except that none of them, of course, contains anything like the suicide scene introduced by Apuleius. One of the parallel witch stories to which Klinger calls attention is a modern Greek tale published by N. G. Politis in his Παραδόσεις in the Βιβλιοθήκη Μαρασλή, two others come from citations in J. Grimm's *Deut. Myth.* (Göttingen, 1844), and the fourth from a Polish collection of folktales published in 1876.

It is unfortunate that the great folklorist Walter Anderson, once of far-off Kazan but recently of Kiel (see the obituary by Kurt Ranke in *Fabula* V, Heft 3 [1962]) did not find the opportunity in his harried career to collect folktale variants on the short stories inserted within the framework of the *Metamorphoses*, such as the story of witches here told by Aristomenes. For, as it happened, only the first volume of his work, which deals exclusively and exhaustively with the motif of Lucius' transformation into an ass, the main story, was published. This is a book of 655 pages published at Kazan in 1914 under the title *Roman Apuleja i narodnaja Skazka*, in the preface to which the author announces his intention of dealing in later volumes with the *Metamorphoses* in comparison with the ῎Ονος, with the inserted stories in Apuleius, and with Cupid and Psyche. A valuable study of the folklore variants on the theme of *Eselmensch* had already been published by K. Weinhold in *Sitzungsberichte der Akad. d. Wiss. zu Berlin*, No. 2 (1893), 475–488; but Anderson goes far beyond this, and recently he has summed up his materials and added to them in two articles published in the *Zeitschrift für Volkskunde:* vol. 51 (1954), 215–236 and 54 (1958), 121–125.

²² Apuleius displays a peculiar fondness for the dramatic aspect of trial scenes and forensic pleading, of which there is no trace in the *Onos*; and on many occasions throughout the *Metamorphoses*, in situations where the reader would not naturally look for it in the logic of the circumstances, he shows himself abnormally conscious of the danger of an innocent man's being falsely condemned by means of circumstantial evidence. In my note on this subject in "The Story of Thelyphron in Apuleius," *CPh* 24, (1929), 395, I cited and described circumstantially, and in part quoted, eight passages in the *Metamorphoses* where this abnormal concern with the danger of being falsely condemned, amounting almost to an obsession, is manifested. Here it will be sufficient simply to list the places in the Apuleian text without describing them. They are found in *Met.* III 1, III 29, VII 1–2, VII 25–26, VII 27 (speech of the bad boy's mother), IX 10 (*quam pleurumque insontes periclitantur homines!*), IX 41 (framing of the gardener, contrary to the Greek version), X 6 ff.

²³ See my article "The Story of Thelyphron in Apuleius," pp. 231–238

(see n. 22) for a more detailed analysis of this tripartite story; also my review of B. J. DeJonge's commentary on Bk. II of the *Metamorphoses* in *CPh* 44 (1949), 40–42.

24 R. C. Flickinger in his book on *The Greek Theater* (Chicago, 1926), p. 141, notes a similar self-consciousness on the part of Greek tragedians, which seems to compel them at times "to call to the hearer's attention the very difficulty that they are striving to avoid. Like some scientists who think they have explained a phenomenon if they have provided a name for it, playwrights sometimes act as if they had justified an incongruity if they mention it."

25 Byrne's translation, *The Golden Ass of Apuleius*.

26 The substance of what is here said about the episode of the animated wineskins in relation to that about the Risus festival is dealt with more fully in my article entitled "On Apuleius' *Metamorphoses* II 31–III 20," in *AJPh* 46 (1925), 253–262; cf. also my review of DeJonge in *CPh* 44 (1949), p. 42.

27 The speech of Lucius addressed to Byrrhena's servant after his humiliation at the Risus festival in III 12, including the words *ego formidans et procul perhorrescens etiam domum eius*, was quoted above in n. 18. In II 31, while banqueting at Byrrhena's house before his battle with the accidentally animated goatskins, Byrrhena tells him that a festival in honor of the god Risus, celebrated by the people of Hypata from time immemorial, will be held on the next day, and she expresses the hope that Lucius himself will attend and may contribute some pleasantry of his own in honor of the occasion. To this Lucius replies, with an irony that only the author could appreciate at this point, that he will gladly be there and that he does indeed hope to be able to devise something of his own worthy of so great a god. The two passages here described have no connection with any part of the story except the Risus festival and can be left out just as easily as the festival itself. They have been added deliberately by Apuleius for the purpose of suggesting something that he could not explain logically or persuasively, namely, that Byrrhena had already planned, with the magistrates of Hypata, to make Lucius the butt of public laughter at the festival on the next day.

28 The places in which the Latin text of Apuleius comes close to being a literal translation of the Greek text as we have it in the *Onos* are never long, because the Latin author writes so freely and with so much fanciful invention or alteration of his own, even in relating the same events; but these cases of near-literal translation are numerous and may occur anywhere when the subject matter of the two texts is the same. Note the following by way of example:

Met. VIII 30	*Onos* 38
me renudatum ac de quadam quercu destinatum flagro illo pecuinis ossibus catenato verberantes paene ad extremam confecerant mortem.	γυμνὸν ἤδη προσδέουσι με δένδρῳ μεγάλῳ, εἶτα ἐκείνῃ τῇ ἐκ τῶν ἀστραγάλων μάστιγι παίοντες ὀλίγον ἐδέησαν ἀποκτεῖναι.

29 Byrrhena tells Lucius (II 31) that the people of Hypata are the only people in the world who celebrate this festival of the god of Laughter; and

the full equivalent of it is elsewhere unrecorded in the history of ancient religious festivals. Plutarch twice mentions a cult of Γέλως at Sparta (*Lycurgus* 25, *Cleomenes* 9), but in such a way as to imply that Laughter was there recognized only as one of several deified abstractions, including Fear and Death, and that no elaborate or highly ritualized ceremonies, comparable to those described by Apuleius at Hypata, attended it. It seems to be an invention of Apuleius, a composite made up on the analogy of various spring festivals, of which the *Hilaria* held on March 25 and associated with the worship of Attis and Cybele makes the nearest approach. In an interesting article entitled "A Greek Carnival" published in the *Journal of Hellenic Studies* 39 (1919), 110–115, D. S. Robertson, after analyzing and comparing the Risus festival with the known cults of antiquity, sums up the matter felicitously by declaring (p. 114) that "the Risus of Hypata, 'hodierni diei praesentissimum numen,' seems to be Carnival personified. Puck mocking the brief usurpers of Olympus."

³⁰ In an article entitled "Some Aspects of the Literary Art of Apuleius in the *Metamorphoses*" written in 1923 (*TAPhA* 54, 196–227), I called attention (pp. 206–208) to the fact that, in place of many abstract statements or phrases in the Greek text, Apuleius substitutes a wealth of concrete, realistic details which lengthen the description, or the dialogue, and make it more picturesque. My statement of this matter, however, was too negative and too much from the Lucianic point of view, which tended to imply that the innovations of Apuleius were only curious and characteristically Roman tendencies in working over a Greek text, which is normally more abstract. It remained for Junghanns (*Die Erzählungstechnik*) to put this phenomenon and others like it into proper perspective by showing that they are only the means by which Apuleius strives positively to achieve his artistic ideal; namely, to make the originally brief or abstractly related story or episode more picturesque and interesting by filling in new details, to prolong the dramatic suspense by leading upward to a climax, and to exhibit the πάθος of individuals, many of whom are introduced for no other purpose. After pointing out how what "the robbers" said in *Onos* 22, all to the same effect, is replaced in Apuleius VI 26 by the speeches made by three individual robbers successively, each of which adds something new and of greater effect than the one before it, thus leading upward to a climax, Junghanns (p. 70) comments significantly as follows: "Wir haben hier ein typisches Beispiel dafür, wie Apuleius einen im ″Ovos einfach mitgeteilten Entschluss der Räuber allmählich im Gespräche entstehen lässt. Einen dort einfach hingesetzten Punkt sehen wir hier in eine dramatische Linie mit Ansatz—Steigerung— Höhepunkt verwandelt; was dort Meinungsässerung einer einheitlichen Masse war, ist hier in Ausserungen einzelner Individuen aufgelöst, von denen jede etwas in sich geschlossenes Neuen hinzufügt." Many examples of this procedure on the part of Apuleius are noted by Junghanns, but to describe them all would require a separate monograph on the subject. Here we can only note and emphasize what is typical. As typical of the tendency in Apuleius to prolong the suspense by the addition of new episodes leading upward to a climax, Junghanns (pp. 56–60) describes the series of attempts

made by Lucius in Apuleius, both before and after his capture by the robbers, to find roses to eat in order to transform himself back into a man. In describing these attempts Apuleius brings in many new persons and actions which are not in the *Onos*, although they do not contradict the outcome of events therein briefly stated, and are in part suggested by statements made in it.

I have praised Junghann's work for what I consider to be true and important in it; but, since it was finished in 1928 according to the preface, four years before its publication, it ignores a series of contributions to the subject which I had made between 1920 and 1930 and is for that reason inadequate on all that relates to the stories of Aristomenes, of Thelyphron, and of the Risus festival—as well as on some other topics.

[31] Fielding states explicitly in his title that his *Joseph Andrews* is "written in imitation of the manner of Cervantes, author of *Don Quixote*." Concerning the imposition of sympathetic character portrayal and pathos upon his satirical parody of Richardson's *Pamela* in *Joseph Andrews*, see chap. iii above, p. 116; and, for the same kind of innovation made by Prévost in *Manon Lescaut*, basically a picaresque novel, note 21 on chap. iii.

Bibliography
of Useful Reference

FOR PART I, THE ANCIENT IDEAL ROMANCES

Greek and Latin Texts

Erotici Scriptores Graeci, ed. G. A. Hirschig, Paris (Didot) 1875, but originally published at Leiden in 1853. This contains Parthenius, Achilles Tatius, Longus (*Daphnis and Chloe*), Xenophon of Ephesus, Heliodorus, Chariton, Antonius Diogenes, Iamblichus, *Apollonius of Tyre*, and two Byzantine romances, all with Latin translations.

Erotici Scriptores Graeci, ed. R. Hercher, Leipzig (Teubner) 1858, in 2 vols.; contents the same as in Hirschig, except that Heliodorus and *Apollonius of Tyre*, both elsewhere edited in Teubner texts, are absent, and four Byzantine romances are given instead of two.

Collections of Papyrus Fragments

Br. Lavagnini, *Eroticorum Fragmenta Papyracea*, Leipzig (Teubner) 1922.

R. M. Rattenbury, in *New Chapters in the History of Greek Literature*, 3rd series, edited by J. U. Powell, Oxford 1933, pp. 211–257.

Fr. Zimmermann, *Griechische Roman-Papyri und verwandte Texte*, Heidelberg 1936.

Romances and Romantic Books Severally,
New Texts, Translations, Summaries

Ninus, edited and translated, so far as possible, by R. M. Rattenbury, *New Chapters in the History of Greek Literature*, and by S. Gaselee
in a supplement to J. M. Edmonds' *Daphnis and Chloe* in the Loeb
Classical Library (London, 1935) pp. 382–399. There is also a translation, following Gaselee with explanations, in E. H. Haight's *Essays
on the Greek Romances*, New York (Longmans), 1943, pp. 7–10. Important new data on this romance are described above in sec. 2 of
chap. iv.

Chariton. Greatly improved critical edition by Warren E. Blake,
Oxford, 1938. English translation by the same scholar: *Chariton's
Chaereas and Callirhoe*, Ann Arbor (Univ. of Mich. Press) and London
(Oxford Press) 1939. On Chariton's significance see my article en-
titled "Chariton and His Romance from a Literary-Historical Point
of View" in *AJPh* 51 (1930), 93–134; and Remi Petri, *Über den
Roman des Chariton*, Meisenheim am Glan, 1963 (= *Beiträge zur
klass. Philol.*, hrsg. von R. Merkelbach, Heft 11).

Xenophon of Ephesus. New critical edition with French translation
by G. Dalmeyda, Paris (Les Belles Lettres) 1926. English translation
by Moses Hadas in *Three Greek Romances*, Garden City, N.Y.
(Doubleday & Co.) 1953. For a good summary of this romance,
entitled *Ephesiaca*, *Concerning Anthia and Habrocomes*, see Miss
Haight's *Essays on the Greek Romances*, New York (Longmans), 1943,
pp. 38–60.

Apollonius Prince of Tyre. See Appendix II. Edited by A. Riese,
Leipzig (Teubner) 1871 and 1893. Story retold at length in E. H.
Haight, *More Essays on Greek Romances*, New York (Longmans),
1945, pp. 144–156. See Schanz, *Röm. Litt.* IV 2 (1920) for a short
but excellent critical account of this romance and the problems
connected with its history.

Longus, *Daphnis and Chloe*. Text edited with an English translation
(adapted from that of George Thornley, *ca.* 1685) by J. M. Edmunds
in the Loeb Library, London (Heinemann), 1935. English translation
also by Moses Hadas in *Three Greek Romances* (see above under
Xenophon). Edited with a French translation by G. Dalmeyda, Paris
(Les Belles Lettres) 1934. Critical text edited with a German trans-

lation, a learned and helpful introduction, and valuable explanatory notes, by Otto Schönberger, Berlin (Akademie Verlag) 1960.

Achilles Tatius, *Leucippe and Clitophon*. Text with English translation by S. Gaselee in the Loeb Library, London (Heinemann) 1917. The latest critical edition is by Ebbe Vilborg, published as volume I in the series *Studia Graeca et Latina Gothoburgensia*, Göteborg 1955. Here the text is preceded by a full account of the manuscript tradition and is followed at the end by the citation of testimonies about the book and useful indices. Summary of the story in E. H. Haight, *Essays on the Greek Romance*, pp. 97–101.

Heliodorus, *Aethiopica* or *Theagenes and Chariclea*. New critical text by R. M. Rattenbury and T. W. Lumb, with French translation by J. Maillon, Paris (Les Belles Lettres), 1935. Another critical edition, with prolegomena and all the *testimonia* concerning Heliodorus, by Aristide Colonna, Rome (Regea Officina Polygraphica), 1938. English translation: Undertowne's translation of 1587 with introduction by George Saintsbury, Boston, 1925. Summary in Haight, *Essays on the Greek Romances*, pp. 63–76.

Parthenius, *Love Stories* (*Erotica Pathemata*). Greek text with introduction and English translation by S. Gaselee on pp. 257–347 of J. M. Edmonds' *Daphnis and Chloe* in the Loeb Library. See above under Longus.

Dio Chrysostom, *The Hunters of Euboea*. English translation by Moses Hadas in *Three Greek Romances* (see above under Xenophon), pp. 173–189. This is part of oration no. VII among the *Orations* of Dio, edited by G. de Budé, Leipzig (Teubner) 1915–1919. Text with English translation by J. W. Cohoon in the Loeb Library edition, London (Heinemann), 1932, vol. I.

Clementine Recognitiones. See Appendix I. A lucid account of the complicated history of this book is given in Christ-Schmid-Stählin, *Geschichte der Griechischen Litteratur*,[6] II (1924) 1210–1213. For an English translation by Rev. Thomas Smith and others, see "Pseudo-Clementine Literature VIII" in *The Ante-Nicene Fathers*, New York (Scribners), 1906, 67–346.

Alexander Romance (so called), by Pseudo-Callisthenes. This historical monograph, which is full of romantic fiction, was propagated in antiquity in three principal and widely variant versions, called A, B, and Γ respectively. The A version, which is the most accurate historically considered, is supposed to be the oldest version and has been edited by W. Kroll, *Historia Alexandri Magni*, Berlin (Weidener), 1926. The most romantic version, containing much of interest that is not in A, is the B version, which has not yet been edited separately but is mixed up with A in the *editio princeps* of Ps.-Callisthenes by C. Müller in the back of Dübner's *Arrian* in the Didot series, Paris, 1846. The Byzantine metrical version is based largely but not entirely on the B version and has recently (1963) been critically edited with an introduction by Siegfried Reichmann, as no. 13 in the series called *Beiträge zur klassischen Philologie*, edited by Reinhold Merkelbach, Meisenheim am Glan (Anton Hain). The Γ version, a conflation of B and derivatives of A, has recently been edited in two parts in the *Beiträge* mentioned above, the first part by Ursula von Lauenstein (Heft 4) and the second by Helmut Engelmann (Heft 12). An English translation of the A version on the basis of Kroll's text has been published by E. H. Haight, New York (Longmans, Green and Co.), 1954. A critical edition of the B version, *Der griech. Alexanderroman Rezension β* by Leif Bergson, appeared at Stockholm in 1965, Almqvist and Wiksell.

Photius, *Bibliotheca*. Greek text by I. Bekker, Berlin, 1824, reprinted in Migne's *Patrol. Gr.* vols. 103 and 104. A new critical edition, long needed, is now in the course of being published in the Budé series, prepared by R. Henry and accompanied by a French translation: Tome I containing codices 1–84 and II containing codices 84–185, Paris (Les Belles Lettres), 1959 and 1960. The *Bibliotheca* has been translated into English by J. H. Freese, London and New York (Macmillan), 1920.

Antonius Diogenes, *On the Wonders beyond Thule*. See Photius in cod. 166 of the *Bibliotheca*.

Books about the Greek Romance and the Problem of its Origin

Erwin Rohde, *Der griechische Roman und seine Vorläufer*, third edition with an *Anhang* by W. Schmid, Leipzig (Breitkopf und Härtel), 1914. This is a great storehouse of critical information about the romantic literature of antiquity centering around the extant Greek romances properly so called. As such it is invaluable and will probably never be superseded. Concerning Rohde's theory of how the romance as a form originated, see p. 333, n. 7 on chap. i above.

E. Schwartz, *Fünf Vorträge über den Griechischen Roman*, Berlin,

1896. Second edition with introduction by A. Rehm, Berlin (De Gruyter), 1943. Informative, interesting and reliable so far as it goes. Schwartz does not undertake to explain precisely how the romance as a form originated; he surveys it in broad perspective against the background of ancient literary history and convention.

Bruno Lavagnini, *Le Origini del Romanzo Greco*, Pisa (F. Mariotti) 1921. This is repeated in the author's *Studi* mentioned below. Lavagnini's theory of origin is discussed above in sec. 6 of chap. i.

Jaroslav Ludvíkovsky, *Recky Roman Dobrodružny* (The Greek Romance of Adventures) with a résumé in French at the end, Prague (Filosofika Fakulta University Karlova), 1925. See sec. 6 of chap. i above for our critique of Ludvíkovsky's theory.

George Lukács, *Die Theorie des Romans*, Berlin (P. Cassirer), 1920. This is a philosophical essay concerning the nature and history of the epic form, of which the romance is seen as a latter-day variety. Although this book has very little to do with the Greek romance specifically, it is illuminating and profound.

Books Descriptive of the Greek Romance

A. Chassang, *Histoire du Roman*, Paris (Hachette), 1862. This is a useful survey describing many ancient romances and romantic books.

Elizabeth Hazelton Haight, the following books:

Essays on Ancient Fiction, New York (Longmans, Green and Co.) 1936.

Essays on the Greek Romances, New York (Longmans, Green and Co.) 1943.

More Essays on Greek Romances, New York (Longmans, Green and Co.) 1945.

Martin Braun, *History and Romance in Graeco-Oriental Literature*, Oxford (Blackwell), 1938. This is an important study of the national hero legends cultivated on a low popular level by the subjugated Oriental peoples following the conquests of Alexander.

R. Helm, *Der Antike Roman*, Berlin (Editionsgesellschaft), 1948 (in *Handbuch der Griechischen und Lateinischen Philologie* edited by Bruno Snell and Hartmut Erbse).

B. Lavagnini, *Studi sul Romanzo Greco*, Messina and Firenze (Casa editrice G. D'Anna), 1950. A collection of articles on the Greek romance and recently-discovered papyrus fragments.

S. L. Wolff, *The Greek Romances in Elizabethan Prose Fiction*, New York (Columbia University Press), 1912. In the first part of this book the author gives us a brilliant analysis in detail of the sophistic romances (Heliodorus, Achilles Tatius, and Longus) with reference to "Plot, Character (Humor), Setting, Structure, and Style."

Otto Weinrich, *Der griechische Liebesroman*, Zürich (Artemis Verlag), 1962. Contains up-to-date and reliable information, among other things, about the dating of the romances severally.

The Novella in Greek Literature

Otmar Schissel von Fleschenberg, *Die Griechische Novelle*, Halle (Max Niemeyer), 1913. This book is devoted almost entirely to an analysis of the ancient testimony concerning the *Milesiaca* of Aristides, all of which is here conveniently quoted and discussed.

Sophie Trenkner, *The Greek Novella in the Classical Period*, Cambridge University Press, 1958. Miss Trenkner demonstrates that many long folktales of adventure well known to the Greeks as such are imbedded in Athenian literature, especially in the New Comedy, where they are sketched briefly in prologues and statements about what has happened off stage. See above, p. 82 with note 19; and the review of this important book by B. E. Perry in *AJPh* 81 (1960), 442–447.

FOR PART II, THE COMIC ROMANCES

Petronius. The standard text is that of Bücheler originally published in 1862 and recently reprinted with important supplements by W. Heraeus: *Petronii Satyrae, recensuit Franciscus Bücheler . . . Adiectae sunt Varronis et Senecae saturae similesque reliquiae ex editione sexta anni MDCCCCXXII a Guilelmo Heraeo curata repetita et supplementa*. Berlin (Weidmann), 1958. The *editio minor* of 1922 contains all the texts and indices included in the large edition of 1862 but omits the latter's 40-page introduction and retains only a little of the elaborate critical annotation. E. T. Sage's edition of the *Satyricon*, New York (Century Co.), 1929, is critical and contains brief notes on the text throughout, together with useful excurses. A. Ernout, *Le Satiricon*, critical text with French translation, Paris

(Les Belles Lettres), 1922. M. Heseltine, *Petronius* with an English translation in the Loeb Library, London, (Heinemann), 1930, together with Seneca's *Apocolocyntosis* translated by W. H. D. Rouse in the same volume.

Lucian. Complete works edited by Carl Jacobitz in four volumes with copious indices, Leipzig (Teubner), 1836–1841. The *editio minor* of this text, in three volumes, first published by Teubner in 1851, has often been reprinted. For English translations of the *True History*, the *Philopseudes* or *Lover of Lies*, the *Toxaris*, and the *Ship*, see volumes 2, 3, and 4 in the works of Lucian translated by H. W. and F. G. Fowler, Oxford (Clarendon Press), 1903; and, in the Loeb Library, text and translation by A. M. Harmon and others, not yet completed, volumes 1, 3, 5 and 6 respectively. The only English translation that has ever appeared of *Lucius or the Ass* (*Onos*) was published, together with a translation of the *True History*, by Paul Turner, Bloomington (University of Indiana Press), 1958.

Apuleius, his *Metamorphoses* or *The Golden Ass*. R. Helm's Teubner text of the *Metamorphoses*, vol. I of the complete works, third edition, Leipzig, 1931, has long been standard; but the critical editions of Giarratano (Turin, 1929) and of D. S. Robertson, Paris (Les Belles Lettres), 1940, 3 vols., are equally reliable and have distinct advantages of their own. Robertson's text is accompanied by an excellent French translation by Paul Vallette and by an up-to-date and interesting introduction by the same scholar on the *Metamorphoses* as such and the problems of literary history and interpretation which it involves. There are numerous English translations. Among the best of these are: F. D. Byrne, *The Golden Ass of Apuleius*, London (The Imperial Press), 1904; H. E. Butler, Oxford (Clarendon Press), 1910; W. Adlington's translation of 1566 revised by S. Gaselee in the Loeb Library, London (Heinemann), 1915. An interesting introduction to Apuleius, addressed to the general reader, is Miss E. H. Haight's *Apuleius and his Influence*, New York (Longmans, Green & Co.), 1927.

Analytical Table
of Contents

CHAPTER IV

THE BIRTH OF THE IDEAL
GREEK ROMANCE   Page

Pages 149–180

CHAPTER V

PETRONIUS AND HIS *SATYRICON*   Page

Pages 186–210

Index